Android™ Boot Camp for Developers Using Java™, Comprehensive: A Guide to Creating Your First Android Apps

SECOND EDITION

Android™ Boot Camp for Developers Using Java™, Comprehensive: A Guide to Creating Your First Android Apps

CORINNE HOISINGTON

 CENGAGE
Learning·

Australia • Brazil • Japan • Korea • Mexico • Singapore • Spain • United Kingdom • United States

Android Boot Camp for Developers Using Java, Comprehensive: A Guide to Creating Your First Android Apps Second Edition Corinne Hoisington

Senior Product Manager: Jim Gish

Senior Content Developer: Alyssa Pratt

Development Editor: Lisa Ruffolo

Product Assistant: Gillian Daniels

Senior Content Project Manager: Cathie DiMassa

Art Director: Cheryl Pearl, GEX

Compositor: Integra Software Services Pvt. Ltd.

Cover Designer: Wing-ip Ngan, Ink design, inc. ©

Cover Image Credits:

istockphoto.com/zentilia

istockphoto.com/thesuperph

istockphoto.com/franckreporter

iQoncept/Shutterstock.com

For product information and technology assistance, contact us at **Cengage Learning Customer & Sales Support, 1-800-354-9706.**

For permission to use material from this text or product, submit all requests online at **cengage.com/permissions.** Further permissions questions can be emailed to **permissionrequest@cengage.com.**

Library of Congress Control Number: 2013957890

ISBN-13: 978-1-285-85683-4

ISBN-10: 1-285-85683-X

Cengage Learning
20 Channel Center Street
Boston, MA 02210

Cengage Learning is a leading provider of customized learning solutions with office locations around the globe, including Singapore, the United Kingdom, Australia, Mexico, Brazil, and Japan. Locate your local office at: international.cengage.com/region

Cengage Learning products are represented in Canada by Nelson Education, Ltd.

Visit our corporate website at **cengage.com.**

Some of the product names and company names used in this book have been used for identification purposes only and may be trademarks or registered trademarks of their respective manufacturers and sellers.

Any fictional data related to persons or companies or URLs used throughout this book is intended for instructional purposes only. At the time this book was printed, any such data was fictional and not belonging to any real persons or companies.

Cengage Learning reserves the right to revise this publication and make changes from time to time in its content without notice.

Printed in the United States of America
1 2 3 4 5 6 7 18 17 16 15 14

Brief Contents

Contents

Preface

Welcome to *Android Boot Camp for Developers Using Java, Comprehensive: A Guide to Creating Your First Android Apps, Second Edition.* This book is designed for people who have some programming experience or are new to Java programming and want to move into the exciting world of developing apps for Android mobile devices on a Windows or Mac computer. Google Android is quickly becoming the operating system of choice for mobile devices, including smartphones and tablets, with nearly three-quarters of the world's mobile devices running on the Android platform. To help you participate in the growing Android market, this book focuses on developing apps for Android devices.

Approach

The approach used in *Android Boot Camp for Developers Using Java, Comprehensive, Second Edition,* is straightforward. You review a completed Android app and identify why people use the app, and then analyze the tasks it performs and the problems it solves. You also learn about the programming logic, Java tools, and code syntax you can use to create the app. Next, you work through a hands-on tutorial that guides you through the steps of creating the Android app, including designing the user interface and writing the code. After each step, you can compare your work to an illustration that shows exactly how the interface should look or what the code should contain. Using the illustrations, you can avoid mistakes in creating the app and finish the chapter with an appealing, real-world Android app.

The main tool used in *Android Boot Camp for Developers Using Java, Comprehensive, Second Edition,* is a standard one developers use to create Android apps: Eclipse Classic, a free, open-source integrated development environment (IDE). Eclipse includes an emulator for testing your apps, so you don't need a smartphone or tablet to run any of the apps covered in this book. Instructions for downloading and setting up Eclipse are provided later in this preface.

What This Book Is

This book introduces you to writing apps for Android mobile devices. It familiarizes you with the development software for creating Android apps, programming logic used in the apps, and Java code that puts the software design and logic into practice. You don't need an Android device because you can run the apps you create in this book by using an Android emulator.

What This Book Is Not

Because this book is targeted to those new to developing Android apps, it doesn't cover advanced topics, such as application programming interfaces (APIs) for each platform. Instead, this book provides a launch pad to begin your journey into creating Android apps for fun and for profit.

In addition, this book isn't an exhaustive information resource. You can find a wealth of information, tutorials, examples, and other resources for the Android platform online. You should learn enough from this book that you can modify and make use of code you find to fit your needs. The best way to learn how to create Android apps is to write code, make mistakes, and learn how to fix them.

Organization and Coverage

Chapter 1 introduces the Android platform and describes the current market for Android apps. You create your first Android project using Eclipse and become familiar with the Eclipse interface and its tools. As programming tradition mandates, your first project is called Hello Android World, which you complete and then run in an emulator.

Chapter 2 focuses on the Android user interface. While developing an app for selecting and displaying healthy recipes, you follow a series of steps that you repeat every time you create an Android app. You learn how to develop a user interface using certain types of controls, select a screen layout, and write code that responds to a button event (such as a tap or click). While creating the chapter project, you develop an app that includes more than one screen and can switch from one screen to another. Finally, you learn how to correct errors in Java code.

Chapter 3 covers user input, variables, and operations. You develop an Android app that allows users to enter the number of concert tickets they want to purchase, and then tap or click a button to calculate the total cost of the tickets. To do so, you create a user interface using an Android theme and add controls to the interface, including text fields, buttons, and spinner controls. You also declare variables and use arithmetic operations to perform calculations, and then convert and format numeric data.

Chapter 4 discusses icons and decision-making controls. The sample app provides healthcare professionals with a mobile way to convert the weight of a patient from pounds to kilograms and from kilograms to pounds. You create this project using a custom application icon, learn how to fine-tune the layout of the user interface, and include radio buttons for user selections. You also learn how to program decisions using If statements, If Else statements, and logical operators.

Chapter 5 describes how to use lists, arrays, and Web browsers in an Android app. You design and create an Android app that people can use as a traveler's guide to popular attractions in San Francisco, California. To do so, you work with lists, images, and the Switch decision structure. You also learn how to let users access a Web browser while using an Android app.

Chapter 6 explains how to include audio such as music in Android apps. The sample app opens with a splash screen and then displays a second screen where users can select a song to play. To develop this app, you create and set up a splash screen, learn about the Activity life cycle, pause an Activity, and start, play, stop, and resume music playback.

Chapter 7 demonstrates how to use an Android layout tool called a GridView, which shows thumbnail images in a scrolling grid. When the user clicks a thumbnail, the app displays a larger image below the grid. You also learn how to use an array to manage the images.

In **Chapter 8**, you design a calendar program that includes a DatePicker control for selecting a date to book a reservation. Because this app is designed for a larger tablet interface, you also learn how to design an app for a tablet device and add an Android Virtual Device specifically designed for tablets.

Chapter 9 continues to explore Android apps designed for tablet devices. In this chapter, you create a multipane interface, with a list of options in the left pane, and details about the selected option in the right pane. Each pane displays a different layout and Activity. To create the multipane interface, you work with the Master/Detail Flow template.

Chapter 10 explains how to create two types of animation. Using a frame-by-frame animation, you animate a series of images so that they play in sequence. Using a motion tween animation, you apply an animated effect to a single image.

Chapter 11 shows you how to create an Android app that requests data, stores it, and then modifies that data to produce a result throughout multiple activities. You learn about the ways Android apps can save persistent application data, and then use one—the SharedPreferences class—to store data for an airline's customer rewards app.

In **Chapter 12**, you learn how to publish an Android app to the Google Play Store. Before publishing the app, you test it, prepare it for publication, create a package and digitally sign the app, and then prepare promotional materials.

Features of the Book

Android Boot Camp for Developers Using Java, Comprehensive, Second Edition, includes the following features:

- *Objectives*—Each chapter begins with a list of objectives as an overview of the topics discussed in the chapter and as a useful study aid.

- *GTKs and In the Trenches*—GTK stands for Good to Know. These notes offer tips about Android devices, Android apps, and the Android development tools. The In the Trenches features provide programming advice and practical solutions to typical programming problems.

- *Figures and tables*—The chapters contain a wealth of screen shots to guide you as you create Android apps and learn about the Android marketplace. In addition, many tables are included to give you an at-a-glance summary of useful information.

- *Step-by-step tutorials*—Starting in Chapter 1, you create complete, working Android apps by performing the steps in a series of hands-on tutorials that lead you through the development process.

- *Code syntax features*—Each new programming concept or technique is introduced with a code syntax feature that highlights a type of statement or programming structure. The code is analyzed and explained thoroughly before you use it in the chapter project.

- *Summaries*—At the end of each chapter is a summary list that recaps the Android terms, programming concepts, and Java coding techniques covered in the chapter so that you have a way to check your understanding of the chapter's main points.

- *Key terms*—Each chapter includes definitions of new terms, alphabetized for ease of reference. This feature is another useful way to review the chapter's major concepts.

- *Developer FAQs*—Each chapter contains many short-answer questions that help you review the key concepts in the chapter.

- *Beyond the Book*—In addition to review questions, each chapter provides research topics and questions. You can search the Web to find the answers to these questions and further your Android knowledge.

- *Case programming projects*—Except for Chapter 12, each chapter outlines realistic programming projects, including their purpose, algorithms, and conditions. For each project, you use the same steps and techniques you learned in the chapter to create a running Android app on your own.

- *Quality*—Every chapter project and case programming project was tested using Windows 8 and Mac OS X computers.

Student Resources

Source code and project files for the chapter projects and case programming projects in *Android Boot Camp for Developers Using Java, Comprehensive, Second Edition*, are available at www.cengagebrain.com.

For complete instructions on downloading, installing, and setting up the tools you need to perform the steps in this book, see the section titled "Prelude! Installing the Android Eclipse SDK" later in this preface.

For the Instructor

Android Boot Camp for Developers Using Java, Comprehensive, Second Edition, is intended to be taught as a complete course dedicated to the mobile programming of the Android device or as an exploratory topic in a programming class or literacy course. Students can develop Android applications on a Windows or Mac computer using the Eclipse emulator in a traditional or online class. Offering such a stimulating topic that is relative to today's huge growth in the mobile environment brings excitement to the programming classroom. The Eclipse/Android platform is fully free and open-source, which means all students can access these tools on their home computers.

Instructor Resources

The following teaching tools are available at sso.cengage.com to instructors who have adopted this book:

Instructor's Manual. The electronic Instructor's Manual follows the book chapter by chapter to assist in planning and organizing an effective, engaging course. The manual includes learning objectives, chapter overviews, ideas for classroom activities, and abundant additional resources. A sample course syllabus is also available.

Test Bank. Cengage Learning Testing Powered by Cognero is a flexible, online system that allows you to:

- author, edit, and manage test bank content from multiple Cengage Learning solutions
- create multiple test versions in an instant
- deliver tests from your LMS, your classroom or wherever you want

PowerPoint presentations. This book comes with PowerPoint slides for each chapter. They're included as a teaching aid for classroom presentations, to make available to students on the network for chapter review, or to be printed for classroom distribution. Instructors can add their own slides for additional topics or customize the slides with access to all the figure files from the book.

Solution files. Solution files for all chapter projects and the end-of-chapter exercises are provided.

Prelude! Installing the Android SDK with Eclipse

Setting Up the Android Environment

To begin developing Android applications, you must first set up the Android programming environment on your computer. To establish a development environment, this preface walks you through the installation and setup for a Windows or Mac computer. The Android Software Development Kit (SDK) allows developers to create applications for the Android platform. The Android SDK includes Eclipse along with sample projects including source code, development tools, an emulator, and required libraries to build Android applications, which are written using the Java programming language.

Although installing the Android SDK with Eclipse is easy, you must follow the instructions in this preface to correctly prepare for creating an Android application. Before writing your first application in Chapter 1, complete the following general steps to successfully install the Android SDK with Eclipse on your computer:

1. Prepare your computer for the installation.
2. Download and unzip the Eclipse Integrated Development Environment (IDE).
3. Add an Android SDK.
4. Set up the Android emulator.

Preparing Your Computer

The Android Software Development Kit is compatible with Windows XP (32 bit), Windows Vista (32- or 64-bit), Windows 7 (32- or 64-bit), Windows 8.x (32- or 64- or 128-bit), and Mac OS X (Intel only). To install the basic files needed to write an Android application, your hard drive needs at least 500 MB of available space.

Before getting started, confirm that the latest free Java updates for your computer have been installed. The site java.com allows you to install the latest Java updates to prepare for the Android installation.

Downloading the Android SDK with Eclipse

Before downloading the necessary files, you need to create a folder named Android on the hard drive (C:) of your computer. Next, you download and unzip the software in the Android folder. Windows Vista, Windows 7, and Windows 8.x automatically unzip files, but if you are using Windows XP, you need to first download an unzip program such as WinZip at download.com.

The preferred Java program development software is called the Android SDK, which includes Eclipse plus the ADT plug-in. The Android SDK provides you with the API libraries and developer tools necessary to build, test, and debug apps for Android. The Android SDK with Eclipse is a free and open-source integrated development environment (IDE).

To download the Android SDK with Eclipse and then start Eclipse, complete the following steps:

STEP 1

- Use a browser to open the Web page **http://developer.android.com/sdk/**.

The Get the Android SDK page opens in the browser (Figure 1).

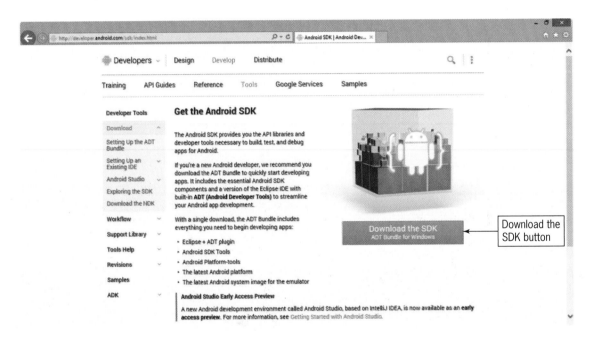

Figure 1 Android SDK download site (http://developer.android.com/sdk/)

STEP 2

- Tap or click the Download the SDK button to download the most recent version of the Android SDK.

The Web site detects whether you are installing the Android SDK on a computer running Windows or Mac OS X. The latest Android system image for the emulator is installed with this installation. If you are downloading to a Windows computer, download the Windows 32-bit or Windows 64-bit version based on your operating system.

- Unzip the downloaded file (adt-bundle-*os_platform*.zip) into the C:\Android folder on your computer.

The zipped file extracts the contents of the Android SDK development environment bundled within Eclipse (Figure 2).

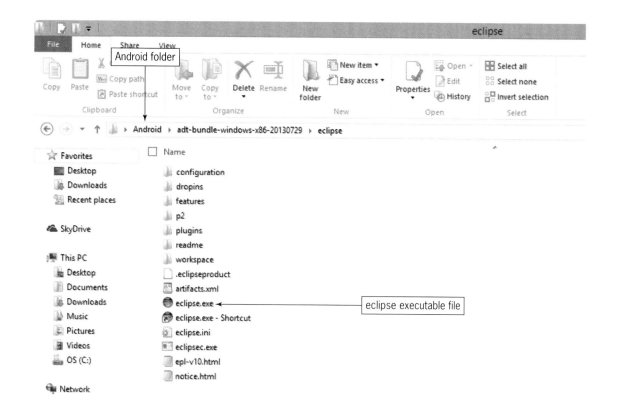

Figure 2 Contents of the Android folder

STEP 2

- Open the adt-bundle-*os_platform*/eclipse/ folder in the Android folder, and then double-tap or double-click eclipse.exe.

Eclipse starts. You may want to create a shortcut on the desktop to make it easier to start Eclipse.

Configuring Eclipse with the Android SDK Manager

After successfully downloading the ADT plug-in, you are ready to begin coding, but if you want to add a recent Android platform such as Jelly Bean or KitKat, the platform most phones are using, or to update to a newer platform, you need to use the Android SDK Manager to configure Eclipse to use these platforms. By default, the most recent SDK was installed with Eclipse, but you may want to program for other Android platforms, which are named after desserts and are described in detail in Chapter 1. Because Google releases updated versions of Android every few months, the best practice in learning or teaching from this text is to download the Jelly Bean, API 18 Android SDK for creating the app project in each chapter. Most of the code does not change in newer versions, but it is helpful for new Android developers to have Eclipse match the images within this text.

To install the multiple repositories for the Android SDK, Google API, and the tools necessary for the emulator, complete the following steps:

STEP 1

- In Eclipse, tap or click the Window menu.

- Tap or click Android SDK Manager to open the Android SDK Manager window.

  On Mac OS X, in Eclipse, tap or click the Window menu and then select Android SDK Manager.

- Select the Android 4.3 (API 18) check box, or select the check box for the platform you want to include.

The Android SDK Manager window opens in Eclipse (Figure 3).

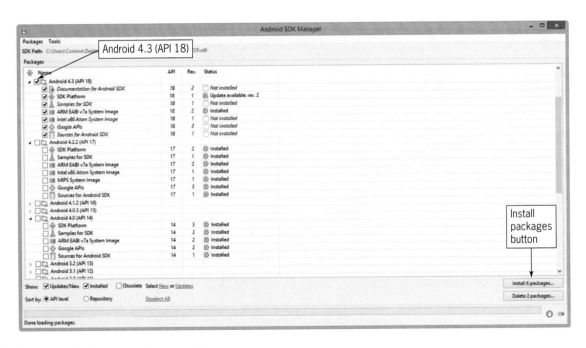

Figure 3 Android SDK Manager window

STEP 2

- Tap or click the Install packages button.

- Tap or click the Accept License option button.

- Tap or click the Install button. The installation may take a few minutes depending on your Internet connection.

Setting Up the Android Emulator

The Android Software Development Kit includes phone and tablet emulators that allow you to develop and test your Android applications. Android mobile devices come in many shapes and sizes and must be tested on a host of emulator layouts to verify the configuration and usability. Each Android device configuration is stored in an Android Virtual Device (AVD).

The Android SDK and the AVD Manager within Eclipse provide multiple emulators you can use to test drive your application without using a physical device. When you run an Android app, it is displayed in the selected emulator. You can then interact with the emulated mobile device just as you would with an actual mobile device. To simulate touching the screen of the emulator, you use a pointing device such as a mouse on your computer.

To use the emulator, you first must create one or more AVD configurations. In each configuration, you specify an Android platform to run in the emulator and the set of hardware options and emulator skin you want to use. (A skin determines the resolution and appearance of the emulator.) When you launch the emulator, you specify the AVD configuration that you want to load. This book uses the Android 4.3 Jelly Bean version emulator. Depending on your actual Android device, you can add emulators to test the devices on which you plan to deploy your apps. You must name the emulator that you set up to use when deploying your Android apps.

To specify an Android emulator, complete the following steps:

STEP 1

- If necessary, open Eclipse, and then tap or click OK in the Workspace Launcher dialog box.

- Tap or click the Window menu, and then tap or click AVD Manager to open the Android Virtual Device Manager dialog box.

- Tap or click the New button to open the Create new Android Virtual Device (AVD) dialog box.

- In the Name text box, type **JellyBean** to name your Android emulator.

- To target your Android app to run using Android 4.3, select **Android 4.3 – API Level 18** from the Target drop-down list. (Newer versions might be listed, but most devices are not using the newest platform).

The Create new Android Virtual Device (AVD) dialog box includes the Name and Target entries (Figure 4).

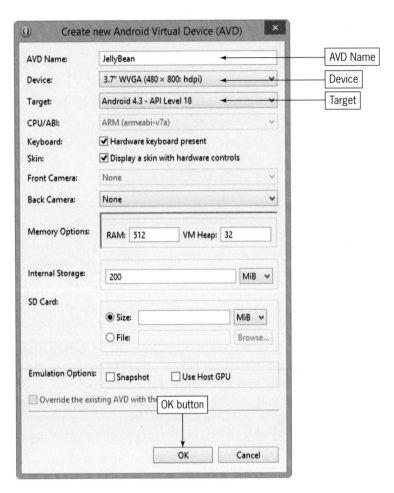

Figure 4 Create new Android Virtual Device (AVD) dialog box

STEP 2

- Tap or click the Create AVD button.

The Android Virtual Device Manager dialog box lists the AVD Name for the Android 4.3 target device, which is JellyBean in this case. Your AVD is now ready to use (Figure 5).

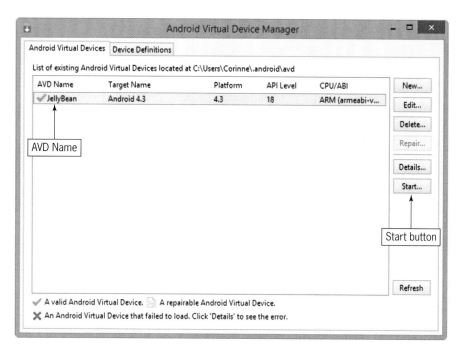

Figure 5   Android Virtual Device Manager dialog box

STEP 3

- To launch and test the emulator with the AVD, tap or click the Start button.

The Android emulator launches (Figure 6).

Figure 6 Android emulator

STEP 4

- Close the emulator window.
- Close Eclipse by tapping or clicking File on the menu bar, and then tapping or clicking Exit.

You are now ready to create your first application. Your adventure begins!

Android Software Development Kit (SDK) Installation Instructions for Mac

To develop Android apps, you need to install the Android Software Development Kit (SDK). In addition, you need another application in which to run the SDK. The most popular version, and the one you use here, is Eclipse. This section provides instructions for installing the Android SDK and Eclipse.

Android currently provides online installation instructions at *http://developer.android.com/sdk/ installing.html.* Eclipse currently provides online installation instructions at *http://developer.android. com/sdk/eclipse-adt.html#installing.* Use the online instructions as a backup if you encounter any unique issues with the installation not covered in this section.

System Requirements

Before you install the software, be sure that your Mac meets the following system requirements by completing the following steps.

STEP 1

- Click the Apple icon on the Mac toolbar, and then click About This Mac to open the About This Mac dialog box and view your current operating system version. Your operating system should be Mac OS X 10.5.8 or later (x86 only).

- In the About This Mac dialog box, verify that your Mac has an Intel processor. If the processor is displayed as Unknown, tap or click the More Info button to display the processor type.

The operating system is later than 10.5.8 and the processor is by Intel (Figure 7).

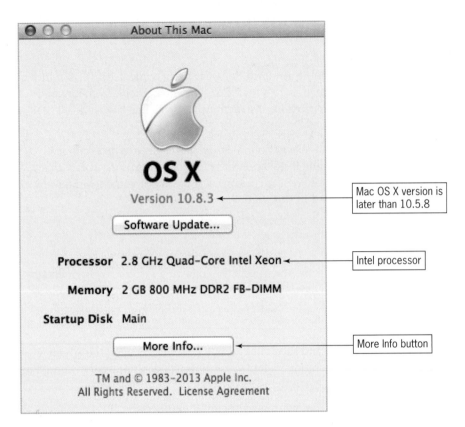

Figure 7   About This Mac dialog box

Source: Apple

Installing the Android Software Development Kit (SDK) and Eclipse

Now that you know your system meets the requirements, you can install the ADT bundle, which includes the Eclipse and the Android Software Development Kit (SDK) starter package. Complete the following steps to install the ADT bundle and then start Eclipse:

STEP 1

- Use your browser to go to **http://developer.android.com/sdk/**.
- Scroll down, if necessary, and then tap or click the DOWNLOAD FOR OTHER PLATFORMS link.

The Web page displays ADT bundles for Windows, Mac OS X, and Linux (Figure 8).

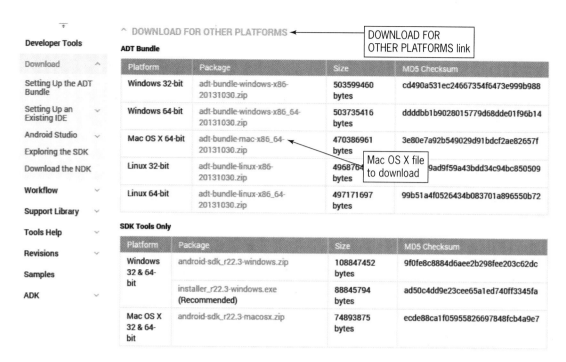

Figure 8   Mac OS X file to download

Source: developer.android.com

STEP 2

- Tap or click the Download the SDK ADT Bundle for Mac button to download the file, which might take a few minutes.

- Open your browser's Downloads folder. To do so in Safari, tap or click the Show downloads button in the upper-right corner of the browser.

- Tap or click the Show in Finder icon next to the .zip file you downloaded.

- Double-tap or double-click the .zip file you downloaded to expand the files.

- Move all the extracted folders to the Applications folder.

Android SDK and Eclipse folders are installed on your computer (Figure 9).

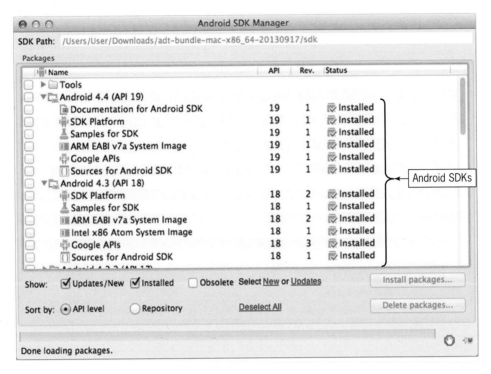

Figure 9   Android SDK and Eclipse are installed

STEP 3

- Open the eclipse folder, and then double-tap or double-click Eclipse.app.

- Tap or click Open if a dialog box is displayed warning that this application has been downloaded from the Internet.

Eclipse starts and the Workspace Launcher dialog box is displayed (Figure 10).

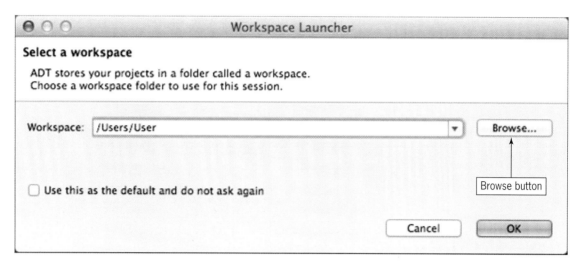

Figure 10   Workspace Launcher dialog box

STEP 4

- To enter the path to the folder where you will save your Android projects, tap or click the Browse button, navigate to the desired location, and then open the location.
- Tap or click the OK button to accept the path.

The Eclipse application is now fully installed and open.

Installing Android Development Tools (ADT) Plugin for Eclipse

Now that Eclipse is installed, the Android Development Tools (ADT) Plugin needs to be added to the program. Complete the following steps to install the ADT Plugin for Eclipse.

STEP 1

- With Eclipse running, tap or click Help on the menu bar and then tap or click Install New Software.

The Install wizard starts and displays the Install dialog box (Figure 11).

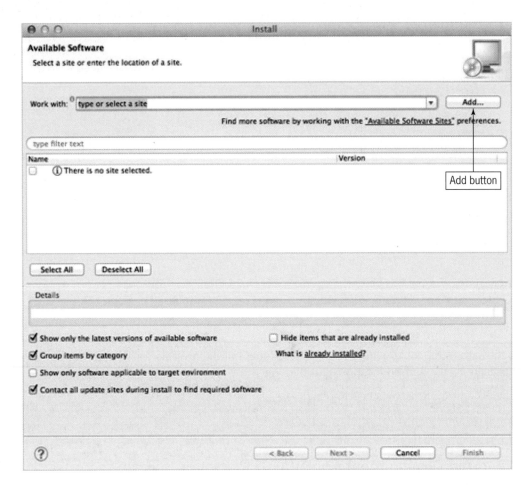

Figure 11 Available Software dialog box in the Install wizard

STEP 2

- Tap or click the Add button to display the Add Repository dialog box.

- In the Name text box, type **ADT Plugin**.

- In the Location text, box, type **https://dl-ssl.google.com/android/eclipse/**.

- If an error message appears, re-enter the Location using http instead of https: **http://dl-ssl. google.com/android/eclipse/**.

The criteria are entered in the Add Repository dialog box (Figure 12).

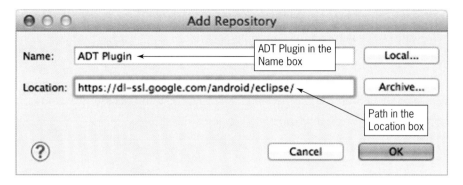

Figure 12   Add Repository dialog box

STEP 3

- Tap or click the OK button to display the Available Software window with an item to install.
- Tap or click the Developer Tools check box to select it.

The Developer Tools item is selected for installation (Figure 13).

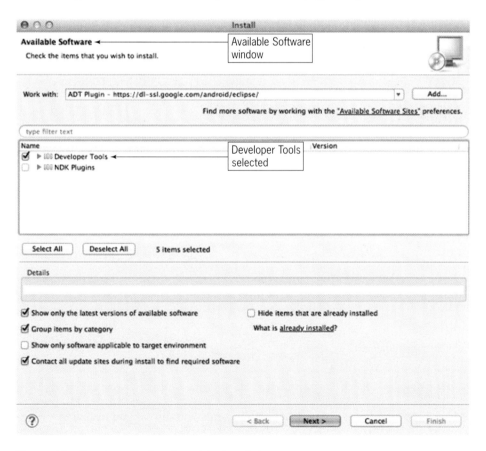

Figure 13   Developer Tools selected for installation

STEP 4

- Tap or click the Next button to display the Install Details screen.

- Tap or click the Next button to accept the defaults in the Install Details list box and display the Review Licenses screen.

- Tap or click each license agreement in the Licenses box, and then read the license agreement.

- Tap or click the "I accept the terms of the license agreement" option button.

The license agreements have been reviewed (Figure 14).

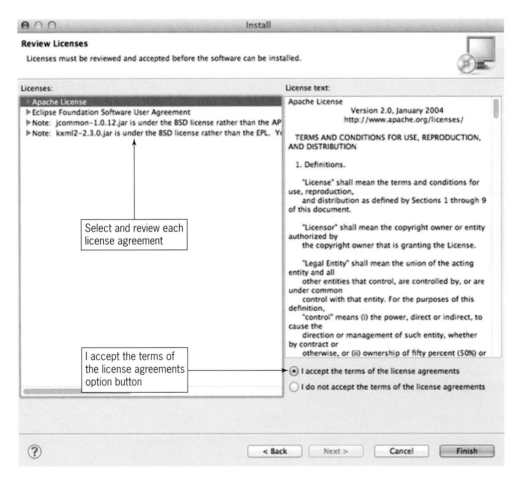

Figure 14   Reviewing license agreements

STEP 5

- Tap or click the Finish button to accept the license agreements and display the Installing Software dialog box.

- Tap or click Run in Background to complete the installation while doing other tasks.

- If a Security Warning dialog box is displayed regarding the authenticity of the software, tap or click OK to clear it.

- When the installation is complete, tap or click Yes in the Software Updates dialog box to restart Eclipse.

- Tap or click OK in the Workspace Launcher dialog box to accept the default location you entered earlier.

Eclipse starts and loads the tools and plug-ins it needs (Figure 15).

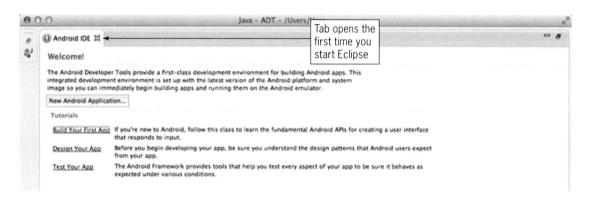

Figure 15   Starting Eclipse

Leave Eclipse open for the next set of instructions. See *http://developer.android.com/tools/sdk/ eclipse-adt.html#* for more installation information, if necessary.

Configuring the ADT Plugin

The ADT Plugin must be connected to the Android Developers SDK directory for it to work correctly. To configure the ADT Plugin, complete the following steps.

STEP 1

- In Eclipse, tap or click ADT on the menu bar and then tap or click Preferences to open the Preferences dialog box.

- In the left pane, tap or click the Android category.

The Eclipse Preferences dialog box displays the Android Preferences (Figure 16).

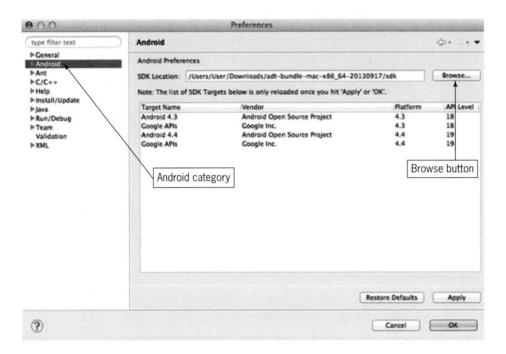

Figure 16   Eclipse Preferences dialog box

STEP 2

- Tap or click the Browse button next to SDK Location.
- Navigate to the Applications folder, and then select the sdk folder.

The sdk folder is selected (Figure 17).

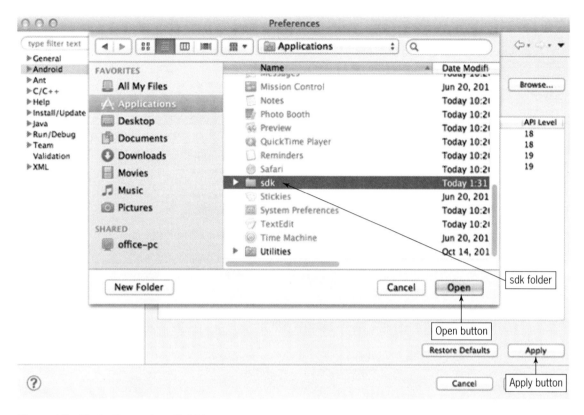

Figure 17   Navigating to the sdk folder

STEP 3

- Tap or click the Open button to select the sdk folder.

- Tap or click the Apply button and then tap or click the OK button to set the SDK location and close the Preferences dialog box.

- Leave Eclipse open for the next set of instructions.

The ADT Plugin is now connected to the correct directory.

Adding Android Platforms and Other Packages to SDK

The final step in this installation is to download essential SDK packages using the Android SDK Manager. To program applications, you need to install at least one Android platform. To add Android platforms to the SDK, complete the following steps:

STEP 1

- In Eclipse, tap or click Window on the menu bar and then tap or click Android SDK Manager to display the Android SDK Manager dialog box.

- Tap or click the Tools check box, if necessary, to select the packages.

The packages are selected for installation (Figure 18).

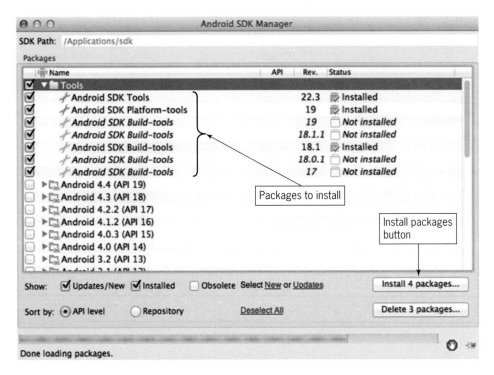

Figure 18   Android SDK Manager dialog box

STEP 2

- Tap or click the Install *x* packages button (where *x* is a number such as 4) to accept the selected tools and display the Choose Packages to Install dialog box.

- Select and read the license agreements, tap or click the Accept License option button for each item to install, and then tap or click Install. The Android SDK Manager Log shows the detailed progress of the download, which might take a few minutes.

- If the Android Tools Updated dialog box is displayed, tap or click the OK button.

- When the Done loading packages message appears, tap or click Close to close the Android SDK Manager Log dialog box.

- Tap or click the Close button on the title bar to close the Android SDK Manager dialog box.

- Tap or click Help on the menu bar, and then tap or click Check for Updates to install the latest updates, if necessary.

See http://developer.android.com/sdk/installing.html for more installation information, if necessary, and details regarding these packages. For Mac users, click the Information for other platforms link to display more information. Your development environment is now ready for you to use to create Android apps.

Acknowledgments

Android Boot Camp for Developers Using Java, Comprehensive: A Guide to Creating Your First Android Apps, Second Edition, is the product of a wonderful team of professionals working toward a single goal: providing students with pertinent, engaging material to further their knowledge and careers. Thank you to the folks at Cengage—specifically Senior Product Manager Jim Gish; Senior Content Developer Alyssa Pratt; Senior Content Project Manager Cathie DiMassa; and Danielle Shaw and Serge Palladino, the MQA testers.

Writing a book is similar to entering a long-term relationship with an obsessive partner. Throughout the journey, life continues around you: teaching classes full time, presenting across the country, and attending family events at every turn. As the world continues, those closest to you allow you to focus on your reclusive writing by assisting with every other task. My husband, Timothy, is credited with taking part in my nomadic life and most of all for his love and patience. Special thanks to my six children, Tim, Brittany, Ryan, Daniel, Breanne, and Eric, for providing much needed breaks filled with pride and laughter. To the newest member of my family, my grandson Liam, who makes me smile like no other, and yes we will go outside in just a minute. And a special thanks to Lisa Ruffolo as my developmental editor and master wordsmith who provided the perfect polish and words of encouragement.

Voilà! Meet the Android

In this chapter, you learn to:

◎ Understand the market for Android applications

◎ Identify the role of the Android device in the mobile market

◎ Describe the features of the Android phone

◎ Identify which languages are used in Android development

◎ Describe the role of Google Play in the mobile marketplace

◎ Create an Android project using Eclipse

◎ Explain the role of the Package Explorer

◎ Specify the use of layout and widget controls in the user interface

◎ Execute an Android application on an emulator

◎ Open a saved Android project in Eclipse

Welcome to the beginning of your journey in creating Android phone applications and developing for the mobile device market. Mobile computing has become the most popular way to make a personal connection to the Internet. Mobile phones and tablets comprise the fastest growing category of any technology in the world. Mobile phone usage has quickly outgrown the simple expectation of voice calls and text messaging. An average data plan for a mobile device, often called a smartphone, typically includes browsing the Web, playing popular games such as Angry Birds or Cut the Rope, using business applications, checking email, listening to music, recording live video, and mapping locations with a GPS (global positioning system).

When purchasing a smartphone, you can choose from many mobile operating systems, including the iOS for the iPhone, Google Android, and Microsoft Phone. Recently the Android phone has become the sales leader, outselling its competitors. The Android market is exploding with more than 1.3 million activations of Android phones per day and close to one billion total activations of Android devices now being used worldwide. Nearly 72 percent of the world's mobile devices run on the Android platform.

IN THE TRENCHES
More than one-third of all U.S. households have canceled their landlines for the convenience of handling only one bill from a mobile carrier.

Creating mobile applications, called **apps**, for the Android phone market is an exciting new job opportunity. Whether you become a developer for a technology firm that creates professional apps for corporations or a hobbyist developer who creates games, niche programs, or savvy new applications, the Android marketplace provides a new means to earn income.

Meet the Android

The Android phone platform is built on a free operating system primarily created by a company called Android, Inc. In 2005, Google obtained Android, Inc., to start a venture in the mobile phone market. Because Google intended the Android platform to be open source, the Android code was released under the Apache license, which permits anyone to download the full open-source Android code for free. Two years later, Google unveiled its first open-standards mobile device called the Android (Figure 1-1). In less than a decade, the Android phone market has grown into the world's best-selling phone platform.

Android is the first open-source technology platform for mobile devices. Being an **open-source operating system** effectively means that no company or individual defines

Figure 1-1   Android phone

the features or direction of the development. Organizations and developers can extract, modify, and use the code for creating any app. The rapid success of the Android phone can be attributed to the collaboration of the **Open Handset Alliance** (*openhandsetalliance.com*), an open-source business alliance of 80 firms that develop standards for mobile devices. The Open Handset Alliance is led by Google. Other members include companies such as Samsung, Sony, Intel, Motorola, Qualcomm, HTC, Texas Instruments, Kyocera, and LG. Competitors such as Apple, which produces the iPhone, and BlackBerry, which produces BlackBerry devices, do not have an open-source coding environment, but instead work with proprietary operating systems. The strength of the open-source community lies in the developers' ability to share their source code. Even though the open-source Android software is free, many developers are paid to build and improve the platform. For example, proprietary software such as the Apple operating system is limited to company employees licensed to build a program within the organization. The Android open-source platform allows more freedom so people can collaborate and improve the source code.

Many phone manufacturers install the Android operating system (OS) on their brand-name mobile phones due to its open-source environment. The open-source structure means that manufacturers do not pay license fees or royalties. With a small amount of customization, each manufacturer can place the Android OS on their latest devices. This minimal overhead allows manufacturers to sell their phones in the retail market for relatively low prices, often less than $100. Low prices on Android mobile devices have increased the sales and popularity of these devices.

The open-source community also makes Android phones attractive for consumers. Android has a large community of developers writing apps that extend the functionality of the devices. Users, for example, can benefit from over 700,000 apps available in the Android marketplace, many of which are free. Because the Android phone platform has become the leader in sales in the mobile market, the Android application market is expected to keep pace.

GTK
On average, each smartphone worldwide runs 41 apps.

Android Phone Device

The Android phone is sold by a variety of companies under names you may recognize, such as Galaxy, Butterfly, Optimus, Droid Razr, Lumia, Prism, Moto, Freeform, Xperia, and Gravity (Figure 1-2).

Figure 1-2   Android models

IN THE TRENCHES
Android has ventured into the television market as well. Chromecast is a thumb drive that enables Web streaming to television.

Android devices come in many shapes and sizes, as shown in Figure 1-2. The Android OS powers all types of mobile devices, including smartphones, tablets, netbooks, e-readers, MP4 players, and Internet TVs. The Kindle by Amazon is based on the Android OS as well. Android devices are available with a variety of screen dimensions. Many devices support a landscape mode where the width and height are spontaneously reversed depending on the orientation of the device. As you design Android apps, the screen size affects the layout of the user interface. To take full advantage of the capabilities of a particular device, you need to design user interfaces specifically for that device. For example, a smartphone and a tablet have not only different physical screen sizes but also different screen resolutions and pixel densities, which change the development process. As you develop an Android app, you can test the results on an **emulator**, which duplicates how the app looks and feels on a particular device. You can change the Android emulators to simulate the layout of a smartphone with a 3.5-inch screen or a tablet with a larger screen, both with high-density graphics. Android automatically scales content to the screen size of the device you choose, but if you use low-quality graphics in an app, the result is often a poorly pixelated display. As a developer, you need to continue to update your app as the market shifts to different platforms and screen resolutions.

The Android phone market has many more hardware case and size options than the 3.5-inch and 4-inch screen options of an iPhone. Several Android phones such as the Galaxy, Droid X, and Nexus offer screens 4 inches or larger. This extra space is excellent for phone users who like to watch movies, play games, or view full Web pages on their phone. In addition, many types of tablets, also called slates, are run on the Android platform. The Galaxy Tab Android tablet is produced by Samsung and offers a 10.1-inch screen with a very high resolution of 1280 × 800 pixels. Amazon also has a 7-inch Android slate device called the Kindle HD Fire (Figure 1-3), currently available for $199. The Android tablets are in direct competition with other tablets and slate computers such as the iPad (various generations) and Windows tablets.

Figure 1-3   Kindle HD Fire

© iStockphoto.com/mphillips007

Features of the Android

As a developer, you must understand a phone's capabilities. The Android offers a wide variety of features that apps can use. Some features vary by model. Most Android phones provide the features listed in Table 1-1.

Feature	Description
3D graphics	The interface can support 3D graphics for a 3D interactive game experience or 3D image rendering.
Facial recognition	Android provides this high-level feature for automatically identifying or verifying a person's face from a digital image or a video frame.
Front- and rear-facing camera	Android phones can use either a front- or a rear-facing camera, allowing developers to create applications involving video calling.
Multiple language support	Android supports multiple human languages.
Onscreen keyboard	The onscreen keyboard offers suggestions for spelling corrections as well as options for completing words you start typing. The onscreen keyboard also supports voice input.
Power management	Android identifies programs running in the background using memory and processor resources. You can close those apps to free up the phone's processor memory, extending the battery power. For optimized gaming, Android supports the use of a gyroscope, gravity and barometric sensors, linear acceleration, and rotation vector, which provide game developers highly sensitive and responsive controls.
Voice-based recognition	Android recognizes voice actions for calling, texting, and navigating with the phone.
Wi-Fi Internet tethering	Android supports tethering, which allows a phone to be used as a wireless or wired hot spot that other devices can use to connect to the Internet.

Table 1-1   Android platform features

Writing Android Apps

Android apps are written using the Java programming language. **Java** is a language and a platform originated by Sun Microsystems. Java is an **object-oriented programming language** patterned after the C++ language. Object-oriented programming encourages good software engineering practices such as code reuse. The most popular tool for writing Java programs is called **Eclipse**, an integrated development environment (IDE) for building and integrating application development tools and open-source projects.

As shown in the preface of this book, the first step in setting up your Android programming environment is to install the free Eclipse Android IDE. The installation includes the Android

Software Development Kit (SDK), which runs in Eclipse. The Android SDK includes a set of development tools that help you design the interface of the program, write the code, and test the program using a built-in Android handset emulator. To write Android programs, an Eclipse plug-in called the **Android Development Tools (ADT)** extends the capabilities of Eclipse to let you quickly set up new Android projects, create an application user interface, and debug your applications. Another language called **XML** (Extensible Markup Language) is used to assist in the layout of the Android emulator.

GTK
You can use Eclipse to develop applications in many programming languages, including Java, C, C++, COBOL, Ada, and Python.

Android Emulator

The Android emulator lets you design, develop, prototype, and test Android applications without using a physical device. When you run an Android program in Eclipse, the emulator starts so you can test the program. You can then use the mouse to simulate touching the screen of the device. The emulator mimics almost every feature of a real Android handset except for the ability to place a voice phone call. A running emulator can play video and audio, render gaming animation, and store information. Multiple emulators are available within the Android SDK to target various devices and versions from early Android phones onward. Developers should test their apps on several versions to confirm the stability of a particular platform. The first Android version, release 1.0, was introduced in September 2008. Each subsequent version adds new features and fixes any known bugs in the platform. Android has adopted a naming system for each version based on dessert items, as shown in Table 1-2. After the first version, dessert names have been assigned in alphabetical order.

Version Name	Release Date
1.0 First version	September 2008
1.5 Cupcake	April 2009
1.6 Donut	September 2009
2.0 Éclair	October 2009
2.2 Froyo (Frozen Yogurt)	May 2010
2.3 Gingerbread	December 2010
3.0 Honeycomb	February 2011
4.0 Ice Cream Sandwich	May 2011
4.1 Jelly Bean	July 2012
4.4 KitKat	October 2013

© 2015 Cengage Learning

Table 1-2   Android version history

Getting Oriented with Market Deployment

The Android platform consists of the Android OS, the Android application development tools, and a marketplace for Android applications. After you write and test a program, you compile the app into an Android package file with the filename extension .apk. Programs written for the Android platform are sold and deployed through an online store called **Google Play** (*play.google.com*), which provides registration services and certifies that the program meets minimum standards of reliability, efficiency, and performance. Google Play requires that you sign an agreement and pay a one-time registration fee (currently $25). After registration, you can publish your app on Google Play, provided the app meets the minimum standards. You can also release updates as needed for your app. If your app is free, Google Play publishes your app at no cost. If you want to charge for your app, the standard split is 70 percent of sales for the developer and 30 percent for the wireless carriers. For example, if you created an app for your city that featured all the top restaurants, hotels, attractions, and festivals and sold the app for $1.99, you would net $1.39 for each app sold. If you sell 5,000 copies of your app, you would earn almost $7,000. You can use Google Play to sell a wide range of content, including downloadable content, such as media files or photos, and virtual content such as game levels or potions (Figure 1-4). As an Android developer, you have the opportunity to develop apps for a fairly new market and easily distribute the app to the millions of Android mobile device owners.

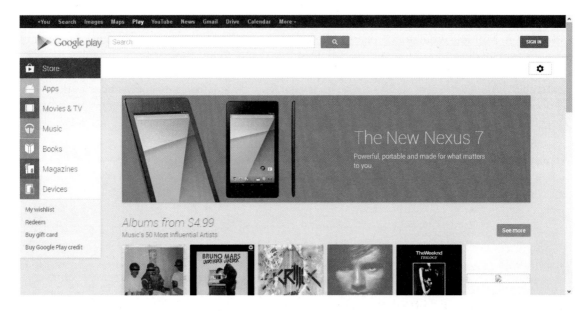

Figure 1-4 Google Play

Source: Google

IN THE TRENCHES

The Apple iTunes App Store charges a $99 yearly registration fee to publish an app through the iPhone Dev Center. The iTunes App Store has a much more rigorous standards approval process than Google Play.

The online company Amazon (*amazon.com*) also has a separate Appstore where Android apps can be deployed and sold. The Amazon Appstore for Android is a department listed on Amazon.com. Customers can shop for apps from their PCs and mobile devices. The Amazon Appstore has an established marketing environment and search engine that displays a trusted storefront and creates app recommendations based on customers' past purchases. The Amazon Appstore charges a $99 annual developer program fee, which covers the application processing and account management for the Amazon Appstore Developer Program. Amazon also pays developers 70 percent of the sale price of the app; in addition, you can post free apps.

First Venture into the Android World

After installing the ADT bundle (*developer.android.com/sdk*) as instructed in the preface of this book, the next step is to create your first Android application. As programming tradition mandates, your first program is called Hello Android World. The following sections introduce you to the elements of the Android SDK and provide a detailed description of each step to create your first app.

Opening Eclipse to Create a New Project

To create a new Android project, you first open Eclipse and then select an Android Application Project. As you create your first project, you provide the following information:

- *Application name*—This is the human-readable title for your application, which will appear on the Android device.

- *Project name*—The Eclipse project name is the name of the directory that will contain the project files.

- *Package name*—This is the Java package namespace where your source code will reside. You need to have at least a period (.) in the package name. Typically, the recommended package name convention is your domain name in reverse order. For example, the domain name of this book is androidbootcamp.net. The package name would be net.androidbootcamp.HelloAndroidWorld. The package name must be unique when posted on Google Play, so it is vital to use a standard domain-style package name for your applications.

- *Minimum Required SDK*—This value specifies the minimum application programming interface (API) level required by your application.

- *Target SDK*—This value specifies the targeted application programming interface (API) level tested by your application.

- *Create Activity*—As the Activity name, use the name for the class that is generated by the plug-in. This will be a subclass of Android's Activity class. An Activity is a class that can run and do work, such as creating a user interface. Creating an Activity is optional, but an Activity is almost always used as the basis for an application.

Creating the Hello World Project

A project is equivalent to a single program or app using Java and the Android SDK. Be sure you have a blank USB (Universal Serial Bus) drive plugged into your computer so you can store the Android project on this USB drive. To create a new Android project, you can take the following steps:

STEP 1

- Open the Eclipse program.

- Tap or click the Browse button in the Workspace Launcher dialog box to select a Workspace folder to store the app on the E: drive (USB drive).

- Expand the This PC folder (or the Computer folder if you are using Windows 7).

- Select the E: drive and tap or click the OK button.

- Type **Workspace** after the E: drive path.

GTK

Throughout the rest of this book, the USB drive is called the E: drive, though you should select the drive on your computer that represents your USB device. If you are using a Mac, enter **/Volumes/USB_DRIVE_NAME** instead of E:\Workspace.

The Workspace location is placed on E:\Workspace drive. A workspace is a directory where Eclipse stores the projects that you define. When you specify this directory name to Eclipse, Eclipse creates files within this directory to manage the project (Figure 1-5).

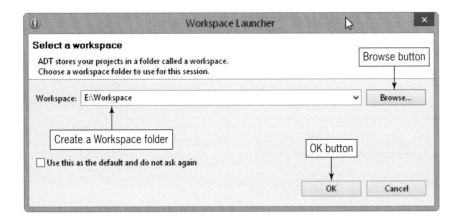

Figure 1-5   Workspace Launcher dialog box

STEP 2

- Tap or click the OK button on the Workspace Launcher dialog box.

- If necessary, tap or click the Close button on the Android IDE tab to close the welcome screen.

- Tap or click the first button on the Standard toolbar, which is the New button.

The New dialog box opens (Figure 1-6).

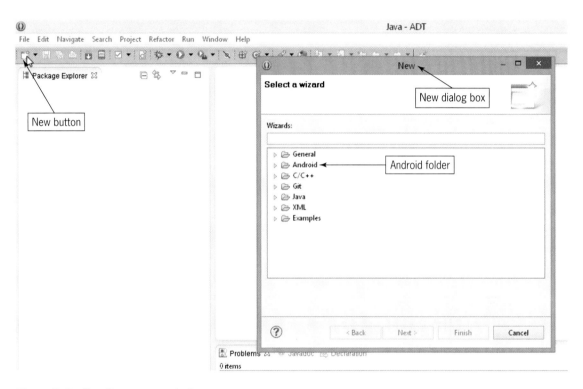

Figure 1-6 Creating a new project

STEP 3

- Expand the Android folder and then select Android Application Project.

Android Application Project is selected in the New dialog box (Figure 1-7).

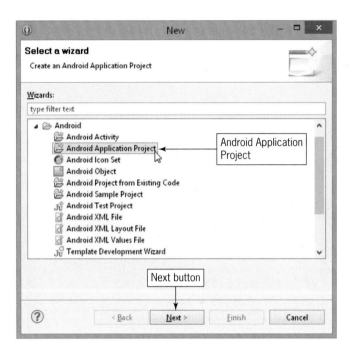

Figure 1-7   Selecting an Android Application Project

STEP 4

- Tap or click the Next button.

- In the New Android Application dialog box, enter the Application Name **Hello Android World**. The Project Name box displays the text that you entered for the Application Name without spaces.

- For the Package Name, type **net.androidbootcamp.helloandroidworld**.

A new application Hello Android World is created (Figure 1-8).

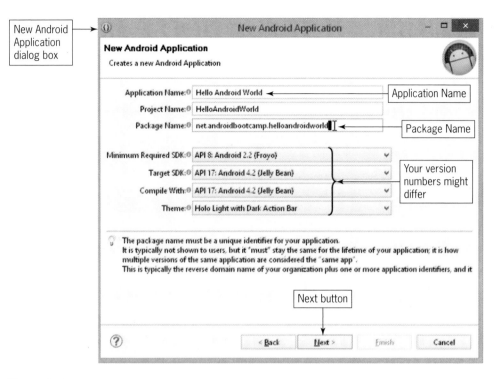

New Android
Application
dialog box

Application Name

Package Name

Your version
numbers might
differ

Next button

Figure 1-8 Naming an Android application

STEP 5

- Tap or click the Next button.
- Click the Create custom launcher icon check box to remove the check mark.

The Create custom launcher icon check box is unchecked (Figure 1-9).

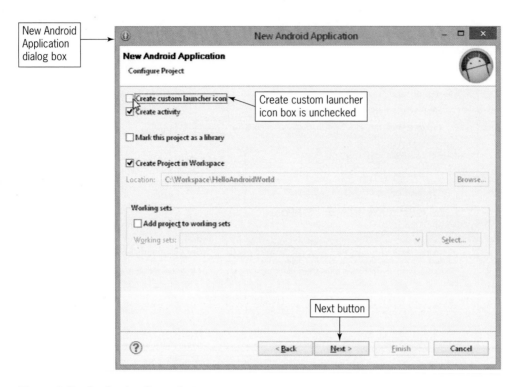

New Android
Application
dialog box

Create custom launcher
icon box is unchecked

Next button

Figure 1-9   Configuring the project

STEP 6

- Tap or click the Next button.

- In the New Android Application - Create Activity dialog box, tap or click the Next button.

A new blank activity is created named MainActivity with the layout activity_main (Figure 1-10).

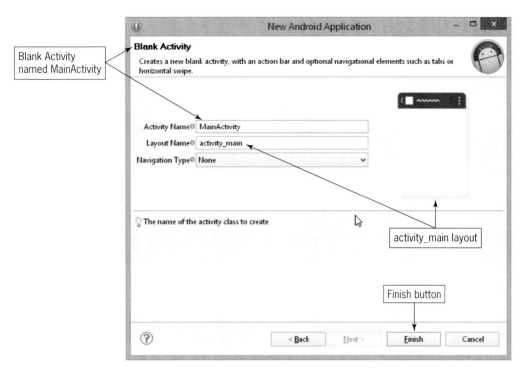

Figure 1-10   Creating a new blank Activity

STEP 7

● Tap or click the Finish button.

The Android project files are created on the USB drive. The HelloAndroidWorld project appears in the left pane.

Building the User Interface

Your first Android app will display the simple message, "Hello World – My First Android App". Beyond the tools and gadgets of the Android environment, what will stand out most is the user experience—how a user feels while using a particular device. Ensuring an intuitive user interface that does not detract from functionality is the key to a successful app. Android supports two ways of building a user interface: through Java code and through XML layout files. The XML method is preferred as it allows you to design the user interface of an application without needing to write large amounts of code. Both methods and more details about building the user interface are covered in later chapters.

Taking a Tour of the Package Explorer

The **Package Explorer** on the left side of the Eclipse program window contains the Hello Android World application folders. When the HelloAndroidWorld project folder is expanded (Figure 1-11), it shows that the Android project includes files in the following folders:

- The **src folder** includes the Java code source files for the project.

- The **gen folder** contains Java files that are automatically generated.

- The **Android Library** contains a single file, android.jar. The android.jar file contains all the class libraries needed to build an Android application for this version.

- The **assets folder** holds any asset files that are accessed through classic file manipulation.

- The **res folder** contains all the resources, such as images, music, and video files, that your application may need. The user interface is in the subfolder of the res folder.

- The **AndroidManifest.xml** file contains all the information about the application that Android needs to run.

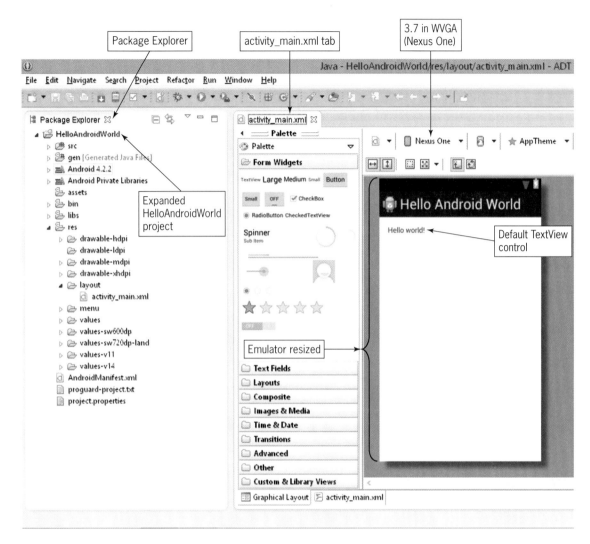

Figure 1-11 Expanded HelloAndroidWorld project folder in Package Explorer

Designing the User Interface Layout

To assist in designing the Android user interface, the Android SDK includes layout files. You can create a layout and then add widgets to the layout. A **layout** is a container that can hold as many widgets as needed. A **widget** is a single element such as a TextView, Button, or CheckBox control, and is also called an object. Upcoming chapters demonstrate many layouts, each with unique properties and characteristics. To open the layout files, follow these steps:

STEP 1

- If the Console pane is open at the bottom of the window, minimize it. Open the Package Explorer (if necessary) by clicking Window on the menu bar, pointing to Show View, and then clicking Package Explorer.

- To select an emulator, tap or click the emulator arrow button directly above the Palette, and then click 3.7in WVGA (Nexus One), if necessary. You can use many phone emulators, but throughout this text, select the 3.7in WVGA (Nexus One) emulator, unless you are instructed to do otherwise.

The activity_main.xml tab and the contents of the main.xml file are displayed in the Project window. The activity_main.xml tab includes an asterisk (*) to indicate that project changes have not been saved. Note that Android placed a default TextView control in the emulator window (Figure 1-12).

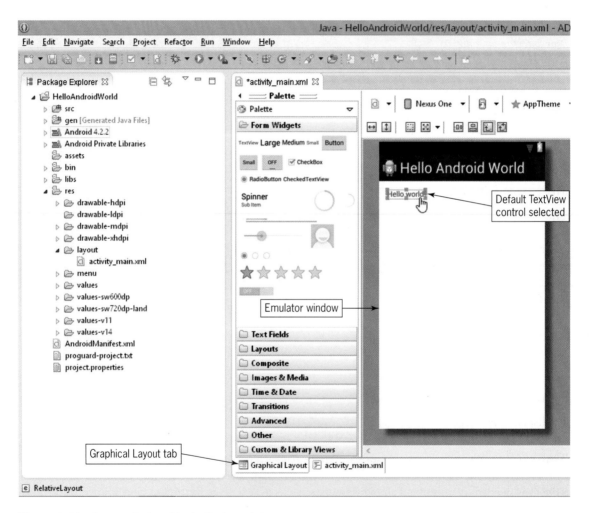

Figure 1-12   Layout displayed in the Project window

STEP 2

- In the emulator window, select the default TextView control, which reads Hello world!

The default TextView control is selected and displayed in a blue selection box (Figure 1-13).

STEP 3

- Press the Delete key.

The default TextView control that Android placed in the user interface is deleted.

GTK

It is best not to target your program only for the latest platform because older phones cannot run the application.

Adding a Form Widget to the User Interface Layout

The Android User Interface Layout editor displays form widgets that you place on the user interface using the drag-and-drop method. Technically, a widget is a View object that functions as an interface for interaction with the mobile user. In other words, a widget is a control such as a message that users read or a button users tap or click. The tabs at the bottom of the emulator identify the Graphical Layout window and the activity_main.xml window, which displays the code behind each form widget. Each window displays a different view of the project: The Graphical Layout view allows you to preview how the controls will appear on various screens and orientations, and the XML view shows you the XML definition of the resource.

Figure 1-13   Selected TextView control

To display a message on the Android device, you must first place a TextView form widget on the emulator and then change the Text property to display the appropriate message. To add a form widget to the user interface layout, follow these steps:

STEP 1

- In the activity_main.xml tab, select TextView in the Form Widgets list in the Palette.

- Drag the TextView control to the emulator window and drop it below the title Hello Android World.

The TextView control is placed in the emulator window (Figure 1-14).

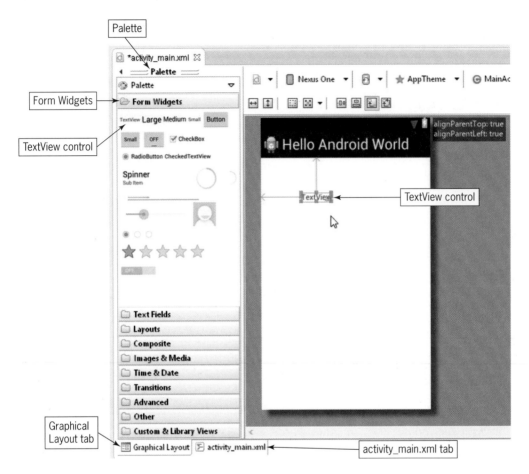

Figure 1-14   TextView control in the emulator

STEP 2

- In the Properties pane on the right side of the window, select the default text to the right of the Text property.

- Type **Hello World – My First Android App** in the Text property, and then press the Enter key.

The Text property displays Hello World – My First Android App in the TextView control in the emulator (Figure 1-15).

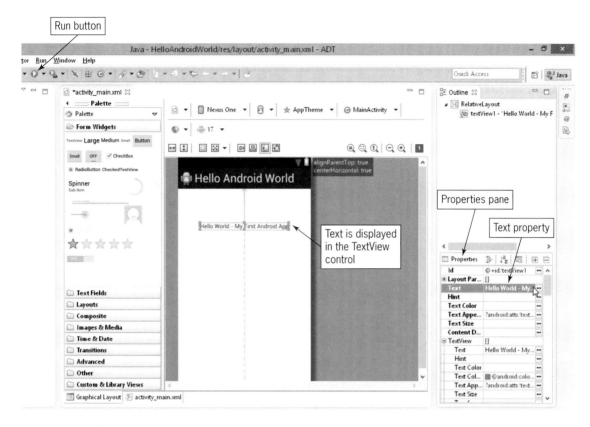

Figure 1-15   Changing the Text property

STEP 3

- If the text you typed does not appear on one line, drag a selection handle on the selected control to increase its width.

- Drag the TextView control to the center of the emulator, using the dashed green line to guide you.

GTK

To deploy your app to an actual Android device instead of the emulator, tap or click Run on the toolbar. In the Run As window that appears, select Android Application, and then tap or click OK.

Testing the Application in the Emulator

Time to see the finished result! Keep in mind that the Android emulator runs slowly. It can take over a minute to display your finished results in the emulator. Even when the emulator is idling, it consumes a significant amount of CPU time, so you should close the emulator when you complete your testing. To run the application, follow these steps:

STEP 1

- Tap or click the Run button on the toolbar.

   Note: If the app does not run, expand the src folder in the Package Explorer. Expand net. androidbootcamp.helloandroidworld. Tap or click the MainActivity.java file, and then tap or click the Run button on the toolbar.

- If necessary, tap or click Android Application in the Run As dialog box, and then click the OK button.

- When the Save Resource dialog box is displayed, click the Yes button to save your changes.

The program slowly begins to execute by displaying the Android logo and then an application window with the Android splash screen on the left. This may take up to one full minute. Next, the Android main screen appears with a lock icon (Figure 1-16).

Figure 1-16   Android emulator lock screen

STEP 2

- Tap or click the lock icon and slide it across the screen to the right to unlock the simulated device. If you are using a Mac, drag the lock icon until it changes to an unlock icon.

After the Android device is unlocked, the emulator displays the text message (Figure 1-17).

STEP 3

- Close the application by tapping or clicking the Close button.

The emulated application window closes. The program is saved each time the program is run. You can close Eclipse by tapping or clicking File on the menu bar and then clicking Exit if you are working on a Windows computer. Press the Command+Q keys to close Eclipse if you are working on a Mac.

Figure 1-17　Message displayed in the emulator

GTK
Ctrl+F11 is the Windows shortcut key combination for running your Android application in Eclipse. On a Mac, the shortcut keys are Command+Shift+F11.

Opening a Saved App in Eclipse

After you save a project and close Eclipse, you might need to open the project and work on it again. To open a saved project, you can follow these steps with Eclipse open:

STEP 1

- If the project is not listed in the Package Explorer, tap or click File on the Eclipse menu bar and select Import.

- In the Import dialog box, expand the Android folder, if necessary, and then tap or click Existing Android Code Into Workspace.

The Import dialog box opens and in the Select an import source area, the Existing Android Code Into Workspace folder is selected (Figure 1-18).

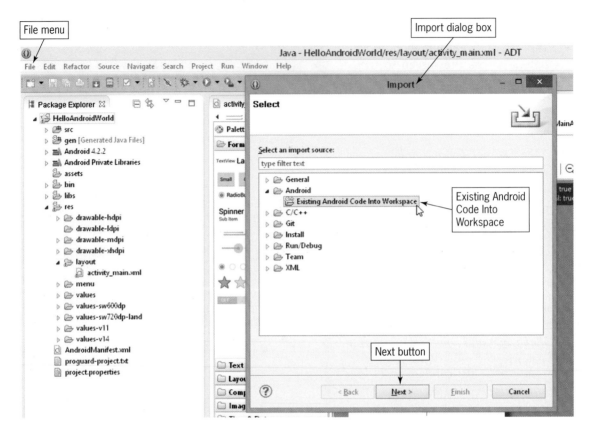

Figure 1-18   Import dialog box

STEP 2

- Tap or click the Next button.

- Tap or click the Browse button next to the Root Directory text box.

- Tap or click the arrow to expand This PC (or Computer in Windows 7) and then tap or click the arrow to expand the USB drive on a Windows computer. (If you are using a Mac, click the USB DEVICE in the left pane of the Finder.)

- Tap or click the arrow to expand the Workspace folder.

- Tap or click to select the HelloAndroidWorld project.

- Tap or click the OK button.

In the Import Projects dialog box, the root directory and the HelloAndroidWorld project are selected (Figure 1-19).

Figure 1-19 Project and directory selected

STEP 3

- Tap or click the Finish button.

The program loads into the Package Explorer. You can now continue working on your user interface and code.

GTK
To delete a project from the project workspace, press and hold or right-click the project name in the Package Explorer. Select Delete on the shortcut menu. Tap or click the OK button. The project is still saved on the USB drive, but is no longer in the Package Explorer.

Wrap It Up—Chapter Summary

This chapter has provided an overview of the Android open-source platform, which is positioned for fast innovation without the restraints of a proprietary system. With the largest market share and its rich feature set, the Android environment allows you to develop useful, inventive Android apps. In the first chapter project, Hello Android World, you completed steps that start your journey to create more interesting applications in future chapters.

- The Android operating system is released under the Apache license, which permits anyone to download the full open-source Android code for free. Android is the first open-source technology platform for mobile devices.

- The Android OS powers all types of mobile devices, including smartphones, tablets, netbooks, MP4 players, and Internet TVs.

- To write Android apps, you can use Eclipse, an integrated development environment for building applications, including Android apps, using Java, an object-oriented programming language.

- The Android emulator lets you design, develop, prototype, and test Android applications without using a physical device. When you run an Android program in Eclipse, the emulator starts so you can test the program as if it were running on a specified Android mobile device.

- The Android platform consists of the Android OS, the Android application development platform, and Google Play, a marketplace for Android applications.

- Android supports two ways of building the user interface of an application: through Java code and through XML layout files. The XML method is preferred as it allows you to design the user interface of an application without needing to write large amounts of code.

- The Package Explorer on the left side of the Eclipse program window contains the folders for an Android project.

- To design a user interface for an Android app, you can create a layout, which is a container that displays widgets such as TextView, Button, and CheckBox controls, also called objects.

- After you create an application, you can run it in the Android emulator to test the application and make sure it runs correctly.

Key Terms

Android Development Tools (ADT)—An Eclipse plug-in that extends the capabilities of Eclipse to create Android projects.

Android Library—A project folder that contains the android.jar file, which includes all the class libraries needed to build an Android application for the specified version.

AndroidManifest.xml—A file containing all the information Android needs to run an application.

app—A mobile application.

assets folder—A project folder containing any asset files that are accessed through classic file manipulation.

Eclipse—The most popular IDE for writing Java programs and for building and integrating application development tools and open-source projects.

emulator—Software that duplicates how an app looks and feels on a particular device.

gen folder—A project folder that contains automatically generated Java files.

Google Play—An online store that sells programs written for the Android platform.

Java—An object-oriented programming language and a platform originated by Sun Microsystems.

layout—A container that can hold widgets and other graphical elements to help you design an interface for an application.

object-oriented programming language—A type of programming language that allows good software engineering practices such as code reuse.

Open Handset Alliance—An open-source business alliance of 80 firms that develop open standards for mobile devices.

open-source operating system—Organizations and developers can extract, modify, and use the source code free of charge and copyright restrictions.

Package Explorer—A pane on the left side of the Eclipse program window that contains the folders for the current project.

res folder—A project folder that contains all the resources, such as images, music, and video files, that an application may need.

Software Development Kit (SDK)—A package containing development tools for creating applications.

src folder—A project folder that includes the Java code source files for the project.

widget—A single element such as a TextView, Button, or CheckBox control, and is also called an object.

XML—An acronym for Extensible Markup Language, a widely used system for defining data formats. XML assists in the layout of the Android emulator.

Developer FAQs

1. What was the first dessert name to describe an Android version?
2. What is the one-time cost for a developer's account at Google Play?
3. When you post an Android app at Google Play, what percentage of the app price does the developer keep?
4. How much is Amazon's annual fee for a developer's account?

5. Which three manufacturers' operating systems can be used to program an Android app?

6. Which two languages are used in creating an Android app in Eclipse?

7. In which folder are the Java source files stored?

8. Name three widgets mentioned in this chapter.

9. What is the name of the widget that was used in the Hello Android World app?

10. Which two key combinations can you press to execute an Android app in Eclipse?

11. Which Android version is KitKat?

12. Using the alphabetical theme for Android version names, name three possible future names for the next versions of Android device operating systems.

13. What does XML stand for?

14. What does SDK stand for?

15. Where are music and image files saved within the Package Explorer?

Beyond the Book

Using the Internet, search the Web for the following answers to further your Android knowledge.

1. Research a particular model of a popular Android smartphone or tablet device and write a paragraph on this device's features, specifications, price, and manufacturer.

2. Name five Android mobile device features not mentioned in the "Meet the Android" section of Chapter 1.

3. What is the current annual cost for a developer's account at the iPhone and Windows Store?

4. Go to Google Play Web site and take a screen-shot of each of the following app categories: education, gaming, mapping, travel, and personal hobby. Place screen-shots in a word processor document and label each one to identify it.

Case Programming Projects

Complete one or more of the following case programming projects. Use the same steps and techniques taught within the chapter. Submit the program you create to your instructor. The level of difficulty is indicated for each case programming project.

Easiest: ★

Intermediate: ★★

Challenging: ★★★

Case Project 1–1: Joke of the Day App ★

Requirements Document

Application title:	Joke of the Day App
Purpose:	In the Joke of the Day app, a joke of your choice is displayed.
Algorithms:	The opening screen displays the joke of the day.
Conditions:	You may change the joke to one of your own (Figure 1-20).

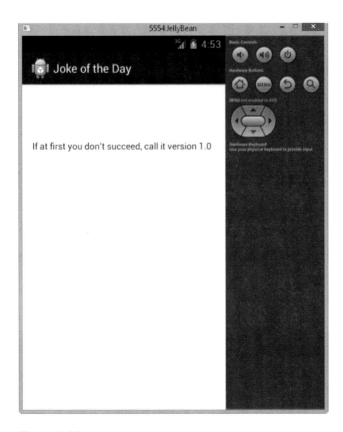

Figure 1-20

Case Project 1–2: Android Dessert Versions App ★★

Requirements Document

Application title:	Android Dessert Versions App
Purpose:	In the Android Terminology app, the version names (desserts) introduced in Chapter 1 are displayed.
Algorithms:	The opening screen displays the dessert names of Android versions listed in this chapter.
Conditions:	Multiple TextView controls are required.

Case Project 1–3: Business Card App ★★★

Requirements Document

Application title:	Business Card App
Purpose:	In the Business Card app, your address and other information are displayed.
Algorithms:	The opening screen displays a simple business card with your personal information. The first line should include your name. The second line should include your future dream job title. The third line should include your address.

CHAPTER 2

Simplify! The Android User Interface

Unless otherwise noted in the chapter, all screenshots are provided courtesy of Eclipse.

In this chapter, you learn to:

- ◎ Develop a user interface using the TextView, ImageView, and Button controls
- ◎ Create an Android project that includes a Button event
- ◎ Describe Relative and Linear layouts for the user interface
- ◎ Create multiple Android Activities
- ◎ Add Activities to the Android Manifest file
- ◎ Add a Java class file
- ◎ Write code using the onCreate method
- ◎ Display content using the setContentView command
- ◎ Open a second screen using a Button event handler
- ◎ Use an OnClickListener to detect user interaction
- ◎ Launch a second screen using a startActivity method
- ◎ Correct errors in Java code
- ◎ Run the completed app in the emulator

Before a mobile app can be coded using Java, it must be designed. Designing a program can be compared with constructing a building. Before cement slabs are poured, steel beams are put in place, and walls are erected, architects and engineers must design the building to ensure it will perform as required and be safe and reliable. The same holds true for a computer app developer. Once the program is designed within the user interface, it can be implemented through the use of Extensible Markup Language (XML) and Java code to perform the functions for which it was designed.

Designing an Android App

To illustrate the process of designing and implementing an Android app, in this chapter you will design and code the Healthy Recipes application shown in Figures 2-1 and 2-2.

Figure 2-1   Healthy Recipes Android app

Figure 2-2   Second window displaying the recipe

The Android app in Figure 2-1 could be part of a larger app that is used to display Healthy Recipes. The Healthy Recipes app begins by displaying the recipe name, which is Guacamole Recipe, and an image illustrating the ingredients. If the user taps the View Recipe button, a second window opens displaying the full recipe, including the ingredients and preparation for making guacamole.

 IN THE TRENCHES
If you own a data plan phone, tablet, or other mobile device, download the free app called Epicurious to get an idea of how this Healthy Recipes app would be used in a much larger application.

The Big Picture

To create the Healthy Recipes application, you follow a set of steps that you repeat every time you create an Android application.

1. Create the user interface, also called an XML layout, for every screen in the application.

2. Create a Java class, also called an Activity, for every screen in the application.

3. Update the Android Manifest file for each Java class in the application.

4. Code each Java class with the appropriate objects and actions as needed.

Using the Android User Interface

Before any code can be written for an Android application, you design the user interface to control the user experience. For an Android application, the user interface is a window on the screen of any mobile device in which the user interacts with the program. The user interface is stored in the res/ layout folder in the Package Explorer. The layout for the user interface is stored as XML code. Special Android-formatted XML code is extremely compact, which means the application uses less space and runs faster on the device. Using XML for layout also saves you time in developing your code; for example, if you developed this recipe app for use in eight human languages, you could use the same Java code with eight unique XML layout files, one for each language. To open the layout of the user interface of the Healthy Recipes app and begin the application, follow these steps:

STEP 1

- Open the Eclipse program.

- Type **E:\Workspace** (if necessary, enter a different drive letter that identifies the USB drive) to select a workspace, and then tap or click the OK button.

- Tap or click the New button on the Standard toolbar and then select Android Application Project.

- Tap or click the Next button.

- In the New Android Application dialog box, enter the Application Name **Healthy Recipes**.

- Enter the Package Name of **net.androidbootcamp.healthyrecipes**.

   Notice the Minimum Required SDK text box displays the API number from the selected Target SDK. If you are deploying to an earlier model of an Android device, you can select an earlier version.

The new Android Healthy Recipes project has an application name and a package name (Figure 2-3).

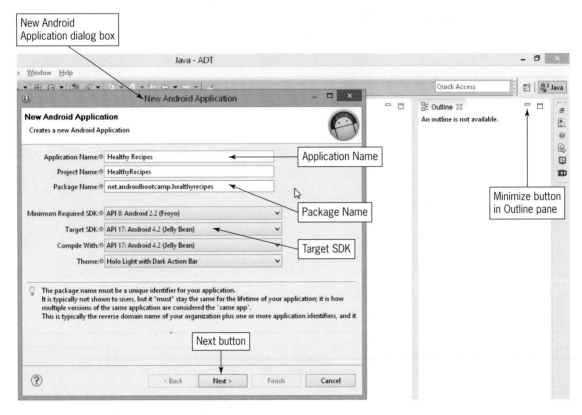

Figure 2-3   Application information for the new Android application

STEP 2

- Tap or click the Next button.

- Tap or click the Create custom launcher icon check box to remove the check mark.

- Tap or click the Next button twice.

- Tap or click the Finish button.

- If necessary, expand the Healthy Recipes project in the Package Explorer, and then double-click the activity_main.xml file to open the Healthy Recipes layout in the emulator.

- Tap or click the Minimize button on the Outline pane.

- Tap or click the Hello world! TextView (displayed by default) in the emulator and then press the Delete key.

The activity_main.xml file is displayed on the Graphical Layout tab and the Hello world TextView widget is deleted (Figure 2-4).

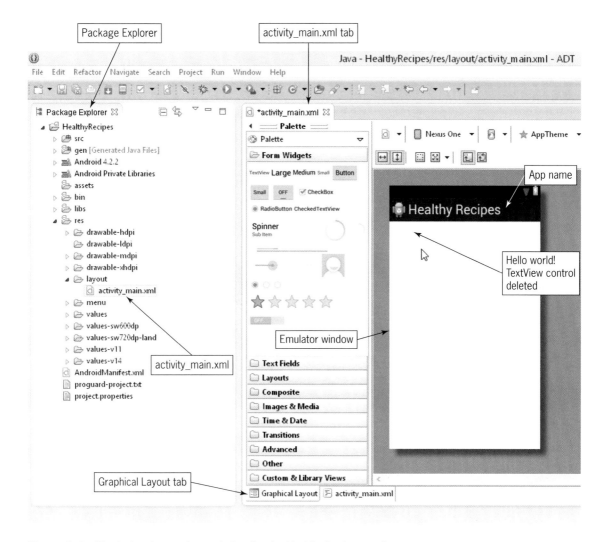

Figure 2-4   Displaying the emulator window for the Healthy Recipes project

GTK

The asterisk (*) on a tab, such as the activity_main.xml tab in Figure 2-4, means the tab contains work that needs to be saved. The asterisk is an indicator Eclipse displays to remind you to save the file.

Relative Layouts and Linear Layouts

The Android user interface includes a layout resource designer that organizes how controls appear on the app's various screens. When you click the Graphical Layout tab shown in Figure 2-4, you display the default user interface for activity_main.xml, which uses a resource file defined as a Relative layout.

A **Relative layout** organizes layout components in relation to each other as shown in Figure 2-5. This provides more flexibility in positioning controls than other layouts. As shown in Figure 2-5, four ImageView controls are placed anywhere the developer desires. Using a Relative layout, you can place an ImageView, TextView, RadioButton, or Button control to the left of, to the right of, above, or below another control. Layout resources are stored as XML code in the res/layout resource directory for the Android application corresponding to the user interface template.

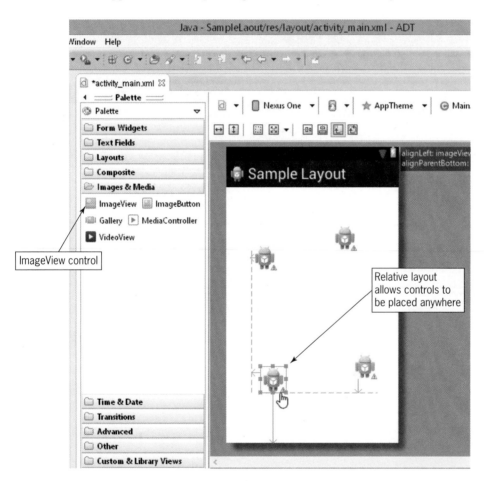

Figure 2-5   Relative layout

Another layout called a **Linear layout** organizes layout components in a vertical column or horizontal row. In Figure 2-6, multiple ImageView controls (Android icons) were dragged onto the emulator window. A Linear layout places each control directly below the previous control to form a vertical column. To change the default Relative layout to a Linear layout, press and hold or right-click the emulator window and then tap or click Change Layout. In the Change Layout dialog box, tap or click the New Layout Type button and then click LinearLayout (Vertical). Tap or click the OK button to change the emulator to a Linear layout. If you select a vertical Linear layout and drag the images onto the emulator, the images are arranged vertically in multiple rows, as shown in Figure 2-6. Linear layouts are common for forms that display controls in a single row or column.

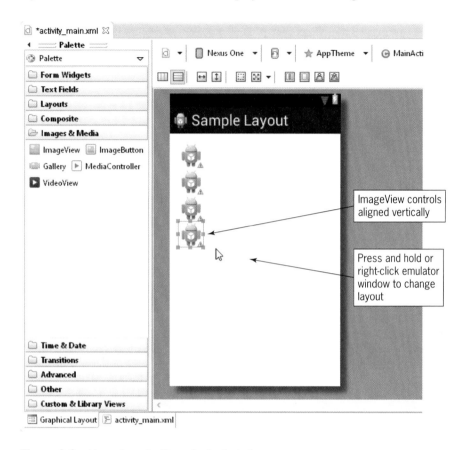

ImageView controls aligned vertically

Press and hold or right-click emulator window to change layout

Figure 2-6   Linear layout with vertical orientation

GTK
Other layouts you can use include a Frame Layout, Table Layout, and TableRow Layout. You also can use a combination of layouts, which means you can nest controls within one another.

Designing the Healthy Recipes Opening User Interface

When the Healthy Recipes app opens, the initial screen as shown in Figure 2-1 displays a TextView control with the text Guacamole Recipe, an ImageView control with a picture of the ingredients for the guacamole, and a Button control with the text View Recipe. Notice that the controls are not in a Linear layout, but use a Relative layout so they are placed freely on the screen. You can modify a control's properties using the Properties pane. To change the property of a control, select the control first, and then change the appropriate property, such as the text or size, in the Properties pane.

Android Text Properties

The most popular text properties change the displayed text, modify the size of the text, and change the alignment of the text. The **Text property** changes the text written within the control. The **Text Size property** can use various units of measurement, as shown in Table 2-1. The preferred unit of measurement is often **sp**, which stands for scaled-independent pixels. The reason for using this unit of measurement is that if a user has set up an Android phone to display a large font size for more clarity and easier visibility, the font in the app will be scaled to meet the user's size preference.

Unit of Measure	Abbreviation	Example
Inches	in	"0.5in"
Millimeters	mm	"20mm"
Pixels	px	"100px"
Density-independent pixels	dp or dip	"100dp" or "100dip"
Scaled-independent pixels	sp	"10sp"

Table 2-1   Measurements used for the Text Size property

On the opening screen of the Healthy Recipes app, the TextView control for the title, ImageView control for the guacamole picture, and Button controls can all be centered on the screen using a guide, a green dashed vertical line that appears when a control is dragged to the emulator window. The Relative layout allows controls to be placed anywhere, but the green dashed line centers each control perfectly.

GTK

All Palette controls such as TextView and ImageView can use a property called Layout margin top. For example, if you type 50dp to the right of the Layout margin top property, the control is placed 50 pixels from the top of the screen to help you design an exact layout. You can also center controls by changing the Layout center horizontal property to true.

GTK

When you add text to a TextView control, a small yellow triangle appears in the right corner of the text in the emulator. If you hover over the triangle, a message appears that the Hardcoded string should use @string resource. In upcoming chapters, the @string resource will be explained and updated.

To center a TextView control on the form using the default Relative layout, follow these steps:

STEP 1

- In the Form Widgets Palette, select the Form Widget named TextView. Drag the TextView control to the emulator window and drop it below the Healthy Recipes title.

- To center the TextView control, drag the control to the center of the window until a green dashed vertical line identifying the window's center is displayed.

- Tap or click the Window menu, select Reset Perspective, and then tap or click the Yes button to reset the Eclipse view layout.

- Tap or click the Minimize button on the Problems pane at the bottom of the screen.

- Select the TextView control again, and then tap or click to the right of the Text property in the Properties pane.

The TextView object is placed in the emulator window, the Properties pane is opened, and the Text property is selected (Figure 2-7).

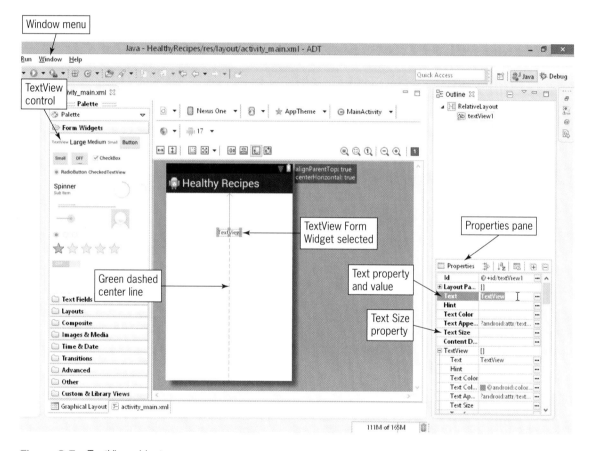

Figure 2-7 TextView object

STEP 2

- Change the Text property to **Guacamole Recipe**.

- In the Properties pane, tap or click to the right of the Text Size property, type **34sp** to represent the scaled-independent pixel size, and then press Enter.

The TextView object has the Text property of Guacamole Recipe and the Text Size is 34sp (Figure 2-8).

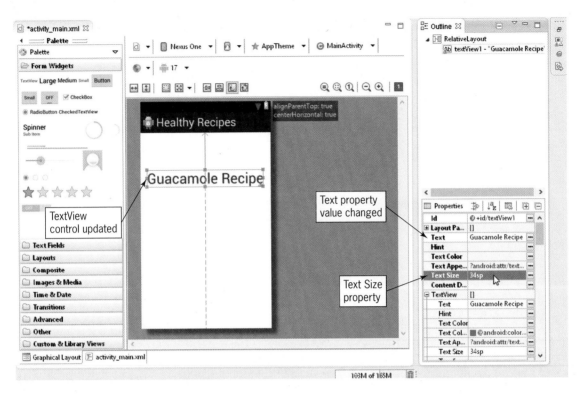

Figure 2-8   Updated Text property

GTK
The top free Android apps are Google Maps, Gmail, Facebook, Angry Birds, YouTube, and Skype, in that order.

GTK
Throughout the book, note that Windows computers have an Enter key, but Mac computers use the Return key.

Adding a File to the Resources Folder

In the Healthy Recipes application, an image of guacamole is displayed in an ImageView control. Before you can insert the ImageView control in the emulator window, you must place the appropriate picture file in the resources folder. In the Package Explorer in the left pane of the Eclipse program window, the res (resource) folder contains three subfolders whose names start with *drawable*. The graphics used by the application can be stored in these folders. Android supports three types of graphic formats: .png (preferred), .jpg (acceptable), and .gif (discouraged).

Android categorizes device screens using two general properties: size and density. You should expect that your app will be installed on devices with screens that vary in both size and density. Android creates a Drawable resource for any of these images when you save them in the res/drawable folder. The four drawable folders are identified with the dpi (dots per inch) densities shown in Table 2-2. To declare different layouts and images for different sized screens, you must place these alternative resources in separate directories, similar to how you do for different language strings. Android automatically scales your layout to properly fit the screen. By using appropriate images, you can achieve the best graphical quality and performance on all screen densities. In this text for brevity, one image will be placed in the hdpi folder for testing purposes.

Name	Description
xhdpi	Resources for extra high-density screens
hdpi	Resources for high-density screens
mdpi	Resources for medium-density screens
ldpi	Resources for low-density screens

© 2015 Cengage Learning

Table 2-2   Drawable folders

Place the guacamole image in the res/drawable-hdpi folder to be used by the ImageView control, which links to the resource image. You should already have the student files for this text that your instructor gave you or that you downloaded from the Web page for this book *(www.cengagebrain.com)*. To place a copy of the guacamole image from the USB drive into the res/drawable-hdpi folder, follow these steps:

STEP 1

- If necessary, copy the student files to your USB drive. Open the USB folder containing the student files.

- In the Package Explorer pane, expand the res folder and then expand the drawable-hdpi folder. A file named ic_launcher.png (the Android logo) is typically contained within this folder already.

- To add the guacamole.png file to the drawable-hdpi resource folder, drag the guacamole.png file to the drawable-hdpi folder until a plus sign pointer appears. Release the mouse button.

The File Operation dialog box opens (Figure 2-9).

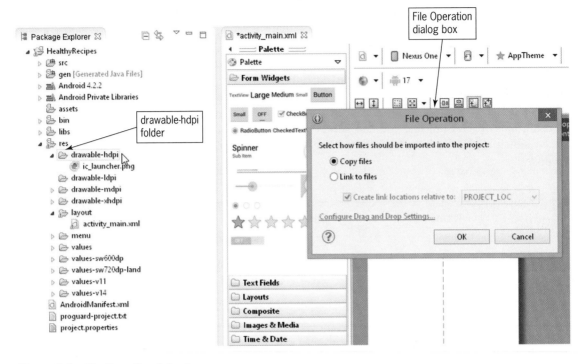

Figure 2-9 File Operation dialog box

STEP 2

- If necessary, tap or click the Copy files option button, and then tap or click the OK button.

A copy of the guacamole.png file appears in the drawable-hdpi folder (Figure 2-10).

GTK
Extra high-density graphics have 320 dots per inch (typically a tablet), high-density graphics have 240 dots per inch, medium-density graphics have 160 dots per inch, and low-density graphics have 120 dots per inch.

Adding an ImageView Control

After an image is placed in a drawable resource folder, you can place an ImageView control in the emulator window. An **ImageView control** can display an icon or a graphic such as a picture file or shape on the Android screen. To add an ImageView control from the Images & Media category of the Palette, follow these steps:

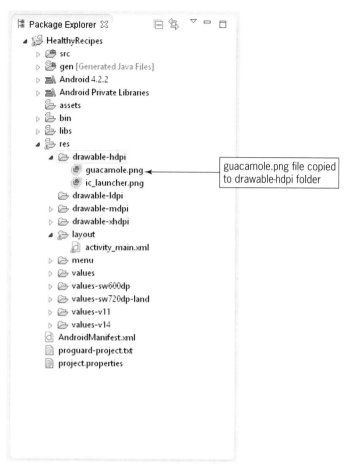

Figure 2-10   Package Explorer

STEP 1

- Tap or click the Images & Media category in the Palette on the Graphical Layout tab.

- Drag an ImageView control (the first control in this category) to the emulator window.

- Drag the control to the center until a green dashed vertical center line appears. Release the mouse button.

The ImageView control is centered and the Resource Chooser dialog box opens (Figure 2-11).

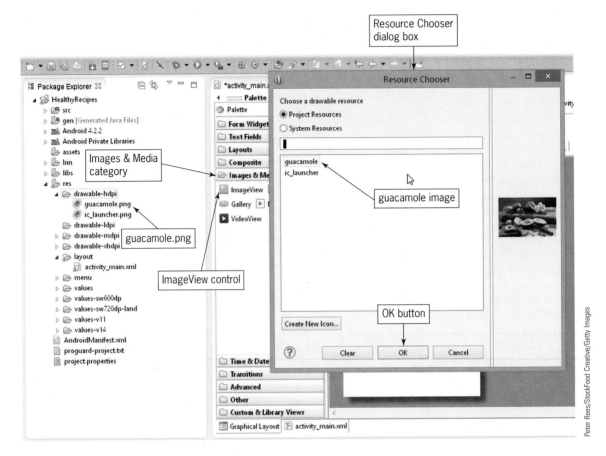

Figure 2-11   Resource Chooser dialog box

STEP 2

- Tap or click guacamole in the Resource Chooser dialog box, and then click the OK button.

The guacamole image is displayed in the emulator window (Figure 2-12).

IN THE TRENCHES
If you have an image that you want to use in your Android app, but the file type is not .png, open the image in Microsoft Paint or a similar type of program. You can convert the file type by saving the image as a .png file.

Adding a Button Control

A Button control is a commonly used object in a graphical user interface. For example, you probably are familiar with the OK button used in many applications. Generally, when the program is running, buttons are used to cause an event to occur. The Android SDK includes four types of button controls: Button, Small Button, ToggleButton, and ImageButton. The Button control is provided in the Form Widgets category in the Palette. In the Healthy Recipes app, the user taps a Button control to display the

Figure 2-12   ImageView control

ImageView control centered

Peter Rees/StockFood Creative/Getty Images

guacamole recipe on a second screen. To name the Button control, you use the Id property. For example, use btnRecipe as the Id property for the Button control in the Healthy Recipes app. The prefix btn represents a button in the code. If you intend to use a control in the Java code, it is best to name that control using the Id property. To add a Button control from the Form Widgets category of the Palette, follow these steps:

STEP 1

- Tap or click the Form Widgets category in the Palette.

- Drag the Button control to the emulator window below the ImageView control until a green dashed vertical center line appears. Release the mouse button.

- If necessary, tap or click the Button control to select it, and then scroll the Properties pane to the Id property, which is set to @+id/button1 by default.

- Change the Id property to **@+id/btnRecipe** to provide a unique name for the Button control, and then press Enter.

- Tap or click the Yes button on the Update References dialog box to update all XML references to the Button control, and then tap or click the OK button.

●   Use the Text property to change the button text to **View Recipe**. Change the Text size property to **30sp** and press Enter.

The Button control is named btnRecipe and displays the text View Recipe, which has the text size of 30sp (Figure 2-13).

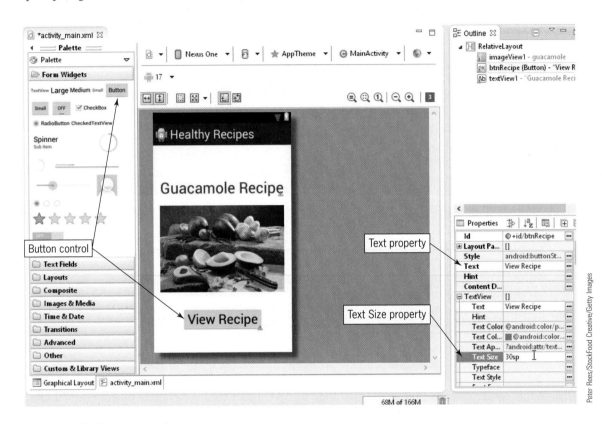

Peter Rees/StockFood Creative/Getty Images

Figure 2-13   Button control

Planning a Program

As you acquire the skills necessary to design an Android user interface, you are ready to learn about the program development life cycle. The program development life cycle is a set of phases and steps that developers follow to design, create, and maintain an Android program. Following are the phases of the program development life cycle:

1. *Gather and analyze the program requirements*—The developer must obtain the information that identifies the program requirements and then document these requirements.

2. *Design the user interface*—After the developer understands the program requirements, the next step is to design the user interface. The user interface provides the framework for the processing that occurs within the program.

3. *Design the program processing objects*—An Android app consists of one or more processing objects that perform the tasks required in the program. The developer must determine what processing objects are required, and then determine the requirements of each object. Your design of the user interface plays an important part in keeping the overall Android experience consistent and enjoyable to use.

4. *Code the program*—After the processing object has been designed, the object must be implemented in program code. Program code consists of the instructions written using XML and Java code that ultimately can be executed.

5. *Test the program*—As the program is being coded, and after the coding is completed, the developer should test the program code to ensure it is executing properly.

Creating Activities

The Healthy Recipes application displays two screens, as shown in Figures 2-1 and 2-2. The system requirement for this app is for the user to select a recipe name and then tap a button to display the recipe details. Screens in the Android environment are defined in layout files. Figure 2-13 shows the completed activity_main.xml design. Next, a second screen named recipe.xml must be created and designed. Each of the two screens is considered an Activity. An **Activity**, one of the core components of an Android application, is the point at which the application makes contact with your users. For example, an Activity might create a menu of Web sites, request a street address to display a map, or even show an exhibit of photographs from an art museum. An Activity is an important component of the life cycle of an Android app. In the chapter project, each screen is an Activity where you capture and present information to the user. You can construct Activities by using XML layout files and a Java class.

Creating an XML Layout File

All XML layout files must be placed in the res/layout directory of the Android project so that the Android packaging tool can find the layout files. To create a second XML layout file to construct the second Activity, follow these steps:

STEP 1

- In the Package Explorer, press and hold or right-click the layout folder.

- On the shortcut menu, point to New and then tap or click Android XML File.

- In the New Android Layout XML File dialog box, type **recipe.xml** in the File text box to name the layout file.

- In the Root Element list, select RelativeLayout.

The XML file is named recipe.xml and the layout is set to RelativeLayout (Figure 2-14).

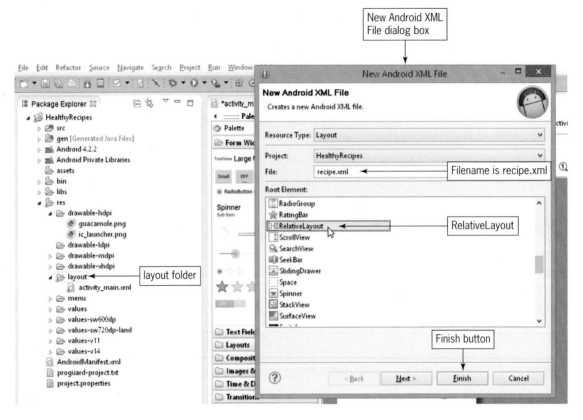

Figure 2-14 Naming the XML file

STEP 2

- Tap or click the Finish button to create a second XML layout named recipe.xml.

- Using the techniques taught earlier in the chapter, create the second user interface, recipe.xml, as shown in Figure 2-15 with multiple TextView controls.

The second user interface, recipe.xml, is designed (Figure 2-15).

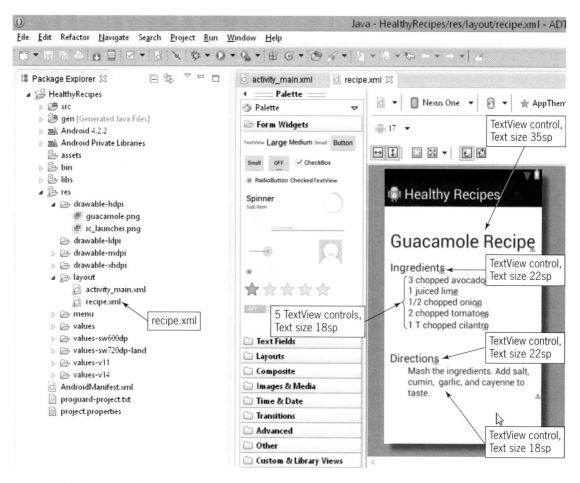

Figure 2-15   User interface for recipe.xml

GTK
You can use comments to document your code. Comments are ignored by the Java compiler. When you want to make a one-line comment, type two forward slashes (//), and then enter your comment. For example:
// This is a single-line comment
Another way to comment is to use block comments. For example:
/* This is a
block comment
*/

Adding a Class File

The src folder in the Package Explorer includes the MainActivity.java file. This file contains the MainActivity class that opens the activity_main.xml screen, which you designed for the app's user interface. In object-oriented terminology, a class describes a group of objects that establishes an introduction to each object's properties. A **class** is simply a blueprint or a template for creating objects by defining its properties. Classes are the fundamental building blocks of a Java program. Classes are categories, and objects are items within each category. An **object** is a specific, concrete instance of a class. When you create an object, you instantiate it. When you **instantiate**, you create an instance of the object by defining one particular variation of the object within a class, giving it a name, and locating it in the memory of the computer. Each class needs its own copy of an object. A class determines what data an object can hold and the way it can behave when using the data.

Later in this chapter, Java code is added to the MainActivity class to recognize the action of tapping the Button control to open the recipe screen. Recall that each screen represents an Activity. In addition, each Activity must have a matching Java class file. The recipe.xml file that was designed as shown in Figure 2-15 must have a corresponding Java class file. It is a Java standard to begin a class name with an uppercase letter, include no spaces, and emphasize each new word with an initial uppercase letter. To add a second Java class to the application, follow these steps:

STEP 1

- Close the recipe.xml and activity_main.xml tabs and save your changes.

- In the Package Explorer, expand the src folder and the net.androidbootcamp.healthyrecipes package to view the MainActivity.java existing class.

- To create a second class, press and hold or right-click the net.androidbootcamp.healthyrecipes folder, point to New on the shortcut menu, and then tap or click Class.

The New Java Class dialog box opens (Figure 2-16).

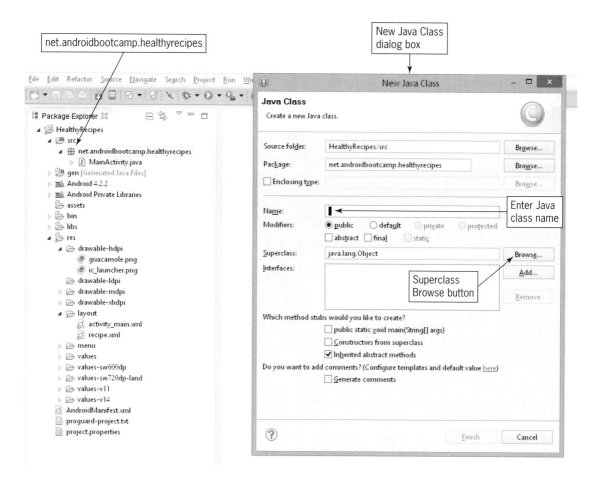

net.androidbootcamp.healthyrecipes

New Java Class dialog box

Enter Java class name

Superclass Browse button

Figure 2-16 New Java Class dialog box

STEP 2

- Type Recipe in the Name text box to create a second class for the recipe Activity.

- Tap or click the Superclass Browse button. Type **Activity** in the Choose a type text box. As you type, matching items are displayed.

- Tap or click Activity - android.app and then tap or click the OK button to extend the Activity class.

A new class named Recipe is created with the Superclass set to android.app.Activity (Figure 2-17).

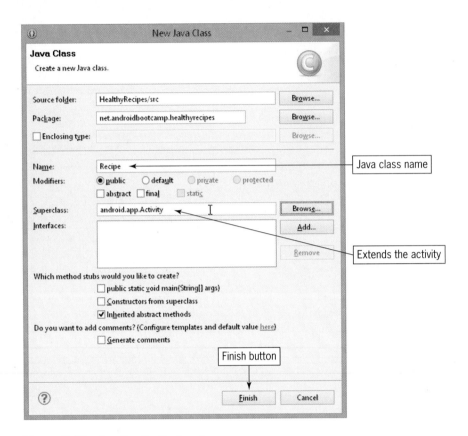

Figure 2-17   Creating the Recipe class

STEP 3

- Tap or click the Finish button to finish creating the Recipe class.

- Display line numbers in the code window, if necessary, by tapping or clicking Window on the menu bar and then tapping or clicking Preferences.

- In the Preferences dialog box, expand General in the left pane.

- Expand Editors, and then tap or click Text Editors.

- Tap or click the Show line numbers check box to select it, and then tap or click the OK button.

  If you are using a Mac, click ADT on the menu bar, and then click Preferences to open the Preferences dialog box. Double-click General, double-click Editors, and then click Text Editors.

The Recipe.java class is created and line numbers are displayed (Figure 2-18).

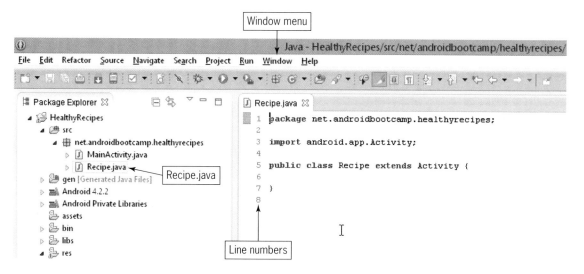

Figure 2-18 New Recipe class in the Healthy Recipes project

GTK
Using an uppercase letter to begin a Java class name and starting each new word with an uppercase letter is known as **Pascal case**.

The Android Manifest File

An Android project is made up of far more than the XML layout files that create the user interface. The other important components of any Android project are the Android Manifest file and the Java code in the Java classes. The **Android Manifest** file is necessary in every Android application and must be named AndroidManifest.xml exactly. The Android Manifest file provides all the essential information to the Android device, such as the name of your Java application, a listing of each Activity, any permissions needed to access other Android functions such as the use of the Internet, services, broadcast receivers, and the minimum level of the Android API. This file lets the Android system know what the components are and under what conditions they can be launched. AndroidManifest.xml is like a project manager of a business process that determines which activities are scheduled, the permissions that are necessary, and the device versions needed to get the job done.

Adding an Activity to the Android Manifest

Eclipse automatically creates the initial Android Manifest file, but this file must be updated to include every Activity in the app. In the Healthy Recipes app, the Android Manifest is only aware of the initial Activity named MainActivity. When an application has more than one Activity, the Android Manifest file must have an **intent** to navigate among multiple activities. To see which Activities an application contains, double-tap or double-click the AndroidManifest.xml file in the Package Explorer, and then tap or click the AndroidManifest.xml tab at the bottom of the window as shown in Figure 2-19. Notice that Line 17 calls an Activity named MainActivity. The intent in Lines 19-23 launches the opening screen.

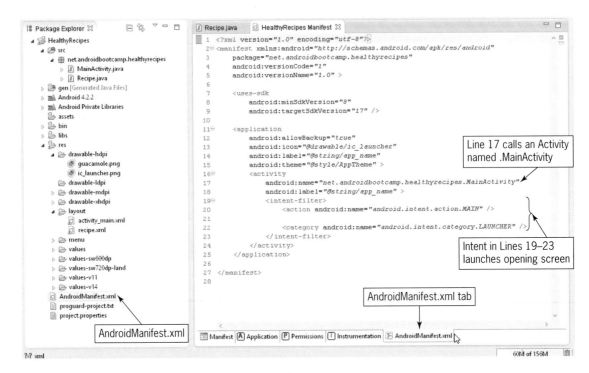

Figure 2-19   Displaying the Activities in an application

The AndroidManifest.xml file must contain an entry for each Activity. In the case of the Healthy Recipes app, the second Activity named Recipe must be added to the Android Manifest file or the app will not execute properly. To add the second Activity to the Android Manifest file, follow these steps:

STEP 1

- In the Package Explorer, double-tap or double-click the AndroidManifest.xml file.

- Minimize the Outline pane on the right side of the window.

- To add the Recipe class to the Android Manifest, tap or click the Application tab at the bottom of the HealthyRecipes Manifest page.

- Scroll down to display the Application Nodes section and to view the MainActivity, which is automatically added to the Android Manifest file.

The AndroidManifest.xml file is opened to the Application tab (Figure 2-20).

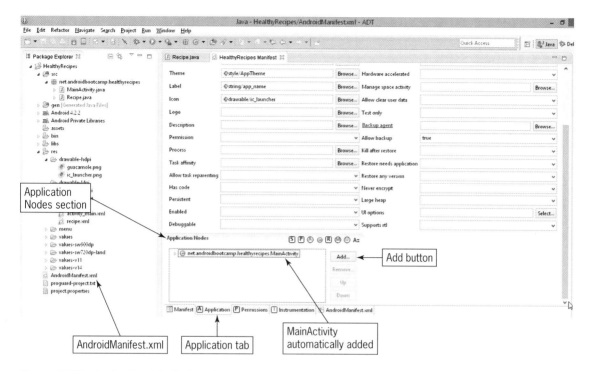

Figure 2-20 Application tab displayed

STEP 2

- In the Application Nodes section, tap or click the Add button.

- Select Activity in the Create a new element at the top level, in Application dialog box.

The Create a new element at the top level, in Application dialog box opens and Activity is selected (Figure 2-21).

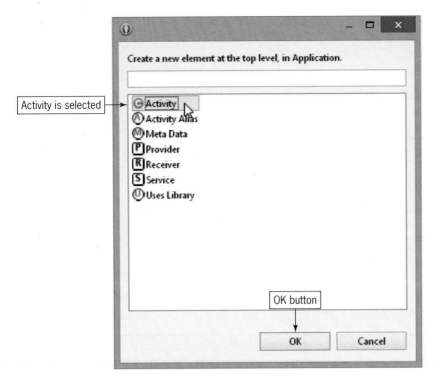

Figure 2-21   Creating an element

STEP 3

- Tap or click the OK button to add the Activity. The Attributes for Activity section opens in the Application tab.

- In the Name text box, type **.Recipe**, which is a period followed by the class name, to add the Recipe Activity to the AndroidManifest.xml file.

- Tap or click the Save All button on the toolbar to save the application.

The class .Recipe is entered in the Name text box of the Attributes for Activity section and added to the Android Manifest (Figure 2-22).

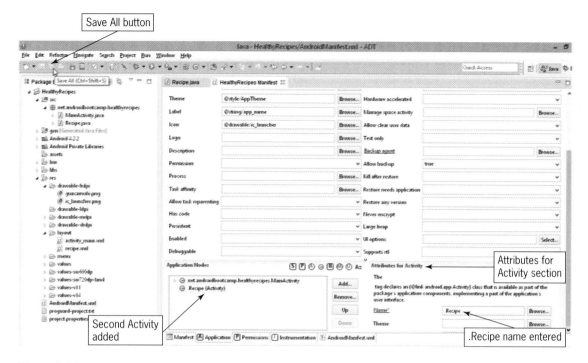

Figure 2-22 Adding the Recipe Activity

STEP 4

- To view the MainActivity and Recipe Activities in the code, tap or click the AndroidManifest.xml tab at the bottom of the window.

The AndroidManifest.xml code includes the .Recipe Activity in Line 25 (Figure 2-23).

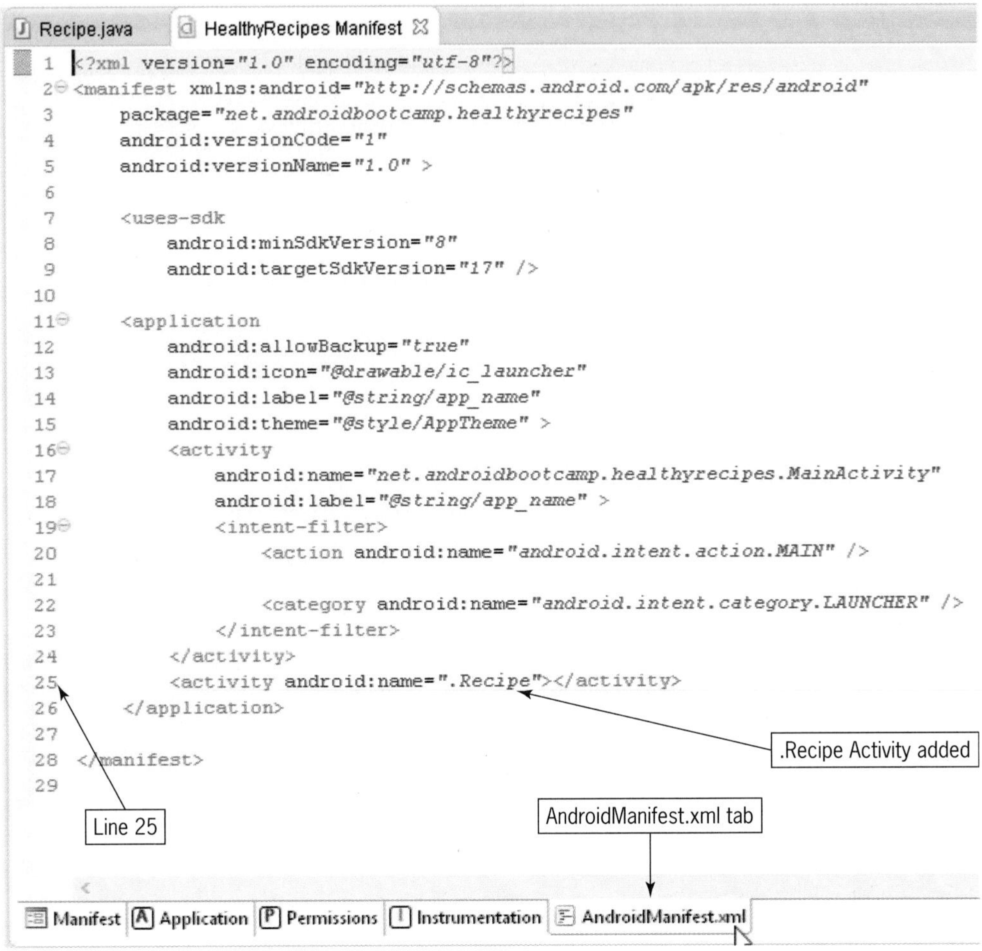

Figure 2-23 AndroidManifest.xml code

Coding the Java Activity

When the user taps an application icon on his or her Android phone or tablet, the MainActivity.java code is read by the device processor. The entry point of the Activity class is the onCreate( ) event handler, which is called a method. A **method** is a set of Java statements that can be included inside a Java class. The **method body** contains a collection of statements that defines what the method does. The onCreate method is where you initialize the Activity. Imagine a large stack of papers on your desk. The paper on top of the stack is what you are reading right now. The Android also has a stack of Activities. The onCreate method places this new Activity on top of the stack.

Coding an onCreate Method

In the chapter project, the first Activity displayed in the title screen layout designed in activity_main.xml is the currently running Activity. When the user presses the View Recipe button, the activity_main.xml screen closes and a new Activity that displays the actual recipe (recipe.xml) is placed on top of the stack and becomes the running Activity. The syntax for the onCreate method is:

Code Syntax

```
public void onCreate(Bundle savedInstanceState) {
super.onCreate(savedInstanceState);
}
```

The method begins with *public void*, which are special keywords that Java uses to determine the type of method. They must always be in all lowercase letters. Void is called the return type of the method. A void return type means that the method does not return anything. At the end of the public void statement is an opening curly brace. The closing curly brace appears at the end of the method. Inside the braces is the onCreate method, where the first user interface must be opened. Activities have no clue which user interface should be displayed on the screen. For a particular user interface to open, code must be added inside the onCreate method to place that specific Activity on top of the stack. The Java code necessary to display the content of a specific screen is called **setContentView**, which has the following syntax:

Code Syntax

```
setContentView(R.layout.activity_main);
```

In the code syntax, R.layout.*activity_main* represents the user interface of the activity_main.xml layout (the opening screen), which displays the opening title, guacamole image, and View Recipe button. The R represents the term *Resource*, as the layout folder resides in the res folder.

Displaying the User Interface

The MainActivity.java file was created automatically by Eclipse and already contains the onCreate method and setContentView(R.layout.activity_main) code, as shown in Lines 11 and 12 in Figure 2-24. Line 10 starts the method and Line 12 displays the activity_main.xml layout when the application begins.

```
  Recipe.java      MainActivity.java  ⊠
  1  package net.androidbootcamp.healthyrecipes;
  2
  3⊕ import android.os.Bundle;
  6
  7  public class MainActivity extends Activity {
  8
  9⊖      @Override
▲10      protected void onCreate(Bundle savedInstanceState) {
 11          super.onCreate(savedInstanceState);          ────── onCreate method
 12          setContentView(R.layout.activity_main);
 13      }
 14                                          setContentView(R.layout.activity_main) code
 15⊖      @Override
▲16      public boolean onCreateOptionsMenu(Menu menu) {
 17          // Inflate the menu; this adds items to the action bar if it is present.
 18          getMenuInflater().inflate(R.menu.main, menu);
 19          return true;
 20      }
 21
 22  }
 23
```

Figure 2-24   MainActivity.java code

To display the second screen (recipe.xml), the onCreate method is necessary to place the second Activity on top of the Activity stack. Next, the setContentView command displays the recipe.xml layout. To add the onCreate and setContentView code to the Recipe.java file, follow these steps:

STEP 1

- Close the HealthyRecipes Manifest tab.

- If necessary, tap or click the Recipe.java tab to display its code. Notice that the Recipe file extends the Activity, as indicated in Line 5 of the code.

- Tap or click Line 6 to move the insertion point between the two curly braces that open and close the method.

- Press Tab to indent the line, type **oncreate,** and then press Ctrl+spacebar (simultaneously). When you press Ctrl+spacebar, Eclipse displays an auto-complete listing with all the possible entries that are valid at that point in the code. A yellow Help window may also appear to the right.

The onCreate method is entered in the Recipe class. A list of possible onCreate methods is displayed after pressing Ctrl+spacebar (Figure 2-25).

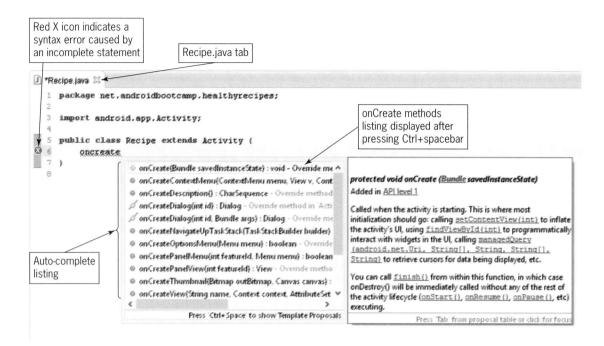

Figure 2-25 Listing of onCreate methods

STEP 2

● Double-tap or double-click the first onCreate method in the auto-complete listing to generate the method structure.

The onCreate method is generated in the Recipe class (Figure 2-26).

```
 *Recipe.java
 1   package net.androidbootcamp.healthyrecipes;
 2
 3   import android.app.Activity;
 4   import android.os.Bundle;
 5
 6   public class Recipe extends Activity {
 7       @Override
 8       protected void onCreate(Bundle savedInstanceState) {
 9           // TODO Auto-generated method stub
10           super.onCreate(savedInstanceState);
11       }
12   }
13
```

onCreate method added

Figure 2-26 Inserting the onCreate method

STEP 3

- Tap or click at the end of Line 10 and then press Enter to insert a blank line.

- Type **setContentView(R.** to display an auto-complete listing.

The setContentView(R. command is entered to display an auto-complete listing of resource files (Figure 2-27).

Figure 2-27 Code for displaying the Resources

STEP 4

- Double-tap or double-click layout.

- Type a period. Another auto-complete listing requests the XML layout file you intend to display.

The setContentView(R.layout. command is entered to display an auto-complete listing of layout files (Figure 2-28).

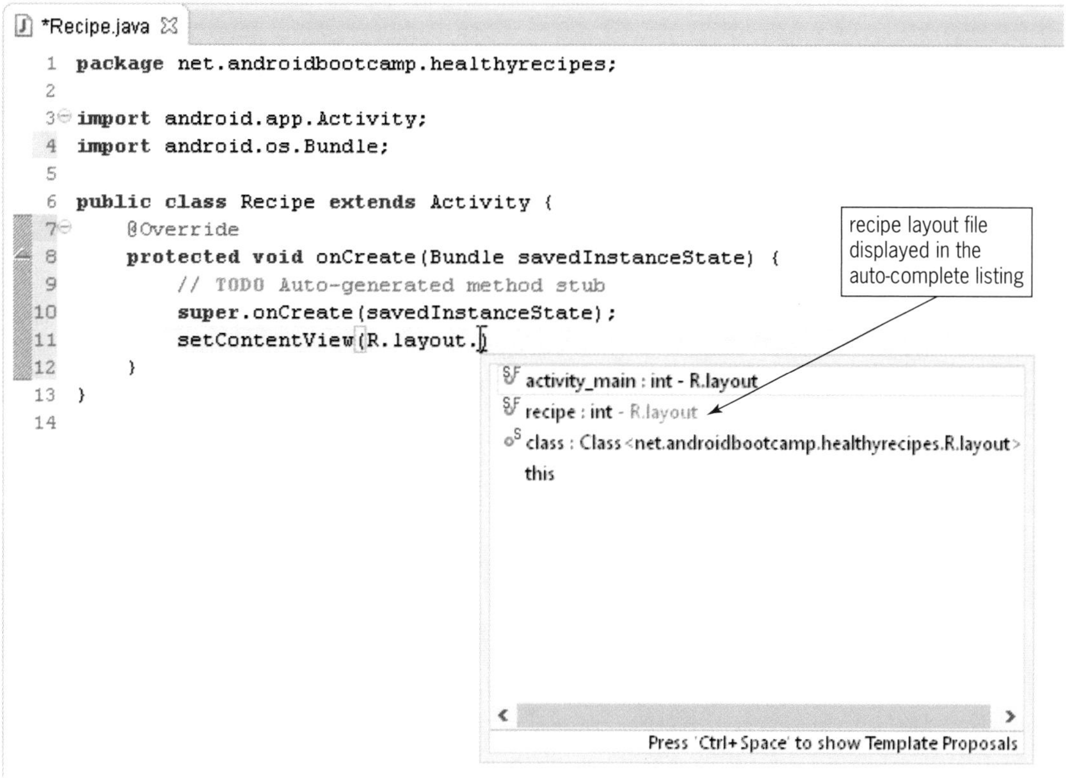

Figure 2-28   Layout files

STEP 5

- Double-tap or double-click recipe : int.

- Type a semicolon after the parenthesis to complete the statement.

The setContentView command is entered to display the recipe.xml file (Figure 2-29).

```
J  *Recipe.java ⊠
 1  package net.androidbootcamp.healthyrecipes;
 2
 3  import android.app.Activity;
 4  import android.os.Bundle;
 5
 6  public class Recipe extends Activity {
 7      @Override
 8      protected void onCreate(Bundle savedInstanceState) {
 9          // TODO Auto-generated method stub
10          super.onCreate(savedInstanceState);
11          setContentView(R.layout.recipe);
12      }
13  }
14
```

recipe file name turns blue to indicate that the layout file has been located in the layout folder

Figure 2-29   recipe XML layout file

Creating a Button Event Handler

Android phones and tablets have touchscreens that create endless possibilities for user interaction, allowing the user to tap, swipe, and pinch in or out to change the size of the screen. As you program with this event-driven language, users typically see an interface containing controls, buttons, menus, and other graphical elements. After displaying the interface, the program waits until the user touches the device. When the user reacts, the app initiates an event, which executes code in an **event handler**, which is a part of the program coded to respond to the specific event. In the Healthy Recipes app, users have only one interaction—they can tap the Button control to start an event that displays the guacamole recipe. When the user taps the Button control, code for an event listener is necessary to begin the event that displays the recipe.xml file on the Android screen. This tap event is actually known as a click event in Java code. In the Healthy Recipes application, the MainActivity.java code must first contain the following sections:

- Class property to hold a reference to the Button object

- OnClickListener( ) method to await the button click action

- onClick( ) method to respond to the click event

The Healthy Recipes application opens with a Button control on the screen. To use that button, a reference is required in the MainActivity.java file. To reference a Button control, use the following syntax to create a Button property:

Code Syntax

```
Button b=(Button)findViewById(R.id.btnRecipe);
```

The syntax for the Button property includes the findViewById( ) method, which is used by any Android Activity. This method finds a layout view in the XML files that you created when designing the user interface. The variable b in the code contains the reference to the Button control.

After the code is entered to reference the Button control, you can press Ctrl+spacebar to import the Button type as an Android widget. When you **import** the Button type as an Android widget, you make the classes from the Android Button package available throughout the application. An import statement is automatically placed at the top of the Java code. An **import statement** is a way of making more Java functions available to your specific program. Java can perform almost endless actions, and not every program needs to do everything. So, to limit the size of the code, Java has its classes divided into packages that can be imported at the top of your code.

After the Button property is referenced in MainActivity.java, an OnClickListener( ) method is necessary to detect when the user taps an onscreen button. Event listeners wait for user interaction, which is when the user taps the button to view the recipe in the case of the chapter project. When an OnClickListener is placed in the code window, Java creates an onClick auto-generated stub. A **stub** is a piece of code that actually serves as a placeholder to declare itself, and it has just enough code to link to the rest of the program. The following syntax is needed for an OnClickListener method that listens for the Button control:

Code Syntax

```
b.setOnClickListener(new OnClickListener() {
public void onClick(View v) {
    // TODO Auto-generated method stub
    }
});
```

The last step to code is to call the startActivity( ) method, which opens the second Activity displaying the recipe.xml user interface. The startActivity( ) method creates an intent to start another Activity such as to start the recipe Activity class. The intent needs two parts known as parameters: a context and the name of the Activity that is being opened. A context in Android coding means that any time you request that program to launch another Activity, a context is sent to the Android system to show which initiating Activity class is making the request. The context of the chapter project is MainActivity.this, which references the MainActivity.java class. The following syntax line launches the Recipe Java class:

Code Syntax

```
startActivity(new Intent(MainActivity.this, Recipe.class));
```

Coding a Button Event Handler

When the activity_main.xml layout is initially launched by the MainActivity.java class, it is necessary to code how the Button control interacts with the user. When this View Recipe button is tapped, the MainActivity.java class must contain code to launch the Recipe.xml layout (Activity) and to begin the second Java class called Recipe.java. To initialize the Button control and code the Button handler to launch the second Activity class, follow these steps:

STEP 1

- In the Package Explorer, double-tap or double-click MainActivity.java to open its code window.

- Tap or click to the right of the setContentView(R.layout.activity_main); line, and then press Enter to insert a new blank line.

- To initialize and reference the Button control with the Id name of btnRecipe, type
  Button b = (Button) findViewById(R.id.btnRecipe);

- After the code is entered to reference the Button control, point to the red curly line below the first Button command.

  If you are using a Mac, error indicators in the code are red dashed lines.

The Button control named btnRecipe is referenced in MainActivity.java. By tapping or clicking the Button command, an auto-complete listing is displayed to import the Button library (Figure 2-30).

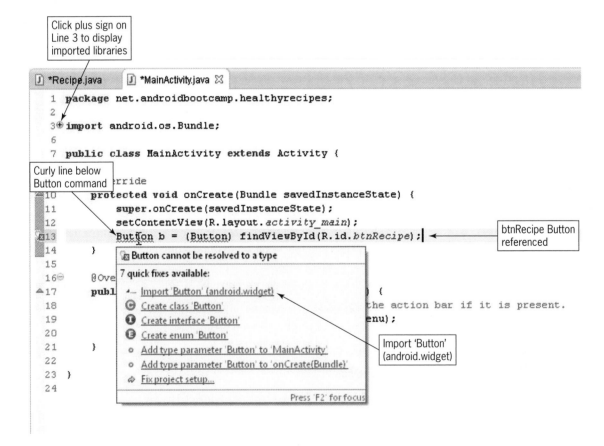

Figure 2-30   Importing the Button library

STEP 2

- Select Import 'Button' (android.widget) to import the Button library.

- Tap or click the Save All button on the Standard toolbar to save your work.

The Button library is imported into this project. The b *variable is flagged to indicate that this local variable has not been used in the code yet (Figure 2-31).*

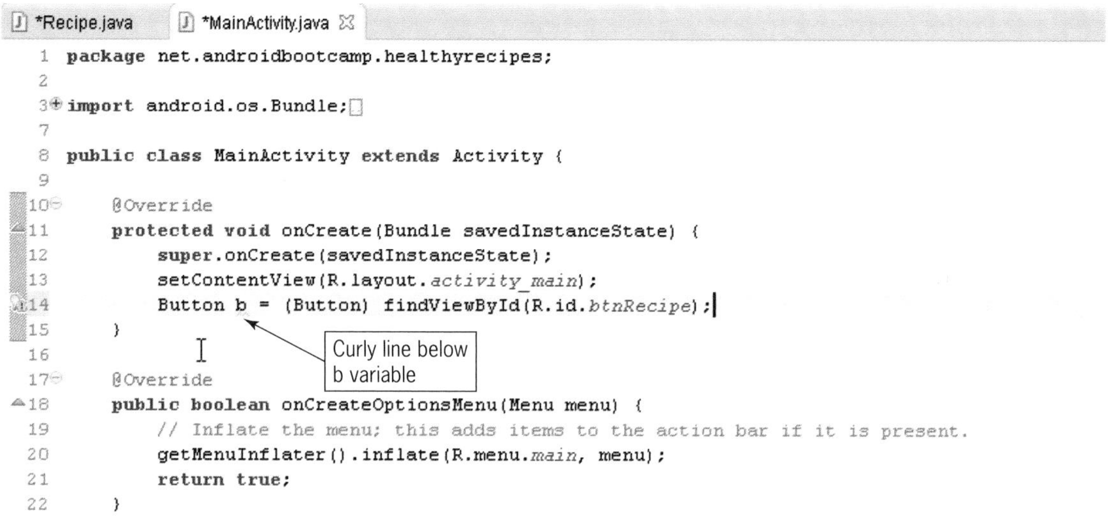

```java
1   package net.androidbootcamp.healthyrecipes;
2
3⊕ import android.os.Bundle;
7
8   public class MainActivity extends Activity {
9
10⊝     @Override
11      protected void onCreate(Bundle savedInstanceState) {
12          super.onCreate(savedInstanceState);
13          setContentView(R.layout.activity_main);
14          Button b = (Button) findViewById(R.id.btnRecipe);
15      }
16
17⊝      @Override
18      public boolean onCreateOptionsMenu(Menu menu) {
19          // Inflate the menu; this adds items to the action bar if it is present.
20          getMenuInflater().inflate(R.menu.main, menu);
21          return true;
22      }
```

Curly line below b variable

Figure 2-31   Button instantiated

STEP 3

- Press Enter to insert a new blank line.

- To code the button listener that awaits user interaction, type **b.seton** and press Ctrl+spacebar.

- Double-tap or double-click the first setOnClickListener to select it from the auto-complete listing.

- In the parentheses, type **new on** and press Ctrl+spacebar to display an auto-complete listing.

- Double-tap or double-click the first choice, which lists an OnClickListener with an Anonymous Inner Type event handler.

- Point to the red curly line below OnClickListener on Line 17.

- Select Import 'OnClickListener' (android.view.View).

- On Line 24, type **;** (semicolon) after the closing parenthesis to complete the auto-generated stub.

An OnClickListener auto-generated stub appears in the code (Figure 2-32).

```
 1  package net.androidbootcamp.healthyrecipes;
 2
 3⊕ import android.os.Bundle;▯
 9
10  public class MainActivity extends Activity {
11
12⊖     @Override
13      protected void onCreate(Bundle savedInstanceState) {
14          super.onCreate(savedInstanceState);
15          setContentView(R.layout.activity_main);
16          Button b = (Button) findViewById(R.id.btnRecipe);
17⊖         b.setOnClickListener(new OnClickListener() {
18
19⊖             @Override
20              public void onClick(View v) {
21                  // TODO Auto-generated method stub
22
23
24          }});
25      }
26
27⊖     @Override
28      public boolean onCreateOptionsMenu(Menu menu) {
29          // Inflate the menu; this adds items to the action bar if it is present.
30          getMenuInflater().inflate(R.menu.main, menu);
31          return true;
32      }
33
34  }
35
```

Button OnClickListener—most of this code was automatically generated

Semicolon closes stub

Figure 2-32   Inserting the Button OnClickListener stub

STEP 4

- To launch the Recipe.java class when the Button control is tapped, tap or click Line 23, which is inside the public void onClick(View v) braces after the TODO comment.

- Type **startactivity** and press Ctrl+spacebar. Select the first option, startActivity(Intent intent) : void - Activity.

- In the parentheses, change the intent text by typing **new int** and then pressing Ctrl+spacebar.

- In the auto-complete listing, scroll if necessary and select Intent(Context packageContext, Class<?> cls).

- In the next set of parentheses, change packageContext to **MainActivity.this** and change cls to **Recipe.class**.

- Type **;** (semicolon) at the end of the line after the parenthesis.

- Tap or click the Save All button on the toolbar.

The startActivity code launches the intent to open Recipe.class (Figure 2-33).

```
 1  package net.androidbootcamp.healthyrecipes;
 2
 3⊕ import android.os.Bundle;▯
10
11  public class MainActivity extends Activity {
12
13⊖     @Override
▲14     protected void onCreate(Bundle savedInstanceState) {
15          super.onCreate(savedInstanceState);
16          setContentView(R.layout.activity_main);
17          Button b = (Button) findViewById(R.id.btnRecipe);
18⊖         b.setOnClickListener(new OnClickListener() {
19
20⊖             @Override
▲21             public void onClick(View v) {
22                  // TODO Auto-generated method stub
23                  startActivity(new Intent(MainActivity.this, Recipe.class));     I
24              }
25          });
26      }
27
28⊖     @Override
▲29     public boolean onCreateOptionsMenu(Menu menu) {
30          // Inflate the menu; this adds items to the action bar if it is present.
31          getMenuInflater().inflate(R.menu.main, menu);
32          return true;
33      }
34
35 }
36
```

startActivity code

Figure 2-33   Complete code for MainActivity.java

GTK
In Step 4, the packageContext is replaced with MainActivity because it is the name of the present Activity. The term *this* refers to the present Activity.

IN THE TRENCHES
In years past, a software developer would have to wait many months for his or her software to be published and placed in stores for sale. In today's mobile market, app stores have become the de facto app delivery channel by reducing time-to-shelf and time-to-payment and by providing developers with unprecedented reach to consumers.

Correcting Errors in Code

Using the built-in auto-complete listing to assist you when entering code considerably reduces the likelihood of coding errors. Nevertheless, because you could create one or more errors when entering code, you should understand what to do when a coding error occurs. One possible error you could commit would be to forget a semicolon at the end of a statement. In

Figure 2-34, when the application is run, a dialog box opens stating "your project contains error(s), please fix them before running your application." A red curly line identifies the error location. Also notice that Line 16 has an error icon (a red X) at the beginning of the line to identify the line containing the error. When you point to the error icon, Java suggests the possible correction to the syntax error in the code. After a semicolon is placed at the end of the line, the application is run again and the program functions properly.

```
J  Recipe.java        J  *MainActivity.java  ⊠

 1  package net.androidbootcamp.healthyrecipes;
 2
 3⊕ import android.os.Bundle;▯
10
11  public class MainActivity extends Activity {
12
13⊖     @Override
14      protected void onCreate(Bundle savedInstanceState) {
15          super.onCreate(savedInstanceState);
16          [Syntax error, insert ";" to complete Statement].activity_main)|
17          Button b = (Button) findViewById(R.id.btnRecipe);
18⊖         b.setOnClickListener(new OnClickListener() {
19
20⊖             @Override
                ublic void onClick(View v) {
                    // TODO Auto-generated method stub
                    startActivity(new Intent(MainActivity.this, Recipe.class));

25              });
26          }
27
28⊖         @Override
29          public boolean onCreateOptionsMenu(Menu menu) {
30              // Inflate the menu; this adds items to the action bar if it is present.
31              getMenuInflater().inflate(R.menu.main, menu);
32              return true;
33          }
34
35  }
36
```

Figure 2-34   Syntax error

Saving and Running the Application

Each time an Android application is tested in the emulator, the programming design and code are automatically saved. If you start your project and need to save it before completion, tap or click the Save All button on the toolbar. As shown in Chapter 1, tap or click the Run button on the toolbar to test the application in the emulator. A dialog box that requests how to run the application opens the first time the application is executed. Select Android Application and tap or click the OK button. When the emulated Android main screen appears, unlock the emulator. The application opens in the emulator window, where you can click the View Recipe button to view the guacamole recipe.

Wrap It Up—Chapter Summary

This chapter described the steps to create the graphical user interface for the Healthy Recipes program. As you can see, many of the steps required are somewhat repetitive in the design; that is, the same technique is used repeatedly to accomplish similar tasks. When you master these techniques, together with the principles of user interface design, you will be able to design user interfaces for a variety of programs.

- Relative layouts arrange screen components freely on the screen. Linear layouts arrange screen components in a vertical column or horizontal row.

- Popular text properties for controls include the Text property, which specifies the text displayed in the control, and the Text size property, which specifies the size of the text.

- To display graphics such as pictures and icons in an Android app, you use an ImageView control. Before you can place an ImageView control in the emulator window, you must place a graphics file in the resources folder.

- An Activity is the point at which the application makes contact with your users and is one of the core components of the Android application. The chapter project has two Activities, one for each screen.

- Each screen represents an Activity and each Activity must have a matching Java class file. To create a Java class file, you can extend the built-in Activity class.

- Every Android application has an Android Manifest file (named AndroidManifest.xml), which provides essential information to the Android device, such as the name of your Java application and a listing of each Activity. Eclipse automatically creates the initial Android Manifest file, but you must update this file to include every Activity in the app.

- When an application has more than one Activity, the Android Manifest file must have an intent so the application can navigate among multiple Activities.

- A method is a set of Java statements that can be included inside a Java class. The onCreate method is where you initialize an Activity. You use the setContentView command to display the content of a specific screen.

- When the user taps a Button control in an Android app, the code for an event listener, or click event, begins the event associated with the Button control. Event listeners such as the OnClickListener method wait for user interaction before executing the remaining code.

- In an Android app that contains more than one Activity, or screen, you use the startActivity( ) method to create an intent to start another Activity. The intent should contain two parameters: a context and the name of the Activity being opened. A context shows which initiating Activity class is making the request.

- When you run an Android application, a dialog box opens if your project contains any errors. Look for red error icons and red curly lines, which identify the location of the errors. Point to a red curly line to have Java suggest a correction to a syntax error in the code.

Key Terms

Activity—An Android component that represents a single screen with a user interface.

Android Manifest—A file with the filename AndroidManifest.xml that is required in every Android application. This file provides essential information to the Android device, such as the name of your Java application and a listing of each Activity.

class—A group of objects that establishes an introduction to each object's properties.

event handler—A part of a program coded to respond to the specific event.

ImageView control—A control that displays an icon or a graphic from a picture file.

import—To make the classes from a particular Android package available throughout the application.

import statement—A statement that makes more Java functions available to a program.

instantiate—To create an object of a specific class.

intent—Code in the Android Manifest file that allows an Android application with more than one Activity to navigate among Activities.

Linear layout—A layout that arranges components in a vertical column or horizontal row.

method—A set of Java statements that can be included inside a Java class.

method body—The part of a method containing a collection of statements that defines what the method does.

object—A specific, concrete instance of a class.

Pascal case—Text that begins with an uppercase letter and uses an uppercase letter to start each new word.

Relative layout—A layout that arranges components in relation to each other. Relative layout is the default layout of the emulator.

setContentView—The Java code necessary to display the content of a specific screen.

sp—A unit of measurement that stands for scaled-independent pixels.

stub—A piece of code that serves as a placeholder to declare itself, containing just enough code to link to the rest of the program.

Text property—A property that changes the text written within a control.

Text Size property—A property that sets the size of text in a control.

Developer FAQs

1. How many drawable folders are available in the res folder?

2. If you were creating an app in many different languages, would you have to write the entire program from scratch for each language? What part of the program would stay the same? What part of the program would be different?

3. In which subfolder in the Package Explorer are the XML files stored?

4. Which three controls were used in the chapter project?

5. What is the difference between a Linear layout and a Relative layout?

6. Is the default layout for an Android screen Linear or Relative?

7. Which measurement is most preferred for text size? Why?

8. What does px stand for?

9. What does sp stand for?

10. What does dpi stand for?

11. Which picture file types are accepted for an ImageView control?

12. Which picture file type is preferred?

13. In the Palette in the layout folder, in which category is the ImageView control found?

14. Which three properties were changed in the chapter project for the Button control?

15. What is the property that defines the name of a Button control?

16. Write one line of code that would launch a second class named Garden from the present MainActivity class.

17. Write one line of code that declares a Button control with the variable bt that references a button in the XML layout with the Id property of btnOpinion.

18. Write one line of code that opens the XML layout named lemon.

19. Which two keys are pressed to auto-complete a line of Java code?

20. What character is placed at the end of most lines of Java code?

Beyond the Book

Using the Internet, search the Web for the following answers to further your Android knowledge.

1. Linear and Relative layouts are not the only types of Android layouts. Name three other types of layouts and write a paragraph describing each type.

2. Why are .png files the preferred type of image resource for the Android device? Write a paragraph that gives at least three reasons.

3. How much does an average Android app developer profit from his or her apps? Research this topic and write 150–200 words on your findings.

4. Research the most expensive Android apps currently available at Google Play. Name three expensive apps, their price, and the purpose of each.

Case Programming Projects

Complete one or more of the following case programming projects. Use the same steps and techniques taught within the chapter. Submit the program you create to your instructor. The level of difficulty is indicated for each case programming project.

Easiest: ★

Intermediate: ★★

Challenging: ★★★

Case Project 2–1: Hotel Room App ★

Requirements Document

Application title:	Hotel Room App
Purpose:	In a hotel room reservations app, a hotel is selected and an address and other information are displayed.
Algorithms:	1. The opening screen displays the name of a hotel, an image, and a Button control (Figure 2-35).
	2. When the user selects a hotel, an address and a cost range are displayed in a second screen (Figure 2-36).
Note:	The hotel room image is provided with your student files.

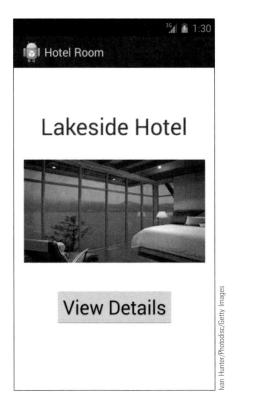

Figure 2-35

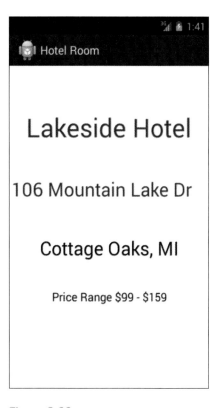

Figure 2-36

Case Project 2–2: Motor Scooter Rental App ★

Requirements Document

Application title:	Motor Scooter Rental App
Purpose:	In a motor scooter rental app, the type of scooter is selected and the motor scooter image is displayed with rental information.
Algorithms:	1. The opening screen displays the type of scooter rental, scooter specifications, and a Button control (Figure 2-37).
	2. When the user selects a scooter, an image displaying the motor scooter and daily price is shown (Figure 2-38).
Note:	The motor scooter image is provided with your student files.

Figure 2-37

Figure 2-38

Ryan McVay/Digital Vision/Getty Images

Case Project 2–3: Your School App ★★

Requirements Document

Application title: Your School App

Purpose: This large app provides information on every school in your country. Create two screens for the app. You use the app to select the name of a school, and then display information about the selected school.

Algorithms: 1. The opening screen displays the name of your school, a picture of your school, and a Button control. Create your own layout.

2. The second screen displays the name of your school, a picture of your logo, the school address, and the phone number. Create your own layout.

Case Project 2–4: Hostel App for Travel ★★

Requirements Document

Application title: Hostel App for Travel

Purpose: This large app provides information about every hostel (small youth hotel) in Italy. Create two screens for the hostel app. You use the app to select the name of a hostel, and then display detailed hostel room information.

Algorithms: 1. The opening screen displays the name of the Italian hostel, an exterior image of the hostel, and a Button control. Create your own layout.

2. The second screen displays the name of the hostel, a picture of the interior room, the street address, the Web address, and the rate. Create your own layout.

Case Project 2–5: Your Contacts App—Address Book ★★★

Requirements Document

Application title:	Your Contacts App—Address Book
Purpose:	This large app provides business contact information in an address book. Create two screens for contacts for the app. You use the app to select a particular contact, and then display that person's information.
Algorithms:	1. The opening screen displays two names of contacts with the last name starting with the letter J. Each contact has a separate Button control below the name. Create your own layout.
	2. The second screen displays the name, address, phone number, and picture of the contact. Create your own layout.
Conditions:	Three Java classes and three XML layouts are needed.

Case Project 2–6: Latest Music Scene App ★★★

Requirements Document

Application title:	The Latest Music Scene
Purpose:	This large app called The Latest Music Scene contains the latest music news. Create two screens for two music news stories. You use the app to select a particular music news story title, and then display an image and a paragraph about the music news story.
Algorithms:	1. The opening screen displays two music news story titles that you can create based on the music stories in the news. Each music news story has a separate Button control below the name and displays a small image. Create your own layout.
	2. The second screen displays the name of the music story and a paragraph detailing the news. Create your own layout.
Conditions:	Three Java classes and three XML layouts are needed.

CHAPTER 3

Engage! Android User Input, Variables, and Operations

In this chapter, you learn to:

◎ Use an Android theme
◎ Add a theme to the Android Manifest file
◎ Develop the user interface using Text Fields
◎ State the role of different Text Fields
◎ Display a hint using the Hint property
◎ Develop the user interface using a Spinner control
◎ Add text to the String table
◎ Add a prompt to a Spinner control
◎ Declare variables to hold data
◎ Code the GetText( ) method
◎ Understand arithmetic operations
◎ Convert numeric data
◎ Format numeric data
◎ Code the SetText( ) method
◎ Run the completed app in the emulator

In the Healthy Recipes app developed in Chapter 2, when the user tapped or clicked the button in the user interface, events were triggered, but the user did not enter data. In many applications, users enter data and then the program uses the data in its processing. Engaging the user by requesting input customizes the user experience each time the application is executed. When processing data entered by a user, a common requirement is to perform arithmetic operations on the data in order to generate useful output information. Arithmetic operations include adding, subtracting, multiplying, and dividing numeric data.

To illustrate the use of user data input and arithmetic operations, the application in this chapter allows the user to enter the number of concert tickets to be purchased from an Android app. The application then calculates the total cost to purchase the concert tickets. The user interface for the app named Concert Tickets is shown in Figure 3-1 with the company name Ticket Vault displayed at the top of the screen.

In Figure 3-2, the user entered 4 as the number of tickets to purchase. When the user clicked the Find the Cost button, the program multiplied 4 times the concert ticket cost ($79.99) and then displayed the result as the total cost of the concert tickets, as shown in Figure 3-2. To create this application, the developer must understand how to perform the following processes, among others:

1. Apply a theme to the design of the Android screen.

2. Define all text displayed in a String table.

Figure 3-1   Concert Tickets Android app

3. Define a Text Field for data entry. For this app, a number is expected for the quantity of tickets. Using a specific Text Field for positive integers, an incorrect value cannot be entered.

4. Define a Spinner control to allow users to select the performance group.

5. Convert data so it can be used for arithmetic operations.

6. Perform arithmetic operations with the data the user enters.

7. Display formatted results.

Android Themes

To prevent each Android app from looking too similar, the Android SDK includes multiple themes that provide individual flair to each application. A **theme** is a style applied to an Activity or an entire application. Themes are Android's mechanism for applying a consistent style to an app or activity. The style specifies the visual properties of the elements that make up your user interface, such as color, height, padding, and font size. Some themes change the background wallpaper of the Activity, while others hide the title bar or display an action bar. Some

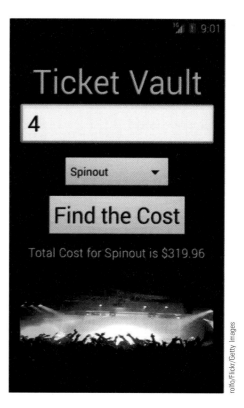

Figure 3-2 Four tickets purchased for a concert

themes display a background depending on the size of the mobile device. Themes can be previewed in the emulator window in activity_main.xml. The default theme shows the title bar (often gray) with a white background, as shown in Figure 3-3. Figure 3-4 displays a Theme. Holo.Light.Dialog theme with a light translucent background and no title bar. The light and transparent themes are sheer and allow you to see the initial home screen through the background. Figure 3-5 displays a black background with the default Android icon and an action bar.

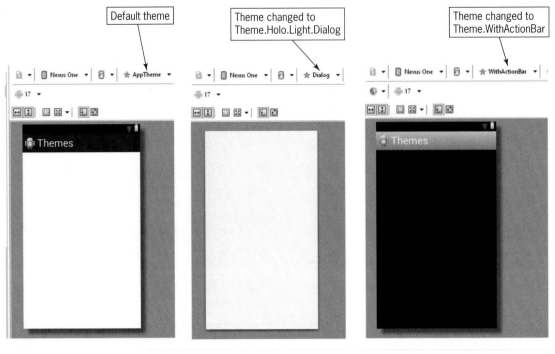

Figure 3-3   Default theme   **Figure 3-4**   Holographic theme   **Figure 3-5**   Action bar theme

Previewing a Theme

By changing the theme in the emulator window in the activity_main.xml file, you can preview what the new theme looks like, but to permanently change it in the application, you must define the themes in the Android Manifest for each Activity. You can code a predefined system theme or a customized theme of your own design. The Concert Tickets chapter project uses the predefined system theme named Theme.Black.NoTitleBar. To initiate the Concert Tickets application and preview the Theme. Black.NoTitleBar theme, follow these steps:

STEP 1

- Open the Eclipse program.

- Type **E:\Workspace** (if necessary, enter a different drive letter that identifies the USB drive) to select a workspace and tap or click the OK button.

- Tap or click the New button on the Standard toolbar and then select Android Application Project.

- Tap or click the Next button.

- In the New Android Application Project dialog box, enter the Application Name **Concert Tickets**.

- Enter the Package Name **net.androidbootcamp.concerttickets**.

The new Android Concert Tickets project has an application name, a package name, and a Main Activity (Figure 3-6).

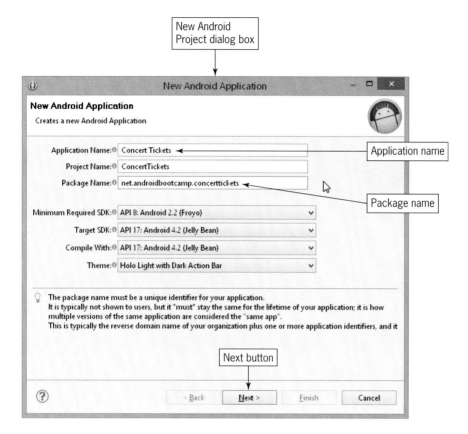

Figure 3-6   Setting up the Concert Tickets project

STEP 2

- Tap or click the Next button.

- Tap or click the Create custom launcher icon box to uncheck the option.

- Tap or click the Next button twice.

- Tap or click the Finish button.

- If necessary, expand the Concert Tickets project in the Package Explorer. If necessary, click the activity_main.xml tab.

- Tap or click the Hello world! TextView (displayed by default) in the emulator and press the Delete key.

The activity_main.xml file is displayed on the Graphical Layout tab and the Hello world TextView widget is deleted (Figure 3-7).

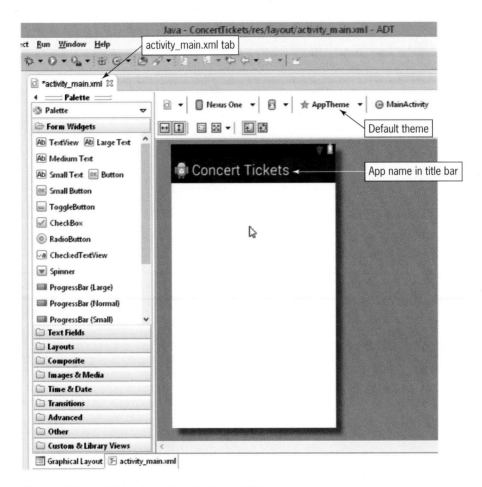

Figure 3-7 activity_main.xml for the Concert Tickets project

STEP 3

- Tap or click the AppTheme button and select Theme to display the list of built-in themes.

- Select Theme.Black.NoTitleBar.

The theme is changed to Theme.Black.NoTitleBar. The title bar in the emulator is removed and the background is black (Figure 3-8).

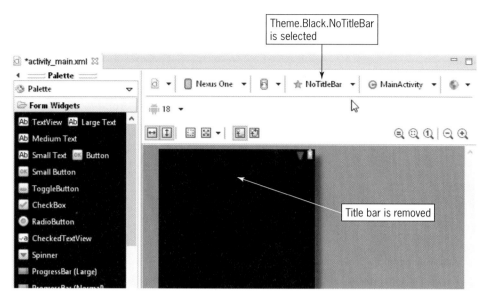

Figure 3-8   New theme applied

Updating the Theme in the Android Manifest File

At this point, the theme only appears in the activity_main.xml graphical layout, but to actually display the theme in the application, the Android Manifest must be made aware of the change in the theme layout. The AndroidManifest.xml file must be updated to include the updated theme. To update the theme within the AndroidManifest file, follow these steps:

STEP 1

- In the Package Explorer, double-tap or double-click the AndroidManifest.xml file.
- Tap or click the Application tab at the bottom of the ConcertTickets Manifest window to view the Application Attributes, which includes the Theme.

The default theme is displayed on the Application tab of the Android Manifest (Figure 3-9).

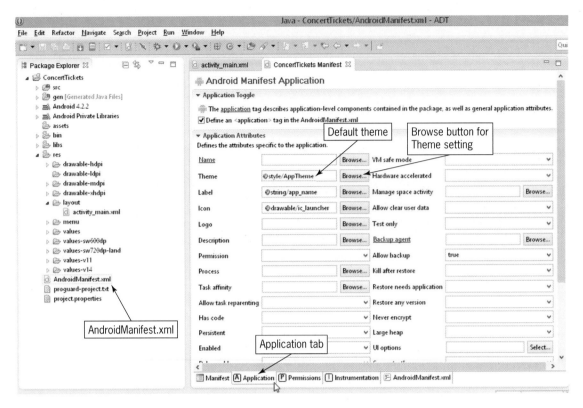

Figure 3-9   Android Manifest file for the Concert Tickets project

STEP 2

- Tap or click the Browse button for the Theme in the Application Attributes.

- Tap or click the System Resources option button in the Resource Chooser dialog box.

- Scroll down and select Theme.Black.NoTitleBar.

- Tap or click the OK button.

The Android theme is updated within the Activity in the Android Manifest file (Figure 3-10).

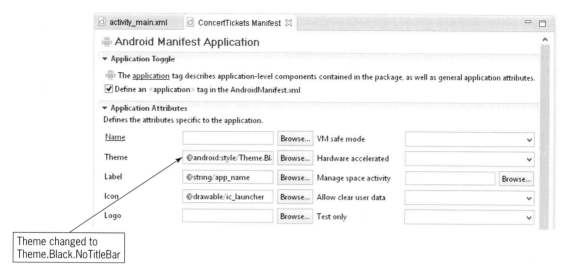

Figure 3-10 Theme changed in AndroidManifest.xml

STEP 3

- Tap or click the Save All button on the Standard toolbar.

- Tap or click the AndroidManifest.xml tab at the bottom of the window.

Line 15 of the AndroidManifest.xml has been automatically updated to include the theme named Theme.Black.NoTitleBar (Figure 3-11).

```
    *Android Manifest Editor ⊠
 1  <?xml version="1.0" encoding="utf-8"?>
 2  <manifest xmlns:android="http://schemas.android.com/apk/res/android"
 3      package="com.example.concerttickets"
 4      android:versionCode="1"
 5      android:versionName="1.0" >
 6
 7      <uses-sdk
 8          android:minSdkVersion="8"
 9          android:targetSdkVersion="17" />
10
11      <application
12          android:allowBackup="true"
13          android:icon="@drawable/ic_launcher"
14          android:label="@string/app_name"
15          android:theme="@style/Theme.Black.NoTitleBar" >
16          <activity
17              android:name="com.example.concerttickets.MainActivity"
18              android:label="@string/app_name" >
19              <intent-filter>
20                  <action android:name="android.intent.action.MAIN" />
21
22                  <category android:name="android.intent.category.LAUNCHER" />
23              </intent-filter>
24          </activity>
25      </application>
26
27  </manifest>
28
```

Theme changed to Theme.Black.NoTitleBar

AndroidManifest.xml tab

Manifest |A| Application |P| Permissions |I| Instrumentation |≡| AndroidManifest.xml

Figure 3-11   AndroidManifest.xml

Simplifying User Input

On the Android phone, users can enter text in multiple ways that include entering input through an onscreen soft keyboard, an attached flip button hard keyboard, and even voice-to-text capabilities on most phone models. The onscreen keyboard is called a **soft keyboard**, which is positioned at the bottom of the screen over the application window. Touch input can vary from tapping the screen to using gestures. Gestures are multitouch interactions such as pressing two fingers to pan, rotate, or zoom. The primary design challenge for mobile Web applications is how to simplify the user experience for an application that appears on screens measuring from a few inches square to much larger tablets. To meet the challenge and maximize the user experience, you need to use legible fonts, simplify input, and optimize each device's capabilities. Certain Android Form Widgets such as those in the Text Fields category allow specific data types for user input, which simplifies data entry. For example, a numeric Text Field only allows numbers to be entered from the onscreen keyboard, limiting accidental user input, such as by touching the wrong location on a small touchscreen.

Figure 3-12   Text Fields category

IN THE TRENCHES

A decade ago, nearly every mobile phone offered an alphanumeric keypad as part of the device. Today a touchscreen full QWERTY keyboard is available to allow users to enter information, engage in social networking, surf the Internet, and view multimedia.

Using Android Text Fields

In the Concert Tickets application shown in Figure 3-1, the user enters the quantity of tickets that he or she intends to purchase to attend the concert event. The most common type of mobile input is text entered by touch input from the soft (onscreen) keyboard or the attached keyboard. User keyboard input can be requested with the Text Fields in the Eclipse Palette (Figure 3-12). With Text Fields, the input can be received on the mobile device with an onscreen keyboard or the user can use the physical keyboard on the emulator.

A mobile application's Text Field controls can request different input types, such as free-form plain text; numbers; a person's name, password, email address, and phone number; a date; and multiline text. You need to select the correct Text Field for the specific type of data you are requesting. As shown in Figure 3-13, each Text Field control allows you to enter a specific data type from the keyboard. For example, if you select the Phone Text Field, Android deactivates the letters on the keyboard because letters are not part of a phone number.

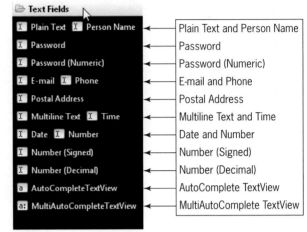

Figure 3-13 Types of Text Field controls

GTK

The AutoComplete TextView control can suggest the completion of a word after the user begins typing the first few letters. For example, if the input control is requesting the name of a city where the user wants to book a hotel, you could suggest the completed name from a coded listing of city names that match the prefix entered by the user.

In the chapter project, the Concert Tickets application requests the number of concert tickets. This quantity is an integer value because you cannot purchase part of a ticket. By selecting the Number Text Field, only positive integers can be entered from the keyboard. Letters and symbols from the keyboard are not accepted, which saves you time as the developer because you do not have to write lengthy data validation code.

IN THE TRENCHES

An application with an appealing graphical design is preferred over applications that are mostly text. Good graphic design communicates simplicity and engages the user.

Adding a Text Field

In the Concert Tickets application, a single screen opens when the application runs, with a Number Text Field requesting the number of concert tickets desired. To name a Text Field, use the Id property in the Properties pane to enter a name that begins with the prefix txt, which represents a text field in the code. The Id property of any widget is used in the Java code to refer to the widget. A descriptive variable name such as txtTickets can turn an unreadable piece of code into one that is well documented and easy to debug.

Using the String Table

Instead of adding text directly in a TextView's Text property, Android prefers that text not be placed statically in a Text property, but in one central file location named strings.xml. For example, suppose you are hired to write an app and you enter text in the Text property of each control. After testing the app, your customer decides to change all the text within the app. Now you have to check for the original text control by control, file by file, including .xml and .java files, for all the text you have inserted, and then replace it. As a time-saving alternative, Android provides a very useful way to use text and sentences in an application: using the strings.xml file inside the Resources folder. If your customer wants to change all the text within the app, you can go to a single file location to make the changes.

The string items that are displayed in the TextView control in this app will not be typed directly in the Properties pane, but instead in a string array in the res/values folder. A file named **strings.xml** is a default file that is part of every Android application and contains commonly used strings for an application. You enter text in this file using the String table because it can easily be changed without changing code. A **string** is a series of alphanumeric characters that can include spaces. Android loads text resources from the project's String table. The String table can also be used for localization. **Localization** is the use of the String table to change text based on the user's preferred language. For example, Android can select text in Spanish from the String table, based on the current device configuration and locale. The developer can add multiple translations in the String table.

In the Concert Tickets app, the first TextView control displays the text Ticket Vault, and the Button control displays the text Find the Cost. You also need text to prompt users to enter text and to display a description of the concert image shown on the screen. To add the Name and Value text for Text Field, Button, and ImageView controls to the strings.xml file, follow these steps.

STEP 1

- Tap or click the Save All button on the Standard toolbar, and then close the ConcertTickets Manifest tab.

- In the Package Explorer, expand the values folder within the res folder.

- Double-tap or double-click the strings.xml file to display the Android Resources.

The strings.xml tab is displayed with the Android Resources. Notice that three default String values are already in the strings.xml file (Figure 3-14).

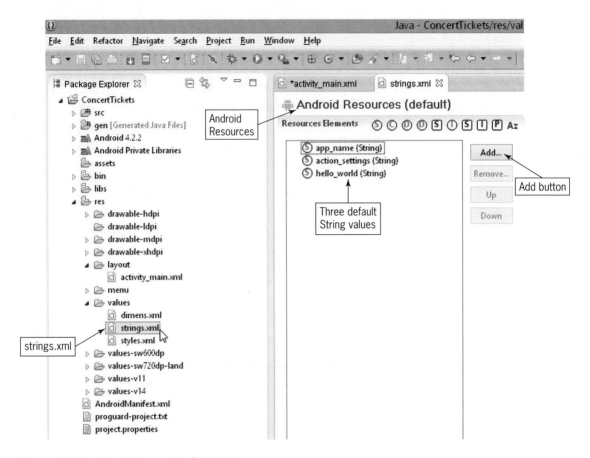

Figure 3-14   Android Resources–String table

STEP 2

• Tap or click the Add button.

A dialog box opens displaying the elements that can be added to the Android Resources (Figure 3-15).

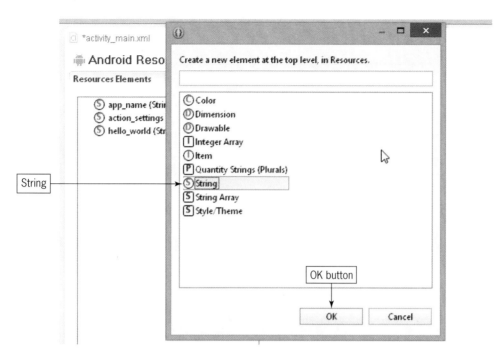

Figure 3-15 Adding a String resource

STEP 3

- If necessary, tap or click String and then tap or click the OK button.
- In the Name text box, type **txtTitle** to name the String.
- In the Value text box, type **Ticket Vault** to define the text.

The Name and Value settings of the TextView control are entered into the strings.xml file (Figure 3-16).

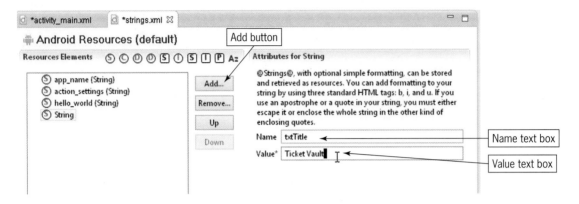

Figure 3-16   TextView control name and value

STEP 4

- Tap or click the Add button.
- If necessary, tap or click String and tap or click the OK button.
- In the Name text box, type **txtTickets** to name the String.
- In the Value text box, type **Number of Tickets** to define the text that will be displayed as a Hint within the Text Field control.
- Tap or click the Add button.
- If necessary, tap or click String and tap or click the OK button.
- In the Name text box, type **prompt** to name the String.
- In the Value text box, type **Select Group** to define the text that will be displayed as a Hint within the Text Field control.
- Tap or click the Add button.
- If necessary, tap or click String and tap or click the OK button.
- In the Name text box, type **description** to name the String.
- In the Value text box, type **Concert Image** to define the text.
- Tap or click the Add button.
- If necessary, tap or click String and tap or click the OK button.
- In the Name text box, type **btnCost** to name the String.
- In the Value text box, type **Find the Cost** to define the text.

The Name and Value settings of the Text Field, Button, and ImageView controls are entered into the strings.xml file (Figure 3-17).

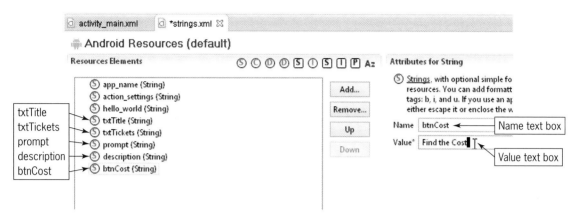

Figure 3-17   Multiple Strings added to the strings.xml file

String Arrays

The TextView, Spinner, Button, and ImageView controls each reference an individual string of text assigned in the strings.xml file, but if a control holds multiple text strings, it is best to use a **string array** that can be referenced from the String Resources in the application. In the Concert Tickets app, the user can select one of three performance groups: Cracked Eggs, Spinout, and Zig Zag. The text representing the performance groups can be placed in strings.xml as a string array resource tied together within one array name. A control such as a Spinner can be populated with a string array resource without using any code. To add a string array to the strings.xml file, follow these steps.

STEP 1

- In the Android Resources window of the strings.xml tab, tap or click the Add button.
- Tap or click String Array and then tap or click the OK button.
- Type **txtGroup** in the Name text box to name the String Array.

The String Array is named txtGroup (Figure 3-18).

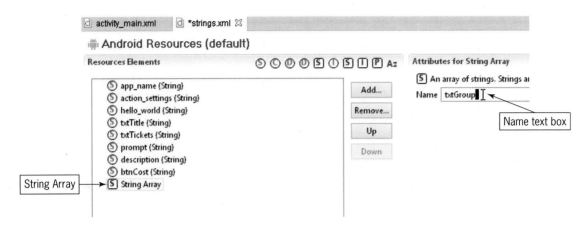

Figure 3-18   String Array

STEP 2

- Tap or click the Add button.

- Tap or click Item and then tap or click the OK button.

- In the Value box, type **Cracked Eggs** as the name of the first item.

- Tap or click the Add button and then tap or click Item.

- Tap or click the OK button.

- In the Value box, type **Spinout** as the name of the second item.

- Tap or click the Add button again, select Item, and then click the OK button.

- In the Value box, type **Zig Zag** as the name of the last item.

Three items are added to the txtGroup String Array (Figure 3-19).

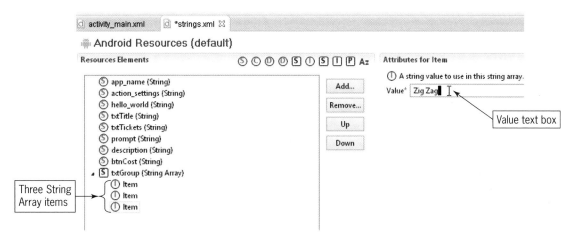

Figure 3-19   String Array items

After the strings and string arrays are set, you can add controls to the emulator. To begin the design of the emulator screen and to add a TextView and Text Field control, follow these steps:

STEP 1

- Tap or click the Save All button on the Standard toolbar.

- Close the strings.xml tab.

- With activity_main.xml open and displaying the emulator screen, tap or click the Form Widgets category in the Palette, if necessary.

- Drag and drop the TextView control onto the top part of the emulator user interface.

- To center the TextView control, drag the control to the center of the screen until a green dashed vertical line identifying the screen's center is displayed.

- In the Text property in the Properties pane, tap or click the ellipsis button (...).

The Resource Chooser dialog box opens with a listing of string resources (Figure 3-20).

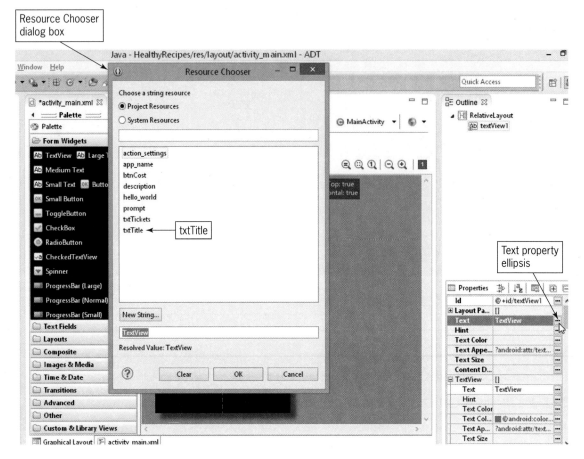

Figure 3-20 Resource Chooser dialog box

STEP 2

- Tap or click txtTitle in the Resource Chooser dialog box to select the assigned string, and then tap or click the OK button.

- In the Text Size property, type **48sp** and then press the Enter key.

- If necessary, resize the TextView control so its text is displayed on one line.

A TextView control is added to the emulator to represent the company name with the text Ticket Vault from strings.xml and size of 48sp (Figure 3-21).

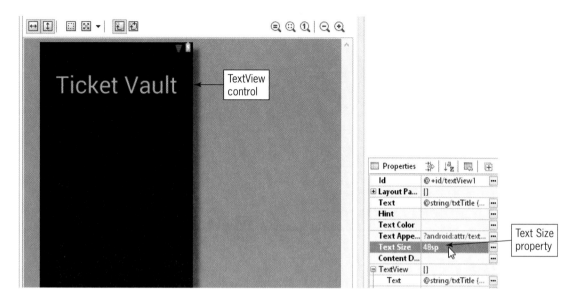

Figure 3-21   TextView control updated with String text

STEP 3

- Tap or click the Text Fields category in the Palette.

- Scroll down to the Number Text Field.

- Drag and drop the Number Text Field control onto the emulator's user interface below the Ticket Vault text.

- Drag the control to the center of the screen until a green dashed vertical line identifying the screen's center is displayed.

- Change the Id property of the Text Field to **@+id/txtTickets** to reference this control later in the Java code, and then press the Enter key.

- Tap or click the Yes button on the Update References? dialog box to update the id of this control in the XML code.

- Tap or click the OK button in the Rename Resource dialog box to update the new name.

- Set the Text Size property to **32sp** and press the Enter key.

A Number Text Field control named txtTickets with the size of 32sp is added to the emulator to allow the user to enter the number of tickets (Figure 3-22).

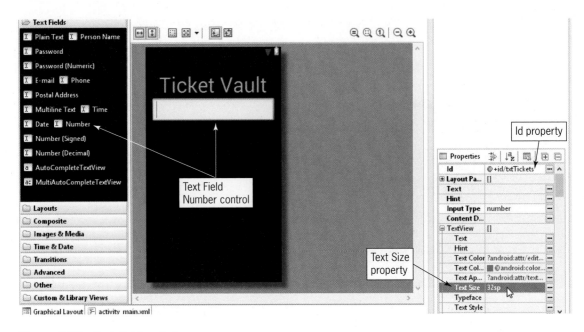

Figure 3-22   Text Field control

GTK
You might need to tap or click controls in the emulator to select them to display the correct properties for that control.

IN THE TRENCHES
Chromecast, a popular Google online entertainment system, provides HDTV movies, television shows, and music from Google Play apps.

Setting the Hint Property for the Text Field

When the Concert Tickets program is executed, the user needs guidelines about the input expected in the Text Field control. These guidelines can be included in the Hint property of the Text Field control. A **hint** is a short description of a field that is visible as light-colored text (also called a watermark) inside a Text Field control. Instead of typing the hint directly into the Hint property, the preferred way is to enter the value in the String table. When the user taps or clicks the control, the hint is removed and the user is free to type the requested input. The purpose of the hint in Figure 3-23 is to request what is expected in this field, without the user having to select and delete default text.

Figure 3-23   Hint in a Text Field control

To set the Hint property for the Text Field control, follow these steps:

STEP 1

- With the txtTickets Text Field control selected on the emulator screen, tap or click the ellipsis button of the Hint property.

The Resource Chooser dialog box opens with a listing of string resources (Figure 3-24).

STEP 2

- Tap or click txtTickets in the Resource Chooser dialog box to select the assigned string and then tap or click the OK button.

A watermark hint indicates that the number of tickets is needed as input in the Text Field control (Figure 3-25).

GTK
If your activity_main.xml emulator window fails to update, try saving your project to update the emulator. You can also refresh your Android project by tapping or clicking Project on the menu bar, tapping or clicking Clean, and then tapping or clicking the OK button.

Figure 3-24   Resource Chooser dialog box

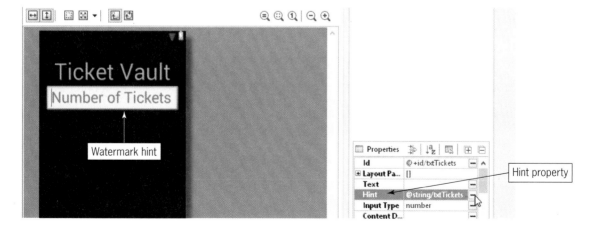

Figure 3-25   Hint added to Text Field control

Using the Android Spinner Control

After the user enters the number of tickets, the next step is to select which concert to attend. Three musical groups are performing next month: Cracked Eggs, Spinout, and Zig Zag. Due to possible user error on a small onscreen keyboard, it is much easier for a user to use a Spinner control instead of actually typing the group names. A **Spinner control** is a widget similar to a drop-down list for selecting a single item from a fixed listing, as shown in Figure 3-26. The Spinner control displays a prompt with a list of strings called **items** in a pop-up window without taking up multiple lines on the initial display.

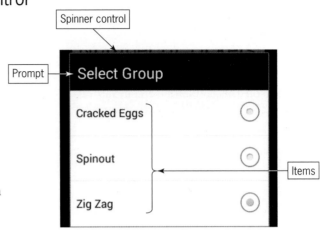

Figure 3-26   Spinner control and items

In the Concert Tickets app, a String Array for the Spinner control named txtGroup is necessary to hold the three concert group names as individual string resources in strings.xml. The strings.xml resources file provides an easy way to update commonly used strings throughout your project, instead of searching through code and properties to alter a string array within the application. For example, each month the concert planners can simply change the text in the strings.xml file to reflect their new concert events. A **prompt**, which can be used to display instructions at the top of the Spinner control, also is stored in strings.xml and is named prompt.

The Spinner property called **Entries** connects the String Array to the Spinner control for display in the application. The Spinner control is located in the Form Widgets category. The following steps add the Spinner control to the Android application:

STEP 1

- With the activity_main.xml tab open, tap or click the Form Widgets category in the Palette.
- Drag and drop the Spinner control below the Text Field and center it horizontally.
- Change the Id property of the Spinner control to **@+id/txtGroup** and then press Enter.
- Tap or click the Yes button and then tap or click the OK button.

The Spinner control is added to the emulator window and named txtGroup (Figure 3-27).

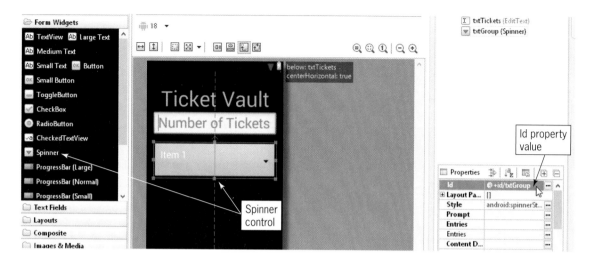

Figure 3-27 Entries property for the Spinner control

STEP 2

- In the Properties pane, tap or click the Prompt property ellipsis button.
- In the Reference Chooser dialog box, tap or click the expand arrow for String.
- Select prompt.
- Tap or click the OK button to close the Reference Chooser dialog box.
- To display the String Array, tap or click the ellipsis button to the right of the first Entries property.
- In the Reference Chooser dialog box, tap or click the expand arrow for Array.
- Select txtGroup and tap or click the OK button.

The Prompt property connects to the resource named @string/prompt. The Entries property connects to the resources of the String Array @array/txtGroup. The actual groups are displayed in the Spinner when the app is executed in the emulator (Figure 3-28).

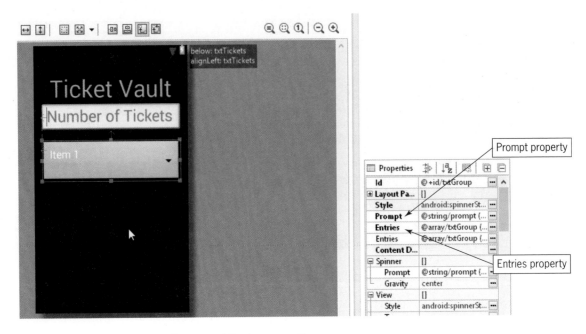

Figure 3-28 Spinner control Prompt and Entries properties

Adding the Button, TextView, and ImageView Controls

After the user enters the number of tickets and the concert group name, the user taps the Find the Cost button to calculate the cost with a Button event. After the total cost is calculated by multiplying the number of tickets by the cost of each ticket ($79.99), the name of the group and total cost of the tickets are displayed in a TextView control.

An ImageView control displayed on an Android device should be accessible to everyone. Accessibility should be addressed for people with limited or no vision, who might be using a built-in screen reader to assist them in using the app. An ImageView control should have a content description for those who cannot see the image. For example, in the Concert Tickets app, a picture of a concert is displayed. By setting the Content Description property for the ImageView control to the String text "Concert Image", the viewer can imagine what the image looks like based on your description.

An image file named concert.png, provided with your student files, is displayed in an ImageView control for the Concert Tickets app. You should already have the student files for this text that your instructor gave you or that you downloaded from the Web page for this book (www.cengagebrain.com). To add the Button, TextView, and Image View controls to the emulator window, follow these steps:

- In the activity_main.xml tab, drag the Button control from the Form Widgets category in the Palette to the emulator and center it below the Spinner control.

- In the Properties pane, change the Id property to **@+id/btnCost**, and then press Enter. Tap or click the Yes button and then tap or click the OK button.

- Tap or click the ellipsis button to the right of the Text property, select btnCost, and then tap or click the OK button.

- Change the Text Size property to **32sp**. Save your work.

The Button control named btnCost displays the text Find the Cost from the btnCost String and the size is changed to 32sp (Figure 3-29).

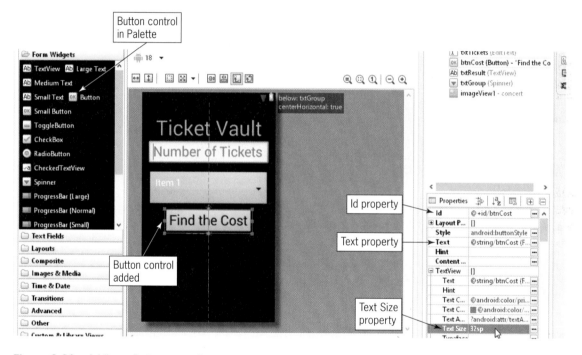

Figure 3-29   Adding a Button control

- From the Form Widgets category in the Palette, drag the TextView control to the emulator and center it below the Button control.

- In the Properties pane, change the Id property of the TextView control to **@+id/txtResult**, and then press Enter.

- Tap or click the Yes button and then tap or click the OK button.

- Change the Text Size property to **18sp**.
- Tap or click to the right of the Text property and delete the text.

The txtResult TextView control is added to the emulator window with the Text property deleted (Figure 3-30).

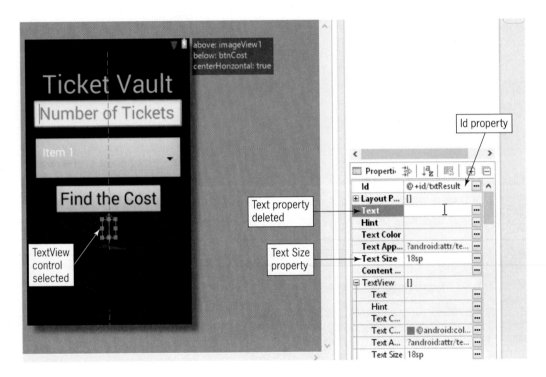

Figure 3-30 Adding a TextView control to display results

STEP 3

- To add the ImageView control, first copy the student files to your USB drive (if necessary).
- Open the USB folder containing the student files.
- In the Package Explorer, expand the drawable-hdpi folder. Drag the concert.png file to the drawable-hdpi folder until a plus sign pointer appears. Release the mouse button.
- Tap or click the OK button in the File Operation dialog box.
- In the activity_main.xml tab, tap or click the Images & Media category in the Palette.
- Drag the ImageView control to the emulator and center it below the TextView control at the bottom of the emulator window.
- Tap or click concert in the Resource Chooser dialog box, and then tap or click the OK button.

- With the image selected, tap or click the ellipsis button to the right of the Content Description property in the Properties pane. Select description, and then click the OK button.

The concert image is displayed at the bottom of the emulator window with a content description for accessibility purposes (Figure 3-31).

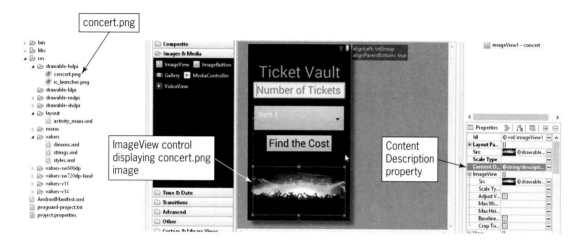

Figure 3-31   Adding an ImageView control

GTK

An Android app will not run in the emulator until you open the MainActivity.java code.

Coding the EditText Class for the Text Field

To handle the input that the user enters into the numeric Text Field control in the chapter project, you use the EditText class, which extracts the text and converts it for use in the Java code. The extracted text must be assigned to a variable. A **variable** is used in a Java program to contain data that changes during the execution of the program. In the chapter project, a variable named tickets holds the text entered in the Text Field for the number of tickets. The following code syntax declares (or initializes) the tickets variable, which contains the extracted EditText class text from the user's input. Notice the code syntax begins with the word **final**, indicating that tickets is a final variable. A final variable can only be initialized once and any attempt to reassign the value results in a compile error when the application is executed.

Code Syntax

```
final EditText tickets=(EditText)findViewById(R.id.txtTickets);
```

Recall that if you want to refer to a control in the Java code, you need to use the Id property to name the control when you add it to the interface. For example, the Text Field control was assigned the id txtTickets. Now you can access the control in the code using the findViewById( ) method. In the parentheses, the R refers to resources available to the app, such as a layout control, the id indicates that the resource is identified by the Id property, and txtTickets is the assigned id.

Next, the txtTickets Text Field control should be assigned to the variable named tickets. To collect the ticket input from the user, code the EditText class for the Text Field by following this step:

STEP 1

- In the Package Explorer, expand src and net.androidbootcamp.concerttickets, and then double-tap or double-click MainActivity.java to open the code window.

- If necessary, close the Outline/Properties pane.

- Tap or click to the right of the line setContentView(R.layout.*activity_main*);.

- Press the Enter key to insert a blank line.

- To initialize and reference the EditText class with the Id name of txtTickets, type **final EditText tickets=(EditText)findViewById(R.id.txtTickets);**.

- Point to the red curly line under EditText and select Import 'EditText' (android.widget) on the pop-up menu to import the Java library for the EditText control.

The EditText class extracts the value from the user's input for the number of tickets and assigns the value to the variable named tickets. Notice variables that have not been used in the program have a curly underline. This underline is removed when a value is assigned later in the program (Figure 3-32).

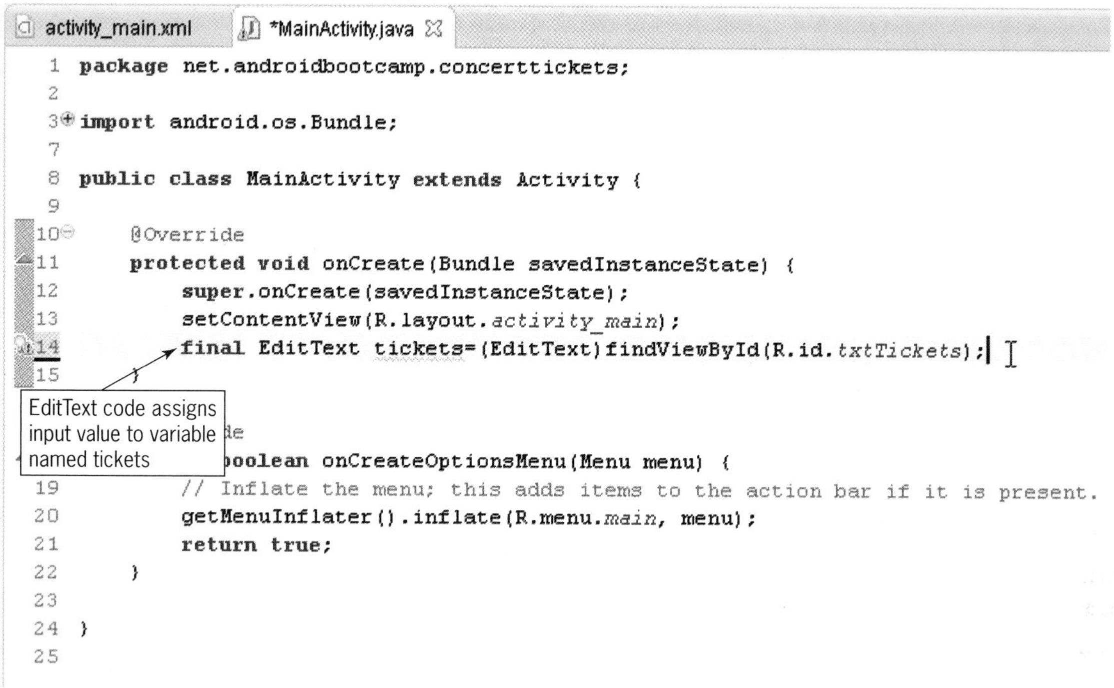

```
 activity_main.xml      *MainActivity.java

 1  package net.androidbootcamp.concerttickets;

 2

 3 import android.os.Bundle;

 7

 8  public class MainActivity extends Activity {

 9

10      @Override

11      protected void onCreate(Bundle savedInstanceState) {

12          super.onCreate(savedInstanceState);

13          setContentView(R.layout.activity_main);

14          final EditText tickets=(EditText)findViewById(R.id.txtTickets); I

15      }
```

EditText code assigns
input value to variable
named tickets

```
        boolean onCreateOptionsMenu(Menu menu) {

19          // Inflate the menu; this adds items to the action bar if it is present.

20          getMenuInflater().inflate(R.menu.main, menu);

21          return true;

22      }

23

24  }

25
```

Figure 3-32   Coding the EditText class for the Text Field

Coding the Spinner Control

The user's selection of the concert group also must be assigned to a variable and stored in the computer's memory. For this application, the selection made from the Spinner control (txtGroup) is assigned to a variable named group using the following code:

Code Syntax

```
final Spinner group = (Spinner)findViewById(R.id.txtGroup);
```

To collect the input from the user's group selection, code the Spinner control by following this step:

STEP 1

- After the EditText line, press the Enter key to create a new line.

- To initialize and reference the Spinner control with the Id name of txtGroup, type
  final Spinner group = (Spinner) findViewById(R.id.txtGroup);.

- Point to the red curly line under Spinner and select Import 'Spinner' (android.widget) on the pop-up menu.

The Spinner control assigns the value from the user's input to the variable named group. (Figure 3-33).

```
activity_main.xml        *MainActivity.java

 1  package net.androidbootcamp.concerttickets;
 2
 3  import android.os.Bundle;
 8
 9  public class MainActivity extends Activity {
10
11      @Override
12      protected void onCreate(Bundle savedInstanceState) {
13          super.onCreate(savedInstanceState);
14          setContentView(R.layout.activity_main);
15          final EditText tickets=(EditText)findViewById(R.id.txtTickets);
16          final Spinner group = (Spinner)findViewById(R.id.txtGroup);  I
17      }
18
19      @Override
20      public boolean onCreateOptionsMenu(Menu menu) {
21          // Inflate the menu; this adds items to the action bar if it is present.
22          getMenuInflater().inflate(R.menu.main, menu);
23          return true;
24      }
```

Spinner code assigns input value to variable named group

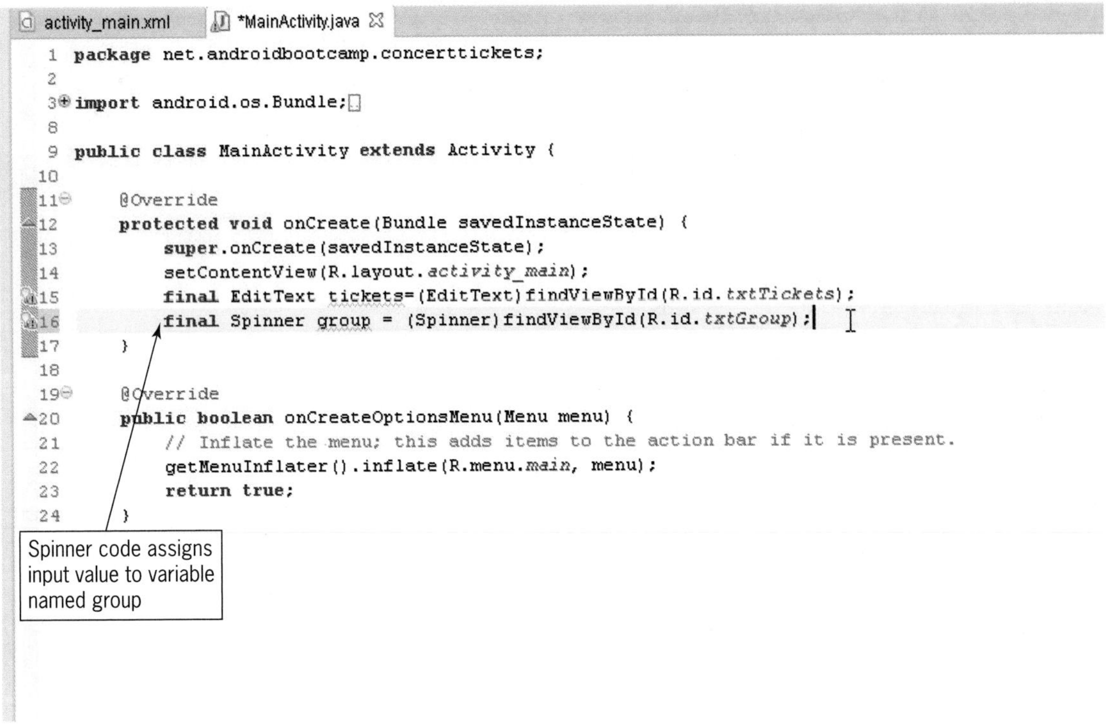

Figure 3-33 Coding the Spinner control

Coding the Button Control

After the user inputs the number of tickets and the concert group name, the user taps the Find the Cost button to calculate the cost in a Button event. After the total cost is calculated by multiplying the number of tickets by the cost of each ticket ($79.99), the name of the group and total cost of the tickets are displayed in a TextView control. The TextView control is assigned to the variable named result using the following code:

Code Syntax

```
final TextView result = ((TextView)findViewById(R.id.txtResult));
```

To initialize the Button control, set up the Button listener, and initiate the TextView control to display the results, follow these steps:

STEP 1

- If necessary, tap or click to the right of the code line that assigned the Spinner control to the variable named group. Press the Enter key.

- To initialize the Button control with the Id name of btnCost, type **Button cost = (Button) findViewById(R.id.btnCost);**.

- Point to Button and import the Button type as an Android widget. Press the Enter key.

The Button control is initialized and the Button type is imported (Figure 3-34).

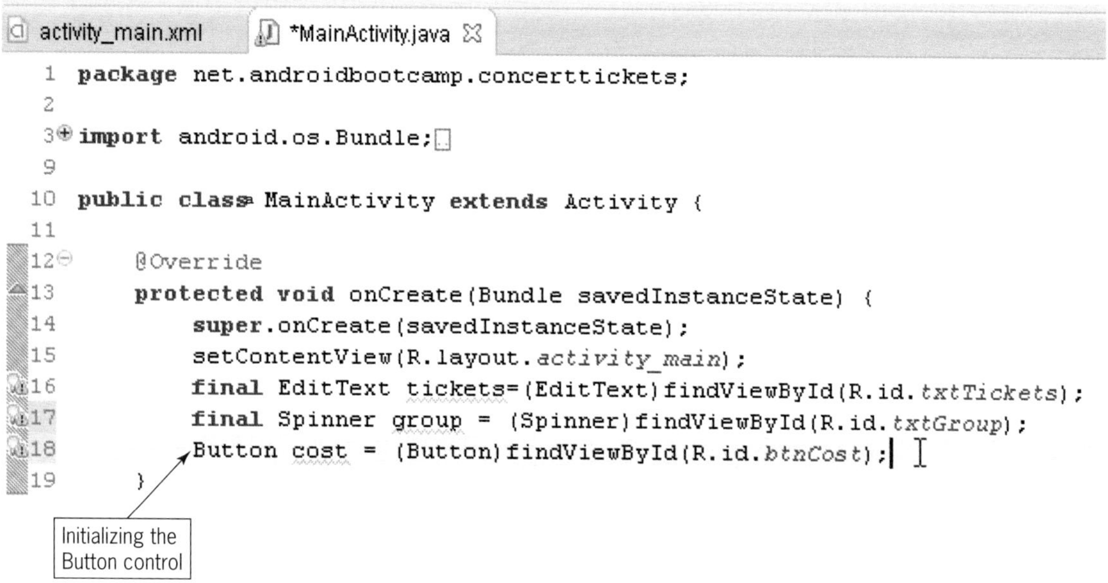

```
 activity_main.xml      *MainActivity.java 

  1  package net.androidbootcamp.concerttickets;
  2
  3⊕ import android.os.Bundle;
  9
 10  public class MainActivity extends Activity {
 11
 12⊖     @Override
 13      protected void onCreate(Bundle savedInstanceState) {
 14          super.onCreate(savedInstanceState);
 15          setContentView(R.layout.activity_main);
 16          final EditText tickets=(EditText)findViewById(R.id.txtTickets);
 17          final Spinner group = (Spinner)findViewById(R.id.txtGroup);
 18          Button cost = (Button)findViewById(R.id.btnCost);
 19      }
```

Initializing the Button control

Figure 3-34   Coding the button

STEP 2

- To code the button listener that awaits user interaction, type **cost.setOn** to display an auto-complete listing.

- Double-tap or double-click the first setOnClickListener displayed in the auto-complete listing.

- Inside the parentheses, type **new on** and press Ctrl+spacebar to display an auto-complete listing.

- Double-tap or double-click the first choice, which lists an OnClickListener with an Anonymous Inner Type event handler.

- Point to OnClickListener and select Import 'OnClickListener' (android.view.View).
- Place a semicolon at the end of the auto-generated stub closing brace and parenthesis on Line 28.

The Button control is initialized and an OnClickListener auto-generated stub appears in the code window (Figure 3-35).

activity_main.xml | *MainActivity.java

```java
1  package net.androidbootcamp.concerttickets;
2
3  import android.os.Bundle;
11
12 public class MainActivity extends Activity {
13
14     @Override
15     protected void onCreate(Bundle savedInstanceState) {
16         super.onCreate(savedInstanceState);
17         setContentView(R.layout.activity_main);
18         final EditText tickets=(EditText)findViewById(R.id.txtTickets);
19         final Spinner group = (Spinner)findViewById(R.id.txtGroup);
20         Button cost = (Button)findViewById(R.id.btnCost);
21         cost.setOnClickListener(new OnClickListener() {
22
23             @Override
24             public void onClick(View v) {
25                 // TODO Auto-generated method stub
26
27             }
28         });
29     }
30
```

Button OnClickListener

Figure 3-35 Initializing the Button control

STEP 3

- After the line of code beginning with cost.setOnClickListener, in Line 22 type **final TextView result = ((TextView)findViewById(R.id.txtResult));**.
- Import 'TextView' (android.widget).

The TextView control txtResult is assigned to the variable named result (Figure 3-36).

```
  activity_main.xml      *MainActivity.java ⊠
   1  package net.androidbootcamp.concerttickets;
   2
   3⊕ import android.os.Bundle;▯
  12
  13  public class MainActivity extends Activity {
  14
  15⊖      @Override
▲16      protected void onCreate(Bundle savedInstanceState) {
  17          super.onCreate(savedInstanceState);
  18          setContentView(R.layout.activity_main);
  19          final EditText tickets=(EditText)findViewById(R.id.txtTickets);
  20          final Spinner group = (Spinner)findViewById(R.id.txtGroup);
  21          Button cost = (Button)findViewById(R.id.btnCost);
  22⊖          cost.setOnClickListener(new OnClickListener() {
  23          final TextView result = ((TextView)findViewById(R.id.txtResult)); I
  24⊖              @Override
▲25          public void onClick(View v) {
  26              // TODO Auto-generated method stub
  27
  28          }
  29      });
  30      }
  31
```

txtResult TextView control assigned to result variable

Figure 3-36   TextView control code

GTK

Variable names are case sensitive and should be mixed case (camel case) when they include more than one word, as in costPerItem. Java variables cannot start with a number or special symbol. Subsequent characters in the variable name may be letters, digits, dollar signs, or underscore characters.

Declaring Variables

As you have seen, the user can enter data in the program using a Text Field control. In the Concert Tickets app, a mathematical equation multiplies the number of tickets by the cost of the tickets to calculate the total cost. When writing programs, it is convenient to use variables instead of the actual data such as the cost of a ticket ($79.99). As you learned in the previous section, two steps are necessary in order to use a variable:

1. Declare the variable.

2. Assign a value to the variable.

The declared type of a value determines which operations are allowed. At the core of Java code are eight built-in primitive (simple) types of data.

Primitive Data Types

Java requires all variables to have a data type. Table 3-1 lists the primitive data types that are supported across all computer platforms, including the Android SDK.

Type	Meaning	Range	Default Value
byte	Often used with arrays	–128 to 127	0
short	Often used with arrays	–32,768 to 32,767	0
int	Most commonly used number value	–2,147,483,648 to 2,147,483,647	0
long	Used for numbers that exceed int	–9,223,372,036,854,775,808 to 9,223,372,036,854,775,807	0
float	A single precision 32-bit floating-point number	+/–3.40282347 ^{38}	0
double	Most common for decimal values	+/–1.79769313486231570 ^{308}	0
char	Single character	Characters	0
boolean	Used for conditional statement	True or false	False

Table 3-1   Primitive data types in Java

In the Concert Tickets program, the tickets cost $79.99 each. This cost is best declared as a double data type, which is appropriate for decimal values. A statement should both declare the variable and assign a value for costPerTicket, as shown in the following code syntax. The requested quantity of tickets is assigned to a variable named numberOfTickets, which represents an integer. To multiply two values, the values must be stored in one of the numeric data types. When the total cost of the tickets is computed, the value is assigned to a variable named totalCost, also a double data type, as shown in the following code:

Code Syntax

```
double costPerTicket=79.99;
int numberOfTickets;
double totalCost;
```

String Data Type

In addition to the primitive data types, Java has another data type for working with text. The String type is a class and not a primitive data type. Most strings that you use in the Java language are an object of type String. A string can be a character, word, or phrase. If you assign a phrase to a String variable, place the phrase between double quotation marks. In the Concert Tickets app, after the user selects a musical group from the Spinner control, that group is assigned to a String type variable named groupChoice, as shown in the following code:

Code Syntax

```
String groupChoice;
```

GTK

When defining variables, good programming practice dictates that the variable names you use should reflect the actual values to be placed in the variable. That way, anyone reading the program code can easily understand the use of the variable.

Declaring the Variables

Variables in an Android application are typically declared at the beginning of an Activity. A variable must first be declared before the variable can be used in the application. To initialize, or declare, the variables, follow this step:

STEP 1

- In MainActivity.java on Line 14 within the class, press the Tab key to indent the text, and then insert the following four lines of code to initialize the variables in this Activity:

    double costPerTicket=79.99;

    int numberOfTickets;

    double totalCost;

    String groupChoice;

The variables are declared at the beginning of the Activity (Figure 3-37).

```
 ⓐ activity_main.xml      🗐 *MainActivity.java ⊠

  1  package net.androidbootcamp.concerttickets;
  2
  3⊕ import android.os.Bundle;▯
 12
 13  public class MainActivity extends Activity {
 14        ⌈ double costPerTicket=79.99;
 15        │ int numberOfTickets;
 16        │ double totalCost;
■17        ⌊ String groupChoice;▏  I
 18⊖        @Override
▲19          protected void onCreate(Bundle savedInstanceState) {
 20              super.onCreate(savedInstanceState);
 21              setContentView(R.layout.activity_main);
 22              final EditText tickets=(EditText)findViewById(R.id.txtTickets);
 23              final Spinner group = (Spinner)findViewById(R.id.txtGroup);
 24              Button cost = (Button)findViewById(R.id.btnCost);
 25⊖            cost.setOnClickListener(new OnClickListener() {
 26              final TextView result = ((TextView)findViewById(R.id.txtResult));
 27⊖                @Override
▲28                public void onClick(View v) {
✓29                    // TODO Auto-generated method stub
 30
 31                }
 32            });
 33        }
 34
```

variables declared

Figure 3-37 Declaring variables for the Activity

GetText( ) Method

At this point in the application development, all the controls have been assigned variables to hold their values. The next step is to convert the values in the assigned variables to the correct data type for calculation purposes. After the user enters the number of tickets and the concert group name, the Find the Cost button is clicked. Inside the OnClickListener code for the button control, the text stored in the tickets EditText control can be read with the **GetText( )** method. By default, the text in the EditText control is read as a String type. A String type cannot be used in a mathematical function. To convert a string into a numerical data type, you use a **Parse** class. Table 3-2 displays the Parse types that convert a string to a common numerical data type.

Numerical Data Type	Parse Types
Integer	Integer.parseInt( )
Float	Float.parseFloat( )
Double	Double.parseDouble( )
Long	Long.parseLong( )

© 2015 Cengage Learning

Table 3-2   Parse type conversions

To extract the string of text typed into the EditText control and convert it to an integer data type for the number of tickets, the following syntax is necessary:

Code Syntax

```
numberOfTickets = Integer.parseInt(tickets.getText( ).toString( )) ;
```

To code the GetText( ) method and convert the value in the tickets variable into an integer data type, and assign it to a variable named numberOfTickets, follow this step:

STEP 1

- In MainActivity.java, inside the OnClickListener onClick method stub on line 30, press the Tab key, and then type **numberOfTickets = Integer.parseInt(tickets.getText( ).toString( ));**.

The GetText( ) method extracts the text from tickets, converts the string to an integer, and assigns the value to numberOfTickets (Figure 3-38).

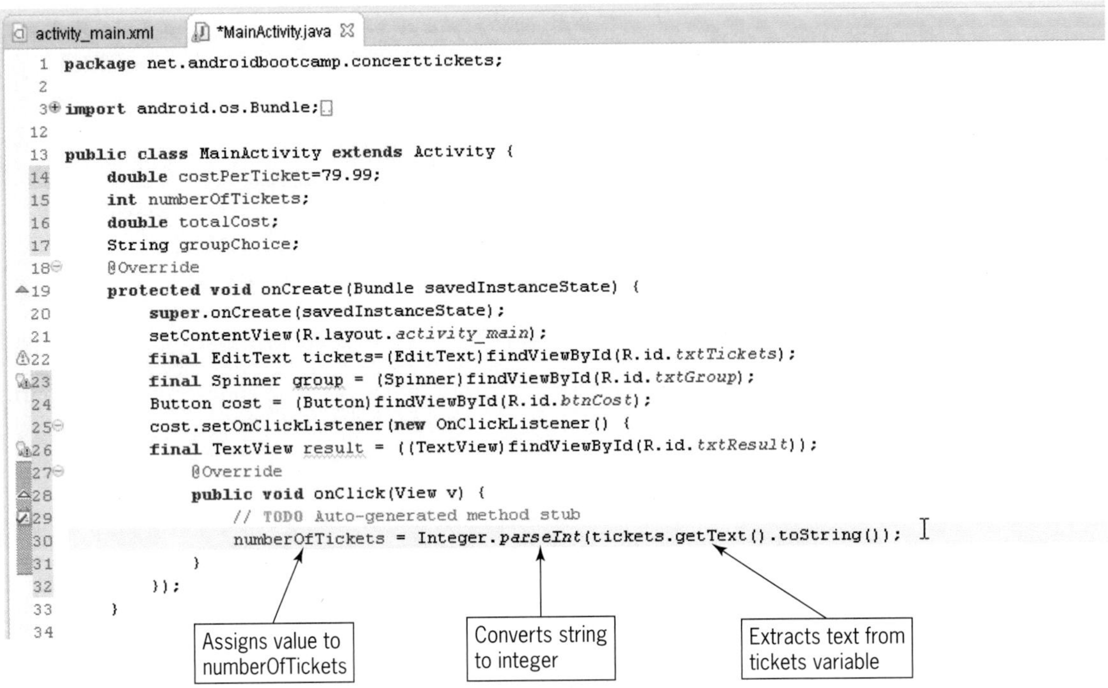

```
  activity_main.xml      *MainActivity.java

   1  package net.androidbootcamp.concerttickets;
   2
   3⊕ import android.os.Bundle;□
  12
  13  public class MainActivity extends Activity {
  14      double costPerTicket=79.99;
  15      int numberOfTickets;
  16      double totalCost;
  17      String groupChoice;
  18⊖     @Override
 ▲19     protected void onCreate(Bundle savedInstanceState) {
  20          super.onCreate(savedInstanceState);
  21          setContentView(R.layout.activity_main);
 ⚠22         final EditText tickets=(EditText)findViewById(R.id.txtTickets);
 ⚠23         final Spinner group = (Spinner)findViewById(R.id.txtGroup);
  24          Button cost = (Button)findViewById(R.id.btnCost);
  25⊖         cost.setOnClickListener(new OnClickListener() {
 ⚠26             final TextView result = ((TextView)findViewById(R.id.txtResult));
  27⊖             @Override
 ▲28             public void onClick(View v) {
 ☑29                 // TODO Auto-generated method stub
  30                 numberOfTickets = Integer.parseInt(tickets.getText().toString());  I
  31             }
  32          }});
  33      }
  34  }
```

| Assigns value to numberOfTickets | Converts string to integer | Extracts text from tickets variable |

Figure 3-38   Converting a string to an integer

Working with Mathematical Operations

The ability to perform arithmetic operations on numeric data is fundamental to many applications. Many programs require arithmetic operations to add, subtract, multiply, and divide numeric data. For example, in the Concert Tickets app in this chapter, the cost of each ticket must be multiplied by the number of tickets in order to calculate the total cost of the concert tickets.

Arithmetic Operators

Table 3-3 shows a listing of the Java arithmetic operators, along with their use and an example of an arithmetic expression showing their use.

Arithmetic Operator	Use	Assignment Statement
+	Addition	value = itemPrice + itemTax;
–	Subtraction	score = previousScore – 2;
*	Multiplication	totalCost = costPerTicket * numberOfTickets;
/	Division	average = totalGrade / 5.0;
%	Remainder	leftover = widgetAmount % 3; If widgetAmount = 11 the remainder = 2
++	Increment (adds 1)	golfScore ++
– –	Decrement (subtracts 1)	points – –

Table 3-3 Java arithmetic operators

© 2015 Cengage Learning

When multiple operations are included in a single assignment statement, the sequence of performing the calculations is determined by the rules shown in Table 3-4, which is called the order of operations.

For example, the result of 2 + 3 * 4 is 14 because the multiplication is of higher precedence than the addition operation.

Highest to Lowest Precedence	Description
( )	Parentheses
++ – –	Left to right
* / %	Left to right
+ –	Left to right

Table 3-4 Order of operations

© 2015 Cengage Learning

Formatting Numbers

After the total ticket cost is computed, the result should be displayed in currency format, which includes a dollar sign and commas if needed in larger values, and rounds off to two places past the decimal point. Java includes a class called **DecimalFormat** that provides patterns for formatting numbers for output on the Android device. For example, the pattern "$###,###.##" establishes that a number begins with a dollar sign character, displays a comma if the number has more than three digits, and rounds off to the nearest penny. If the pattern "###.#%" is used, the number is multiplied by 100 and rounded to the first digit past the decimal point. To establish a currency decimal format for the result of the ticket cost, the following code syntax is assigned to a variable named currency and later applied to the totalCost variable to display a currency value:

Code Syntax

```
DecimalFormat currency = new DecimalFormat("$###,###.##");
```

To code the calculation computing the cost of the tickets and to create a currency decimal format, follow this step:

STEP 1

- In MainActivity.java, after the last line entered, insert a new line, type **totalCost = costPerTicket * numberOfTickets;** and then press Enter.

- To establish a currency format, type **DecimalFormat currency = new DecimalFormat("$###,###.##");**.

- Import the 'DecimalFormat' (java.text) class.

The equation computes the total cost of the tickets and DecimalFormat creates a currency format that is used when the total cost is displayed (Figure 3-39).

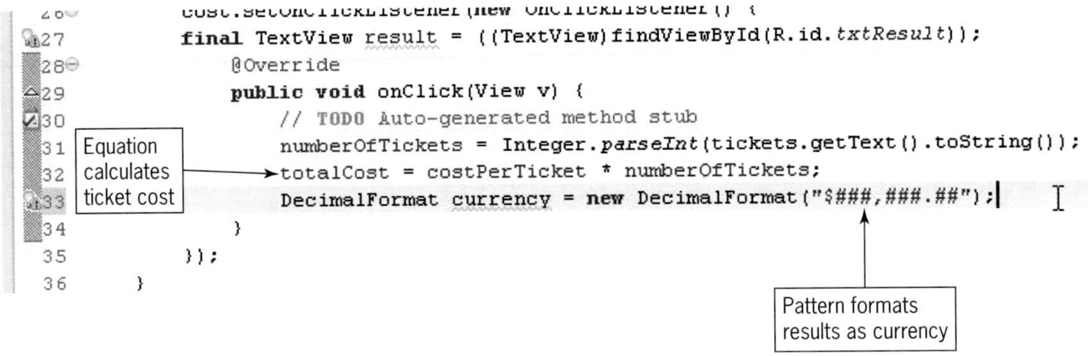

```
26      cost.setOnClickListener(new OnClickListener() {
27          final TextView result = ((TextView) findViewById(R.id.txtResult));
28          @Override
29          public void onClick(View v) {
30              // TODO Auto-generated method stub
31              numberOfTickets = Integer.parseInt(tickets.getText().toString());
32              totalCost = costPerTicket * numberOfTickets;
33              DecimalFormat currency = new DecimalFormat("$###,###.##");
34          }
35      });
36  }
```

Equation calculates ticket cost → (pointing to line 32)

Pattern formats results as currency (pointing to line 33)

Figure 3-39   Calculating and formatting the ticket cost

Displaying Android Output

In Java, computing the results does not mean displaying the results. To display the results that include the name of the group and the final cost of the tickets, first the name of the group must be assigned to a String variable.

GetSelectedItem( ) Method

To obtain the text name of the concert group that was selected by the user in the Spinner control, you use a method named GetSelectedItem( ). The **GetSelectedItem( )** method returns the text label of the currently selected Spinner item. For example, if the user selects Zig Zag, the GetSelectedItem( ) method assigns this group to a String variable named groupChoice that was declared at the beginning of the Activity, as shown in the following code:

Code Syntax

```
groupChoice = group.getSelectedItem( ).toString( );
```

GTK

A method named GetSelectedIndex( ) can be used with a Spinner control to determine if the user selected the first, second, or subsequent choice. For example, if GetSelectedIndex( ) is equal to the integer 0, the user selected the first choice.

SetText( ) Method

Earlier in the Android project, the method GetText( ) extracted the text from the Text Field control. In an opposite manner, the method SetText( ) displays text in a TextView control. SetText( ) accepts a string of data for display. To join variable names and text, you can concatenate the text with a plus sign (+). In the following example, the variable completeSentence is assigned *Android is the best phone platform*. This sentence is displayed in a TextView object named result.

Example:

```
String mobile = "Android";
String completeSentence = mobile + " is the best phone platform";
result.setText(completeSentence);
```

The syntax for the SetText( ) method is shown in the following code. In this example, the result is displayed in the TextView control named result, and includes the string that uses the concatenation operator, the plus sign connecting variables to the string text.

Code Syntax

```
result.setText("Total Cost for " + groupChoice + " is " +
currency.format(totalCost));
```

The currency.format portion of the code displays the variable totalCost with a dollar sign and rounds off to the nearest penny. The output for result is displayed in Figure 3-2: Total Cost for Spinout is $319.96. To code the GetSelectedItem( ) method and the SetText( ) method, follow these steps to complete the application:

STEP 1

- In MainActivity.java after the last line of code entered, insert a new line and type **groupChoice = group.getSelectedItem( ).toString( );** to assign the concert group to the String variable groupChoice.

- Insert a new line, and then type **result.setText("Total Cost for " + groupChoice + " is " + currency.format(totalCost));** to display the output.

The getSelectedItem( ) method identifies the selected group and setText( ) displays the selected group with the total cost of the tickets (Figure 3-40).

```
 activity_main.xml       MainActivity.java 

  1  package net.androidbootcamp.concerttickets;
  2
  3 import java.text.DecimalFormat;
 13
 14  public class MainActivity extends Activity {
 15       double costPerTicket=79.99;
 16       int numberOfTickets;
 17       double totalCost;
 18       String groupChoice;
 19       @Override
 20       protected void onCreate(Bundle savedInstanceState) {
 21            super.onCreate(savedInstanceState);
 22            setContentView(R.layout.activity_main);
 23            final EditText tickets=(EditText)findViewById(R.id.txtTickets);
 24            final Spinner group = (Spinner)findViewById(R.id.txtGroup);
 25            Button cost = (Button)findViewById(R.id.btnCost);
 26            cost.setOnClickListener(new OnClickListener() {
 27            final TextView result = ((TextView)findViewById(R.id.txtResult));
 28                @Override
 29                public void onClick(View v) {
 30                     // TODO Auto-generated method stub
 31                     numberOfTickets = Integer.parseInt(tickets.getText().toString());
 32                     totalCost = costPerTicket * numberOfTickets;
 33                     DecimalFormat currency = new DecimalFormat("$###,###.##");
 34                     groupChoice = group.getSelectedItem( ).toString();
 35                     result.setText("Total Cost for " + groupChoice + " is " + currency.format(totalCost)); |
 36                }
 37            });
 38       }
 39
```

Figure 3-40   Completed code

STEP 2

- To view the finished application, tap or click the Run As button on the Standard toolbar to test the application in the emulator.

- A dialog box opens the first time the application is executed to request how to run the application. Select Android Application and then tap or click the OK button.

- Save all the files in the next dialog box and then unlock the emulator.

- When the application opens in the emulator, enter the number of tickets using the onscreen keyboard and then select a group from the Spinner control. To view the results, tap or click the Find the Cost button.

The Concert Tickets Android app is executed (Figure 3-1 and 3-2).

Wrap It Up—Chapter Summary

In this chapter, you have learned to declare variables and write arithmetic operations. New controls such as the Text Field to enter text and the Spinner control to select from multiple items were used in the chapter project. GetText( ) and SetText( ) methods were used to extract and display data, respectively. An Android theme was also applied to the application.

- You can assign a theme to an Activity or entire application to define its appearance and style and to prevent each Android app you develop from looking too similar.

- Preview a theme by clicking the AppTheme button in the emulator window, clicking Theme, and then selecting a theme. To permanently change the theme in the application, define the theme in the Android Manifest file for each Activity.

- Use Text Fields to request input from users, who can enter characters using an onscreen keyboard or a physical keyboard. You need to select the correct type of Text Field control for the type of data you are requesting.

- The strings.xml file is part of every Android application by default and contains strings used in the application, such as text displayed in a TextView, Spinner, or Button control. You can edit a string in strings.xml to update the text wherever it is used in the application. In strings.xml, you can also include prompt text that provides instructions in a Spinner control. In the Java code, use the GetSelectedItem( ) method to return the text of the selected Spinner item.

- To provide guidelines so users enter the correct data in a Text Field control, use the control's Hint property to display light-colored text describing what to enter. The user clicks the control to remove the hint and type the requested input.

- To handle the input that users enter into a Text Field control, you use the EditText class, which extracts the text and converts it for use in the Java code. The extracted text must be assigned to a variable, which holds data that changes during the execution of the program. To extract the string of text entered in an EditText control, use the GetText( ) method. To display the extracted text in a TextView control, use the SetText( ) method.

- To use a variable, you must first declare the variable and then assign a value to it. The declared type of a value determines which mathematical operations are allowed. Variables in an Android application are typically declared at the beginning of an Activity.

- After assigning variables to hold the values entered in controls, you often need to convert the values in the assigned variables to the correct data type so the values can be used in calculations. To use string data in a mathematical function, you use the Parse class to convert the string into a numerical data type.

Key Terms

DecimalFormat—A class that provides patterns for formatting numbers in program output.

Entries—A Spinner property that connects a string array to the Spinner control for display.

final—A type of variable that can only be initialized once; any attempt to reassign the value results in a compile error when the application is executed.

GetSelectedItem( )—A method that returns the text of the selected Spinner item.

GetText( )—A method that reads text stored in an EditText control.

hint—A short description of a field that appears as light text in a Text Field control.

item—In a Spinner control, a string of text that appears in a list for user selection.

localization—The use of the String table to change text based on the user's preferred language.

Parse—A class that converts a string into a number data type.

prompt—Text that displays instructions at the top of the Spinner control.

soft keyboard—An onscreen keyboard positioned over the lower part of an application's window.

Spinner control—A widget similar to a drop-down list for selecting a single item from a fixed listing.

string—A series of alphanumeric characters that can include spaces.

string array— Two or more text strings.

strings.xml—A default file that is part of every Android application and holds commonly used strings in an application.

theme—A style applied to an Activity or an entire application.

variable—A name used in a Java program to contain data that changes during the execution of the program.

Developer FAQs

1. What is an Android theme?

2. Which theme was used in the chapter project?

3. In an app, suppose you want to use the theme named Theme.Holo.Light. What code is needed in the AndroidManifest.xml file to support this theme?

4. What is a soft keyboard? Be sure to include its location in your answer.

5. Which five controls were used in the chapter project?

6. Which Text Field control is best for entering an amount that contains a paycheck amount?

7. Which property of the Spinner control adds text at the top of the control such as instructions?

8. What is the name of the file that holds commonly used phrases (arrays) of text in an application?

9. What is a single string of information called in a string array?

10. Which property do you assign to the string array that you create for a Spinner?

11. Write the following variable in camel case: NUMBEROFBOXES.

12. Write a declaration statement for each of the following variables using the variable type and variable name that would be best for each value. Assign values if directed.

   a. The population of the state of Idaho

   b. Your weekly pay using the most common type for this type number

   c. The smallest data type you can use for your age

   d. Assign the first initial of your first name

   e. Assign the present minimum wage using the most common type for this type of number

   f. Assign the name of the city in which you live

   g. The answer to a true/false question

13. Name two numeric data types that can contain a decimal point.

14. What is the solution to each of the following arithmetic expressions?

   a. 3 + 4 * 2 + 7

   b. 16 / 2 * 4 + 3

   c. 40 − (6 + 2) / 2

   d. 3 + 68 % 9

15. Write a GetText( ) statement that converts a variable named deficit to a double data type and assigns the value to the variable named financeDeficit.

16. Assign the text of the user's choice of a Spinner control named collegeName to the variable named topCollege.

17. If a variable named amount is assigned to the value 47,199.266, what would these statements display in the variable called price?

```
DecimalFormat money = new DecimalFormat("$###,###.##");
price.setText("Salary = " + money.format(amount));
```

18. Write a line of Java code that assigns the variable jellyBeans to a decimal format with six digits and a comma if needed, but no dollar sign or decimal places.

19. Write a line of Java code to use concatenation to join the phrase "Welcome to the ", versionNumber (an int variable), and the phrase "th version" to the variable combineStatement.

20. Write a line of Java code that assigns a number to the variable numberChoice, which indicates the user's selection. If the user selects the first group, the number 0 is assigned; if the user selects the second group, the number 1 is assigned; and if the user selects the third group, the number 2 is assigned with the same variables used in the chapter project.

Beyond the Book

Using the Internet, search the Web for the answers to the following questions to further your Android knowledge.

1. Name 10 themes used in your Android SDK not mentioned in this chapter.

2. Search the Internet for three real Android apps that sell any type of tickets. Name five features of each of the three apps.

3. A good Android developer always keeps up with the present market. Open the page https://play.google.com. Find this week's featured tablet apps and write about the top five. Write a paragraph on the purpose and cost of each for a total of five paragraphs.

4. Open the search engine *Bing.com* and then click the News tab. Search for an article about Androids with this week's date. Insert the URL link at the top of a new document. Write a summary of the article containing 150–200 of your own words.

Case Programming Projects

Complete one or more of the following case programming projects. Use the same steps and techniques taught within the chapter. Submit the program you create to your instructor. The level of difficulty is indicated for each case programming project.

Easiest: ★

Intermediate: ★ ★

Challenging: ★ ★ ★

Case Project 3–1: Car Ferry Fare App ★

Requirements Document	
Application title:	Car Ferry Fare App
Purpose:	For a car ferry that transports cars and passengers from Cape Marie to the Star Island, a simple app determines how many tickets are needed and whether the ticket is to Cape Marie or Star Island. The app displays the total price for the fare for the ferry.
Algorithms:	1. The app displays a title; an image; and a Text Field, Spinner, and Button control (Figure 3-41). The two options in the Spinner control include To Cape Marie and To Star Island. Each single passenger ticket is $18 for one way.
	2. When the user taps or clicks the Button control, the number of tickets and the total cost of the fare is displayed (Figure 3-42).
Conditions:	Use a theme, Spinner prompt, string array, and Hint property.

Figure 3-41

Figure 3-42

Case Project 3–2: Volleyball Tickets App ★

Requirements Document

Application title: Volleyball Tickets App

Purpose: A volleyball ticket app allows the ticket taker at the court to sell entry tickets to a tournament.

Algorithms: 1. The volleyball ticket app has one Text Field that requests the number of adult tickets ($18).
A Spinner control allows the student to select one of the three possible games: Friday afternoon, Friday night, and Saturday night. The app also displays a title, an image, and a Button control (Figure 3-43).

2. After the user taps or clicks the Button control, the selected game and the total ticket cost are displayed in a TextView control (Figure 3-44).

Conditions: Use a theme, a title, an image, a Spinner prompt, a string array, and a Hint property.

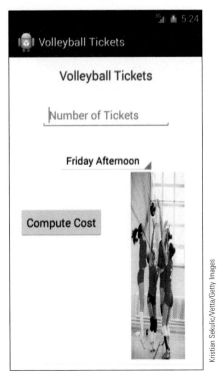

Figure 3-43

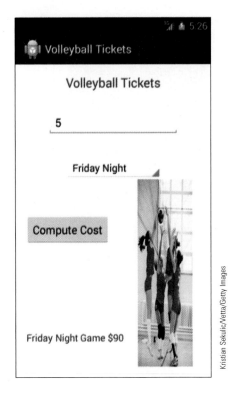

Figure 3-44

Case Project 3–3: New York City Cab Fare App ★★

Requirements Document

Application title:	NYC Cab Fare App
Purpose:	Create an app that estimates the cost for cab fare in New York City. The app calculates the cost of the trip and requests a reservation for a smart car, traditional sedan, or minivan.
Algorithms:	1. The app requests the distance in miles for the cab ride and your preference for the requested cab: a smart car, traditional sedan, or minivan. The cab fare has an initial rate of $3.00. A mileage rate of $3.25 per mile is also charged.
	2. The app displays the name of a cab company, a picture of a logo, and the results of the requested type of cab with the cost of the fare. Create your own layout.
Conditions:	Use a theme, Spinner prompt, string array, and Hint property. Decimal mileage is possible.

Case Project 3–4: Paint Calculator App ★★

Requirements Document

Application title:	Paint Calculator App
Purpose:	The paint calculator app is needed in the paint section of a large home store to calculate the number of gallons needed to paint a room. The amount of paint in gallons is displayed.
Algorithms:	1. The app displays a title; an image; two Text Fields; and a Spinner, Button, and TextView control. The Spinner control allows five colors of paint to be selected. The room's height in feet and the distance in feet around the room are entered.
	2. The color and the exact number of gallons in decimal form are displayed.
Conditions:	A gallon is needed for every 250 square feet for a single coat of paint. Display the result rounded to two decimal places. Select five names for paint for the Spinner control. Use a theme, Spinner prompt, string array, and Hint property.

Case Project 3–5: Split the Bill App ★★★

Requirements Document

Application title:	Split the Bill App
Purpose:	You are out with friends at a nice restaurant and the bill comes! This app splits the bill, including the tip, among the members of your party.
Algorithms:	1. A welcome screen displays the title, image, and button that takes the user to a second screen. The input/output screen requests the restaurant bill and the number of people in your group. The Spinner control asks about the quality of service: Excellent, Average, or Poor.
	2. Calculate an 18 percent tip and divide the restaurant bill with the tip included among the members of your party. Display the service and the individual share of the bill.
Conditions:	Use a theme, Spinner prompt, string array, and Hint property.

Case Project 3–6: Piggy Bank Children's App ★★★

Requirements Document

Application title:	Piggy Bank Children's App
Purpose:	A piggy bank app allows children to enter the number of quarters, dimes, nickels, and pennies that they have. The child can select whether to save the money or spend it. Calculate the amount of money and display the amount that the child is saving or spending. Create two screens: a welcome screen and an input/output screen.
Algorithms:	1. A welcome screen displays the title, image, and button that takes the user to a second screen. The input/output screen requests the number of quarters, dimes, nickels, and pennies. A Spinner control should indicate whether the children are saving or spending their coins. Create your own layout.
	2. The results display how much the child is saving or spending.
Conditions:	Use a theme, Spinner prompt, string array, and Hint property.

Explore! Icons and Decision-Making Controls

In this chapter, you learn to:

◎ Create an Android project with a custom icon
◎ Change the text color in controls using hexadecimal colors
◎ Align controls using the Change Gravity tool
◎ Determine layout with the Change Margins tool
◎ Place a RadioGroup and RadioButtons in Android applications
◎ Write code for a RadioGroup control
◎ Make decisions using an If statement
◎ Make decisions using an If Else statement
◎ Make decisions using logical operators
◎ Display an Android toast notification
◎ Test the isChecked property
◎ Make decisions using nested If statements

Developers can code Android applications to make decisions based on the input of users or other conditions that occur. Decision making is one of the fundamental activities of a computer application. In this chapter, you learn to write decision-making statements in Java, which allows you to test conditions and perform different operations depending on the results of that test. You can test for a condition being true or false and change the flow of what happens in a program based on the user's input.

The sample program in this chapter is designed to run on an Android phone or tablet device at a hospital. The Medical Calculator application provides nurses a mobile way to convert the weight of a patient from pounds to kilograms and kilograms to pounds. Most medication amounts are prescribed based on the weight of the patient. Most hospital scales display weight in pounds, but the prescribed medication is often based on the weight of a patient in kilograms. For safety reasons, the exact weight of the patient must be correctly converted between pounds and kilograms. The nurse enters the weight of the patient and selects a radio button, as shown in Figure 4-1, to determine whether pounds are being converted to kilograms or kilograms are being converted to pounds. The mobile application then computes the converted weight based on the conversion formulas. The conversion formulas are as follows: kilograms = pounds * 2.2 and pounds = kilograms / 2.2. To validate that correct weights are entered, if the value is greater than 500 for the conversion from pounds to kilograms or greater than 225 for the conversion from kilograms to pounds, the user is asked for a valid entry. If the user enters a number out of the acceptable range, a warning called a toast message appears on the screen. When the app is running, a nurse enters 225 for the value of the weight of the patient and selects the Convert Pounds to Kilograms radio button shown in Figure 4-1. After tapping the Convert Weight button, the application displays 102.3 kilograms (rounded off to the nearest tenth place) in a red font, as shown in Figure 4-2. By using a mobile device, the nurse can capture patient information such as weight directly at the point of care anywhere and anytime and reduce errors made by delaying entry on a traditional computer in another location.

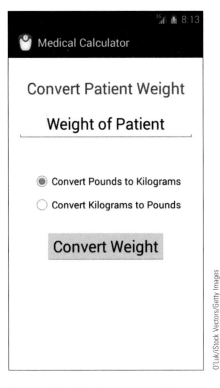

Figure 4-1 Opening screen of the Medical Calculator

Figure 4-2 Results screen of the Medical Calculator

To create this application, the developer must understand how to perform the following processes:

1. Create a customized launcher icon.
2. Define a TextField for the data entry of the weight of the patient.
3. Define a RadioGroup to select pounds to kilograms or kilograms to pounds.
4. Display a Toast message for data validation.
5. Convert data so it can be used for arithmetic operations.
6. Perform arithmetic operations on data the user enters.
7. Display formatted results.

IN THE TRENCHES
Medical device apps are changing the entire patient point-of-care system. Apps now used in hospitals include mobile patient records, drug prescription references, medical journals, surgical checklists, dosage calculators, radiology imagery, and disease pathology.

Using the Launcher Icon

By default, Android places a standard Android icon as the graphic to represent your application on the device's home screen and in the Launcher window. To view the opening icon called the **launcher icon** on the home screen, tap or click the application listing icon at the bottom of the emulator when an application begins to execute, as shown in Figure 4-3. Instead of a default icon, each app published to Google Play should have a custom graphic (Figure 4-3) representing the contents of your application. Launcher icons form the first impression of your app on prospective users in Google Play. With so many apps available, a high-quality launcher icon can influence users to purchase your Android app.

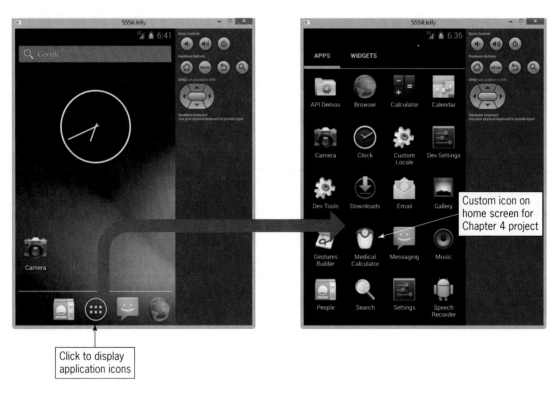

Figure 4-3   Android home screen and launcher icons

An icon is a graphic that takes up a small portion of screen space and provides a quick, intuitive representation of an app. As you design a launcher icon, consider that an icon can establish brand identity. A unique image logo and program name can communicate your brand to potential customers. In the Medical Calculator app, the scale icon shown in Figure 4-4 clearly communicates that this icon launches a program about weight. A simple image with a clear visual cue like the scale has a memorable impact. It also helps users find the app on the Google Play site. Google Play suggests icons should be simple and bold in design. For example, for a paint graphics program, an icon shaped like a thin art paintbrush may be hard to distinguish from a pencil image, but a large cartoonlike paintbrush can convey its purpose easily.

Google Play also specifies the size and format of all launcher icons for uniformity. Launcher icons should be saved in the .png file format. Based on your target device, Table 4-1 specifies the size of a finished launcher icon. You can use programs such as Microsoft Paint, Mac Paintbrush, and Adobe Photoshop to resize the icon to the correct number of pixels. In the chapter project, the icon dimension is 48 × 48 pixels for the high-density screen used by the application. If you are creating an application that can be deployed on any Android device, you can use the same name for the icon, but resize it four times and place each image in the appropriate res/drawable folder.

Figure 4-4 Launcher icon for the Medical Calculator app

Resolution	Dots per Inch (dpi)	Size (px)
ldpi (low-density screen)	120	36 × 36
mdpi (medium-density screen)	160	48 × 48
hdpi (high-density screen)	240	72 × 72
xhdpi (extra high-density screen)*	320	96 × 96
xxhdpi (extra extra high-density screen)*	440	144 × 144

Table 4-1 Launcher icon sizes

* Used by some tablets

GTK

When you publish an app to Google Play, you must provide a 512 × 512 pixel, high-resolution application icon in the developer console as you upload your program. This icon is displayed on the Google Play site to provide a description of the app and does not replace your launcher icon.

Google Play recommends a naming convention for launcher icons. Typically, the prefix ic_launcher is used to name launcher icons for Android apps. In the case of the Medical Calculator app, the launcher icon is named ic_launcher_weight.png. After a custom icon is placed within the project, Android renames the icon to the name ic_launcher-web.png.

GTK

Vector-based graphics are best to use for icon design because the images can be scaled without the loss of detail and are easily resized.

Customizing a Launcher Icon

To display a custom launcher icon instead of the default icon on the home screen, the custom icon image can be automatically placed in the res\drawable folder when you name and set up the app. In addition, the Android Manifest file must be updated to include the new filename of the image file. The application code within the Android Manifest file for the chapter project should be changed to android: icon = "ic_launcher_weight.png". To perform the following steps, you need an image file named ic_launcher_weight.png, provided with your student files, to use as the custom launcher icon for the Medical Calculator app. You should already have the student files for this text that your instructor gave you or that you downloaded from the Web page for this book (*www.cengagebrain.com*). To begin the chapter project and add a customized launcher icon, follow these steps:

STEP 1

- Open the Eclipse program.

- Type **E:\Workspace** (if necessary, enter a different drive letter that identifies the USB drive) to select a workspace and then tap or click the OK button.

- Tap or click the New button on the Standard toolbar and then select Android Application Project.

- Tap or click the Next button.

- In the New Android Application Project dialog box, enter the Application Name **Medical Calculator**.

- Enter the Package Name of **net.androidbootcamp.medicalcalculator**.

The new Android Medical Calculator project has an application name, a package name, and a Main Activity (Figure 4-5).

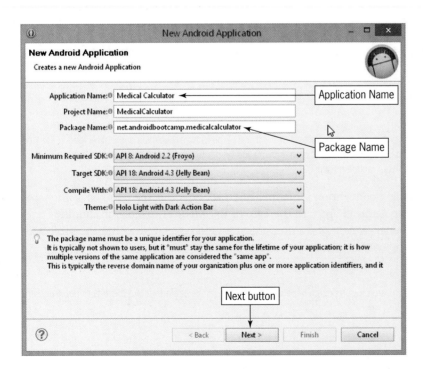

Figure 4-5   New Android Application dialog box

STEP 2

- Tap or click the Next button to configure the project.

The first check box is checked by default to create a custom launcher icon (Figure 4-6).

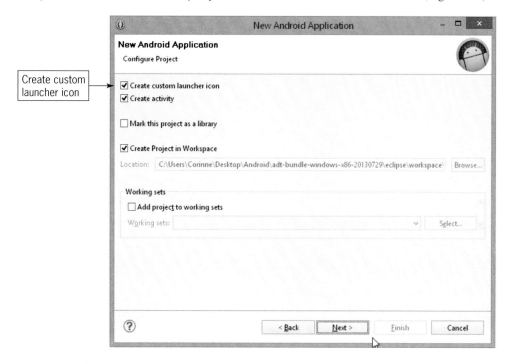

Create custom launcher icon

Figure 4-6 Creating a custom launcher icon

STEP 3

- Tap or click the Next button to view the default launcher icons for the resolutions of various devices.

- Tap or click the Browse button.

- To add the custom launcher icon, copy the student files to your USB drive (if necessary). Open the USB folder containing the student files to locate and then select the file ic_launcher_weight.png.

- Tap or click the Open button to add the custom launcher icon.

The custom icon launcher of a scale is displayed in different sizes (Figure 4-7).

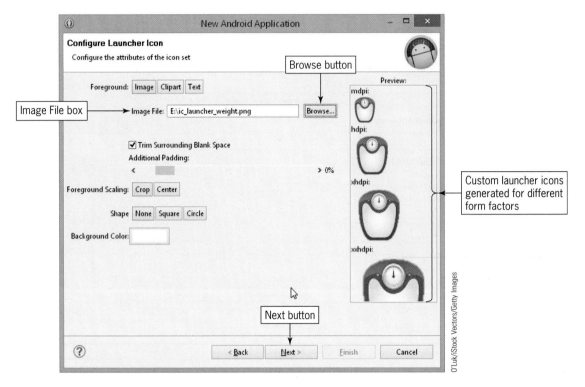

Figure 4-7 Configuring the launcher icon

STEP 4

- Tap or click the Next button twice.

- Tap or click the Finish button.

- If necessary, select the activity_main.xml tab. Tap or click the Hello world! TextView (displayed by default) in the emulator and then press the Delete key.

The activity_main.xml file is displayed on the Graphical Layout tab and the new custom launcher icon is displayed in the emulator (Figure 4-8).

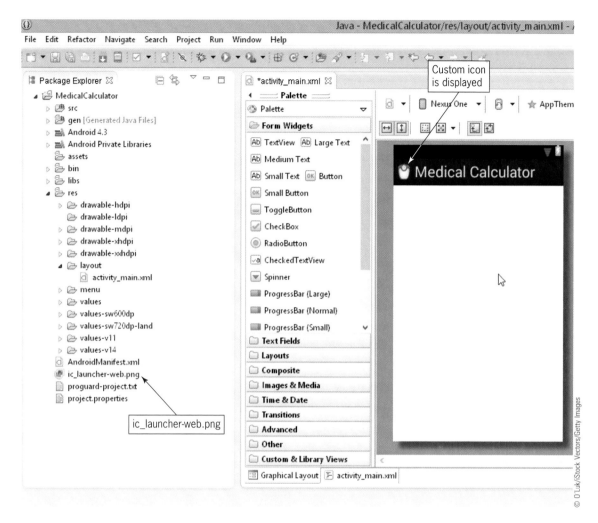

Figure 4-8 Custom icon displayed in the emulator

String Table

In the Medical Calculator app, the String resources are stored within the /res/values/strings.xml file of the resource hierarchy for the text displayed in the TextView, RadioButton, EditText, and Button controls. Any strings you add to the strings.xml file are accessible within your application. In the following steps, you insert the string names and values shown in Table 4-2.

String Name	String Value
hint	Weight of Patient
radLbToKilo	Convert Pounds to Kilograms
radKiloToLb	Convert Kilograms to Pounds
btnConvert	Convert Weight

© 2015 Cengage Learning

Table 4-2   String names and values to add

To begin the design of the Android user interface and create the String table, follow this step:

STEP 1

- In Package Explorer, open the strings.xml file in the res\values folder.

- Tap or click the Add button.

- Tap or click String and then tap or click the OK button.

- Type **txtTitle** in the Name text box to name the String.

- In the Value box, type **Convert Patient Weight** as the name.

- Tap or click the Add button again and continue to repeat the same process to add the remaining items listed in Table 4-2.

The strings.xml file is populated with the text used in the app (Figure 4-9).

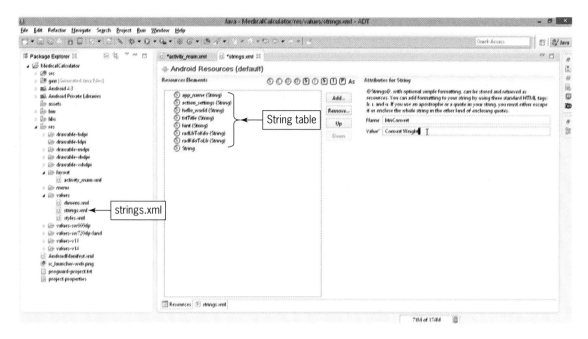

Figure 4-9 strings.xml

RadioButton and RadioGroup Controls

RadioButton controls are used to select or deselect an option. In the chapter project, the user can select which mathematical conversion is needed. When a RadioButton is placed on the emulator, by default each control is arranged vertically. If you prefer the RadioButton controls to be listed horizontally, you can set the orientation property to horizontal. Each RadioButton control has a label defined by the Text property and a Checked property set to either true or false. RadioButton controls are typically used together in a **RadioGroup**. Checking one radio button unchecks the other radio buttons within the group. In other words, within a RadioGroup control, only one RadioButton control can be selected at a time. When the RadioGroup control on the Palette is placed on the emulator window, three RadioButton controls are included in the group by default. If you need additional RadioButton controls, drag them from the Palette into the group. In the case of the Medical Calculator app, only two radio buttons are needed, so the third radio button is deleted.

To make the user's input as simple as possible, offer a default selection. For example, nurses more often convert weight from pounds to kilograms, so that RadioButton option should be checked initially. The Checked property of this RadioButton control is set to true to provide a default selection.

GTK

Like RadioButton controls, a CheckBox control allows a user to check or uncheck a listing. A user may select any number of check boxes, including zero, one, or several. In other words, each check box is independent of all other check boxes in the list, so checking one box does not uncheck the others. The shape of a radio button is circular and the check box is square.

Changing the Text Color of Android Controls

Thus far, each application in this text used the default color of black or white for the text color based on the theme for each Android control. The Android platform uses a color system called hexadecimal color codes to display different colors. A **hexadecimal color code** is a triplet of three colors. Colors are specified first by a pound sign, followed by how much red (00 to FF), how much green (00 to FF), and how much blue (00 to FF) are in the final color. For example, the hexadecimal color of #FF0000 is a true red. The TextView and RadioGroup controls displayed in the chapter project have light gray text, which you designate by typing #CCCCCC as the Text color property. To look up these color codes, search for hexadecimal color codes in a search engine or refer to *http://html-color-codes.com*.

Changing the Margins

After placing a control on the user interface, you can change the alignment by adjusting the gravity of the control. For more flexibility in controlling your layout, use **margins** to change the spacing around each object. Each control in the Medical Calculator app can use margins to add a certain amount of blank space measured in density independent pixels (dp) on each of its four sides. Instead of "eyeballing" the controls on the user interface for alignment, the Change Margins tool creates equal spacing around controls. Using the Change Margins tool helps make your user interface more organized and ultimately easier to use. The Change Margins tool is displayed when a control is selected on the user interface.

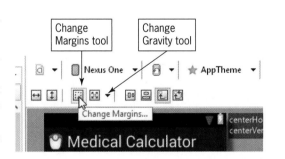

Figure 4-10   Change Margins and Change Gravity tools

See Figure 4-10. As you design the user interface, use the same specified margins around each control to provide a symmetrical layout.

Changing the Layout Gravity

The Medical Calculator app displays controls from the palette with Relative Layout. Relative Layout is the default setting for layout on the Android emulator. At times, you may find the emulator displaying a control in a different location from where you placed it on the screen. Layout can be set for each control using a property named Layout gravity to center a control horizontally as well as positioning it at other places on the screen. After each control is placed on the emulator, a toolbar appears above the emulator screen. The gravity can be changed using the properties listing or with a shortcut on the toolbar. The **Change Gravity** tool, shown in Figure 4-10, changes the linear alignment. Layout gravity is similar to the alignment feature in Microsoft Office, which allows a control to snap to the left, center, right, top, or bottom.

Adding the RadioButton Group

Before the RadioButton group is placed on the emulator, a strings.xml must be created to hold the text used within the app. The String table is necessary to assign the TextView title, the hint property of the EditText control, the text on both RadioButton controls, and the Button control text. The Medical Calculator app displays a TextView control, Number Text Field, and RadioGroup control, all centered horizontally. The TextView and RadioGroup controls use the text color of gray. To name a RadioButton control, use the Id property in the Properties pane to enter a name that begins with the prefix rad, which represents a radio button in the code. To add a TextView, EditText, and RadioGroup controls to the Medical Calculator app, follow these steps:

STEP 1

- Tap or click the Save All button on the toolbar.

- Close the strings.xml tab.

- With activity_main.xml open and displaying the emulator screen, tap or click the Form Widgets category in the Palette, if necessary, to open it.

- Drag and drop the TextView control onto the top part of the emulator user interface.

- To center the TextView control, drag the control to the center of the screen until a green dashed vertical line identifying the screen's center is displayed.

- Drag the top edge of the Properties pane to expand it, and in the Text property, tap or click the ellipsis button (three dots).

- Tap or click txtTitle in the Resource Chooser dialog box to select the assigned string and then tap or click the OK button.

- Change the Text Size property to **25sp**.

- Tap or click the Text Color property, type **#FF0000**, and then press Enter to change the text color to red to match the launcher icon.

- With the control selected, tap or click the Change Margins tool on the toolbar.

- In the Top text box of the Edit Margins dialog box, enter **15dp**.

The Edit Margins dialog box is displayed with 15dp entered in the Top text box. The TextView control is added to the form with the text, size, and text color changed (Figure 4-11).

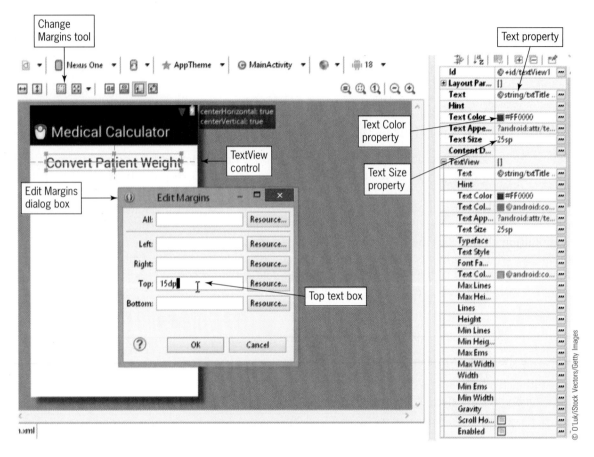

Figure 4-11   TextView control and Edit Margins Dialog Box

STEP 2

- Tap or click the OK button to place 15 pixels of space above the control.

- To add the Number Text Field, tap or click the Text Fields category in the Palette.

- Drag and drop the Number Text Field Number control onto the emulator's user interface below the TextView control in the center.

- Change the Id property of the Number Text Field to **@+id/txtWeight**, press Enter, and then tap or click Yes and the OK buttons.

- Tap or click the ellipsis button in the Hint property.

- Tap or click hint in the Resource Chooser dialog box to select the assigned string and then tap or click the OK button.

- Change the Text size property to **25sp**.

- Tap or click the Change Gravity tool and then select Center Horizontal to center the hint within the control.

- Select the control, tap or click the Change Margins tool, in the Top text box of the Edit Margins dialog box, enter **15dp**, and then tap or click the OK button to place 15 pixels of space between the TextView and the Number Text Field control.

A Number Text Field control is placed on the emulator with the id, text size, text hint, gravity, and margins changed (Figure 4-12).

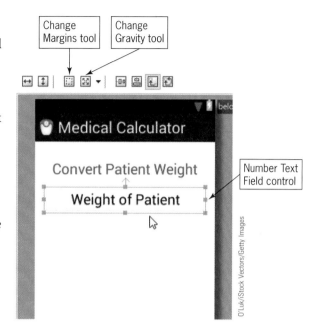

Figure 4-12   Number Text Field control

STEP 3

- In the Palette, select the Form Widgets category, scroll down and select the Form Widget named RadioGroup, and then drag and drop the RadioGroup control onto the user interface below the Number Text Field.

- Only two radio buttons are needed for this app, so tap or click the third RadioButton control and press the Delete key.

- Select the first RadioButton control and in the Properties pane, change the Id property of the RadioButton control to **@+id/radLbToKilo**, and then press Enter. Tap or click the Yes button and the OK button.

- Tap or click the ellipsis button in the Text property, tap or click radLbToKilo in the Resource Chooser dialog box to select the assigned string, and then tap or click the OK button.

- Change the Text size property to **16sp**. Notice the Checked property is preset as true, indicating that the first radio button is the default selection.

- Tap or click the Change Margins tool to open the Edit Margins dialog box.

- In the Left text box, type **2dp** and in the Top text box, type **15dp**. Tap or click the OK button.

- Select the second RadioButton control and in the Properties pane, change the Id property to **@+id/radKiloToLb**, and then press Enter. Tap or click the Yes and OK buttons.

- Tap or click the ellipsis button in the Text property, and then tap or click radKiloToLb in the Resource Chooser dialog box to select the assigned string. Tap or click the OK button.

- Change the Text size property to **16sp**.

- Tap or click the Change Margins tool to open the Edit Margins dialog box. In the Left text box, type **2dp** and in the Top text box, type **5dp** to keep the RadioButtons close to one another within the group.

- Tap or click the OK button.

The RadioGroup object is placed on the emulator with the id, text, size, and margin properties changed (Figure 4-13).

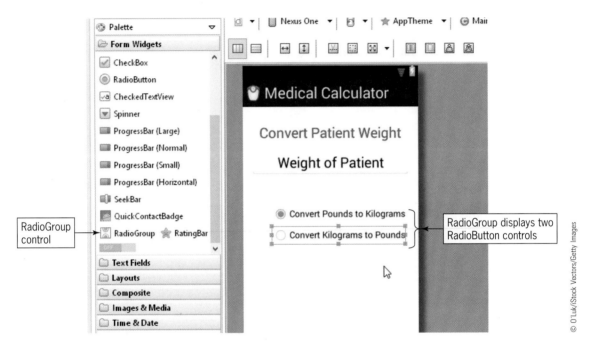

Figure 4-13   RadioGroup control

Completing the User Interface

As you design the Android interface, it is important to have a clean layout and use the entire screen effectively. To complete the user interface by adding a Button control and a TextView control and code the Button and TextView controls, follow these steps:

STEP 1

- In the activity_main.xml tab, drag the Button control from the Palette to the emulator below the RadioGroup.

- In the Properties pane, change the Id property of the Button control to **@+id/btnConvert**, press Enter, and then tap or click the Yes and OK buttons.

- Tap or click the ellipsis button in the Text property, and then select btnConvert to change the text display.

- Change the Text Size property to **25sp**.

- Tap or click the Change Gravity tool on the toolbar, and then, if necessary, tap or click Center Horizontal to center the control.

- Tap or click the Change Margins tool, in the Top text box of the Edit Margins dialog box, enter **15dp**, and then tap or click the OK button to place 15 pixels of space above the control.

The Button control named btnConvert displays the text Convert Weight and its id, text size, gravity, and margins are changed (Figure 4-14).

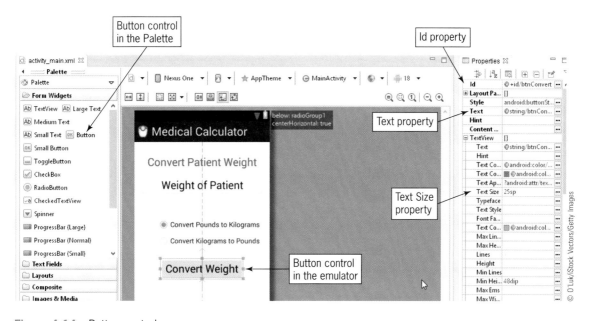

Figure 4-14 Button control

STEP 2

- Drag another TextView control to the emulator below the Button.

- Change the Id property of the TextView control to **@+id/txtResult**, and then press Enter. Tap or click the Yes button and then the OK button.

- Change the Text size property to **25sp**.

- For the Text color property, enter **#FF0000** (red).

- Tap or click the Change Margins tool, and in the Top text box of the Edit Margins dialog box, enter **25dp** to place 25 pixels of space above the control. Tap or click the OK button.

- Delete the text in the Text property, and then press Enter.

- Tap or click the Save All button on the Standard toolbar.

The TextView control is placed on the emulator with an empty Text property (Figure 4-15).

Coding a RadioButton Control

Each of the RadioButton controls placed on the emulator need to be referenced by using the findViewById Java command. In the following code syntax, lbToKilo and kiloToLb reference the two RadioButton controls in the Medical Calculator application:

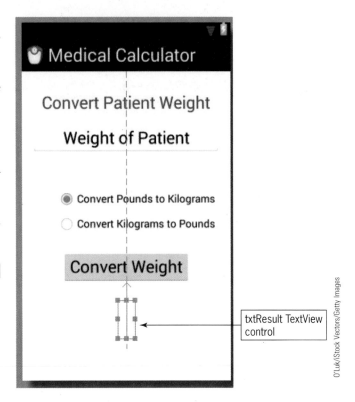

Figure 4-15　Button control

Code Syntax

```
final RadioButton lbToKilo = (RadioButton) findViewById (R.id.radLbToKilo);
final RadioButton kiloToLb = (RadioButton) findViewById(R.id.radKiloToLb);
```

The keyword **final** represents that the variable can be assigned only once. This variable can only be referenced within this class. After the RadioButton controls have been referenced, the next priority is to determine which of the two radio buttons the user selected. If the user selected the Convert Pounds to Kilograms radio button, the weight entered is divided by 2.2, but if the user selected the Convert Kilograms to Pounds radio button, the weight is multiplied by 2.2. A variable named conversionRate is assigned the decimal value 2.2. The variables weightEntered and convertedWeight contain the patient weight and converted weight result, respectively.

To create the Java code to declare the variables used in the application and to assign variables to reference the controls, follow these steps:

STEP 1

- In the Package Explorer, expand src and net.androidbootcamp.medicalcalculator, and then double-tap or double-click MainActivity.java to open the code window.

- Tap or click in the blank line (Line 8) inside the MainActivity class, and then press Tab to indent the line.

- To initialize the conversion rate value of 2.2, type **double conversionRate** = **2.2;** and press the Enter key.

- To initialize the weightEntered variable, type **double weightEntered;** and press the Enter key.

- To initialize the variable that will hold the converted weight, type **double convertedWeight;** and press the Enter key.

Three variables are declared in the Java code (Figure 4-16).

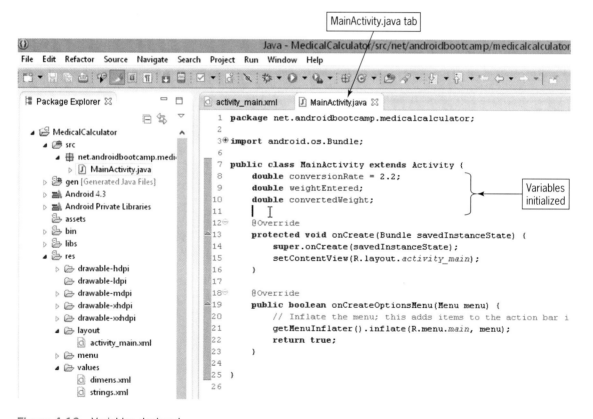

Figure 4-16 Variables declared

STEP 2

- Tap or click at the end of the Line 15, setContentView(R.layout.activity_main);, and press the Enter key.

- To initialize and reference the EditText class with the Id name of txtWeight, type **final EditText weight = (EditText) findViewById(R.id.txtWeight);**.

- Point to the red curly line under EditText and select Import 'EditText' (android.widget) on the pop-up menu. After the closing semicolon, press the Enter key.

- To initialize and reference the RadioButton class with the Id name of radLbToKilo, type **final RadioButton lbToKilo = (RadioButton) findViewById(R.id.radLbToKilo);**.

- Point to the red curly line under RadioButton and select Import 'RadioButton' (android.widget). After the closing semicolon, press the Enter key.

- To initialize and reference the RadioButton class for the second radio button with the Id name of radKiloToLb, type **final RadioButton kiloToLb = (RadioButton) findViewById(R.id.radKiloToLb);**.

- Save your work.

The EditText class extracts the value from the user's input for the patient weight and the RadioButton class extracts the checked value from the radio buttons (Figure 4-17).

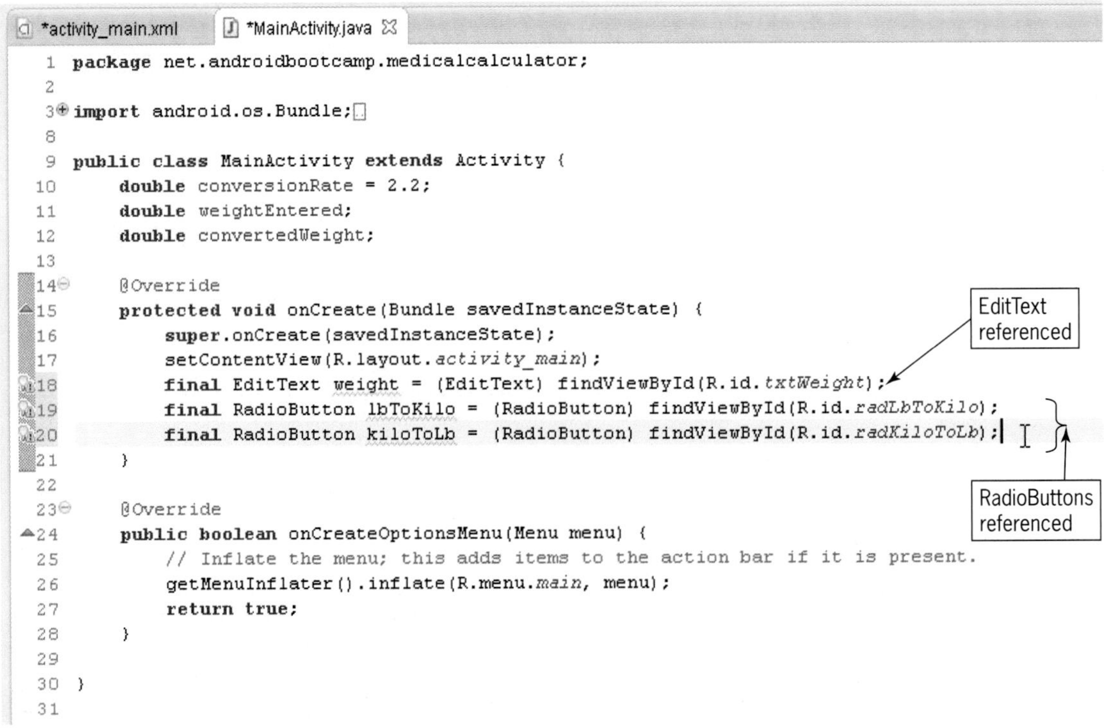

```
 1  package net.androidbootcamp.medicalcalculator;
 2
 3⊕ import android.os.Bundle;
 8
 9  public class MainActivity extends Activity {
10      double conversionRate = 2.2;
11      double weightEntered;
12      double convertedWeight;
13
14⊖     @Override
15      protected void onCreate(Bundle savedInstanceState) {
16          super.onCreate(savedInstanceState);
17          setContentView(R.layout.activity_main);
18          final EditText weight = (EditText) findViewById(R.id.txtWeight);
19          final RadioButton lbToKilo = (RadioButton) findViewById(R.id.radLbToKilo);
20          final RadioButton kiloToLb = (RadioButton) findViewById(R.id.radKiloToLb);
21      }
22
23⊖     @Override
24      public boolean onCreateOptionsMenu(Menu menu) {
25          // Inflate the menu; this adds items to the action bar if it is present.
26          getMenuInflater().inflate(R.menu.main, menu);
27          return true;
28      }
29
30  }
31
```

EditText referenced

RadioButtons referenced

Figure 4-17 EditText and RadioButtons referenced

Coding the Button Control

The Button control detects user interaction using an event listener. The following steps initialize the second TextView control, the Button control, and the OnClickListener.

- After the two lines of code referring to the RadioButton controls, type a new line with the code **final TextView result = (TextView) findViewById(R.id.txtResult);**.

- Import the 'TextView' (android.widget).

The TextView control is initialized to the variable result (Figure 4-18).

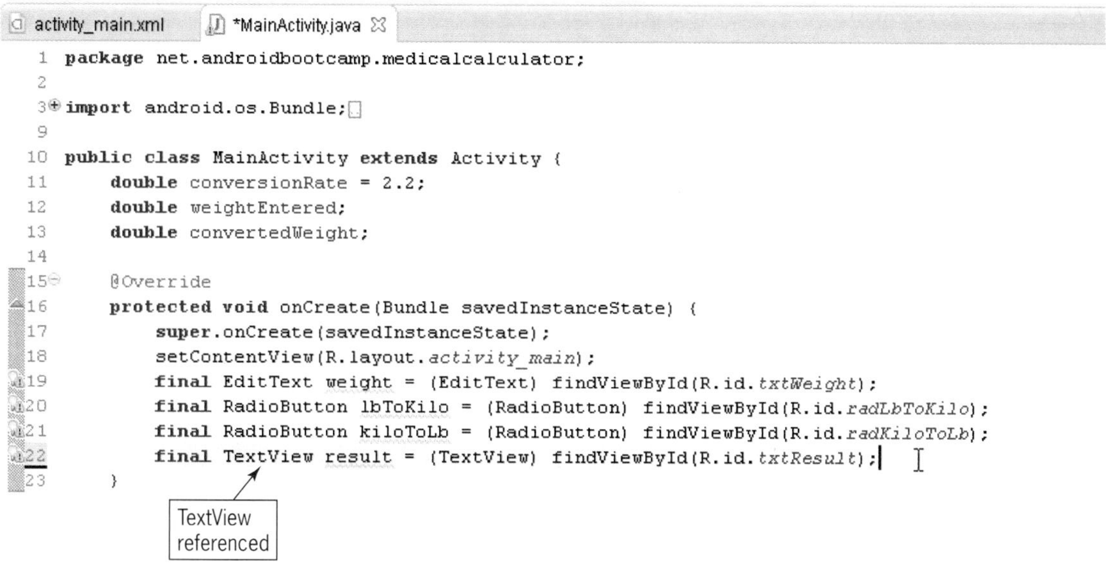

```
 activity_main.xml      *MainActivity.java

  1  package net.androidbootcamp.medicalcalculator;
  2
  3⊕ import android.os.Bundle;□
  9
 10  public class MainActivity extends Activity {
 11      double conversionRate = 2.2;
 12      double weightEntered;
 13      double convertedWeight;
 14
 15⊝     @Override
 16      protected void onCreate(Bundle savedInstanceState) {
 17          super.onCreate(savedInstanceState);
 18          setContentView(R.layout.activity_main);
 19          final EditText weight = (EditText) findViewById(R.id.txtWeight);
 20          final RadioButton lbToKilo = (RadioButton) findViewById(R.id.radLbToKilo);
 21          final RadioButton kiloToLb = (RadioButton) findViewById(R.id.radKiloToLb);
 22          final TextView result = (TextView) findViewById(R.id.txtResult);│  I
 23      }
```

TextView referenced

Figure 4-18 TextView control referenced

- After the closing semicolon, press the Enter key.

- To code the button, type **Button convert = (Button) findViewById(R.id.btnConvert);**.

- Point to Button and import the Button type as an Android widget.

- After the closing semicolon, press the Enter key two times to separate the variables from the rest of the code.

- To code the Button listener, type **convert.setOn** and then press Ctrl+spacebar to display an auto-complete code listing.

- Double-tap or double-click the first setOnClickListener displayed in the auto-complete listing.

- Inside the parentheses, type **new on** and press Ctrl+spacebar to display the auto-complete listing.

- Double-tap or double-click the first choice, which lists an OnClickListener with an Anonymous Inner Type event handler.

- Point to OnClickListener and select Import 'OnClickListener' (android.view.View).

- On Line 5, place a semicolon at the end of the auto-generated stub closing brace and parenthesis.

The btnConvert Button control and OnClick Listener are coded (Figure 4-19).

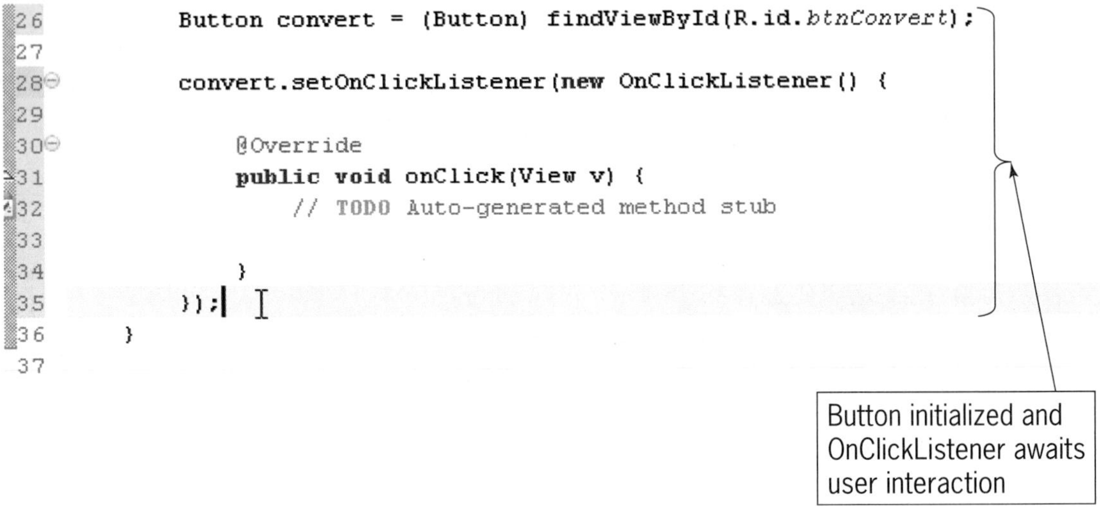

```
26      Button convert = (Button) findViewById(R.id.btnConvert);
27
28⊖     convert.setOnClickListener(new OnClickListener() {
29
30⊖         @Override
31          public void onClick(View v) {
32              // TODO Auto-generated method stub
33
34          }
35      });
36  }
37
```

Button initialized and OnClickListener awaits user interaction

Figure 4-19   OnClickListener

Making Decisions with Conditional Statements

In the Medical Calculator chapter project, which converts the weight entered to either pounds or kilograms, the user selects one of two radio buttons. Then, based on the choice, the application either divides by 2.2 or multiplies by 2.2.

Java uses decision structures to deal with the different conditions that occur based on the values entered into an application. A **decision structure** is a fundamental control structure used in computer programming. A statement that tests the radio button is called a conditional statement and the condition checked is whether the first or second radio button is selected. If the first radio button is selected, the weight is divided by 2.2. When a condition is tested in a Java program, it is either true or false. Conditional statements allow the user to make a decision and to follow a path after the decision is made. To execute a conditional statement and the statements that are executed when a condition is true, Java uses the If statement and its variety of formats.

Using an If Statement

In the chapter program, an **If statement** is used to determine which RadioButton control is selected. The simplest form of the If statement is shown in the following code:

Code Syntax

```
if (condition){
    //Statements completed if true
}
```

The statement(s) between the opening and closing braces are executed if the condition is true. If the condition is not true, no statements between the braces are executed, and program execution continues with the statement(s) that follows the closing brace.

Using If Else Statements

In many applications, the logic requires one set of instructions to be executed if a condition is true and another set of instructions to be executed if a condition is false. For example, a program requirement may specify that if a student's test score is 60 or greater, a message stating "You passed the examination" is displayed, but if the test score is less than 60, a message stating "You failed the examination" is displayed.

To execute one set of instructions if a condition is true, and another set of instructions if the condition is false, you can use the **If Else statement**, as shown in the following code:

Code Syntax

```
if (condition){
    //Statements completed if condition is true
} else {
    //Statements completed if condition is false
}
```

GTK

Java automatically indents statements to be executed when a condition is true or not true to indicate that the lines of code are within the conditional If structure.

Relational Operators

In the syntax of the condition portion of the If statement, a condition is tested to determine if it is true or false. The conditions that can be tested are as follows:

- Is one value equal to another value?
- Is one value not equal to another value?
- Is one value greater than another value?
- Is one value less than another value?
- Is one value greater than or equal to another value?
- Is one value less than or equal to another value?

To test these conditions, Java provides relational operators that are used within the conditional statement to express the relationship between the numbers being tested. Table 4-3 shows these relational operators.

Relational Operator	Meaning	Example	Resulting Condition
==	Equal to	6 == 6	True
! =	Not equal to	4 ! = 7	False
>	Greater than	3 > 2	True
<	Less than	8 < 1	False
>=	Greater than or equal to	5 >= 5	True
<=	Less than or equal to	9 <= 6	False

Table 4-3   Relational operators

© 2015 Cengage Learning

In the chapter project, an If Else statement determines if the entered weight is valid. If the nurse is converting pounds to kilograms, the weight entered must be less than or equal to 500 to be considered within a valid range of acceptable entries. If the entered weight is valid, the weight is converted by dividing it by the conversion rate of 2.2, as shown in the following code:

Code Syntax

```
if (weightEntered <= 500){
        convertedWeight = weightEntered / conversionRate;
} else {
        //Statements completed if condition is false
}
```

GTK
The most common mistake made with an If statement is the use of a single equal sign to compare equality. A single equal sign (=) is used for assigning a value to a variable, not for comparison.

In addition to numbers, strings can also be compared in a conditional statement. A string value comparison compares each character in two strings, starting with the first character in each string. All characters found in strings, including letters, numbers, and special characters, are ranked in a sequence from low to high based on how the characters are coded internally on the computer. The relational operators in Table 4-3 cannot be used with string comparisons. If you are comparing equality, string characters cannot be compared with the == operator. Java strings are compared with the **equals method** of the String class.

If you are comparing whether a string is alphabetically before another string, use the compareTo method to determine the order of strings. Do not use the less-than or greater-than symbols as shown in Table 4-3 to compare string data types. The compareTo method returns a negative integer if the first string precedes the second string. It returns zero if the two strings being compared are equal. It returns a positive integer if the first string follows the second string. Examples of the equals and compareTo methods are shown in Table 4-4 using the following initialized variables:

```
String name1 = "Sara";
String name2 = "Shawna";
String name3 = "Ryan";
```

If Statement	Comparison	Resulting Condition
if (name1.equals(name2))	Strings are not equal	False
if (name1.compareTo(name1) == 0)	Strings are equal	True
if (name1.compareTo(name3) == 0)	Strings are not equal	False
if (name1.compareTo(name2) > 0)	The first string precedes the second string; returns a negative number	False
if (name1.compareTo(name3) < 0)	The first string precedes the third string; returns a negative number	True
If (name3.compareTo(name2) > 0)	The first string follows the second string; returns a positive number	True

Table 4-4   Examples of the equals and compareTo methods

© 2015 Cengage Learning

Logical Operators

An If statement can test more than one condition within a single statement. In many cases, more than one condition must be true or one of several conditions must be true in order for the statements within the braces to be executed. When more than one condition is included in an If statement, the conditions are called a **compound condition**. For example, consider the following business traveling rule: "If the flight costs less than $400.00 and the hotel is less than $120.00 per night, the business trip is approved." In this case, both conditions (flight less than $400.00 and hotel less than $120.00 per night) must be true for the trip to be approved. If either condition is not true, then the business trip is not approved.

To create an If statement that processes the business traveling rule, you must use a logical operator. The most common set of logical operators is listed in Table 4-5.

Logical Operator	Meaning	Example
&&	And—all conditions must be true	if (flight < 400 && hotel < 120)
||	Or—at least one condition must be true	if (stamp < 0.49 || rate == 2)
!	Not—reverses the meaning of a condition	if (! (grade > 70))

© 2015 Cengage Learning

Table 4-5   Common logical operators

Data Validation

In the chapter project, it is important to confirm that the number entered by the user is not a typo or other type of mistake. If a value greater than 500 is entered for the conversion from pounds to kilograms or greater than 225 for the conversion from kilograms to pounds, the user should be notified and asked for a valid entry. To alert the user that an incorrect value was entered, a message called a toast notification (or toast message) can appear on the screen temporarily.

Toast Notification

A **toast notification** communicates messages to the user. These messages pop up as an overlay onto the user's current screen, often displaying a validation warning message. For example, a weather application may display a toast notification if a town is under a tornado warning. An instant messaging app might display a toast notification stating that a text message has been sent. In the chapter project, a toast notification displays a message warning the user that an invalid number was entered. A toast message only fills the amount of space required for the message to be displayed, while the user's current activity remains visible and interactive. The notification automatically fades in and out on the screen.

The toast notification code uses a Toast object and the MakeText( ) method with three parameters: the context (displays the activity name), the text message, and the duration of the interval that the toast is displayed (LENGTH_SHORT or LENGTH_LONG). To display the toast notification, a show( ) method displays the Toast object.

Code Syntax

```
Toast toast = Toast.makeText(context, text, duration).show( );
```

The toast message is best used for short messages. If the user enters an invalid number into the Medical Calculator, a warning toast notification fades in and then out on the screen. Notice in the following syntax that the text notification message displays *Pounds must be less than 500.*

Code Syntax

```
Toast.makeText(MainActivity.this,"Pounds must be less than 500",
Toast.LENGTH_LONG).show( );
```

GTK

An ex-Microsoft employee of Google is credited with coining the term *toast,* which is a small notification window that slides upward into view, like toast popping out of a toaster.

Using the isChecked( ) Method of RadioButton Controls

You will recall that the RadioButton controls in the Medical Calculator Android application allow the user to select one conversion option. When the user selects the second radio button, a shaded small circle is displayed in that radio button. When a RadioButton is selected, the Checked property of the second RadioButton control changes from False (unselected) to True (selected). The Java code must check each RadioButton to determine if that RadioButton has been selected by the user. This checked property can be tested in an If statement using the **isChecked( ) method** to determine if the RadioButton object has been selected.

Code Syntax

```
if (lbToKilo.isChecked){
     //Statements completed if condition is true
} else {
     //Statements completed if condition is false
}
```

If the user selects the lbToKilo RadioButton control, the statements within the If portion between the braces are completed. If the user selects the kiloToLb RadioButton control, the statements within the Else portion are completed.

Using Nested If Statements

At times, more than one decision must be made to determine what processing must occur. For example, if one condition is true, a second condition might need to be tested before the correct code is executed. To test a second condition only after determining that a first condition is true (or false), you must place an If statement within another If statement. When you do this, the inner If statement is said to be **nested** within the outer If statement. In the chapter Android app, if the user checks the first radio button to convert pounds to kilograms and if the entered weight is equal to 500 pounds or less, then the weight can be converted. If the weight is above 500 pounds, a toast notification appears with a warning. A second nested If statement evaluates whether the second radio button is checked and if the user entered 225 kilograms or less as part of the final code.

Code Syntax

```
if (lbToKilo.isChecked( )){
    if (weightEntered <=500){
        convertedWeight = weightEntered / conversionRate;
    } else {
        Toast.makeText(MainActivity. this, "Pounds must be less than 500",
Toast.LENGTH_LONG).show( ) ;
    }
}
```

Coding the Button Event

After the user enters the weight and selects the desired RadioButton, the Button control is tapped. The OnClickListener event is triggered and the conversion of the weight entered occurs. Within the onClick method, the weight entered must be converted to double data. The syntax **Double.parseDouble** converts input to a Double data type and Integer.parseInt converts input to an Integer data type. A DecimalFormat layout is necessary to format the result to one place past the decimal point ("#.#"). If you would like two places past the decimal point, use the format ("#.##"). To convert the weight to a double data type and establish the format for the output, follow these steps:

STEP 1

- On Line 33 inside the OnClick method stub of the MainActivity.java code, type **weightEntered=Double.parseDouble(weight.getText( ).toString( ));** to convert the weight entered to a double data type.

The weight entered by the user is converted to a double data type (Figure 4-20).

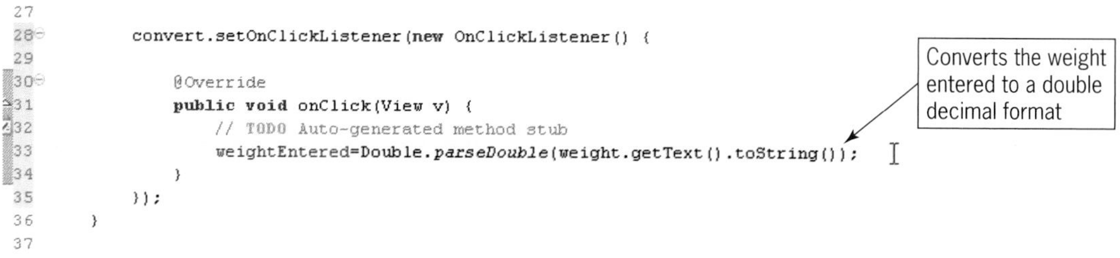

```
27
28      convert.setOnClickListener(new OnClickListener() {
29
30          @Override
31          public void onClick(View v) {
32              // TODO Auto-generated method stub
33              weightEntered=Double.parseDouble(weight.getText().toString());
34          }
35      });
36  }
37
```

Converts the weight entered to a double decimal format

Figure 4-20   Weight converted to a double data type

STEP 2

● After the closing semicolon, press the Enter key.

● To create a decimal layout that changes the weight to a decimal rounded to the nearest tenth for use in the result later in the code, type **DecimalFormat tenth = new DecimalFormat("#.#");**.

● Point to the red curly line below DecimalFormat and select Import 'DecimalFormat' (java.text).

The DecimalFormat code rounds off to the nearest tenth (Figure 4-21).

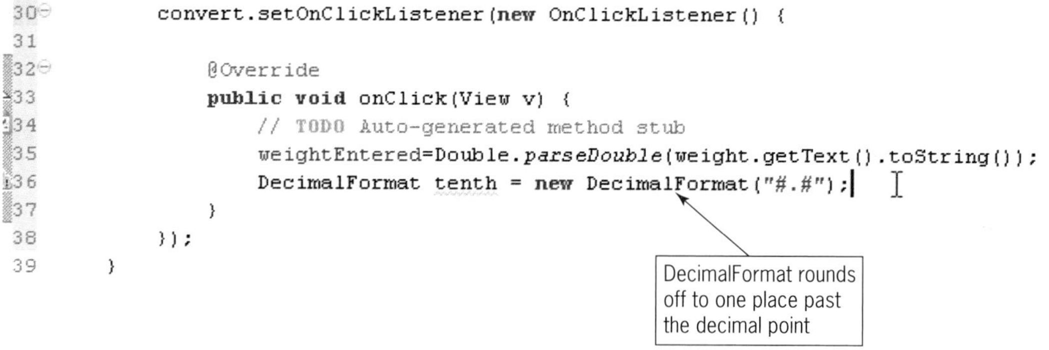

```
30      convert.setOnClickListener(new OnClickListener() {
31
32          @Override
33          public void onClick(View v) {
34              // TODO Auto-generated method stub
35              weightEntered=Double.parseDouble(weight.getText().toString());
36              DecimalFormat tenth = new DecimalFormat("#.#");
37          }
38      });
39  }
```

DecimalFormat rounds off to one place past the decimal point

Figure 4-21   DecimalFormat—Rounding

Coding the Nested If Statements

After the weight entered is converted to a double and a format is set, code is necessary to determine which RadioButton was selected by using the isChecked property. Within each RadioButton If statement, the weight entered is converted to the appropriate weight unit and displayed only if that weight is within the valid weight ranges (500 pounds or 225 kilograms). If the weight is not within the valid range, a toast notification appears warning the user to enter a value within the acceptable range. To code a nested If statement to display the result, follow these steps:

STEP 1

- After the DecimalFormat line of code, to determine if the first RadioButton control is selected, type **if(lbToKilo.isChecked( ))** { and press the Enter key. Java automatically adds the closing brace.

An If statement determines if the lbToKilo RadioButton control is checked (Figure 4-22).

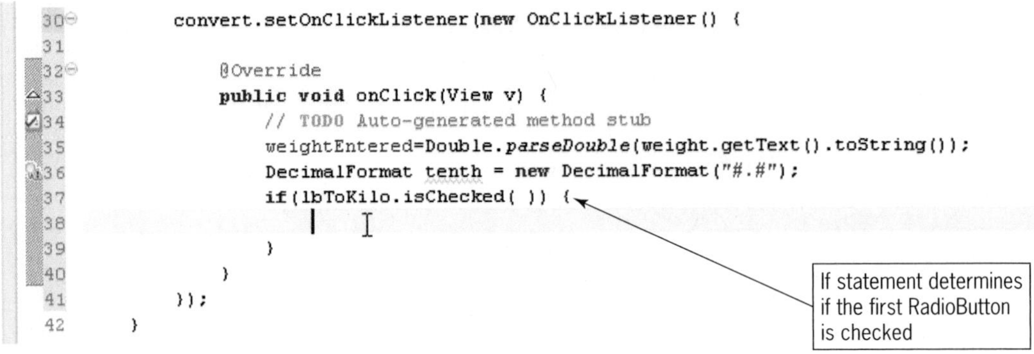

```
30⊖            convert.setOnClickListener(new OnClickListener() {
31
32⊖                @Override
33                 public void onClick(View v) {
34                     // TODO Auto-generated method stub
35                     weightEntered=Double.parseDouble(weight.getText().toString());
36                     DecimalFormat tenth = new DecimalFormat("#.#");
37                     if(lbToKilo.isChecked( )) {
38
39                     }
40                 }
41            });
42        }
```

If statement determines if the first RadioButton is checked

Figure 4-22 If statement

STEP 2

- Within the first If statement, braces create a nested If Else statement that determines if the weight entered for pounds is less than or equal to 500. Type **if (weightEntered <=500)** { and press the Enter key. Java automatically adds the closing brace.

- On Line 41, after the closing brace, type **else** { and press the Enter key. Java automatically adds the closing brace.

A nested If Else statement determines if the number of pounds entered is valid (Figure 4-23).

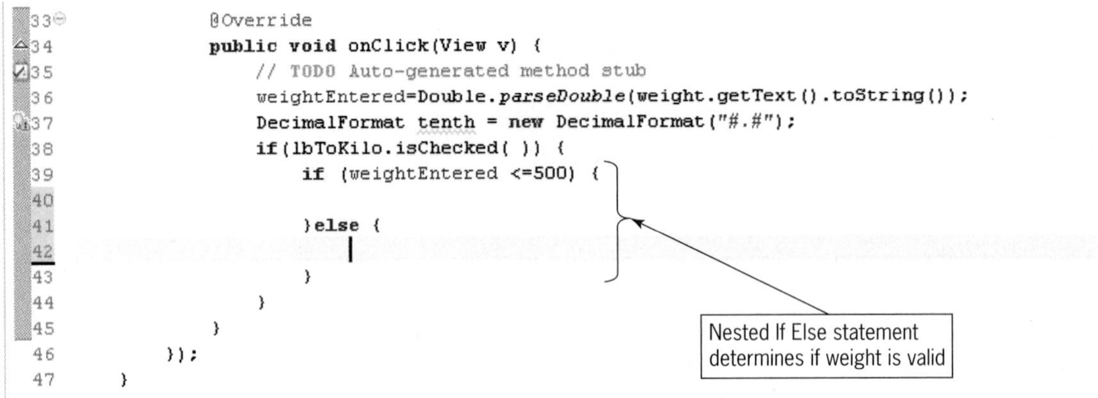

```
33⊖                @Override
34                 public void onClick(View v) {
35                     // TODO Auto-generated method stub
36                     weightEntered=Double.parseDouble(weight.getText().toString());
37                     DecimalFormat tenth = new DecimalFormat("#.#");
38                     if(lbToKilo.isChecked( )) {
39                         if (weightEntered <=500) {
40
41                         }else {
42
43                         }
44                     }
45                 }
46            });
47        }
```

Nested If Else statement determines if weight is valid

Figure 4-23 Nested If Else statement

STEP 3

- After the pounds variable is validated, the weight must be converted. Inside the nested If statement after the weightEntered <= 500) { line, type **convertedWeight = weightEntered / conversionRate;** and press the Enter key to divide the weight by the conversion rate of 2.2.

- To display the result of the equation rounded to one place past the decimal point, type **result.setText(tenth.format(convertedWeight) + " kilograms");.**

The number of pounds is converted to kilograms and displayed in the result TextView control (Figure 4-24).

```
31      convert.setOnClickListener(new OnClickListener() {
32
33          @Override
34          public void onClick(View v) {
35              // TODO Auto-generated method stub
36              weightEntered=Double.parseDouble(weight.getText().toStr   Equation to convert
37              DecimalFormat tenth = new DecimalFormat("#.#");            pounds to kilograms
38              if(lbToKilo.isChecked()) {
39                  if (weightEntered <=500) {
40                      convertedWeight = weightEntered / conversionRate;
41                      result.setText(tenth.format(convertedWeight) + " kilograms");
42                  }else {
43
44                  }
45              }                                                          Converted weight
46          }                                                             displayed
47      }});
48      }
```

Figure 4-24 Equation for weight conversion and displayed results

STEP 4

- If the weight is not within the valid range, a toast message requesting that the user enter a valid weight is displayed briefly. Tap or click the line after the Else statement and type **Toast.makeText(MainActivity.this,"Pounds must be less than 500", Toast.LENGTH_LONG).show( );.**

- Point to Toast and select Import 'Toast' (android.widget).

A toast message displays a reminder to enter a valid weight (Figure 4-25).

```
32
33⊖            @Override
34            public void onClick(View v) {
35                // TODO Auto-generated method stub
36                weightEntered=Double.parseDouble(weight.getText().toString());
37                DecimalFormat tenth = new DecimalFormat("#.#");
38                if(lbToKilo.isChecked( )) {
39                    if (weightEntered <=500) {
40                        convertedWeight = weightEntered / conversionRate;
41                        result.setText(tenth.format(convertedWeight) + " kilograms");
42                    }else {
43                        Toast.makeText(MainActivity.this,"Pounds must be less than 500", Toast.LENGTH_LONG).show( );
44                    }
45                }
46            }
47        });
48    }
49
```

Toast message

Figure 4-25 Toast message

STEP 5

- If necessary, type a closing brace for the If statement in Figure 4-25.

- For when the user selects the Convert the Kilograms to Pounds RadioButton control, type the following lines of code, as shown in Figure 4-26:

```
if(kiloToLb.isChecked( )) {
    if (weightEntered <=225) {
        convertedWeight = weightEntered * conversionRate;
        result.setText(tenth.format(convertedWeight) + " pounds");
    }else {
      Toast.makeText(MainActivity.this, "Kilos must be less than 225",
Toast.LENGTH_LONG).show( );
        }
    }
```

The nested If statement is executed if the second RadioButton control is selected (Figure 4-26).

```
] MainActivity.java ⋈
26      final RadioButton lbToKilo = (RadioButton) findViewById(R.id.radLbToKilo);
27      final RadioButton kiloToLb = (RadioButton) findViewById(R.id.radKiloToLb);
28      final TextView result = (TextView) findViewById(R.id.txtResult);
29      Button convert = (Button) findViewById(R.id.btnConvert);
30
31⊖     convert.setOnClickListener(new OnClickListener() {
32
33⊖         @Override
34         public void onClick(View v) {
35             // TODO Auto-generated method stub
36             weightEntered=Double.parseDouble(weight.getText().toString());
37             DecimalFormat tenth = new DecimalFormat("#.#");
38             if(lbToKilo.isChecked( )) {
39                 if (weightEntered <=500) {
40                     convertedWeight = weightEntered / conversionRate;
41                     result.setText(tenth.format(convertedWeight) + " kilograms");
42                 }else {
43                     Toast.makeText(MainActivity.this,"Pounds must be less than 500", Toast.LENGTH_LONG).show( );
44                 }
45             }
46             if(kiloToLb.isChecked( )) {
47                 if (weightEntered <=225) {
48                     convertedWeight = weightEntered * conversionRate;
49                     result.setText(tenth.format(convertedWeight) + " pounds");
50                 }else {
51                     Toast.makeText(MainActivity.this, "Kilos must be less than 225",Toast.LENGTH_LONG).show();
52                 }
              }
          }
56  }
57
```

Second nested if statement

Figure 4-26   Completed code

Running and Testing the App

An app can be run and tested on an actual Android device or the emulator. It is best to leave the emulator running and run the app to test your code each time you make a change. To run your app, follow this step.

STEP 1

- To view the finished application, tap or click Run As on the menu bar, and then select Android Application in the Run As dialog box, then click OK.

- Save all the files in the next dialog box and unlock the emulator. The application opens in the emulator where you enter a weight and select a radio button.

- If the app does not run, tap or click Run on the menu and select Run Configurations. Tap or click the Target tab. Confirm that the AVD that you are using is checked, and then tap or click the Run button again.

- To view the results, tap or click the Convert Weight button.

The Medical Calculator Android app is executed (see Figures 4-1 and 4-2).

Wrap It Up—Chapter Summary

Beginning with a customized icon, this chapter has covered the steps to create the graphical user interface including a RadioGroup control for the Medical Calculator program. The decision structure including a nested If Else statement determines different outcomes based on user input. If necessary, a toast message reminds the user of the expected input. You have learned to customize feedback and make decisions based on any user's input.

- To display a custom launcher icon instead of the default icon on the home screen of an Android device, copy the custom icon image to the res/drawable-hdpi folder for the project and then update the Android Manifest file to include the filename of the image file.

- Include RadioButton controls to allow users to select or deselect an option. Each RadioButton control has a label defined by the Text property and a Checked property set to either true or false. In a RadioGroup control, only one RadioButton control can be selected at a time.

- Android apps use hexadecimal color codes to set the color displayed in controls.

- For more flexibility in controlling your layout, use the Change Margins tool to change the spacing between objects. Use the Layout gravity property to position a control precisely on the screen. You can change this property using the Properties pane or the Change Gravity tool on the toolbar.

- A decision structure includes a conditional statement that checks whether the condition is true or false. To execute a conditional statement and the statements that are executed when a condition is true, Java uses the If statement and its variety of formats, including the If Else statement. An If statement executes one set of instructions if a specified condition is true and takes no action if the condition is not true. An If Else statement executes one set of instructions if a specified condition is true and another set of instructions if the condition is false.

- To test the conditions in a conditional statement such as an If statement, Java provides relational operators that are used within the conditional statement to express the relationship between the numbers being tested. For example, you can use a relational operator to test whether one value is greater than another.

- If more than one condition is tested in a conditional statement, the conditions are called a compound condition. To create an If statement that processes a compound condition, you must use a logical operator such as && (And).

- After including code that validates data, you can code a toast notification (also called a toast message) to display a brief message indicating that an incorrect value was entered.

- To test a second condition only after determining that a first condition is true or false, you nest one If statement within another If statement.

Key Terms

Change Gravity—A tool that changes the linear alignment of a control, so that it is aligned to the left, center, right, top, or bottom of an object or the screen.

compound condition—More than one condition included in an If statement.

decision structure—A fundamental control structure used in computer programming that deals with the different conditions that occur based on the values entered into an application.

equals method—A method of the String class that Java uses to compare strings.

hexadecimal color code—A triplet of three colors using hexadecimal numbers, where colors are specified first by a pound sign followed by how much red (00 to FF), how much green (00 to FF), and how much blue (00 to FF) are in the final color.

If Else statement—A statement that executes one set of instructions if a specified condition is true and another set of instructions if the condition is false.

If statement—A statement that executes one set of instructions if a specified condition is true and takes no action if the condition is not true.

isChecked( ) method—A method that tests a checked property to determine if a RadioButton object has been selected.

launcher icon—An icon that appears on the home screen to represent the application.

margin—Blank space that offsets a control by a certain amount of density independent pixels (dp) on each of its four sides.

nest—To place one statement, such as an If statement, within another statement.

RadioGroup—A group of RadioButton controls; only one RadioButton control can be selected at a time.

toast notification—A message that appears as an overlay on a user's screen, often displaying a validation warning.

Developer FAQs

1. What is the name of the icon on the Android home screen that opens an app?

2. What is the preferred prefix for a filename and file extension of the icon described in question 1?

3. What is the pixel size for the icon described in question 1 for a high-density pixel image?

4. To display a custom icon, you must perform two steps. First, add the icon image file to the drawable-hdpi folder. What is the second step?

5. Which TextView property is changed to identify the color of the control?

6. Which primary color is represented by the hexadecimal code of #0000FF?

7. What is the name of the tool used to center an EditText control Hint property horizontally?

8. Using the Change Margins tool, in which text box would you type 18dp to move a control 18 density pixels down from the upper edge of the emulator?

9. When a RadioGroup control is placed on the emulator, the first RadioButton control is selected by default. Which property is set as true by default?

10. Write an If statement that tests if the value in the variable age is between 17 and 21 years of age, inclusive, with empty braces.

11. Write an If statement that tests if the radio button named *gender* is selected with empty braces.

12. Rewrite the following line of code without a Not logical operator but keeping the same logical processing: if ! (height <= 60) {

13. Write an If statement to compare if a string variable named *company* is equal to *Verizon* with empty braces.

14. Fix this statement: if (hours < 1 | | > 8) {

15. How many radio buttons can be selected at one time in a RadioGroup control?

16. Write an If statement that compares if wage is equal to 7.25 with empty braces.

17. If you compare two strings and the result is a positive number, what is the order of the two strings?

18. Using a relational operator, write an If statement that evaluates if a variable named *tipPercent* is not equal to .15 with empty braces.

19. Write a warning message that would display the comment "The maximum credits allowed is 18" with a long interval.

20. Write a quick reminder message that would display the comment "File saved" with a short interval.

Beyond the Book

Using the Internet, search the Web for the answers to the following questions to further your Android knowledge.

1. You have developed an application on music downloads. Search using Google Images to locate an appropriate icon and resize the icon using a paint-type program for use as a tablet app launcher icon (xhdpi).

2. Search the Google Play site for a popular app that has a Sudoku puzzle. Take a screenshot of one Sudoku puzzle's launcher icon and another screenshot of the larger graphic used for the description of the app.

3. An Android toast message can also be coded to appear at an exact location on the screen. Explain how this works and give an example of the code that would do this.

4. Research the average price of an individual paid app. Write 75–100 words on the average selling prices of Android and iPhone apps.

Case Programming Projects

Complete one or more of the following case programming projects. Use the same steps and techniques taught within the chapter. Submit the program you create to your instructor. The level of difficulty is indicated for each case programming project.

Easiest: ★

Intermediate: ★ ★

Challenging:★ ★ ★

Case Project 4–1: Tool Rental App ★

Requirements Document

Application title:	Daily Tool Rental App
Purpose:	The app determines the cost of power washer or tiller.
Algorithms:	1. The opening screen requests the number of days that the power tool will be rented (Figure 4-27).
	2. The user selects a radio button labeled Power Washer or Tiller and then selects the Compute Cost button.
	3. The final cost is displayed for the number of days rented (Figure 4-28).
Conditions:	1. The result is rounded off to the nearest penny.
	2. The power washer costs $55.99 for each day rented and the tiller costs $68.99 a day.
	3. Do not enter more than 7 days.
	4. Use a custom launcher icon named ic_launcher_tools.png.

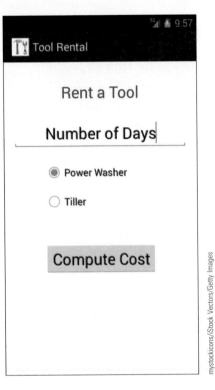

Figure 4-27

Figure 4-28

Case Project 4–2: Zip Car Rental App ★

Requirements Document

Application title:	Zip Car Rental App
Purpose:	Large cities rent cars called Zip cars on daily basis. The Zip Car Rental app charges a daily fee based on whether you rent a compact, mid-size, or luxury car with insurance coverage (Figure 4-29).
Algorithms:	1. The opening screen requests the number of days to rent a Zip car.
	2. The user selects which size Zip car: compact car for $59.99 per day, mid-size car for $65.99 per day, or luxury car for $89.99 per day.
	3. When the Compute Cost button is selected, the total price is displayed for the number of months subscribed (Figure 4-30).
Conditions:	1. The app allows you to rent a car for up to 10 days.
	2. Use a customized launcher icon (ic_launcher_car.png).
	3. Only one RadioButton control can be selected.

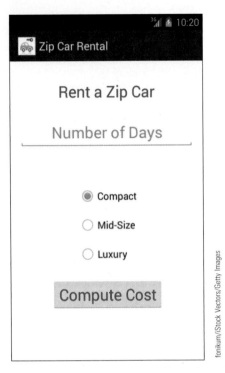

Figure 4-29

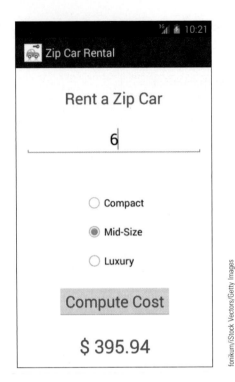

Figure 4-30

Case Project 4–3: Floor Tiling App ★★

Requirements Document

Application title:	Floor Tiling App
Purpose:	The tiling app allows you to calculate how many tiles you need to cover a rectangular area.
Algorithms:	1. The opening screen requests the length and the width of a room in whole feet.
	2. The user selects whether the tiles are 12 inches by 12 inches or 18 inches by 18 inches.
	3. The number of tiles needed to cover the area in square feet is displayed.

Case Project 4–4: Math Flash Cards App ★★

Requirements Document

Application Title:	Math Flash Cards App
Purpose:	The Math Flash Cards App is designed for children to practice their basic math skills.
Algorithms:	1. The opening screen requests two integer values.
	2. The user can select addition, subtraction, or multiplication.
	3. The entire math problem is displayed with the result.
Conditions:	1. The integer values must be between 1 and 20.
	2. Use a customized launcher icon.

Case Project 4–5: Currency Conversion App ★★★

Requirements Document

Application title:	Currency Conversion App
Purpose:	The Currency Conversion app converts U.S. dollars into euros, Mexican pesos, or Canadian dollars.
Algorithms:	1. The opening screen requests the amount of U.S. dollars to be converted.
	2. The user selects euros, Mexican pesos, or Canadian dollars.
	3. The conversion of U.S. dollars to the selected currency is displayed.
Conditions:	1. Use *http://xe.com* to locate current conversion rates.
	2. The program only converts values below $100,000 U.S. dollars.
	3. Use a customized launcher icon.

Case Project 4–6: Average Income Tax by Country App ★★★

Requirements Document

Application title:	Average Income Tax by Country App
Purpose:	The Average Income Tax by Country app allows the user to enter the amount of taxable income earned in the past year. The user selects his or her country of residence and the yearly income tax is displayed.
Algorithms:	1. The opening screen requests two integer values.
	2. The user can select addition, subtraction, or multiplication.
	3. The entire math problem is displayed with the result.
Conditions:	The following table displays the annual income tax percentages.

Country	Average Income Tax (%)
China	25
Germany	32
Sweden	34
USA	18

CHAPTER 5

Investigate! Android Lists, Arrays, and Web Browsers

In this chapter, you learn to:

◎ Create an Android project using a list

◎ Develop a user interface that uses ListView

◎ Extend the ListActivity class

◎ Use an array to create a list

◎ Code a setListAdapter to display an array

◎ Design a custom ListView layout with XML code

◎ Display an image with the ListView control

◎ Change the default title bar text

◎ Code a custom setListAdapter for a custom layout

◎ Call the onListItemClick method when a list item is selected

◎ Write code using the Switch decision structure

◎ Call an intent to work with an outside app

◎ Open an Android Web browser

◎ Launch a Web site through the use of a URI using an Android browser

◎ Test an application with multiple decisions

Displaying a list is one of the most common design patterns used in mobile applications. This morning you likely read the news designed as a listing of articles on a phone or tablet. You scrolled down the list of news articles and selected one by tapping the screen to display a full story with text, images, and hyperlinks. As you walked to class today, you probably scrolled a list of songs on a mobile device and listened to your favorite tunes.

From a list, you can open an article, play a song, open a Web site, or even launch a video. A list created with a ListView control may be one of the most important Android design elements because it is used so frequently. To select a list item, a design structure is necessary to route your request to the intended content. In Chapter 4, you learned about the decision structure called an If statement, one of the major control structures used in computer programming. In this chapter, you learn about another decision structure called the Switch statement.

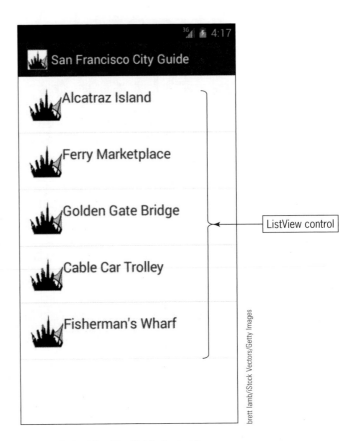

To demonstrate the process of using a list to navigate to different content, you design a travel city guide for San Francisco, California, highlighting the best attractions the city has to offer. The City Guide application shown in Figure 5-1 provides a list of city attractions. A city guide for a large city can provide easy access to all its sights, activities, and restaurants in one handy guide for your phone.

Figure 5-1   The City Guide Android app

The Android app in Figure 5-1 could be part of a larger app that displays city maps, detailed site information, and restaurant recommendations. This mobile app provides information about popular places tourists visit in San Francisco. The City Guide app displays five San Francisco attractions. When the user taps one of the attractions, a second window opens displaying either an image or a Web site providing more information about the site or activity. The first two items on the list link to Web sites, as shown in Figure 5-2. A browser opens to display a Web site for Alcatraz Island or Ferry Marketplace. If the user selects Golden Gate Bridge, Cable Car Trolley, or Fisherman's Wharf, an image appears on a second screen, as shown in Figure 5-3. By pressing the left Hardware Button on the emulator, you can return to the list of the attractions.

Figure 5-2   Alcatraz and Ferry Marketplace Web sites

Figure 5-3   San Francisco attractions

IN THE TRENCHES
To see a professional city guide app in action, download a free app created by Trip Advisor or Triposo.

To create this application, the developer must understand how to perform the following processes, among others:

1. Create a list using a ListView control.

2. Define an array to establish the items of the list.

3. Add the images used in the project.

4. Define an XML file to design the custom list with a leading image.

5. Code a Switch decision structure to handle the selection of items.

6. Open an Android Web browser to display a specified Uniform Resource Identifier (URI).

7. Create multiple classes and XML layout files to display pictures of attractions.

Creating a List

The San Francisco City Guide app begins with a vertical list of attractions on the opening screen, as shown in Figure 5-1. The Java View class creates the list and makes it scrollable if it exceeds the length of the screen. Lists can be used to display a to-do list, your personal contacts, recipe names, shopping items, weekly weather, Twitter messages, and Facebook postings, for example. You use a ListView control to contain the list attraction items. Android also has a TableLayout view that looks similar to a ListView, but a ListView allows you to select each row in the list for further action. Selecting an item opens a Web browser to a related Web page or displays an image of the attraction. You can directly use the ListView control in the Composite category of the Palette in the layout of the emulator (Figure 5-4) as you can with any other user interface component, but coding the list in Java is the preferred method and is used in the chapter project.

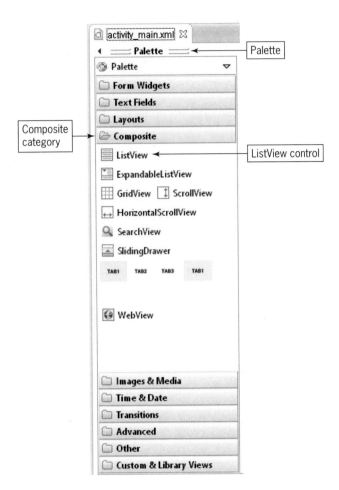

Figure 5-4   ListView control on the Palette

Extending a ListActivity

You begin creating a list by opening MainActivity.java and changing the type of Activity in the code. In the previous chapters, each opening class statement (public class Main extends Activity) extended the basic Activity class. If the primary purpose of a class is to display a ListView control, use a class named **ListActivity** instead, which makes it simple to display a list of items within the app. To add a custom icon launcher and extend the ListActivity class of MainActivity.java of the City Guide app, follow these steps to begin the application:

STEP 1

- Open the Eclipse program.

- Type **E:\Workspace** (if necessary, enter a different drive letter that identifies the USB drive) to select a workspace, and then tap or click the OK button.

- Tap or click the New button on the Standard toolbar, and then select Android Application Project.

- Tap or click the Next button.

- In the New Android Application dialog box, enter the Application Name **City Guide**.

- Enter the Package Name of **net.androidbootcamp.cityguide**. Notice the Minimum Required SDK text box displays the API number from the selected Target SDK. If you are deploying to an earlier model of an Android device, you can select an earlier version.

The new Android City Guide project has an application name and a package name (Figure 5-5).

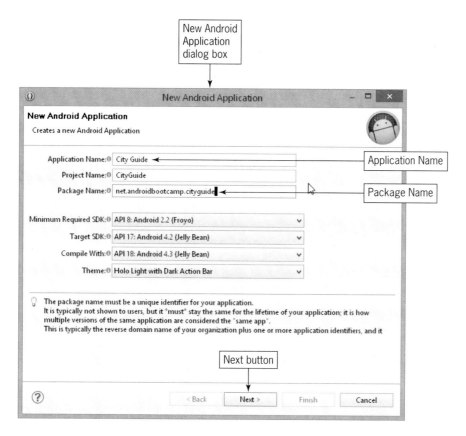

Figure 5-5 Application information for the new Android project

STEP 2

- Tap or click the Next button to configure the project.

- Tap or click the Next button to view the default launcher icons for the different resolution sizes of various devices.

- Tap or click the Browse button.

- To add the custom launcher icon, copy the student files to your USB drive (if necessary). Open the USB folder containing the student files to locate the file ic_launcher_sf.png.

- Tap or click the Open button to add the custom launcher icon.

The custom icon launcher of a city skyline is displayed in different sizes (Figure 5-6).

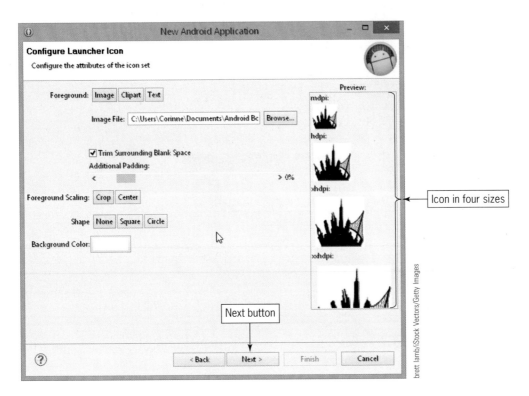

Figure 5-6 Custom Icon Launcher dialog box

STEP 3

- Tap or click the Next button twice.

- Tap or click the Finish button.

- Tap or click the Minimize button on the Outline pane, if necessary.

- Double-tap or double-click MainActivity.java to open its code window, if necessary.

- Tap or click to the left of *Activity* in the public class MainActivity extends Activity { line, and then change Activity to **ListActivity**.

- Point to ListActivity and then tap or click Import 'ListActivity' (android.app).

- Delete the line import android.app.Activity; and then delete the line setContentView(R.layout. activity_main); because the layout will be custom coded later in the XML code.

Main extends ListActivity, which contains predefined methods for the use of lists (Figure 5-7).

MainActivity.java

```
 1  package net.androidbootcamp.cityguide;
 2
 3  import android.app.ListActivity;
 4  import android.os.Bundle;
 5  import android.view.Menu;
 6
 7  public class MainActivity extends ListActivity {
 8
 9      @Override
10      protected void onCreate(Bundle savedInstanceState) {
11          super.onCreate(savedInstanceState);
12      }
13
14      @Override
15      public boolean onCreateOptionsMenu(Menu menu) {
16          // Inflate the menu; this adds items to the action bar if it is present.
17          getMenuInflater().inflate(R.menu.main, menu);
18          return true;
19      }
20
21  }
22
```

ListActivity

Figure 5-7 Main extends ListActivity

IN THE TRENCHES

Another type of a ListView control is the ExpandableListView, which provides a two-level list. For example, if you were renting a car, a list of all the compact cars would be listed in one category on the top half of your phone and the economy cars in a separate category at the bottom. ExpandableListView provides two separate listings.

Creating an Array

Before the list of attractions can be displayed, the string of attraction names must be declared. By using an **array variable**, which can store more than one value, you can avoid assigning a separate variable for each item in the list. Every application developed thus far involved a limited number of variables. Professional programming applications commonly require much larger sets of data using multiple variables. You learned that data type variables can store only one value at a time. If you changed a variable's value, the previous value would be deleted because a typical variable can store only one value at a time. Each individual item in an array that contains a value is called an **element**.

Arrays provide access to data by using a numeric index, or subscript, to identify each element in the array. Using an array, you can store a collection of values of similar data types. For example, you can store five string values without having to declare five different variables. Instead, each value is stored in an individual element of the array, and you refer to each element by its index within the array. The index used to reference a value in the first element within an array is zero. Each subsequent element is referenced by an increasing index value, as shown in Table 5-1.

Element	Value
Attraction[0]	Alcatraz Island
Attraction[1]	Ferry Marketplace
Attraction[2]	Golden Gate Bridge
Attraction[3]	Cable Car Trolley
Attraction[4]	Fisherman's Wharf

© 2015 Cengage Learning

Table 5-1   Attraction array with index values

In Table 5-1, an array named Attraction holds five attractions. Each attraction is stored in an array element, and each element is assigned a unique index. The first string is stored in the element with the index of 0. The element is identified by the term Attraction[0], pronounced "attraction sub zero."

Declaring an Array

Like declarations for variables of other types, an array declaration has two components: the array's data type and the array's name. An array is a container object that holds a fixed number of values of a single type. You can declare an array containing numeric values as in the following coding examples:

```
int[] age={16,21,38,88};
double[] weather={72.3, 65.0, 25.7, 99.5};
char[] initials={'P','N','D'};
```

Declare a String array containing the text values used in the chapter project with the following code:

Code Syntax

```
String[] attraction={"Alcatraz Island", "Ferry Marketplace",
"Golden Gate Bridge", "Cable Car Trolley", "Fisherman's Wharf"};
```

The attraction list initialized in the array can easily be expanded to include more items at any time. To assign the listing of attractions to the String data type in an array named attraction, follow these steps:

STEP 1

- After the super.onCreate(savedInstanceState); statement in MainActivity.java, insert a new line.

- Type **String[ ] attraction={"Alcatraz Island", "Ferry Marketplace", "Golden Gate Bridge", "Cable Car Trolley", "Fisherman's Wharf"};**.

The String array named attraction is assigned the five attraction locations (Figure 5-8).

```
activity_main.xml    *MainActivity.java ⊠
 1  package net.androidbootcamp.cityguide;
 2
 3  import android.app.ListActivity;
 4  import android.os.Bundle;
 5  import android.view.Menu;
 6
 7  public class MainActivity extends ListActivity {
 8
 9      @Override
10      protected void onCreate(Bundle savedInstanceState) {
11          super.onCreate(savedInstanceState);
12          String[ ] attraction={"Alcatraz Island", "Ferry Marketplace", "Golden Gate Bridge",
13                  "Cable Car Trolley", "Fisherman's Wharf"}; I
14      }
15
16      @Override
17      public boolean onCreateOptionsMenu(Menu menu) {
18          // Inflate the menu; this adds items to the action bar if it is present.
19          getMenuInflater().inflate(R.menu.main, menu);
20          return true;
21      }
22
23  }
24
```

> Press Enter after typing comma to place statement on two lines

> String array initialized

Figure 5-8 String array initialized with attractions

STEP 2

- Save your work.

GTK

To declare an array without assigning actual values, allocate the size of the array in the brackets to reserve the room needed in memory, as in int[ ] ages = new int[100];. The first number assigned to the ages array is placed in ages [0]. This array holds 101 elements in the array, one more than the maximum index.

Using a setListAdapter and Array Adapter

In the City Guide application, once the array is assigned, you can display an array listing using adapters. An **adapter** provides a data model for the layout of the list and for converting the data from the array into list items. The ListView and adapter work together to display a list. For example, if you want to share an iPad screen with a group, you need an adapter to connect to a projector to display the image on a large screen. Similarly, a **setListAdapter** projects your data to the onscreen list on your device by connecting the ListActivity's ListView object to the array data. A setListAdapter contains the information to connect the onscreen list with the attraction array in the chapter project. Calling a setListAdapter in the Java code binds the elements of the array to a ListView layout. In the next portion of the statement, a ListAdapter called an **ArrayAdapter<String> i** supplies the String array data to the ListView. The three parameters that follow ArrayAdapter refer to the *this* class, a generic layout called simple_list_item_l, and the array named attraction. The following code syntax shows the complete statement:

Code Syntax

```
setListAdapter(new ArrayAdapter<String>(this
    android.R.layout.simple_list_item_1, attraction));
```

Later in the chapter, instead of using the generic layout called simple_list_item_1, you design an XML layout to customize the layout to include the City Guide's logo. You can change the setListAdapter statement to reference the custom layout when you finish designing it. Follow these steps to add the setListAdapter that displays the array as a list:

STEP 1

- After the second line of code initializing the String array, press the Enter key.
- Type **setListAdapter(new ArrayAdapter<String>(this, android.R.layout.simple_list_item_1, attraction));**.
- Press the Enter key.
- Point to ArrayAdapter and tap or click Import 'ArrayAdapter' (android.widget).

The setListAdapter displays the attraction array in a generic ListView layout (Figure 5-9).

```
 7
 8  public class MainActivity extends ListActivity {
 9
10    @Override
11    protected void onCreate(Bundle savedInstanceState) {
12        super.onCreate(savedInstanceState);
13        String[ ] attraction={"Alcatraz Island", "Ferry Marketplace", "Golden Gate Bridge",
14            "Cable Car Trolley", "Fisherman's Wharf"};
15        setListAdapter(new ArrayAdapter<String>(this, android.R.layout. simple_list_item_1, attraction));
16    }
17
```

setListAdapter command

Generic built-in layout named simple_list_item_1

Figure 5-9 setListAdapter displays an array

STEP 2

- To display the attraction list in the generic ListView layout, tap or click Run on the menu bar, and then select Run.
- Select Android Application and tap or click the OK button. Save MainActivity.java in the next dialog box, if necessary, and unlock the emulator when the app starts.

The application opens in the emulator window displaying the ListView control with the five attractions in San Francisco with the launcher icon (Figure 5-10).

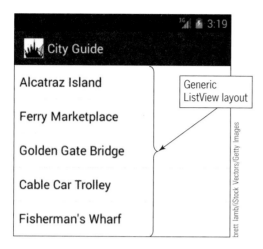

Figure 5-10   ListView built-in layout

STEP 3

- Close the emulated application window.

GTK

Other generic layouts that you might want to try with ListView include simple_list_item_2, simple_list_item_checked (displays check boxes), and simple_list_item_multiple_choice.

Adding the Images to the Resources Folder

The City Guide application uses several images throughout the app. An icon logo called ic_launcher_sf.png displays the skyline of San Francisco and is used multiple times on the opening screen. Images of the Golden Gate Bridge, Cable Car Trolley, and Fisherman's Wharf appear when the user selects those items from the opening list. To place a copy of the images from the USB drive into the res/drawable-hdpi folder, follow these steps:

STEP 1

- If necessary, copy the student files to your USB drive. Open the USB folder containing the student files.

- In the Package Explorer, expand the drawable-hdpi folder in the res folder.

- Delete the file named ic_launcher.png (the Android logo).

- To add the four image files to the drawable-hdpi resource folder, drag ic_launcher_sf.png, bridge.png, trolley.png, and wharf.png files to the drawable-hdpi folder until a plus sign pointer appears.

- Release the mouse button. If necessary, tap or click the Copy files option button, and then tap or click the OK button.

Copies of the four files appear in the drawable-hdpi folder (Figure 5-11).

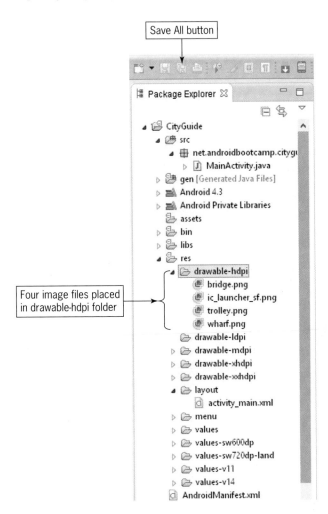

Figure 5-11   Images copied

STEP 2

- Tap or click the Save All button on the Standard toolbar to save your work.

IN THE TRENCHES

When publishing apps, you must follow copyright laws relative to copyrighted images used within your Android apps. Copyright is the legal protection extended to the authors or owners of original published and unpublished artistic and intellectual works, and you must seek copyright permissions. A copyright holder can also seek monetary or statutory damages for the violation of copyright. However, if the image is accompanied by the statement "This work is dedicated to the public domain," the image is available for fair use in your app.

Changing the Title Bar Text

Developers often want a custom title to appear on the title bar at the top of the window instead of the actual application name. A string named app_name in the strings.xml file displays the project name in the title bar by default. To change the title bar on the opening screen of the City Guide app to *San Francisco City Guide* and add three strings for the three ImageView control descriptions, follow these steps:

STEP 1

- Expand the res\values folder and then double-tap or double-click the strings.xml file.

- Tap or click app_name (String) in the Android Resources window.

- Change the text in the Value text box to **San Francisco City Guide**.

- Tap or click the Add button, select String, and then tap or click the OK button.

- Type **bridge** in the Name text box and then type **Bridge Image** in the Value text box.

- Tap or click the Add button, select String, and then tap or click the OK button.

- Type **trolley** in the Name text box and then type **Trolley Image** in the Value text box.

- Tap or click the Add button, select String, and then tap or click the OK button.

- Type **wharf** in the Name text box and then type **Wharf Image** in the Value text box.

The app_name value and image values are entered in the String table (Figure 5-12).

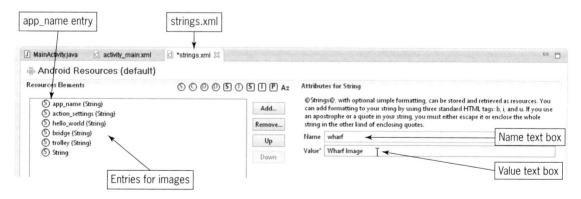

Figure 5-12 String table

STEP 2

- Save your work and close the strings.xml tab.

Creating a Custom XML Layout for ListView

You can design a layout by using the emulator window on the Graphical Layout tab and then drag and drop controls from the Palette, or you can code the activity_main.xml file using XML code. The XML code uses an auto-complete feature that assists you as you type XML code. As soon as you start typing an XML command or phrase, the xml code editor shows a list containing the probable words or phrases that you want to enter without requiring you to type it completely. This feature makes the application easier to use and improves user experience.

It is often easier to use the Palette for a simple layout, but understanding how to manipulate XML code can assist you greatly in app design. The opening screen for the City Guide chapter project shown in Figure 5-1 requires a custom layout for the list that includes a San Francisco City Guide logo and unique size and spacing of the attraction names. In the XML code, you must add a TextView control with the id of the name travel. The text property of android:text="@+id/travel" is used in the setListAdapter in the Java code (MainActivity.java) and the actual items in the array named attraction display instead of the text object named travel. Next the layout is identified, and the textSize property is set to 20sp. To display the ic_launcher_sf image file in front of the city attractions TextView object, the location source of the file is entered. The android:drawableLeft directs that the drawable image be drawn to the left of the text. Other commands such as drawableRight would place the image after the text or drawableTop would place the image above the text. To create a custom XML layout for activity_main.xml, follow these steps:

STEP 1

- In the res\layout folder, double-tap or double-click activity_main.xml.
- Delete the Hello world! TextView control.
- Tap or click the activity_main.xml tab at the bottom of the window to display the XML code.
- By default, RelativeLayout is already set.
- Tap or click in front of the closing statement </RelativeLayout> in Line 11, and then press the Enter key.
- On Line 11, type **<TextView** and press the Enter key.

The TextView control is added by typing XML code instead of dragging the TextView control to the emulator from the Palette (Figure 5-13).

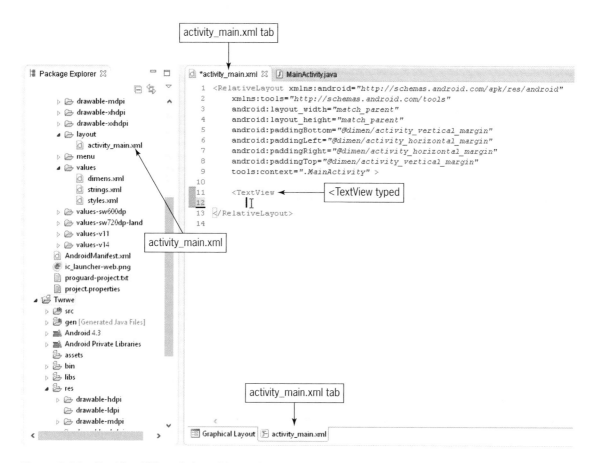

Figure 5-13 TextView XML code in activity_main.xml

STEP 2

- Type the following code using auto-completion as much as possible:

```
android:id="@+id/travel"
android:layout_width="fill_parent"
android:layout_height="wrap_content"
android:textSize="20sp"
android:text="@+id/travel"
android:drawableLeft="@drawable/ic_launcher_sf" />
```

- Press the Enter key and save your work.

The TextView control is customized in the activity_main.xml file to display an image to the left of the attractions text from the array (Figure 5-14).

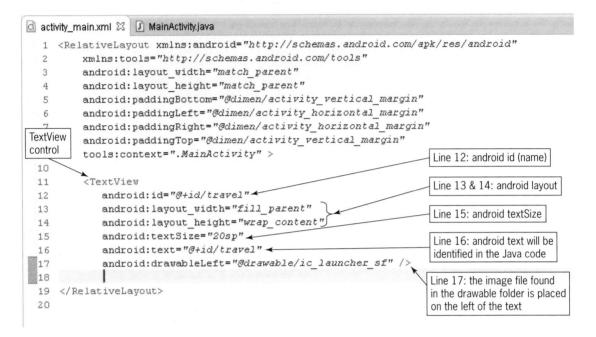

Figure 5-14   TextView XML code

Coding a setListAdapter with a Custom XML Layout

When the setListAdapter was coded and executed as shown in Figure 5-10, the attractions list was displayed within a built-in layout called simple_list_item_1 in the following statement:

```
setListAdapter(new ArrayAdapter<String>(this,
android.R.layout.simple_list_item_1, attraction));
```

Instead of using a standard layout in the setListAdapter, the custom XML layout you designed in activity_main.xml in Figure 5-14 adds the San Francisco City Guide logo and updates the TextView properties. The syntax changes from the default in two significant ways:

1. The second parameter in the default statement (android.R.layout.*simple_list_item_1*) is changed to R.layout.*activity_main*. The android reference is removed because the Android library default layout is not being used. Instead R.layout.*activity_main* references the activity_main.xml custom layout design for the TextView control.

2. A third parameter is added before the attraction array name to reference the variable travel, which identifies the TextView control created in the activity_main.xml file. The variable is substituted for the actual attraction locations initialized in the attraction array.

The following code syntax shows the code for a custom XML layout:

Code Syntax

```
setListAdapter(new ArrayAdapter<String>(this,
    R.layout.activity_main, R.id.travel, attraction));
```

To edit the setListAdapter to use the custom XML layout, follow these steps:

STEP 1

- Close the activity_main.xml window.

- In the setListAdapter statement of MainActivity.java, tap or click after the comma following the *this* command.

- Change the android.R.layout.simple_list_item_1, text to **R.layout.activity_main, R.id.travel,** to add the custom layout named activity_main.xml.

The default setListAdapter is edited to include the custom layout (Figure 5-15).

```
 8  public class MainActivity extends ListActivity {
 9
10    @Override
11    protected void onCreate(Bundle savedInstanceState) {
12        super.onCreate(savedInstanceState);
13        String[ ] attraction={"Alcatraz Island", "Ferry Marketplace", "Golden Gate Bridge",
14            "Cable Car Trolley", "Fisherman's Wharf"};
15        setListAdapter(new ArrayAdapter<String>(this, R.layout.activity_main,R.id.travel, attraction));
16        }
17
```

Custom layout formatted by activity_main.xml;

Figure 5-15 setListAdapter with custom layout for list

STEP 2

- Run and save the application to view the custom layout of the ListView.

The emulator displays the opening screen with a custom ListView (Figure 5-16).

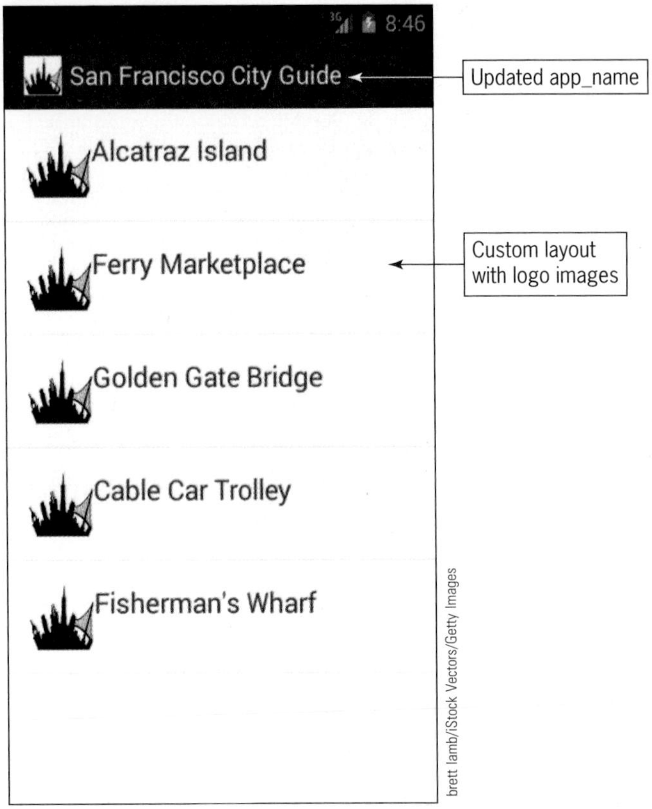

Figure 5-16　ListView custom layout in emulator

STEP 3

- Close the emulated application window.

Using the onListItemClick Method

The City Guide opening screen has a custom list shown in Figure 5-16. Each of the attractions displayed in the list can be selected by tapping the attraction name on the mobile device. The method **onListItemClick( )** is called when an item in the list is selected. The onListItemClick is similar to the Button OnClickListener, which awaits user interaction. When an attraction in the list is selected, the **position** of the item is passed from the onListItemClick and evaluated with a decision structure, as shown in the following code syntax. If the user selects the first attraction, the position parameter is assigned an integer value of 0. The second item is assigned the position of 1, and so forth. The first position or index of an array is always zero.

Code Syntax

```
protected void onListItemClick(ListView l, View v, int position, long id){
    }
```

To code the onListItemClick method to respond to the event of the user's selection, follow these steps:

STEP 1

- In MainActivity.java, press the Enter key after the closing brace of the onCreate method to insert a new line.

- To respond to the user's selection, type **protected void onListItemClick(ListView l, View v, int position, long id)** to create an onListItemClick method to await the user's selection from the ListView items. (Be sure to type a lowercase l after ListView, not the number 1.)

- Type an opening brace after the statement and press the Enter key. A closing brace is automatically placed in the code.

- After the code is entered to reference the ListView and View, point to the red error line below ListView and select Import 'ListView' (android.widget).

- Point to the red error line below View and select Import 'View' (android.view).

The onListItemClick method detects the selection's position (Figure 5-17).

```
J *MainActivity.java ⊠
  1  package net.androidbootcamp.cityguide;
  2
  3⊕ import android.app.ListActivity;☐
  9
 10  public class MainActivity extends ListActivity {
 11
 12⊖     @Override
▲13     protected void onCreate(Bundle savedInstanceState) {
 14         super.onCreate(savedInstanceState);
 15         String[ ] attraction={"Alcatraz Island", "Ferry Marketplace", "Golden Gate Bridge",
 16                 "Cable Car Trolley", "Fisherman's Wharf"};
 17         setListAdapter(new ArrayAdapter<String>(this, R.layout.activity_main,R.id.travel, attraction));
 18     }
 19⊖     protected void onListItemClick(ListView l, View v, int position, long id){
 20         I
 21     }
 22
 23
 24⊖     @Override
▲25     public boolean onCreateOptionsMenu(Menu menu) {
 26         // Inflate the menu; this adds items to the action bar if it is present.
 27         getMenuInflater().inflate(R.menu.main, menu);
 28         return true;
 29     }
 30
 31  }
 32
```

onListItemClick method

Lowercase l, not number 1

Figure 5-17   onListItemClick method

STEP 2

- Save your work.

Decision Structure—Switch Statement

Each item in the list produces a different result when selected, such as opening a Web browser or displaying a picture of the attraction on a second screen. In Chapter 4, If statements evaluated the user's selection and the decision structure determined the results. You can use another decision structure called a Switch statement with a list or menu. The **Switch** statement allows you to choose from many statements based on an integer or char (single character) input. The switch keyword is followed by an integer expression in parentheses, which is followed by the cases, all enclosed in braces, as shown in the following code syntax:

Code Syntax

```
switch(position){
    case 0:
        //statements that are executed if position == 0
    break;
    case 1:
        //statements that are executed if position == 1
    break;
    default:
        //statements that are executed if position !=  any of the cases
}
```

The integer named *position* is evaluated in the Switch statement and executes the corresponding case. The **case** keyword is followed by a value and a colon. Typically the statement within a case ends with a **break** statement, which exits the Switch decision structure and continues with the next statement. Be careful not to omit the break statement or the subsequent case statement will be executed as well. If there is no matching case value, the default option is executed. A default statement is optional. In the chapter project, a default statement is not necessary because the user must select one of the items in the list for an action to occur.

In the City Guide app, five attractions make up the list, so the following positions are possible for the Switch statement: case 0, case 1, case 2, case 3, and case 4. To code the Switch decision structure, follow these steps:

Step 1

- Within the braces of the onListItemClick method, type **switch(position){** and press the Enter key for the closing brace to appear.

The Switch decision structure is coded within the onListItemClick method (Figure 5-18).

```
12    @Override
13    protected void onCreate(Bundle savedInstanceState) {
14        super.onCreate(savedInstanceState);
15        String[ ] attraction={"Alcatraz Island", "Ferry Marketplace", "Golden Gate Bridge",
16            "Cable Car Trolley", "Fisherman's Wharf"};
17        setListAdapter(new ArrayAdapter<String>(this, R.layout.activity_main,R.id.travel, attraction));
18    }
19    protected void onListItemClick(ListView l, View v, int position, long id){
20        switch(position){
21            I
22        }
23    }
24
25
```

Beginning of switch statement decision structure

Figure 5-18   Switch statement

STEP 2

- Within the braces of the switch statement, add the case integer options. Type the following code, inserting a blank line after each case statement:

```
case 0:
    break;
case 1:
    break;
case 2:
    break;
case 3:
    break;
case 4:
    break;
```

The case statements for the five selections from the attractions list each are coded (Figure 5-19).

```
19    protected void onListItemClick(ListView l, View v, int position, long id){
20        switch(position){
21            case 0:
22
23                break;
24            case 1:
25
26                break;
27            case 2:
28
29                break;
30            case 3:
31
32                break;
33            case 4:
34
35                break;
36        }
37    }
38
39
```

case statements each conclude with break statement

Figure 5-19   Case statements

STEP 3

- Save your work.

GTK
Switch statements do not allow ranges such as 10–50. Use If statements when evaluating a range of number or specific strings.

Android Intents

When the user selects one of the first two list items in the project, Alcatraz Island or Ferry Marketplace, a built-in Android browser launches a Web site about each attraction. A browser is launched with Android code using an intent. Android intents send and receive activities and services that include opening a Web page in a browser, calling a phone number, locating a GPS position on a map, posting your notes to a note-taking program such as Evernote, opening your contacts list, sending a photo, or even posting to your social network. Additional Android intents are explored throughout the rest of this book. Android intents are powerful features that allow apps to talk to each other in a very simple way.

To better understand an intent, imagine a student sitting in a classroom. To ask a question or make a request, the student raises a hand. The teacher is alerted to the hand and responds to the student. An intent works the same way. Your app raises its hand and the other apps state that they are ready to handle your request. When the chapter project sends an intent, the browser app handles the request and opens the Web site.

IN THE TRENCHES
Android platform devices have many options for supported browsers. Popular Android browsers include Chrome, Dolphin, Opera Mini, Skyfire, Mozilla Firefox, and Boat.

Launching the Browser from an Android Device

Android phones have a built-in browser with an intent filter that accepts intent requests from other apps. The intent sends the browser a **URI** (Uniform Resource Identifier), a string that identifies the resources of the Web. You might already be familiar with the term **URL** (Uniform Resource Locator), which means a Web site address. A URI is a URL with additional information necessary for gaining access to the resources required for posting the page.

Depending on the lists of browsers installed on an Android device, Android selects a suitable browser (usually a user-set preferred browser), which accepts the action called ACTION_VIEW (must be in caps) and displays the site. **ACTION_VIEW** is the most common action performed on data. It is a generic action you can use to send any request to get the most reasonable action to occur. As shown in the following code syntax, a startActivity statement informs the present Activity that a new Activity is being started and the browser opens the Web site:

Code Syntax

```
startActivity(new Intent(Intent.ACTION_VIEW,
    Uri.parse("http://alcatrazcruises.com/")));
```

When the user selects the Alcatraz Island item from the attractions list, the Switch statement sends a zero integer value to the case statements. The case 0: statement is true, so the program executes the startActivity statement, which sends the browser a parsed string containing the URI Web address. The browser application then launches the Alcatraz Web site. When you tap or click the Back button in some browser windows or the left arrow to the right of the menu button on the right side of the emulator, the previous Activity opens. In the chapter project, the attractions list ListView activity is displayed again. To code the startActivity that launches a Web site in an Android browser, follow these steps:

STEP 1

- In MainActivity.java, tap or click the blank line after the line containing case 0: inside the Switch decision structure.

- Type **startActivity(new Intent(Intent.ACTION_VIEW, Uri.parse ("*http://alcatrazcruises.com/*")));**.

- Point to Intent and tap or click Import 'Intent' (android.content).

- Point to Uri and then tap or click Import 'Uri' (*android.net*).

The startActivity code launches the Alcatraz Web site when the user selects the first list item (Figure 5-20).

Opens Web browser to display Alcatraz site

```
21    protected void onListItemClick(ListView l, View v, int position, long id){
22        switch(position){
23        case 0:
24            startActivity(new Intent(Intent.ACTION_VIEW, Uri.parse ("http://alcatrazcruises.com/")));
25            break;
26        case 1:
27
```

Figure 5-20   Code for launching the Alcatraz Web site

STEP 2

- In MainActivity.java, tap or click the blank line after the line containing case 1:.

- Type **startActivity(new Intent(Intent.ACTION_VIEW, Uri.parse ("*http://www.ferrybuildingmarketplace.com*")));**.

The startActivity code launches the Ferry Marketplace Web site when the user selects the second list item (Figure 5-21).

```
20          }
21⊝    protected void onListItemClick(ListView l, View v, int position, long id){
22          switch(position){
23          case 0:
24              startActivity(new Intent(Intent.ACTION_VIEW, Uri.parse ("http://alcatrazcruises.com/")));
25              break;
26          case 1:
27              startActivity(new Intent(Intent.ACTION_VIEW,Uri.parse ("http://www.ferrybuildingmarketplace.com")));
28              break;
29          case 2:
30
31              break;
```

Opens Web browser
to display Ferry
Marketplace site

Figure 5-21   Code for launching the Ferry Marketplace Web site

STEP 3

- To display the Alcatraz Island Web site in the browser, tap or click Run on the menu bar, and then select Run.

- If necessary, select Android Application and tap or click the OK button.

- Save all the files in the next dialog box, if necessary, and unlock the emulator.

- Select the Alcatraz Island list item.

The first item is selected from the list in the emulator and the Android browser displays the Alcatraz Island Web site. The site loads slowly in the emulator. Some Web sites are especially designed for mobile devices (Figure 5-22).

Android browser
displays Alcatraz
Web site in emulator

Figure 5-22   Browser opens in the emulator

- Close the emulated application window.

IN THE TRENCHES
Be sure to test any links within your Android apps often. If you have hundreds of links, verifying Web links can be simple in concept but very time consuming in practice. A good place to start is with the World Wide Web Consortium's free Web Site Validation Service (http://validator.w3.org).

Designing XML Layout Files

The last three case statements open a second screen that displays a picture of the selected attraction. Three XML layout files must be designed to display an ImageView control with an image source file. To create an XML layout file, follow these steps:

STEP 1

- In the Package Explorer, press and hold or right-click the layout folder.

- On the shortcut menu, point to New and then tap or click Android XML File.

- In the New Android Layout XML File dialog box, type **bridge.xml** in the File text box to name the layout file.

- In the Root Element list, select RelativeLayout.

- Tap or click the Finish button to open the emulator window.

- In the Images & Media category in the Palette, drag the ImageView control to the emulator to open the Resource Chooser dialog box.

- Select bridge, and then tap or click the OK button.

- Resize the image to fill the entire window.

- If necessary, display the Properties pane and tap or click the ellipsis for the Content Description property.

- Select bridge within the String category and then tap or click the OK button.

The bridge XML file is designed with an image of the Golden Gate Bridge (Figure 5-23).

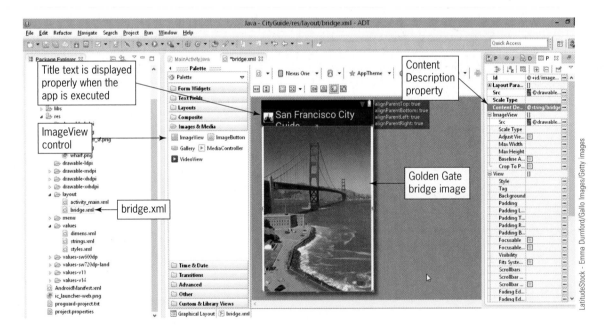

Figure 5-23   bridge.xml layout file

STEP 2

- Close the bridge.xml file tab and save your work.
- Press and hold or right-click the layout folder, point to New on the shortcut menu, and then tap or click Android XML Layout File.
- In the New Android Layout XML File dialog box, type **trolley.xml** in the File text box to name the layout file.
- In the Root Element list, select RelativeLayout.
- Tap or click the Finish button to open the emulator window.
- In the Images & Media category in the Palette, drag the ImageView control to the emulator to open the Resource Chooser dialog box.
- Select trolley, and then tap or click the OK button.
- Resize the image to fill the entire window.
- If necessary, display the Properties pane and tap or click the ellipsis for the Content Description property.
- Select trolley within the String category and then tap or click the OK button.

The trolley XML file is designed with an image of the cable car trolley (Figure 5-24).

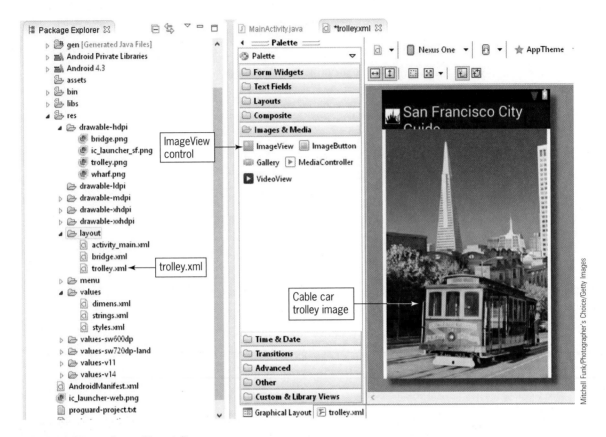

Figure 5-24 trolley.xml layout file

STEP 3

- Close the trolley.xml file tab and save your work.

- Press and hold or right-click the layout folder, point to New on the shortcut menu, and then tap or click Android XML File.

- In the New Android XML File dialog box, type **wharf.xml** in the File text box to name the layout file.

- In the Root Element list, select RelativeLayout.

- Tap or click the Finish button to open the emulator window.

- In the Images & Media category in the Palette, drag the ImageView control to the emulator to open the Resource Chooser dialog box.

- Select wharf, and then tap or click the OK button.

- Resize the image to fill the entire window.

STEP 4

- Close the Wharf.java file tab and save your work.
- To add the reference to these Java class files in the Android Manifest file, in the Package Explorer, scroll down, if necessary, and double-tap or double-click the AndroidManifest.xml file.
- Tap or click the Application tab at the bottom of the City Guide Manifest page.
- Scroll down to display the Application Nodes section.
- Tap or click the Add button.
- Select Activity in the Create a new element at the top level, in Application dialog box.
- Tap or click the OK button. The Attributes for Activity section opens in the Application tab.
- In the Name text box, type the class name preceded by a period **.Bridge** to add the Bridge Activity.
- Tap or click the Add button again.
- Tap or click the first radio button (Create a new element at the top level, in Application) and then select Activity.
- Tap or click the OK button.
- In the Name text box, type the class name preceded by a period **.Trolley** to add the Trolley Activity. Tap or click the Add button again.
- Tap or click the first radio button (Create a new element at the top level, in Application) and select Activity.
- Tap or click the OK button.
- In the Name text box, type the class name preceded by a period **.Wharf** to add the Wharf Activity and save your work.

The AndroidManifest.xml file includes the three Activities (Figure 5-29).

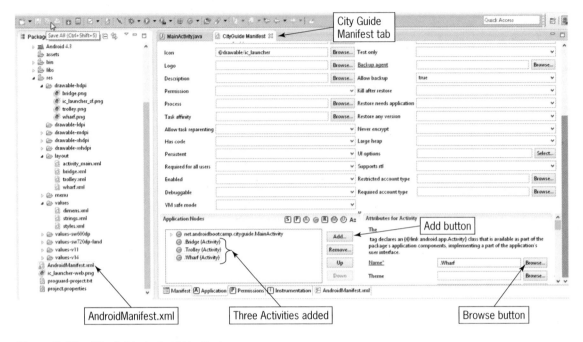

Figure 5-29　City Guide Android Manifest

Opening the Class Files

The last step in the development of the San Francisco City Guide app is to open the class files when the user selects Golden Gate Bridge (case 2), Cable Car Trolley (case 3), or Fisherman's Wharf (case 4) from the ListView control. A startActivity method opens the next Activity, which in turn launches the appropriate XML layout displaying an image of the attraction. To code the remaining case statement within the Switch decision structure that starts each of the Activities, follow these steps:

STEP 1

- Close the City Guide Manifest tab.

- In MainActivity.java, tap or click the blank line below the one containing case 2: and type **startActivity(new Intent(MainActivity.this, Bridge.class));**.

- Tap or click the blank line below the one containing case 3: and type **startActivity(new Intent(MainActivity.this, Trolley.class));**.

- Tap or click the blank line below the one containing case 4: and type **startActivity(new Intent(MainActivity.this, Wharf.class));**.

The case statements 2 through 4 are coded with a startActivity that executes the appropriate class (Figure 5-30).

```
  J  *MainActivity.java  ⊠
  11
  12  public class MainActivity extends ListActivity {
  13
  14⊖      @Override
▲15      protected void onCreate(Bundle savedInstanceState) {
  16          super.onCreate(savedInstanceState);
  17          String[ ] attraction={"Alcatraz Island", "Ferry Marketplace", "Golden Gate Bridge",
  18                  "Cable Car Trolley", "Fisherman's Wharf");
  19          setListAdapter(new ArrayAdapter<String>(this, R.layout.activity_main,R.id.travel, attraction));
  20          }
  21⊖      protected void onListItemClick(ListView l, View v, int position, long id){
  22          switch(position){
  23          case 0:
  24              startActivity(new Intent(Intent.ACTION_VIEW, Uri.parse ("http://alcatrazcruises.com/")));
  25              break;
  26          case 1:
  27              startActivity(new Intent(Intent.ACTION_VIEW,Uri.parse ("http://www.ferrybuildingmarketplace.com")));
  28              break;
  29          case 2:
  30              startActivity(new Intent(MainActivity.this, Bridge.class));
  31              break;
  32          case 3:
  33              startActivity(new Intent(MainActivity.this, Trolley.class));
  34              break;
  35          case 4:
  36              startActivity(new Intent(MainActivity.this, Wharf.class));
  37              break;
  38          }
  39      }
  40
  41
```

Figure 5-30   Complete code for MainActivity.java

STEP 2

- Compare your code to Figure 5-30, make changes as necessary to match the code in the figure, and then save your work.

Running and Testing the Application

As you save and run the San Francisco City Guide application, be sure you test every option of this app. Before publishing to the Android Market, it is critical to make sure all the fields can gracefully handle any tap or click or any value entered in any Android app. Tap or click Run on the menu bar, and then select Run to save and test the application in the emulator. A dialog box requesting how you would like to run the application opens the first time the application is executed. Select Android Application and tap or click the OK button. Save all the files in the next dialog box, if necessary, and unlock the emulator. The application opens in the emulator window where you can test each list item in the San Francisco City Guide app, as shown in Figures 5-1, 5-2, and 5-3.

IN THE TRENCHES

Testing an Android app is called usability testing. In addition to the traditional navigation and ease of use, Section 508 compliance is a third component to be tested. The 1998 Amendment to Section 508 of the Rehabilitation Act spells out accessibility requirements for individuals with certain disabilities. For more details, refer to *www.section508.gov*.

Wrap It Up—Chapter Summary

This chapter described the steps to create a list with items users select to launch Web sites and XML layouts through the use of a Switch decision structure in the City Guide program. The introduction of intents to outside services such as a Web browser begins our adventure of many other intent options used throughout the rest of this book.

- The Java View class creates a list and makes it scrollable if it exceeds the length of the screen. To contain the list items, use a ListView control, which allows you to select each row in the list for further action, such as displaying an image or Web page.

- Instead of extending the basic Activity class in MainActivity.java by using the public class Main extends Activity opening class statement, when you want to display a ListView control, extend the ListActivity class in MainActivity.java with the statement public class Main extends ListActivity.

- Before you can specify the items in a list, declare the item names using an array variable, which can store more than one value of similar data types. For example, you can store five string values in an array without having to declare five variables.

- Arrays provide access to data by using a numeric index to identify each element in the array. Each value is stored in an element of the array, which you refer to by its index. The index for the first element in an array is zero. For example, Attraction[0] is the first element in the Attraction array.

- To declare an array, specify the array's data type and name followed by the values in braces, as in String[ ] attraction={"Alcatraz Island", "Ferry Marketplace", "Golden Gate Bridge", "Cable Car Trolley", "Fisherman's Wharf"};.

- You can display the values in an array using an adapter, which provides a data model for the layout of the list and for converting the array data into list items. A ListView control is the container for the list items, and an adapter such as the setListAdapter command connects the array data to the ListView control so the items are displayed on the device screen. In other words, calling a setListAdapter in the Java code binds the elements of an array to a ListView layout.

- To design a simple layout, you drag controls from the Palette to the emulator on the Graphical Layout tab. To design a custom layout, you add code to the main XML file for the application, such as activity_main.xml.

- By default, the application name is displayed in an app's title bar. To display text other than the application name, change the app_name value in the strings.xml file.

- A setListAdapter statement has three parameters: One refers to the *this* class, the second refers to the layout used to display the list, and the third refers to the array containing the list values to display. For the second parameter, setListAdapter can use a standard layout, as in android.R. layout.*simple_list_item_1,* which specifies the built-in simple_list_item_1 layout to display the list. To use a custom layout instead, replace the name of the standard layout with the name of the custom layout, as in R.layout.*activity_main,* which references a custom layout named activity_main.xml. You also remove the *android* reference because you are no longer using an Android library default layout.

- To have an app take action when a user selects an item in a list, you code the onListItemClick method to respond to the event of the user's selection.

- You can use the Switch decision structure with a list or menu. In a Switch statement, an integer or character variable is evaluated and the corresponding case is executed. Each case is specified using the *case* keyword followed by a value and a colon. For example, if a list contains five items, the Switch statement will have five cases, such as case 0, case 1, case 2, case 3, and case 4. End each case with a break statement to exit the Switch decision structure and continue with the next statement.

- Android intents send and receive activities and services, including opening a Web page in a browser. An intent can use the ACTION_VIEW action to send a URI to a built-in Android browser and display the specified Web site.

- As you develop an application, you must test every option and possible user action, including incorrect values and selections. Thoroughly test an Android app before publishing to the Android Market.

Key Terms

ACTION_VIEW—A generic action you can use to send any request to get the most reasonable action to occur.

adapter—Provides a data model for the layout of a list and for converting the data from the array into list items.

array variable   A variable that can store more than one value.

ArrayAdapter<String> i—A ListAdapter that supplies string array data to a ListView object.

break—A statement that ends a case within a Switch statement and continues with the statement following the Switch decision structure.

case—A keyword used in a Switch statement to indicate a condition. In a Switch statement, the case keyword is followed by a value and a colon.

element—A single individual item that contains a value in an array.

ListActivity—A class that displays a list of items within an app.

onListItemClick( )—A method called when an item in a list is selected.

position—The placement of an item in a list. When an item in a list is selected, the position of the item is passed from the onListItemClick method and evaluated with a decision structure. The first item is assigned the position of 0, the second item is assigned the position of 1, and so forth.

setListAdapter—A command that projects your data to the onscreen list on your device by connecting the ListActivity's ListView object to array data.

Switch—A type of decision statement that allows you to choose from many statements based on an integer or a char input.

URI—An acronym for Uniform Resource Identifier, a URI is a string that identifies the resources of the Web. Similar to a URL, a URI includes additional information necessary for gaining access to the resources required for posting the page.

URL—An acronym for Uniform Resource Locator, a URL is a Web site address.

Developer FAQs

1. Typically in an Android .Java file, the class extends Activity. When the primary purpose of the class is to display a list, what is the opening Main class statement?

2. Which Android control displays a vertical listing of items?

3. When does a scroll bar appear in a list?

4. Initialize an array named lotto with the integers 22, 6, 38, 30, and 37.

5. Answer the following questions about the following initialized array:

   ```
   String[]pizzaToppings = new String[12];
   ```

   a. What is the statement to assign pepperoni to the first array location?

   b. What is the statement to assign green peppers to the fourth location in the array?

   c. How many toppings can this array hold?

   d. Rewrite this statement to initially be assigned the following four toppings only: extra cheese, black olives, mushrooms, and bacon.

6. Write a line of code that assigns the values Samsung, HTC, Sony, Motorola, and Asus to the elements in the array phoneBrands.

7. Fix this array statement:

   ```
   doubles { } driveSize = ["32.0", "64.0", "128.0"]
   ```

8. Write two lines of code that assign an array named languages with the items Java, C#, Python, Visual Basic, and Ruby and display this array as a generic list.

9. Which type of pictures can be used for free fair use without copyright?

10. What does URI stand for?

11. Write a statement that opens the Android Help Site: *http://developer.android.com*

12. Write a single line of XML code that changes the size of the text of a TextView control to 35 scaled-independent pixels.

13. Write a single line of XML code that changes the height of an image to 100 pixels.

14. Write a Switch decision structure that tests the user's age in an integer variable named teenAge and assigns the variable schoolYear as in Table 5-2.

Age	High School Year
14	Freshman
15	Sophomore
16	Junior
17	Senior
Any other age	Not in High School

© 2015 Cengage Learning

Table 5-2

15. Change the following If decision structure to a Switch decision structure:

```
if (count == 3) {
    result = "Password incorrect";
} else {
    result = "Request password";
}
```

16. What is the purpose of a default statement in a decision structure?

17. Name two decision structures.

18. What happens when a Web page opens in the emulator and the Back button is clicked in the chapter project?

19. What does the "R" in R.id.travel stand for?

20. Write a startActivity statement that launches a class named Car.

Beyond the Book

Using the Internet, search the Web for the answers to the following questions to further your Android knowledge.

1. Create a five-item list array program of your own favorite hobby and test out three types of built-in Android list formats. Take a screenshot comparing the three layouts identified by the layout format.

2. Compare four different Android browsers. Write a paragraph about each browser.

3. Research the 508 standards for Android app design. Create a list of 10 standards that should be met while designing Android applications.

4. Besides the 508 standards, research the topic of Android usability testing. Write one page on testing guidelines that assist in the design and testing process.

Case Programming Projects

Complete one or more of the following case programming projects. Use the same steps and techniques taught within the chapter. Submit the program you create to your instructor. The level of difficulty is indicated for each case programming project.

Easiest: ★

Intermediate: ★★

Challenging: ★★★

Case Project 5–1: Photography Studio App ★

Requirements Document

Application title:	Photography Studio App
Purpose:	A photography studio named Picture People would like an app that displays information about their photography services. As each service is selected, a sample photo is displayed.
Algorithms:	1. The opening screen displays a list of services: family photography, portrait photography, and full Web site (Figure 5-31).
	2. When the user selects an item from the list, a full-screen image of the item is displayed for the first two services (Figure 5-32). The third option opens the Web site *http://www.picturepeople.com*.
Conditions:	1. The pictures of the two types of photography are provided with your student files (family.png and portrait.png).
	2. Use the built-in layout *simple_list_item_1*.
	3. Use the Switch decision structure.
	4. Use a String table for image descriptions.

Figure 5-31

Figure 5-32

Case Project 5–2: Sushi Menu App ★

Requirements Document

Application title:	Sushi Menu App
Purpose:	A sushi restaurant named Red Ginger would like an app that lists the specials of the day. As each special is selected, an image is displayed.
Algorithms:	1. The opening screen lists the three specials of the day and displays the restaurant full Web site with a custom icon (Figure 5-33).
	2. When the user selects one of the three specials (seaweed salad, salmon sushi, or mixed sashimi), an image of the special is displayed. If the full Web site is requested, *http://www.eatatginger.com* opens.
Conditions:	1. The sushi icon is provided with your student files and is named ic_launcher_sushi.png. The three images for the specials are named seaweed.png, salmon.png, and sashimi.png.
	2. Design a custom layout similar to Figure 5-33.
	3. Use the Switch decision structure.
	4. Use a String table for image descriptions.

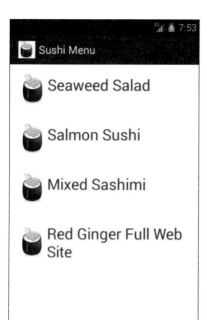

mystockicons/iStock Vectors/Getty Images

Foodcollection RF /Getty Images

ShyMan/Vetta/Getty Images

Kelly Cline/Vetta/Getty Images

Figure 5-33

Case Project 5–3: Rent a Car App ★★

Requirements Document

Application title:	Rent a Car App
Purpose:	A rental car app provides a listing of six nationally known car rental companies. By selecting a car company, a car rental site opens.
Algorithms:	1. An opening screen displays an image of a car and a button.
	2. The second screen displays a listing of six car rental companies. This screen also contains a custom icon and layout.
	3. Each car rental agency can be selected to view a Web site of the corresponding company.
Conditions:	1. Select your own images.
	2. Create a custom layout for the list.

Case Project 5–4: Coffee Finder App ★★

Requirements Document

Application title:	Coffee Finder App
Purpose:	This Coffee Finder App locates four places in your town or city to get a great cup of joe.
Algorithms:	1. The opening screen displays the names of four coffee shops.
	2. When the user selects a coffee shop, a second screen displays the name and address of the selected coffee shop with a picture or logo for the coffee shop.
Conditions:	1. Select your own images.
	2. Create a custom layout for the list.

Case Project 5–5: Tech Gadgets App ★★★

Requirements Document

Application title:	Tech Gadgets App
Purpose:	The Tech Gadgets app shows the top five technology gifts on your wish list.
Algorithms:	1. The opening screen displays names of five technology gadgets of your own choosing.
	2. If the user selects any of the gadgets, a second screen opens that has an image and a button. If the user clicks the button, a Web page opens that displays more information about the tech gadget.
Conditions:	1. Select your own images.
	2. Create a custom layout for the list.

Case Project 5–6: Create Your Own App ★★★

Requirements Document

Application title:	Create Your Own App
Purpose:	Get creative! Create an app with five to eight list items with a custom layout and a custom icon that links to Web pages and other XML layout screens.
Algorithms:	1. Create an app on a topic of your own choice. Create a list.
	2. Display XML layout pages as well as Web pages on different list items.
Conditions:	1. Select your own images.
	2. Use a custom layout and icon.

Jam! Implementing Audio in Android Apps

In this chapter, you learn to:

- ◎ Create an Android project using a splash screen
- ◎ Design a TextView control with a background image
- ◎ Pause the execution of an Activity with a timer
- ◎ Understand the Activity life cycle
- ◎ Open an Activity with onCreate( )
- ◎ End an Activity with finish( )
- ◎ Assign class variables
- ◎ Create a raw folder for music files
- ◎ Play music with a MediaPlayer method
- ◎ Start and resume music playback using the start and pause methods
- ◎ Change the Text property of a control
- ◎ Change the visibility of a control

Playing music on a smartphone is one of the primary uses of a mobile device, especially as MP3 players are losing popularity. The most common phone activities include texting, talking, gaming, and playing music. Talking and texting continue to be mainstream communication channels, but the proportion of users taking advantage of apps, games, and multimedia on their phones is growing. The principal specification when purchasing a smartphone is typically the amount of memory it has. Consumers often purchase a phone with more memory so they can store music.

To demonstrate playing music through an Android built-in media player, the Chapter 6 project is named Latin Music and opens with an image and the text "Sounds of the Caribbean." This opening screen (Figure 6-1), also called a splash screen, is displayed for approximately five seconds, and then the program automatically opens the second window. The Latin Music application (Figure 6-2) plays two songs: Marimba, a type of Latin music made from a set of wooden bars with resonators, and Merengue, a type of dance music originating in the Dominican Republic that has become popular throughout Latin America. If the user selects the first button, the Marimba song plays until the user selects the first button again to pause the Marimba song. If the user selects the second button, the Merengue song plays until the user selects the second button again. The emulator plays the music through your computer's speakers.

Figure 6-1　Latin Music Android app

Figure 6-2　Music played in the app

IN THE TRENCHES

Android music apps can play music on the memory card, download music available for purchase or free from music-sharing sites, tune into Internet-based streaming radio stations, or connect to music saved in a cloud service.

To create this application, the developer must understand how to perform the following processes, among others:

1. Create a splash screen with a timer.

2. Design a TextView control with a background image.

3. Initialize a Timer Task and a timer.

4. Launch a second Activity.

5. Design a second XML layout.

6. Add music files to the raw folder.

7. Initialize the MediaPlayer class.

8. Play and pause music with a Button control.

Creating a Splash Screen

The Latin Music app opens with a window that is displayed for approximately five seconds before automatically launching the next window. Unlike the project in Chapter 2 (Healthy Recipes), which required a button to be tapped to begin a click event that opened a second screen, this program does not require user interaction to open the second Activity class. Many Android applications on the market show splash screens that often include the name of the program, display a brand logo for the application, or identify the author. A splash screen opens as you launch your app, providing time for Android to initialize its resources. Extending the length of time that your splash screen is displayed enables your app to load necessary files.

In the Latin Music app, instead of using Main as the name of the initial Activity, the opening Activity shown in Figure 6-4 is named Splash. A second .java file named MainActivity.java is added later in the chapter. The MainActivity class is responsible for playing the two songs. To start the Latin Music application with a splash screen, complete the following step:

STEP 1

● Open the Eclipse program.

● Type **E:\Workspace** (if necessary, enter a different drive letter that identifies the USB drive) to select a workspace, and then tap or click the OK button.

● Tap or click the New button on the Standard toolbar and then select Android Application Project.

● Tap or click the Next button.

- In the New Android Application dialog box, enter the Application Name **Latin Music**.
- Enter the Package Name of **net.androidbootcamp.latinmusic**.

The new Android Latin Music project has an application name and a package name (Figure 6-3).

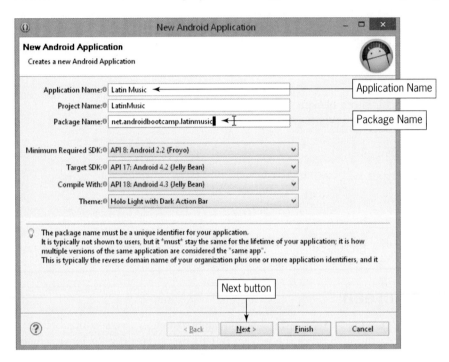

Figure 6-3   Setting up the Latin Music project

STEP 2

- Tap or click the Next button.
- Tap or click the Create custom launcher icon box to uncheck the option.
- Tap or click the Next button twice.
- Replace MainActivity with the text **Splash** in the Activity Name text box.

The new Android Latin Music project has an application name and a Splash Activity (Figure 6-4).

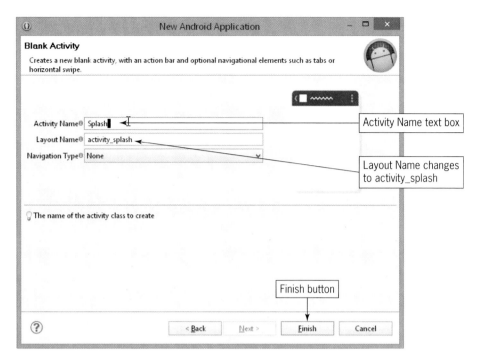

Figure 6-4 Setting up the Splash Activity (splash screen)

Adding a Background Image to a TextView Widget

On the splash screen in Figure 6-1, an image with the text "Sounds of the Caribbean" is displayed. The text for the TextView image as well as the image descriptions for the two ImageView controls and button text are stored in the strings.xml file. This opening image is not an ImageView control, but instead a TextView control with a background image. You use a TextView property named background to specify the image. The image is first placed in the drawable-hdpi folder and then referenced in the TextView background. The TextView background can display an image or a solid-color fill such as the hexadecimal color #CC6600 for light brown. The margins and gravity properties are used to place the text in the location of your choice. To add the images for this project and an activity_splash.xml file with a TextView widget that contains a background image, follow these steps:

STEP 1

- Tap or click the Finish button in the New Android Application dialog box. If necessary, expand the Latin Music project in the Package Explorer.

- Open the USB folder containing the student files.

- In the Package Explorer pane, expand the res folder.

- To add the three image files to the drawable-hdpi resource folder, drag latin.png, marimba.png, and merengue.png to the drawable-hdpi folder until a plus sign pointer appears. Release the mouse button.

- If necessary, tap or click the Copy files option button, and then tap or click the OK button.

Copies of the three image files appear in the drawable-hdpi folder (Figure 6-5).

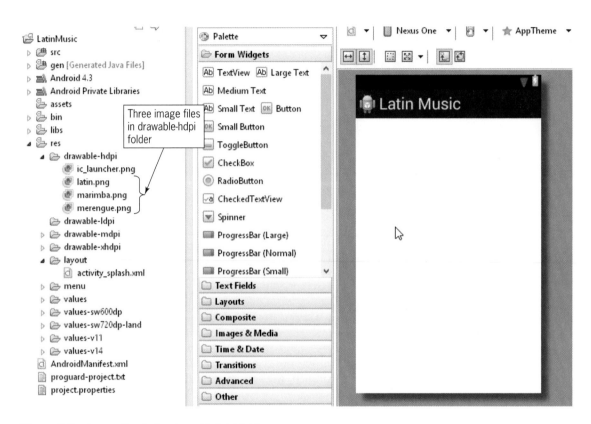

Figure 6-5   Image files in the drawable-hdpi folder

STEP 2

- Expand the res\values folder and then double-tap or double-click the strings.xml file.

- Tap or click the Add button, select String, and then tap or click the OK button.

- Type **txtSplash** in the Name text box and type **Sounds of the Caribbean** in the Value text box.

- Tap or click the Add button, select String, and then tap or click the OK button.

- Type **marimba** in the Name text box and type **Marimba Image** in the Value text box.

- Tap or click the Add button, select String, and then tap or click the OK button.
- Type **merengue** in the Name text box and type **Merengue Image** in the Value text box.
- Tap or click the Add button, select String, and then tap or click the OK button.
- Type **btnMarimba** in the Name text box and type **Play Marimba Song** in the Value text box.
- Tap or click the Add button, select String, and then tap or click the OK button.
- Type **btnMerengue** in the Name text box and type **Play Merengue Song** in the Value text box.

The strings.xml file contains the String values necessary in this app (Figure 6-6).

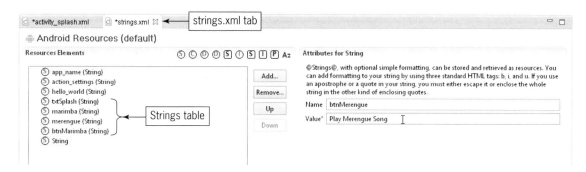

Figure 6-6   The strings.xml file

STEP 3

- Save your work and close the strings.xml tab.
- If necessary, open the activity_splash.xml layout file, and then delete the Hello world! placeholder.
- In the Form Widgets category in the Palette, drag the TextView control to the emulator.
- Display the Properties pane and with the TextView control selected, tap or click the ellipsis button in the Text property and select txtSplash. Tap or click the OK button.
- Type **#CC6600** for the Text Color property.
- Set the Text Size property to **33sp**.
- Tap or click to the right of the Text style property, and then tap or click bold.
- Tap or click the OK button.
- Tap or click to the right of the Gravity property, tap or click the ellipsis button, and then select the top check box and the right check box to place the text in the top right part of the screen.
- Tap or click the OK button.

- If necessary, scroll down the Properties pane, and in the Background property, tap or click the ellipsis button.

- In the Reference Chooser dialog box, expand the Drawable folder and then tap or click latin. Tap or click the OK button.

- Resize the image to fit the emulator window.

A TextView control with an image background is displayed in the activity_splash.xml file (Figure 6-7).

STEP 4

- Close the activity_splash.xml tab and save your work.

Creating a Timer

When most Android apps open, a splash screen is displayed for a few seconds, often preloading database files and information behind the scenes in large-scale applications. In

Figure 6-7 activity_splash.xml displays a TextView control with a background image

the Latin Music app, a timer is necessary to display the splash.xml file for approximately five seconds before the Main Activity intent is called. A **timer** in Java executes a one-time task, such as displaying an opening splash screen, or performs a continuous process, such as a morning wake-up call set to run at regular intervals.

Timers can be used to pause an action temporarily or to time dependent or repeated activities such as animation in a cartoon application. The timer object uses milliseconds as the unit of time. On an Android device, 1,000 milliseconds is equivalent to about one second. This fixed period of time is supported by two Java classes, namely **TimerTask** and **Timer**. To create a timer, the first step is to create a TimerTask object, as shown in the following syntax:

Code Syntax

```
TimerTask task = new TimerTask( ) {
}
```

GTK

Each time a timer runs its tasks, it executes within a single thread. A **thread** is a single sequential flow of control within a program. Java allows an application to have multiple threads of execution running concurrently. You can assign multiple threads so they occur simultaneously, completing several tasks at the same time. For example, a program could display a splash screen, download files needed for the application, and even play an opening sound at the same time.

A TimerTask invokes a scheduled timer. A timer may remind you of a childhood game called hide-and-seek. Do you remember covering your eyes and counting to 50 while your friends found a hiding spot before you began searching for everyone? A timer might only count to five seconds (5,000 milliseconds), but in a similar fashion, the application pauses while the timer counts to the established time limit. After the timed interval is completed, the program resumes and continues with the next task.

After entering the TimerTask code, point to the red error line under the TimerTask( ) to add the run( ) method, an auto-generated method stub, as shown in the following code syntax. Any statements within the braces of the run( ) method are executed after the TimerTask class is invoked.

Code Syntax

```
TimerTask task = new TimerTask( ) {
    @Override
    public void run( ) {
        // TODO Auto-generated method stub
    }
```

The TimerTask must implement a run method that is called by the timer when the task is scheduled for execution. To add a TimerTask class to the Splash Activity, follow these steps:

STEP 1

- In the Package Explorer, expand the src folder, expand net.androidbootcamp.latinmusic, and then double-tap or double-click Splash.java to open the code window.

- Press the Enter key to insert a new line after Line 12, and then type **TimerTask task = new TimerTask( ) {** to add the TimerTask, and then press the Enter key.

- Point to the red error line below TimerTask( ).

The TimerTask class is initiated and the quick fixes are displayed (Figure 6-8).

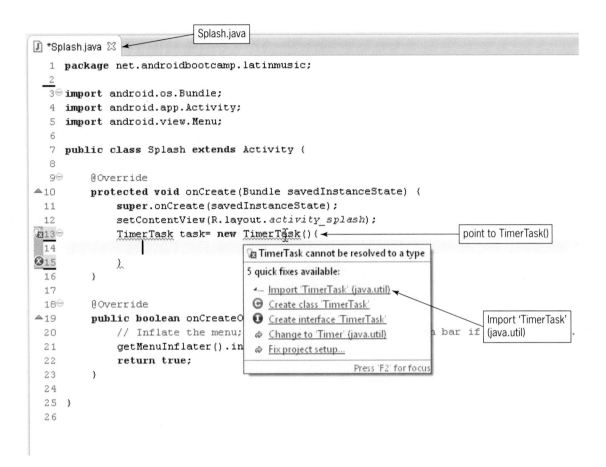

Figure 6-8   setContentView and TimerTask statements

STEP 2

- Add the import statement by tapping or clicking Import 'TimerTask' (java.util).

- Point to TimerTask( ) again to view the quick fix.

- Select Add unimplemented methods to add the auto-generated method stub for the run method.

- To complete the stub, tap or click to right of } in Line 23 at the end of the stub, and then type a semicolon to close the class.

The auto-generated stub for the run method is created automatically (Figure 6-9).

```
 9  public class Splash extends Activity {
10
11      @Override
12      protected void onCreate(Bundle savedInstanceState) {
13          super.onCreate(savedInstanceState);
14          setContentView(R.layout.activity_splash);
15          TimerTask task= new TimerTask(){
16
17              @Override
18              public void run() {
19                  // TODO Auto-generated method stub
20
21              }
22
23          };  I  ◄────── Semicolon ends stub
24      }
```
run( ) method stub
```
26      @Override
27      public boolean onCreateOptionsMenu(Menu menu) {
28          // Inflate the menu; this adds items to the action bar if it is present.
29          getMenuInflater().inflate(R.menu.splash, menu);
30          return true;
31      }
32
33  }
```

Figure 6-9   run( ) method

IN THE TRENCHES
Timers can also be used to display updates of how long an installation is taking by displaying a countdown, monitor what a user is doing, or execute other routines while an Activity is running.

Scheduling a Timer

After including a reference to the TimerTask class, a timer must be scheduled for the amount of time that the splash screen is displayed. The Timer class shown in the following code syntax creates a timed event when the schedule method is called. A delay timer is scheduled in milliseconds using the Timer class. Delay schedules simply prompt an event to occur once at a specified time.

Code Syntax

```
Timer opening = new Timer( );
opening.schedule(task,5000);
```

In the first line of the code syntax, the object named opening initializes a new instance of the Timer class. When the schedule method of the Timer class is called in the second line, two arguments are required. The first parameter (task) is the name of the variable that was initialized for the Timer class. The second parameter represents the number of milliseconds (5,000 milliseconds = about 5 seconds). Follow these steps to add the scheduled timer:

STEP 1

- In the code on the Splash.java tab, after the closing braces for the TimerTask class and the semicolon (Line 23), insert a new line.

- Type **Timer opening = new Timer( );**.

- Point to Timer and tap or click Import 'Timer' (java.util).

An instance of the Timer class is created named opening (Figure 6-10).

```
 9  public class Splash extends Activity {
10
11⊖        @Override
12        protected void onCreate(Bundle savedInstanceState) {
13            super.onCreate(savedInstanceState);
14            setContentView(R.layout.activity_splash);
15⊖            TimerTask task = new TimerTask( ) {
16
17⊖                @Override
18                public void run() {
19                    // TODO Auto-generated method stub
20
21                }                                    Instance of Timer
22
23            };
24            Timer opening = new Timer( );|    I
25        }
26
```

Figure 6-10   Timer class

STEP 2

- To schedule a timer using the schedule method from the Timer class to pause for five seconds, press the Enter key to insert a new line.

- Type **opening.schedule (task,5000);**.

The timer lasting five seconds is scheduled (Figure 6-11).

```
10  public class Splash extends Activity {
11
12⊖      @Override
13      protected void onCreate(Bundle savedInstanceState) {
14          super.onCreate(savedInstanceState);
15          setContentView(R.layout.activity_splash);
16⊖         TimerTask task= new TimerTask(){
17
18⊖             @Override
19             public void run() {
20                 // TODO Auto-generated method stub
21
22             }
23
24          };
25          Timer opening = new Timer( );
26          opening.schedule (task,5000);| I
27      }
28
```

> Timer scheduled for 5 seconds

Figure 6-11 Timer scheduled for 5 seconds

IN THE TRENCHES
Be careful not to code excessively long timers that waste the time of the user. A user-friendly program runs smoothly without long delays.

Life and Death of an Activity

In Line 13 of the Latin Music app, as shown in Figure 6-11, the Splash Activity begins its life in the Activity life cycle with the onCreate( ) method. Each Activity has a **life cycle**, which is the series of actions from the beginning of an Activity to its end. Actions that occur during the life cycle provide ways to manage how users interact with your app. Each Activity in this book begins with an onCreate( ) method. The onCreate( ) method initializes the user interface with an XML layout; the life of the Activity is started. As in any life cycle, the opposite of birth is death. In this case, an **onDestroy( ) method** is the end of the Activity. The onCreate( ) method sets up all the resources required to perform the Activity, and onDestroy( ) releases those same resources to free up memory on your mobile device. The life cycle of the Splash Activity also begins with onCreate( ) and ends with onDestroy( ). Other actions can take place during the life of the Activity. For example, when the scheduled timer starts (Line 25 in Figure 6-11), the Splash Activity is paused. If you open multiple apps on a smartphone and receive a phone call, you must either pause or terminate the other apps to secure enough available memory to respond to the incoming call. To handle the life cycle actions between onCreate( ) and onDestroy( ), you use methods such as onRestart( ), onStart( ), onResume( ), onPause( ), and onStop( ). Each of these methods changes the state of the Activity. The four **states** of an Activity determine whether the activity is active, paused, stopped, or dead. The life cycle of an application affects how an app works and how the different parts are being orchestrated. Table 6-1 shows the development of an Activity throughout its life cycle.

Method	Description
onCreate( )	The onCreate( ) method begins each Activity. This method also provides a Bundle containing the Activity's previously frozen state, if it had one.
onRestart( )	If the Activity is stopped, onRestart( ) begins the Activity again. If this method is called, it indicates your Activity is being redisplayed to the user from a stopped state. The onRestart( ) method is always followed by onStart( ).
onStart( )	If the Activity is hidden, onStart( ) makes the Activity visible.
onResume( )	The onResume( ) method is called when the user begins interacting with the Activity. The onResume( ) method is always followed by onPause( ).
onPause( )	This method is called when an Activity is about to resume.
onStop( )	This method hides the Activity.
onDestroy( )	This method destroys the Activity. Typically, the finish( ) method part of onDestroy( ) is used to declare that the Activity is finished; when the next Activity is called, it releases all the resources from the first Activity.

© 2015 Cengage Learning

Table 6-1   Methods used in the life cycle of an Activity

When an Activity is launched using onCreate( ), the app performs the actions in the Activity. In other words, the Activity becomes the top sheet of paper on a stack of papers. When the methods shown in Table 6-1 are used between the onCreate( ) and onDestroy( ) methods, they shuffle the order of the papers in that stack. When onDestroy( ) is called, imagine that the pile of papers is thrown away. The finish( ) method is part of the onDestroy( ) method and is called when the Activity is completed and should be closed. Typically, the finish( ) method occurs directly before another Activity is launched. As an Android developer, you should be well acquainted with the life cycle of Activities because an app that you publish in the Android market must "play" well with all the other apps on a mobile device. For example, your Android app must pause when a text message, phone call, or other event occurs.

The diagram in Figure 6-12 shows the life cycle of an Activity. The rectangles represent the methods you can implement to perform operations when the Activity moves between states. The colored ovals are the possible major states of the Activity.

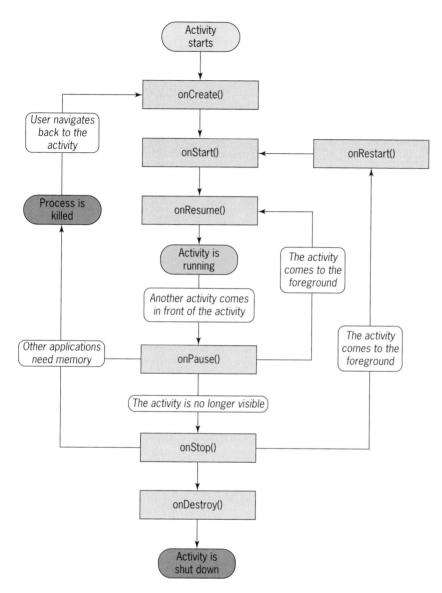

Figure 6-12   Android life cycle
Source: developer.android.com

As an example of the Activity life cycle, the native Android application designed for taking a picture using the built-in camera transitions through each stage in the life cycle. When the user launches the camera app, the camera Activity executes the onCreate( ) method to display the opening screen and the image captured through the camera lens. The user taps a Button control to take a picture. The onStop( ) method is called to hide the live image displayed after the picture is taken. The onRestart( )

method is called after the picture is taken to restart the rest of the app. The onStart( ) method is called to display the picture that was just taken. If the user taps the screen to upload the image to Facebook, the onPause( ) method is called to pause operations of the camera app while the image is uploaded. The onResume( ) method is launched after the picture is uploaded to reactivate the camera. The user can choose to take another image, which repeats the process, or to exit the camera app. If the user selects the exit option, onDestroy( ) or finish( ) frees the saved resources from the temporary memory of the device and closes the camera application.

In the Latin Music application, after the timer pauses the program temporarily, the Splash Activity should be destroyed with onDestroy( ) before launching the second Activity. The app should call the onDestroy( ) method from within the run method of the timer task that was invoked by TimerTask. Doing so guarantees that the ongoing task execution is the last task this timer performs. To close the Splash Activity, follow these steps:

STEP 1

- In Splash.java, tap or click inside the run( ) auto-generated method stub in Line 21 (the blank line below the comment // TODO Auto-generated method stub).

- Type **finish( );**.

The finish( ) statement releases the resources that were created for the Splash Activity and closes the Activity (Figure 6-13).

```
10  public class Splash extends Activity {
11
12    @Override
13    protected void onCreate(Bundle savedInstanceState) {
14        super.onCreate(savedInstanceState);
15        setContentView(R.layout.activity_splash);
16        TimerTask task= new TimerTask(){
17
18            @Override
19            public void run() {
20                // TODO Auto-generated method stub
21                finish();          ⟵  finish( ) method
22            }
23
24        };
25        Timer opening = new Timer( );
26        opening.schedule (task,5000);
27    }
```

Figure 6-13   finish( ) method called

STEP 2

- Save your work.

Launching the Next Activity

After the Activity for the splash screen is destroyed, an intent must request that the next Activity is launched. An XML layout named main.xml already exists as the default layout. A second class named Main must be created before the code can launch this Java class. You must update the Android Manifest file to include the Main Activity. The Main Activity is responsible for playing music. To create a second class and launch the Main Activity, follow these steps:

STEP 1

- In the Package Explorer, press and hold or right-click the net.androidbootcamp.latinmusic folder, point to New on the shortcut menu, and then tap or click Class.

- Type **MainActivity** in the Name text box.

- Tap or click the Superclass Browse button.

- Type **Activity** in the Choose a type text box.

- Tap or click Activity—android.app and then tap or click the OK button to extend the Activity class.

- Tap or click the Finish button to finish creating the MainActivity class.

A second class named MainActivity is created (Figure 6-14).

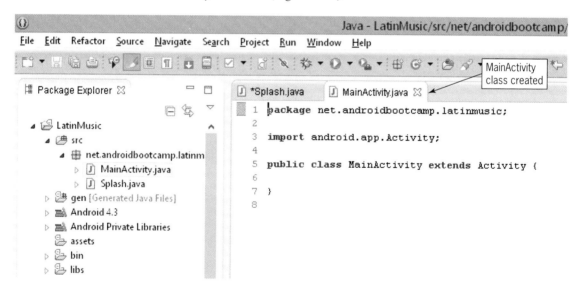

Figure 6-14   Main class created

STEP 2

- In the Package Explorer, scroll down, if necessary, and double-tap or double-click the AndroidManifest.xml file.

- To add the MainActivity class to the Android Manifest, tap or click the Application tab at the bottom of the LatinMusic Manifest page.

- Scroll down to display the Application Nodes section.

- Tap or click the Add button. Select Activity in the Create a new element at the top level, in Application dialog box.

- Tap or click the OK button.

- The Attributes for Activity section opens in the Application tab. In the Name text box in this section, type **.MainActivity**.

- Save your work.

The MainActivity class is added to the Android Manifest file (Figure 6-15).

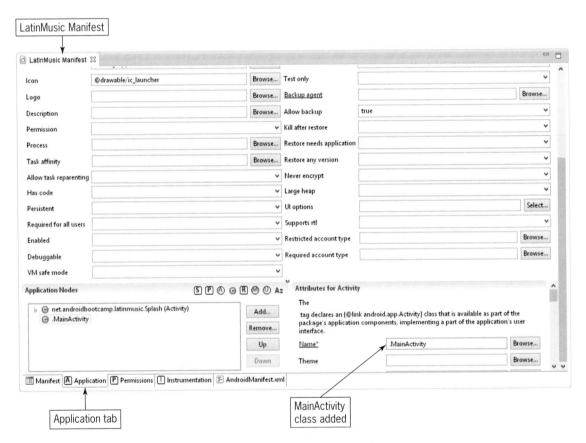

Figure 6-15 Adding the MainActivity class to the Android Manifest

STEP 3

- Close the LatinMusic Manifest tab.

- To launch the MainActivity class from the splash screen, display Splash.java.

- Insert a new line in the run( ) auto-generated method stub after the finish( ); statement.

- Type **startActivity(new Intent(Splash.this, MainActivity.class));** to launch the second Activity.

- Point to the red error line below Intent and select Import 'Intent' (android.content). Save your work.

The second Activity named MainActivity is launched with an Intent statement (Figure 6-16).

```
 1  package net.androidbootcamp.latinmusic;
 2
 3⊕ import java.util.Timer;▯
 9
10  public class Splash extends Activity {
11
12⊝     @Override
▲13     protected void onCreate(Bundle savedInstanceState) {
14         super.onCreate(savedInstanceState);
15         setContentView(R.layout.activity_splash);
16⊝     TimerTask task = new TimerTask( ) {
17
18⊝         @Override
▲19         public void run() {
  20            // TODO Auto-generated method stub
21            finish();
22            startActivity(new Intent(Splash.this, MainActivity.class));▏
23         }
24
25         };
26         Timer opening = new Timer( );
27         opening.schedule (task,5000);
28     }
29
30⊝     @Override
▲31     public boolean onCreateOptionsMenu(Menu menu) {
32         // Inflate the menu; this adds items to the action bar if it is present.
33         getMenuInflater().inflate(R.menu.splash, menu);
34         return true;
35     }
36
37  }
38
```

Opens MainActivity

Figure 6-16   Splash.java complete code

Designing the activity_main.xml File

In the Latin Music app, after the first Activity displaying the splash screen finishes and the second Activity named MainActivity is launched, a second XML layout file is displayed when the onCreate( ) method is called within the MainActivity.java file. The MainActivity.java file uses the default Relative layout with two ImageView and Button controls. To create and design the XML layout for activity_main.xml, follow these steps:

STEP 1

- Close the Splash.java tab.

- To add the activity_main.xml file, right-tap or right-click the layout folder.

- On the shortcut menu, point to New and then tap or click Other.

- In the New dialog box, tap or click Android XML Layout File, and then tap or click the Next button.

- In the New Android Layout XML File dialog box, type activity_main.xml in the File text box to name the layout file. In the Root Element list, select RelativeLayout.

- Tap or click the Finish button. The emulator window opens.

The second layout file named activity_main.xml is created (Figure 6-17).

STEP 2

- Drag an ImageView control from the Images & Media category of the Palette to the emulator window.

- In the Resource Chooser dialog box, tap or click marimba, and then tap or click the OK button.

- Center the image in the upper third of the emulator.

- With the marimba.png image selected, in the Properties pane, tap or click the plus sign in front of Layout Parameters to expand the properties.

- Change the Height property to **150dp** and the Width to **320dp.**

- Tap or click the Change Margins button on the toolbar, type **20dp** in the Top text box, and then tap or click the OK button.

- Tap or click the Content Description ellipsis button, select marimba, and then tap or click the OK button.

- Drag a Button from the Form Widgets category of the Palette and center it below the image.

Figure 6-17   Second XML layout

- Set the Button Id property to **@+id/btnMarimba.** Tap or click the Yes button and OK button.
- Tap or click the ellipsis button for the Text property, select btnMarimba, and then tap or click the OK button.
- Set the Text Size to **22sp**.
- Tap or click the Change Margins button on the toolbar, and type **10dp** in the Top and Bottom text box. Tap or click the OK button.

The image and button to select the first song named Marimba are designed in activity_main.xml (Figure 6-18).

Figure 6-18 ImageView and Button controls in activity_main.xml

STEP 3

- Drag another ImageView control to the emulator and center it below the Button control.
- In the Resource Chooser dialog box, tap or click merengue, and then tap or click the OK button.
- With the merengue.png image selected, in the Properties pane, tap or click the plus sign in front of Layout Parameters to expand the properties.

- Change the Height property to **150dp** and the Width to **320dp**.

- Tap or click the Content Description ellipsis button, select merengue, and then tap or click the OK button.

- Drag another Button from the Form Widgets category to the emulator and center it below the merengue image.

- Set the Button Id property to **@+id/btnMerengue** and then press Enter. Tap or click the Yes button and OK button.

- Tap or click the ellipsis button for the Text property, select btnMerengue, and then tap or click the OK button.

- Set the Text Size to **22sp**.

- Tap or click the Change Margins button on the toolbar, and type **10dp** in the Top and Bottom text box. Tap or click the OK button.

The image and button to select the second song named Merengue are designed in activity_main.xml (Figure 6-19).

Figure 6-19 activity_main.xml layout complete

Class Variables

In the coding examples used thus far in this book, variables have been local variables. **Local variables** are declared by variable declaration statements within a method, such as a primitive integer variable within an onCreate( ) method. The local variable effectively ceases to exist when the execution of the method is complete. The **scope** of a variable refers to the variable's visibility within a class. Variables that are accessible only to a restricted portion of a program such as a single method are said to have local scope. Variables that are accessible from anywhere in a class, however, are said to have global scope. If a variable is needed in multiple methods within a class, the global variable is assigned at the beginning of a class, not within a method. This global scope variable is called a **class variable** in Java and can be accessed by multiple methods throughout the program. In the chapter project, the Button, MediaPlayer (necessary for playing sound), and an integer variable named playing are needed in the onCreate( ) method and within both onClick( ) methods for each Button control. To keep the value of these variables throughout multiple classes, the variables are defined as class variables that cease to exist when their class or activity is unloaded.

After class variables are defined in MainActivity.java, the onCreate( ) method opens the activity_main.xml layout and defines the two Button controls. The Activity waits for the user to select one of the two buttons, each of which plays a song. If a button is clicked twice, the music pauses. Each button must have a setOnClickListener that awaits the user's tap or click. After the user taps a button, the setOnClickListener method implements the Button.OnClickListener, creating an instance of the OnClickListener and calling the onClick method. The onClick method responds to the user's action. For example, in the chapter project, the response is to play a song. The onClick method is where you place the code to handle playing the song. To code the class variables, display the activity_main.xml layout, reference the two Button controls, and set an OnClickListener, follow these steps:

STEP 1

- Close the activity_main.xml window and save your work.

- Open MainActivity.java and after the public class Main extends Activity statement, create two blank lines.

- On the second line, type **Button btMarimba, btMerengue;** to create a class variable referencing the two Button controls.

- Point to Button and tap or click Import 'Button' (android.widget).

- Insert a new line and then type **MediaPlayer mpMarimba, mpMerengue;** to create a class variable reference for the media player.

- Point to MediaPlayer and tap or click Import 'MediaPlayer' (android.media).

- Insert a new line and then type **int playing;** to create a primitive class variable named playing, which keeps track of whether a song is playing.

Class variables that can be accessed by the rest of the program are initialized (Figure 6-20).

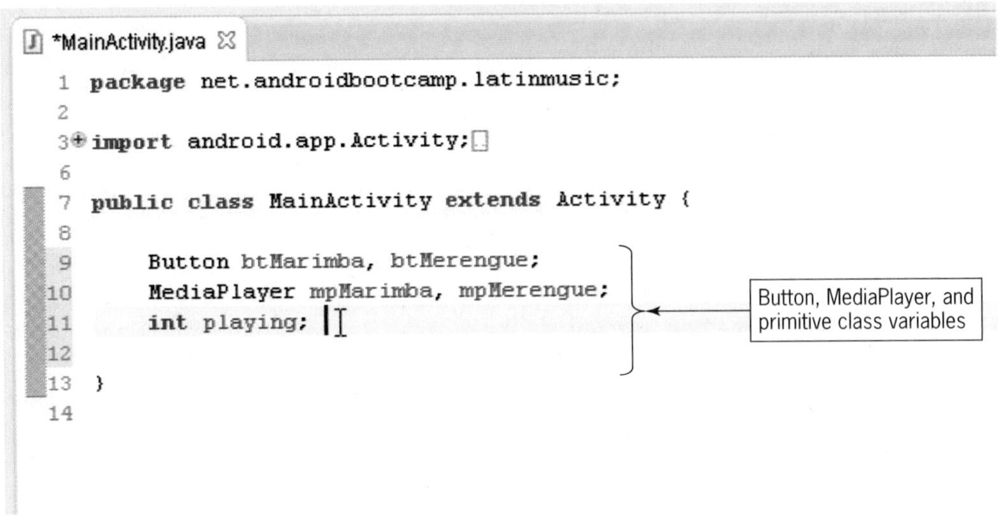

```
 *MainActivity.java  ⌗
  1  package net.androidbootcamp.latinmusic;
  2
  3⊕ import android.app.Activity;
  6
  7  public class MainActivity extends Activity {
  8
  9      Button btMarimba, btMerengue;
 10      MediaPlayer mpMarimba, mpMerengue;
 11      int playing;  |I
 12
 13  }
 14
```

Button, MediaPlayer, and primitive class variables

Figure 6-20   Class variables

STEP 2

- Press the Enter key twice, type **oncreate,** and then press Ctrl+spacebar.

- Double-tap or double-click the first onCreate method in the auto-complete listing to generate the method structure.

- Tap or click after the semicolon, press the Enter key, and then type **setContentView(R.** to display an auto-complete listing.

- Double-tap or double-click layout.

- Type a period and double-tap or double-click activity_main: int—R layout.

- At the end of the line, type a semicolon to complete the statement.

The onCreate method displays the activity_main.xml file (Figure 6-21).

MainActivity.java ⊠

```java
1   package net.androidbootcamp.latinmusic;
2
3⊕ import android.app.Activity;□
7
8   public class MainActivity extends Activity {
9
10      Button btMarimba, btMerengue;
11      MediaPlayer mpMarimba, mpMerengue;
12      int playing;
13
14⊖     @Override
15      protected void onCreate(Bundle savedInstanceState) {
16          // TODO Auto-generated method stub
17          super.onCreate(savedInstanceState);
18          setContentView(R.layout.activity_main);
19      }
20  }
21
```

onCreate method opens activity_main.xml

Figure 6-21   onCreate method

STEP 3

- Both Button references were made as class variables. To create an instance of each Button control, press the Enter key and type **btMarimba = (Button)findViewById(R.id.btnMarimba);**.

- Press the Enter key and then type **btMerengue = (Button)findViewById(R.id.btnMerengue);**.

The Button controls named btnMarimba and btnMerengue are referenced in MainActivity.java (Figure 6-22).

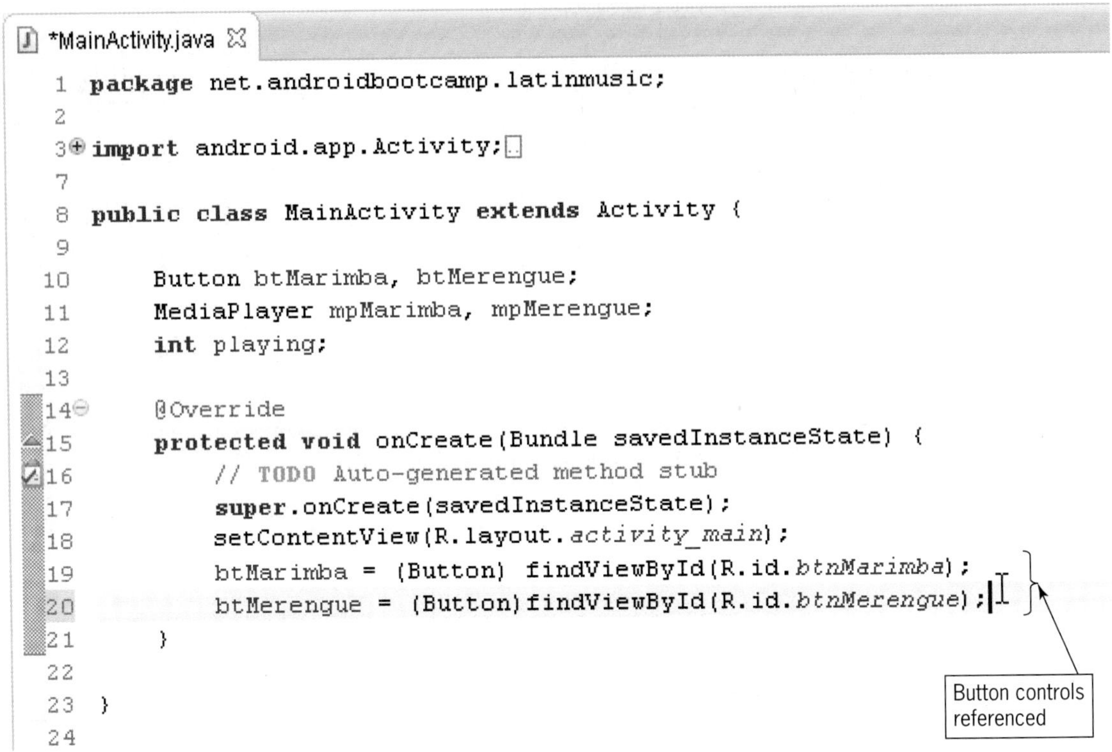

```java
J *MainActivity.java ⊠
 1  package net.androidbootcamp.latinmusic;
 2
 3⊕ import android.app.Activity;
 7
 8  public class MainActivity extends Activity {
 9
10      Button btMarimba, btMerengue;
11      MediaPlayer mpMarimba, mpMerengue;
12      int playing;
13
14⊝     @Override
15      protected void onCreate(Bundle savedInstanceState) {
16          // TODO Auto-generated method stub
17          super.onCreate(savedInstanceState);
18          setContentView(R.layout.activity_main);
19          btMarimba = (Button) findViewById(R.id.btnMarimba);
20          btMerengue = (Button)findViewById(R.id.btnMerengue);
21      }
22
23  }
24
```

Button controls referenced

Figure 6-22 Adding Button controls

STEP 4

- To create a setOnClickListener method so the btMarimba Button waits for the user's tap, press the Enter key and type **btMarimba.setOnClickListener(bMarimba);**.

- To create an instance of the Button OnClickListener, tap or click between the two ending braces (Line 23) and type **Button.OnClickListener bMarimba = new Button.OnClickListener( ) {** and then press the Enter key.

- Place a semicolon after the closing brace on Line 25.

- This OnClickListener is designed for a class variable for a Button. Point to the red error line below Button.OnClickListener and select Add unimplemented methods to add the quick fix.

An OnClickListener auto-generated stub appears in the code for the first button (Figure 6-23).

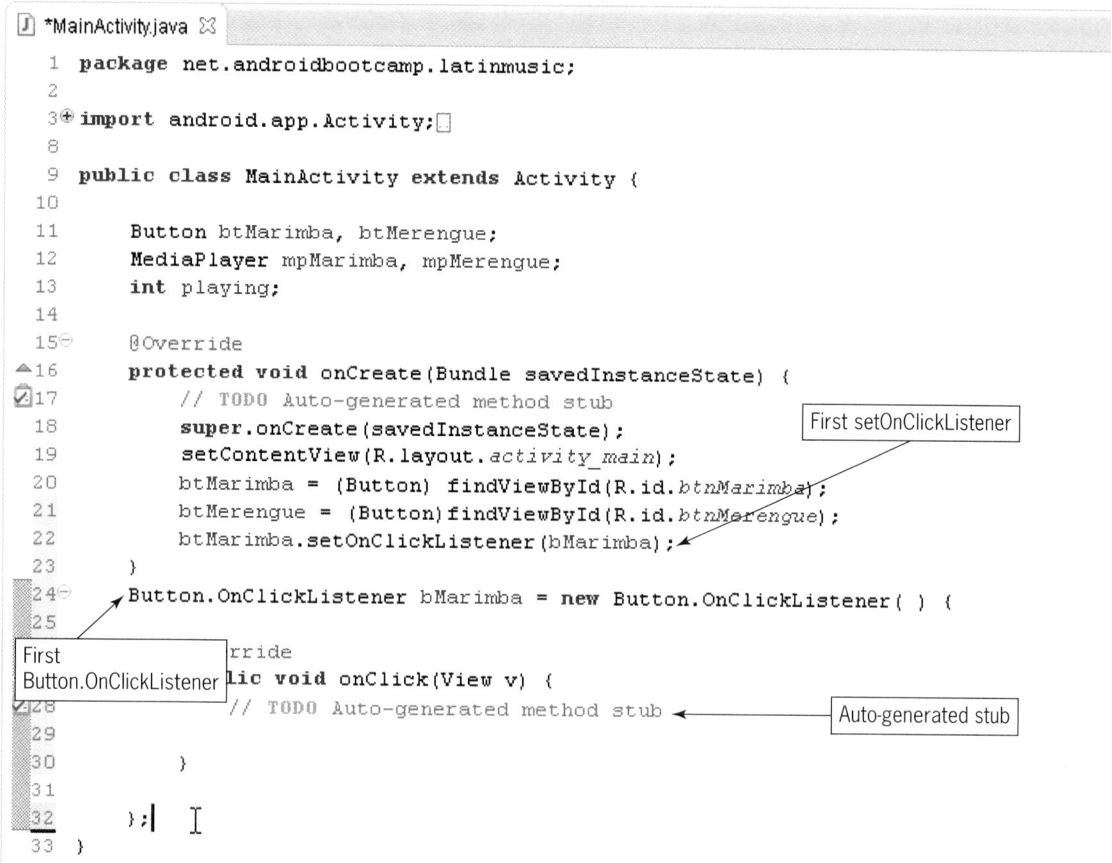

```
J *MainActivity.java ⋈
  1  package net.androidbootcamp.latinmusic;
  2
  3⊕ import android.app.Activity;☐
  8
  9  public class MainActivity extends Activity {
 10
 11       Button btMarimba, btMerengue;
 12       MediaPlayer mpMarimba, mpMerengue;
 13       int playing;
 14
 15⊖      @Override
▲16       protected void onCreate(Bundle savedInstanceState) {
☑17           // TODO Auto-generated method stub
 18           super.onCreate(savedInstanceState);
 19           setContentView(R.layout.activity_main);
 20           btMarimba = (Button) findViewById(R.id.btnMarimba);
 21           btMerengue = (Button) findViewById(R.id.btnMerengue);
 22           btMarimba.setOnClickListener(bMarimba);
 23       }
 24⊖   Button.OnClickListener bMarimba = new Button.OnClickListener( ) {
 25
          rride
          lic void onClick(View v) {
               // TODO Auto-generated method stub
 29
 30           }
 31
 32       };|  I
 33  }
```

First setOnClickListener

First Button.OnClickListener

Auto-generated stub

Figure 6-23 Inserting the first Button.OnClickListener stub

STEP 5

- To create a setOnClickListener method so the btMerengue Button waits for the user's tap or click, tap or click after the btMarimba.setOnClickListener(bMarimba); statement and then press the Enter key.

- Type **btMerengue.setOnClickListener(bMerengue);**.

- To create an instance of the btnMerengue button OnClickListener, tap or click after the brace with the semicolon at the end of the code in line 33 and then press the Enter key.

- Type **Button.OnClickListener bMerengue = new Button.OnClickListener( ) {** and then press the Enter key to create the closing brace.

- Place a semicolon after this closing brace on Line 36.
- Point to the red error line below Button.OnClickListener and select Add unimplemented methods to add the quick fix. Save your work.

An OnClickListener auto-generated stub appears in the code for the second button (Figure 6-24).

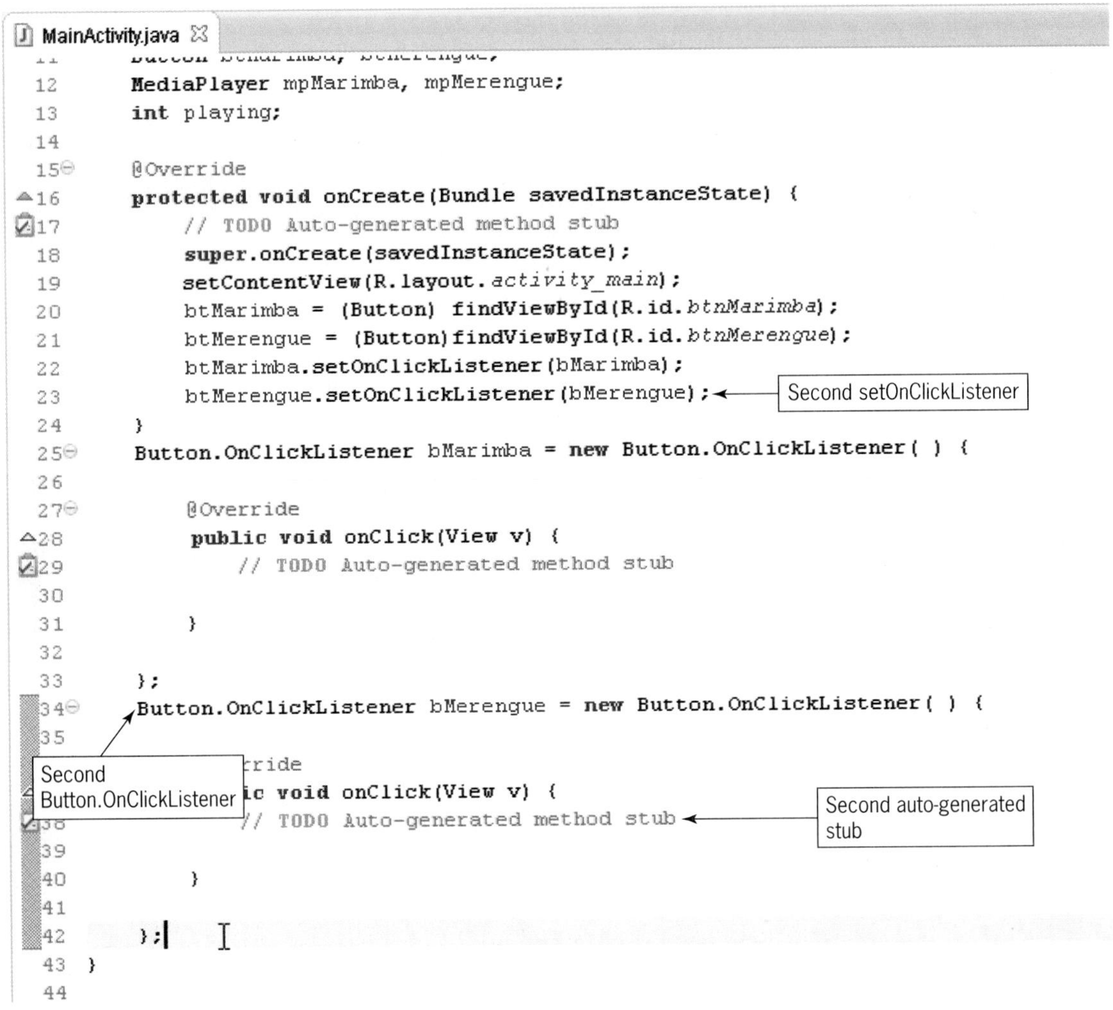
MainActivity.java
12 MediaPlayer mpMarimba, mpMerengue;
13 int playing;
14
15 @Override
16 protected void onCreate(Bundle savedInstanceState) {
17 // TODO Auto-generated method stub
18 super.onCreate(savedInstanceState);
19 setContentView(R.layout.activity_main);
20 btMarimba = (Button) findViewById(R.id.btnMarimba);
21 btMerengue = (Button)findViewById(R.id.btnMerengue);
22 btMarimba.setOnClickListener(bMarimba);
23 btMerengue.setOnClickListener(bMerengue);
24 }
25 Button.OnClickListener bMarimba = new Button.OnClickListener( ) {
26
27 @Override
28 public void onClick(View v) {
29 // TODO Auto-generated method stub
30
31 }
32
33 };
34 Button.OnClickListener bMerengue = new Button.OnClickListener( ) {
35
ride
ic void onClick(View v) {
// TODO Auto-generated method stub
39
40 }
41
42 };
43 }
44
Second setOnClickListener
Second Button.OnClickListener
Second auto-generated stub

Figure 6-24 Inserting the second Button.OnClickListener stub

Playing Music

Every Android phone and tablet includes a built-in music player where you can store your favorite music. You can also write your own applications that offer music playback capabilities. To enable the Latin Music chapter project to play two songs, Android includes a MediaPlayer class that can play both audio and music files. Android lets you play audio and video from several types of data sources. You can play audio or video from media files stored in the application's resources (a folder named raw), from stand-alone files in the Android file system of the device, from an SD (Secure Digital) memory card in the phone itself, or from a data stream provided through an Internet connection. The most common file type of media supported for audio playback with the MediaPlayer class is .mp3, but other audio file types such as .wav, .ogg, and .midi are typically supported by most Android hardware. The Android device platform supports a wide variety of media types based on the codecs included in the device by the manufacturer. A **codec** is a computer technology used to compress and decompress audio and video files.

IN THE TRENCHES

The Android platform provides a class to record audio and video, where supported by the mobile device hardware. To record audio or video, use the MediaRecorder class. The emulator does not provide the capability to capture audio or video, but an actual mobile device can record media input, accessible through the MediaRecorder class.

Creating a Raw Folder for Music Files

In an Android project, music files are typically stored in a subfolder of the res folder called raw. In newer versions of Android, the raw folder must be created before music files can be placed in that folder. The two .mp3 files played in the Latin Music app are named marimba.mp3 and merengue. mp3, and they should be placed in the raw folder. To create a raw folder that contains music files, follow these steps:

STEP 1

- In the Package Explorer, press and hold or right-click the res folder.

- Point to New on the shortcut menu and then tap or click Folder. The New Folder dialog box opens.

- In the Folder name text box, type **raw.**

A folder named raw is created using the New Folder dialog box (Figure 6-25).

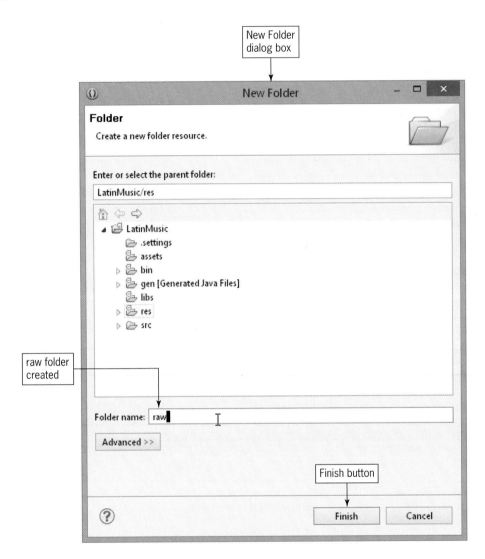

Figure 6-25 New Folder dialog box

STEP 2

- Tap or click the Finish button.

- To add the project music files to the raw folder, open the USB folder containing your student files.

- To add the two music files to the raw resource folder, select marimba.mp3 and merengue.mp3, and then drag the files to the raw folder until a plus sign pointer appears. Release the mouse button.

- If necessary, tap or click the Copy files option button and then tap or click the OK button. Expand the raw folder.

Copies of the music files appear in the raw folder (Figure 6-26).

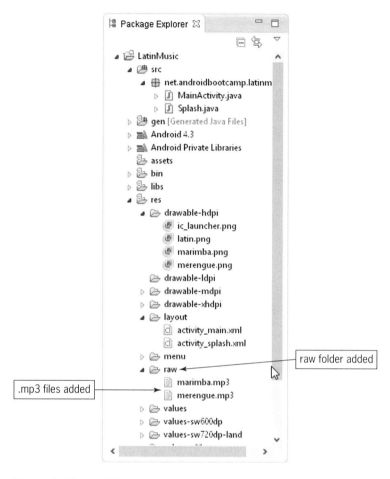

.mp3 files added

raw folder added

Figure 6-26   MP3 files added to raw folder

Using the MediaPlayer Class

The **MediaPlayer class** provides the methods to control audio playback on an Android device. At the beginning of the MainActivity.java code, two MediaPlayer class variables are declared. After the variables are declared, an instance of the MediaPlayer class is assigned to each variable. In the following code syntax, mpMarimba is assigned to an instance of the MediaPlayer class that accesses the marimba music file in the raw folder.

Code Syntax

```
MediaPlayer mpMarimba = MediaPlayer.create(this, R.raw.marimba);
```

The class variables mpMarimba and mpMerengue are assigned the music files from the raw folder. To declare an instance of the MediaPlayer class, follow this step:

STEP 1

- In MainActivity java, press the Enter key after the btMerengue.setOnClickListener(bMerengue); statement (Line 23) to create a new line.

- Type **mpMarimba = new MediaPlayer( );** to create a new instance of MediaPlayer.

- Insert a new line and type **mpMarimba = MediaPlayer.create(this, R.raw.marimba);** to assign the first song to mpMarimba. Press the Enter key after the closing semicolon.

- Type **mpMerengue = new MediaPlayer( );** to add an instance for the second MediaPlayer variable.

- Insert a new line and type **mpMerengue = MediaPlayer.create(this, R.raw.merengue);** to assign the second song to mpMerengue.

The two class variables are assigned an instance of the MediaPlayer class (Figure 6-27).

```
15⊖      @Override
 16      protected void onCreate(Bundle savedInstanceState) {
 17          // TODO Auto-generated method stub
 18          super.onCreate(savedInstanceState);
 19          setContentView(R.layout.activity_main);
 20          btMarimba = (Button) findViewById(R.id.btnMarimba);
 21          btMerengue = (Button) findViewById(R.id.btnMerengue);
 22          btMarimba.setOnClickListener(bMarimba);
 23          btMerengue.setOnClickListener(bMerengue);
 24          mpMarimba = new MediaPlayer( );
 25          mpMarimba = MediaPlayer.create(this, R.raw.marimba);
 26          mpMerengue = new MediaPlayer( );
 27          mpMerengue = MediaPlayer.create(this, R.raw.merengue);
 28      }
 29⊖  Button.OnClickListener bMarimba = new Button.OnClickListe      MediaPlayer
 30                                                                    statements for
 31⊖          @Override                                               both songs
 32          public void onClick(View v) {
 33              // TODO Auto-generated method stub
 34
 35          }
 36
 37      };
 38⊖  Button.OnClickListener bMerengue = new Button.OnClickListener( ) {
 39
```

Figure 6-27 MediaPlayer instance statements

GTK

Music can be used in many ways throughout Android apps. Music can provide sound effects to inform the user of a recent email or to praise you when you reach the winning level on your favorite game. Background music is often used as a soundtrack to create a theme in an adventure game.

The MediaPlayer State

Android uses the MediaPlayer class to control the playing of the audio file. Whether the music file is playing is called the state of the MediaPlayer. The three common states of the audio file are when the music starts, when the music pauses, and when the music stops. The state of the music is established by the MediaPlayer's temporary behavior. Table 6-2 provides an example of the most common MediaPlayer states.

Method	Purpose
start( )	Starts media playback
pause( )	Pauses media playback
stop( )	Stops media playback

Table 6-2   Common MediaPlayer states

© 2015 Cengage Learning

In the Latin Music project, the user first taps a button to start the music playing. The start( ) method is used to begin the playback of the selected music file. When the user taps the same button again, the music temporarily pauses the music file by calling the pause( ) method. To restart the song, the start( ) method must be called again. To determine the state of MediaPlayer, the code must assess if this is the first time the user is tapping the button to start the song or if the user is tapping the same button twice to pause the song. The user can tap the button a third time to start the song again. This cycle continues until the user exits the project. In the chapter project, an integer variable named playing is initially set to zero. Each time the user taps the button, the playing variable changes value. The first time the user taps the button, the variable is changed to the value of 1 to assist the program in determining the state of the MediaPlayer. If the user taps the same button again to pause the song, the variable changes to the value of 0. Android does not have a method for determining the present state of the MediaPlayer, but by using this simple primitive variable, you can keep track of the state of the music. A Switch decision structure uses the variable named playing to change the state of the music. The onClick( ) method is called every time the user selects a button. To initiate the variable used to determine the state of MediaPlayer and to code a Switch decision structure to determine the state, follow these steps:

STEP 1

- In MainActivity.java, press the Enter key after the mpMerengue = MediaPlayer.create(this, R.raw.merengue); statement (Line 27) to create a new line.

- Type **playing = 0;** to initialize the variable named playing as the value 0. When the user clicks a button, the Switch statement follows the path of case 0, which begins the audio playback of one of the songs.

The variable named playing is initialized as the value 0 (Figure 6-28).

```
15⊖        @Override
16        protected void onCreate(Bundle savedInstanceState) {
17            // TODO Auto-generated method stub
18            super.onCreate(savedInstanceState);
19            setContentView(R.layout.activity_main);
20            btMarimba = (Button) findViewById(R.id.btnMarimba);
21            btMerengue = (Button) findViewById(R.id.btnMerengue);
22            btMarimba.setOnClickListener(bMarimba);
23            btMerengue.setOnClickListener(bMerengue);
24            mpMarimba = new MediaPlayer( );
25            mpMarimba = MediaPlayer.create(this, R.raw.marimba);
26            mpMerengue = new MediaPlayer( );
27            mpMerengue = MediaPlayer.create(this, R.raw.merengue)
28            playing = 0; [|
29        }
30⊖    Button.OnClickListener bMarimba = new Button.OnClickListener( ) {
31
32⊖        @Override
33        public void onClick(View v) {
34            // TODO Auto-generated method stub
35
36        }
37
38    };
39⊖    Button.OnClickListener bMerengue = new Button.OnClickListener( ) {
40
```

Variable that changes as state of the music changes

Figure 6-28   Variable named "playing" is set to 0

STEP 2

- Inside the braces of the first onClick method (after the // TODO comment in line 34), tap or click blank Line 35 and then type the following Switch decision structure that is used to determine the state of the music:

```
switch(playing) {
    case 0:
        mpMarimba.start( );
        playing = 1;
        break;
    case 1:
        mpMarimba.pause( );
        playing = 0;
        break;
}
```

The Switch decision structure that determines the state of the music is coded for the first onClick method (Figure 6-29).

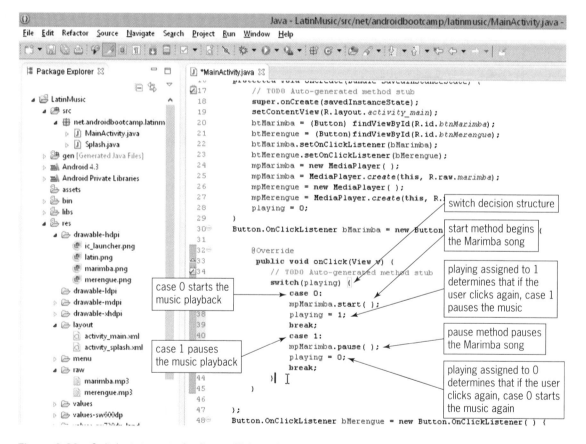

Figure 6-29   Switch statements for first onClick method

IN THE TRENCHES
Music playback control operation may fail due to various reasons, such as unsupported audio/video format, poorly interleaved audio/video, file size overwhelming memory capabilities, or a streaming timeout on the Internet.

Changing the Text Property Using Code

When the user selects a song to play, the Button control with the text "Play Marimba Song" is tapped. To pause the song, the user must tap the same button, but the text should be changed to a more fitting action, such as "Pause Marimba Song." A property can initially be entered in the XML layout or coded in Java. In Chapter 4, the setText( ) method displays text in the TextView control. To change the Text property for a Button control using Java code, the control name and the setText( ) method are separated by a period that precedes a string of text within parentheses, as shown in the following code syntax:

Code Syntax

```
btMarimba.setText("Pause Marimba Song");
```

The btMarimba Button control displays the text "Pause Marimba Song." If the user wants to restart the song, a second setText( ) method changes the text back to "Play Marimba Song." To change the text on the Button control for the first button, follow these steps:

STEP 1

- In MainActivity.java in the first onClick( ) method, press the Enter key after the statement playing = 1; in case 0 (Line 38).
- Type **btMarimba.setText("Pause Marimba Song");** to change the text displayed on the Button control.
- To change the text back to the original text if the user restarts the music, in case 1 of the Switch decision structure, press the Enter key after the statement playing = 0; (Line 43).
- Type **btMarimba.setText("Play Marimba Song");** to change the text displayed on the Button control.

The first button changes text while the music is paused or restarted (Figure 6-30).

```
26          mpMerengue = new MediaPlayer( );
27          mpMerengue = MediaPlayer.create(this, R.raw.merengue);
28          playing = 0;
29      }
30      Button.OnClickListener bMarimba = new Button.OnClickListener( ) {
31
32          @Override
33          public void onClick(View v) {
34              // TODO Auto-generated method stub
35              switch(playing) {
36                  case 0:
37                  mpMarimba.start( );
38                  playing = 1;
39                  btMarimba.setText("Pause Marimba Song");
40                  break;
41                  case 1:
42                  mpMarimba.pause( );
43                  playing = 0;
44                  btMarimba.setText("Play Marimba Song");
45                  break;
46              }
47          }
48
49      };
50      Button.OnClickListener bMerengue = new Button.OnClickListener( ) {
```

setText ( ) changes the Button text

Figure 6-30 The setText( ) method changes the button control in both case statements

STEP 2

- To test the music and text on the first Button control, save and run the program. The second Button control has not been coded yet.

When you tap the first Button control, the Marimba song plays and the Button text is changed. You can restart or pause the music by pressing the button again (Figure 6-31).

Kevin badbuder/Getty Images; Don Bayley /E+/Getty Images

Text will change to Pause Marimba Song when the user taps the Play Marimba Song button

Play Marimba Song

Figure 6-31 Coding the button

Changing the Visibility Property Using Code

When the program is complete, the user can select the button that plays the Marimba song or the Merengue song. One issue that must be resolved is that it is possible to tap the Marimba song button and then tap the Merengue button, playing both songs at once. To resolve this problem, when the user selects one of the songs, the button to the other song can be coded to disappear until the user has paused the current song from playing. The Java property that controls whether a control is displayed on the emulator is the **Visibility property**. By default, the Visibility property is set to display any control you place on the emulator when the program runs. To cause the control not to appear, you must code the setVisibility property to change the view to invisible. To change the visibility of the button to reappear, the setVisibility property is changed to visible, as shown in the following code syntax:

Code Syntax

```
To hide the control:     btMarimba.setVisibility(View.INVISIBLE);
To display the control:  btMarimba.setVisibility(View.VISIBLE);
```

To set the setVisibility property for the Marimba button control to change the view to invisible and to copy and paste the code for the first onClick code to create a Switch decision structure for the second button, you can complete the following steps:

STEP 1

- In MainActivity.java in the first onClick( ) method in the case 0 option, press the Enter key after the statement btMarimba.setText("Pause Marimba Song");

- Type **btMerengue.setVisibility(View.INVISIBLE);** to hide the Merengue button when the Marimba song is playing. When the music is paused, the Merengue button should be visible again.

- In the case 1 option, press the Enter key after the statement btMarimba.setText("Play Marimba Song");.

- Type **btMerengue.setVisibility(View.VISIBLE);** to change the visibility of the Merengue button.

The Merengue button is hidden when the music plays and displayed when the music stops (Figure 6-32).

```
28              playing = 0;
29          }
30⊖      Button.OnClickListener bMarimba = new Button.OnClickListener( ) {
31
32⊖          @Override
33          public void onClick(View v) {
34              // TODO Auto-generated method stub
35              switch(playing) {
36                  case 0:
37                  mpMarimba.start( );
38                  playing = 1;
39                  btMarimba.setText("Pause Marimba Song");
40                  btMerengue.setVisibility(View.INVISIBLE);
41                  break;
42                  case 1:
43                  mpMarimba.pause( );
44                  playing = 0;
45                  btMarimba.setText("Play Marimba Song");
46                  btMerengue.setVisibility(View.VISIBLE);
47                  break;
48              }
49          }
50
51      };
52⊖      Button.OnClickListener bMerengue = new Button.OnClickListener( ) {
53
```

setVisibility( ) method hides Merengue button

setVisibility( ) method displays Merengue button

Figure 6-32   The setVisibility( ) method changes the visibility of the Button control

STEP 2

- To code the second onClick( ) method for Merengue button, select and copy Lines 35–48 in Figure 6-32 by clicking Edit on the menu bar and then clicking Copy. Tap or click Line 57 inside the second onClick() method, tap or click Edit on the menu bar, and then tap or click Paste. Change every reference of mpMarimba to **mpMerengue.** Change every reference of btMarimba to **btMerengue** or vice versa.

- Change the setText messages to read **Pause Merengue Song** and **Play Merengue Song.** You might need to add }; as the second-to-last line of code. Compare your code with the complete code, making changes as necessary.

The second onClick( ) method is coded using a Switch decision structure (Figure 6-33).

```
*MainActivity.java
 1  package net.androidbootcamp.latinmusic;
 2
 3  import android.app.Activity;
 8
 9  public class MainActivity extends Activity {
10
11      Button btMarimba, btMerengue;
12      MediaPlayer mpMarimba, mpMerengue;
13      int playing;
14
15      @Override
16      protected void onCreate(Bundle savedInstanceState) {
17          // TODO Auto-generated method stub
18          super.onCreate(savedInstanceState);
19          setContentView(R.layout.activity_main);
20          btMarimba = (Button) findViewById(R.id.btnMarimba);
21          btMerengue = (Button)findViewById(R.id.btnMerengue);
22          btMarimba.setOnClickListener(bMarimba);
23          btMerengue.setOnClickListener(bMerengue);
24          mpMarimba = new MediaPlayer( );
25          mpMarimba = MediaPlayer.create(this, R.raw.marimba);
26          mpMerengue = new MediaPlayer( );
27          mpMerengue = MediaPlayer.create(this, R.raw.merengue);
28          playing = 0;
29      }
30      Button.OnClickListener bMarimba = new Button.OnClickListener( ) {
31
32          @Override
33          public void onClick(View v) {
34              // TODO Auto-generated method stub
35              switch(playing) {
36                  case 0:
37                  mpMarimba.start( );
38                  playing = 1;
39                  btMarimba.setText("Pause Marimba Song");
40                  btMerengue.setVisibility(View.INVISIBLE);
41                  break;
42                  case 1:
43                  mpMarimba.pause( );
44                  playing = 0;
45                  btMarimba.setText("Play Marimba Song");
46                  btMerengue.setVisibility(View.VISIBLE);
47                  break;
48              }
49          }
50
51      };
52      Button.OnClickListener bMerengue = new Button.OnClickListener( ) {
53
54          @Override
55          public void onClick(View v) {
56              // TODO Auto-generated method stub
57              switch(playing) {
58                  case 0:
59                  mpMerengue.start( );
60                  playing = 1;
61                  btMerengue.setText("Pause Merengue Song");
62                  btMarimba.setVisibility(View.INVISIBLE);
63                  break;
64                  case 1:
65                  mpMerengue.pause( );
66                  playing = 0;
67                  btMerengue.setText("Play Merengue Song");
68                  btMarimba.setVisibility(View.VISIBLE);
```

Merengue button is coded

Figure 6-33   Complete code for MainActivity.java

Running and Testing the Application

Your first experience with media in an Android application is complete. Tap or click Run on the menu bar and then select Run to save and test the application in the emulator. If necessary, select Android Application and tap or click the OK button. Save all the files in the next dialog box, if necessary, and unlock the emulator. The application opens in the emulator window, as shown in Figures 6-1 and 6-2. The splash screen opens for five seconds. The activity_main layout screen opens next, requesting your button selection to play each of the songs. Test both buttons and make sure your speakers are on so you can hear the Latin music play.

Wrap It Up—Chapter Summary

In this chapter, the Android platform created a memorable multimedia experience with the sounds of Latin music. A splash screen provided time to load extra files if needed and displayed an initial logo for brand recognition. Methods such as setText( ) and setVisibility( ) helped to create an easy-to-use Android application that was clear to the user. The state of music using the start and pause methods of MediaPlayer filled your classroom or home with the enjoyment of music.

- An Android application can show a splash screen that displays the name of the program, a brand logo for the application, or the name of the author. The splash screen opens as you launch your app, providing time for Android to initialize its resources.

- A TextView widget can display a background color or image stored in one of the project's drawable folders.

- A timer in Java executes a one-time task such as displaying an opening splash screen, or it performs a continuous process such as a wake-up call that rings each morning at the same time. Timers can be used to pause an action temporarily or to time dependent or repeated activities. The timer object uses milliseconds as the unit of time.

- After including a reference to the TimerTask class in your code, schedule a timer for the amount of time that an event occurs, such as a splash screen being displayed.

- Each Activity has a life cycle, which is the series of actions from the beginning of an Activity to its end. An Activity usually starts with the onCreate( ) method, which sets up all the resources required to perform the Activity. An Activity usually ends with the onDestroy( ) method, which releases those same resources to free up memory on the mobile device. Other actions can take place during the life of the Activity, including onRestart( ), onStart( ), onResume( ), onPause( ), and onStop( ).

- Local variables are declared by variable declaration statements within a method. The local variable effectively ceases to exist when the execution of the method is complete.

- The scope of a variable refers to the variable's visibility within a class. Variables that are accessible only to a restricted portion of a program, such as a single method, have local scope. Variables that are accessible from anywhere in a class, however, have global scope. If a variable is needed in multiple methods within a class, the global variable is assigned at the beginning of a class, not within a method. This global scope variable is called a class variable in Java and can be accessed by multiple methods throughout the program.

- Every Android phone and tablet includes a built-in music player where you can store music. You can also write applications that offer music playback capabilities. The media types an Android device platform supports are determined by the codecs the manufacturer included in the device. A codec is a computer technology used to compress and decompress audio and video files.

- In an Android project, music files are typically stored in the res\raw subfolder. In newer versions of Android, you must create the raw subfolder before storing music files.

- The MediaPlayer class provides the methods to control audio playback on an Android device. First declare the MediaPlayer class variables and then assign an instance of the MediaPlayer class to each variable. Whether the music file is playing is called the state of the MediaPlayer. The three common states of the audio file are when the music starts, when the music pauses, and when the music stops.

- The Java property that controls whether a control is displayed on the emulator is the Visibility property. By default, the Visibility property is set to display any control you place on the emulator when the program runs. To cause the control not to appear, you must code the setVisibility property in Java to change the view to invisible. To change the visibility of the button to reappear, change the setVisibility property to visible.

Key Terms

class variable—A variable with global scope; it can be accessed by multiple methods throughout the program.

codec—A computer technology used to compress and decompress audio and video files.

life cycle—The series of actions from the beginning, or birth, of an Activity to its end, or destruction.

local variable—A variable declared by a variable declaration statement within a method.

MediaPlayer class—The Java class that provides the methods to control audio playback on an Android device.

onDestroy( ) method—A method used to end an Activity. Whereas the onCreate( ) method sets up required resources, the onDestroy( ) method releases those same resources to free up memory.

scope—The scope of a variable refers to the variable's visibility within a class.

state—A stage in an Activity's life cycle that determines whether the Activity is active, paused, stopped, or dead.

thread—A single sequential flow of control within a program.

Timer—A Java class that creates a timed event when the schedule method is called.

timer—A tool that performs a one-time task such as displaying an opening splash screen or performs a continuous process such as a morning wake-up call set to run at regular intervals.

TimerTask—A Java class that invokes a scheduled timer.

Visibility property—The Java property that controls whether a control is displayed on the emulator.

Developer FAQs

1. What is the name of the initial window that typically displays a company logo for a few seconds?

2. Which property of TextView displays a solid color behind the text?

3. Which property of TextView displays an image as a backdrop behind the text?

4. Write a line of code that creates an instance of the TimerTask class with the object named welcome.

5. Write a line of code that creates an instance of the Timer class with the object named stopwatch.

6. Write a line of code that would hold the initial opening screen for four seconds. The Timer object is named stopwatch and the TimerTask object is named welcome.

7. How long (identify units) does this statement schedule a pause in the execution?

   ```
   logo.schedule(task, 3000);
   ```

8. Write a line of code that closes the resources of the existing Activity.

9. Typically, which method begins an Activity?

10. Typically, which method releases the resources used within an Activity and ends the Activity?

11. What are the four states of an Activity?

12. Which method follows an onPause( ) method?

13. Write two statements that initialize the media player necessary to create an instance of a file named blues residing in your raw folder. Name the variable mpJazz.

14. Write a statement that is needed to begin the song playing from question 13.

15. Write a statement that is needed to pause the song playing from question 14.

16. Write a statement that is needed to change the text on a button named btJazz to the text Pause Unforgettable.

17. Write a statement that hides the button in question 16.

18. What is the name of the folder that typically holds media files in the Android project?

19. Why are class variables sometimes used instead of local variables?

20. What is the most common extension for a song played on an Android device?

Beyond the Book

Using the Internet, search the Web for the answers to the following questions to further your Android knowledge.

1. Research the four most common music file types played on an Android device. Write a paragraph about each music file type. Compare the file size, music quality, and usage of each file type.

2. Using a typical weather app as an example, describe the Android life cycle using each of the methods and a process that happens within the weather app. (*Hint:* See the example using the camera app in the chapter.)

3. At Google Play, research five music apps. Write a paragraph on the name, features, and purpose of each app.

4. The MediaPlayer class has a method named seekTo( ). Research the purpose of this method.

Case Programming Projects

Complete one or more of the following case programming projects. Use the same steps and techniques taught within the chapter. Submit the program you create to your instructor. The level of difficulty is indicated for each case programming project.

Easiest: ★

Intermediate: ★ ★

Challenging: ★ ★ ★

Case Project 6–1: Celtic Songs App ★

Requirements Document

Application title:	Celtic Songs App
Purpose:	A music app compares the different types of Celtic music.
Algorithms:	1. A splash screen opens displaying the celtic.png image with the title "Celtic Sounds" for four seconds (Figure 6-34).
	2. Two types of Celtic music are available in this app. An Irish jig named jig.mp3 can be played while displaying an image of Irish dancers. A second selection of a bagpipe music plays bagpipes.mp3 while displaying an image of a man playing bagpipes (Figure 6-35).
Conditions:	1. The pictures of the two types of music (jig and bagpipe) and the two music files are provided with your student files.
	2. The music should be played and paused by a button control.
	3. When a song is playing, the other button should not be displayed.

Figure 6-34

Figure 6-35

Case Project 6–2: Sleep Machine App ★ ★

Requirements Document

Application title:	Sleep Machine App
Purpose:	The Sleep Machine app plays sounds of the ocean waves and a fan to help you sleep.
Algorithms:	1. The opening screen displays an image and the title Sleep Machine for six seconds (Figure 6-36).
	2. The second screen displays two buttons with two images that allow the user to select ocean wave sounds or sounds of an oscillating fan for restful sleeping (Figure 6-37).
Conditions:	1. The waves.png and fan.png images are available in the student files and the sound effects are named waves.mp3 and fan.mp3.
	2. When a sound effect is playing, the other button should not be displayed. Each sound effect can play and pause on the user's selection.

Fuse /Getty Images

Figure 6-36

David Freund/Photodisc/Getty Images; Fuse/Getty Images

Figure 6-37

Case Project 6–3: Serenity Sounds App ⋆ ⋆

Requirements Document

Application title:	Serenity Sounds App
Purpose:	A relaxation app provides songs to allow you to breathe deeply and meditate.
Algorithms:	1. An opening screen displays an image of a relaxing location.
	2. The second screen displays two song names with a description about each song. A button is available that plays each song or pauses each song.
Conditions:	1. Choose your own image for the splash screen from images available on the Web.
	2. Choose your own songs from songs available at free sites online. Listen to each song and create your own description of each song.
	3. When a song is playing, the other button should not be displayed. Each song can play and pause on the user's selection.

Case Project 6–4: Guitar Solo App ⋆

Requirements Document

Application title:	Guitar Solo App
Purpose:	A new guitar performance artist needs an Android app to demo her talent.
Algorithms:	1. The opening screen displays the text "Solo Guitar Demo" and an image of a guitar.
	2. A second screen displays the guitar image and a button. When the user selects the Play Guitar Solo button, a guitar solo plays.
Conditions:	1. The opening screen is displayed for three seconds.
	2. The song can be paused by the user and restarted.
	3. Locate images and music files on free sites online.

Case Project 6–5: Ring Tones App ★ ★ ★

Requirements Document

Application title:	Ring Tones App
Purpose:	The Ring Tones app allows you to listen to three different ring tones using RadioButton controls for selection.
Algorithms:	1. Create an app that opens with a picture of a mobile phone and a title for three seconds.
	2. The second screen shows three RadioButton controls displaying different ring tone titles and a description of each ring tone.
Conditions:	1. Select your own images and free ring tones available by searching the Web.
	2. When a ring tone is playing, the other buttons should not be displayed. Each ring tone can play and pause on the user's selection.

Case Project 6–6: Your Personal Playlist App ★ ★ ★

Requirements Document

Application title:	Your Personal Playlist App
Purpose:	Get creative! Play your favorite three songs on your own personal playlist app.
Algorithms:	1. Create an app that opens with your own picture and a title for six seconds.
	2. The second screen shows three buttons displaying different song titles and an image of the artist or group.
Conditions:	1. Select your own images and music files.
	2. When a song is playing, the other buttons should not be displayed. Each song can play and pause on the user's selection.

Reveal! Displaying Pictures in a GridView

In this chapter, you learn to:

◎ Create an Android project using a GridView control

◎ Add a GridView to display a two-dimensional grid of images

◎ Reference images through an array

◎ Create an ImageAdapter class

◎ Code an OnItemClickListener

◎ Display a custom toast message

◎ Define a Context resource

◎ Understand the use of constructors

◎ Return a value from a method

◎ Determine the length of an array

◎ Assign an ImageView control using setImageResource

◎ Change the scale and layout size of the GridView

Using multimedia within an Android program brings personality and imagery to your app. Images are a powerful marketing tool and add visual appeal to any Android application, but it is essential to create a clean, professional effect with those images. To meet this goal, Android provides a layout tool called a GridView, which shows items in a two-dimensional scrolling grid.

To demonstrate the visual appeal of a GridView control, you will design a grid displaying animals on the endangered species list. The Endangered Species application shown in Figure 7-1 allows users to select the animal they want to symbolically adopt and contribute funds for support groups that work to protect these iconic animals. Users can then scroll the image grid by flicking their fingers across a horizontal listing of thumbnail-sized pictures of the endangered animals. To view a larger image, users can tap a thumbnail to display a full-size image below the grid.

Don Johnston/All Canada Photos/Getty Images; Hyde John/Perspectives/Getty Images; Cultura Travel/Philip Lee Harvey/The Image Bank/Getty Images; Mark Newman/Lonely Planet Images/Getty images; David Jenkins/Robert Harding World Imagery/Getty images

Figure 7-1   Endangered Species Android app

The Android app in Figure 7-1 is more visually appealing than one that simply displays images of the six endangered species in a tiled layout or grid view. The Endangered Species app also provides an easy way for a donor to select an animal to symbolically adopt. The app displays six different animals on the endangered species list, or animals at risk of becoming extinct. The images include an American eagle, Asian elephant, mountain gorilla, giant panda, panther, and polar bear. When a user selects the panda bear in the GridView control, for example, a larger image is displayed with a toast message stating "Selected Species 4," as shown in Figure 7-2. A different image is displayed each time the user selects another thumbnail in the grid.

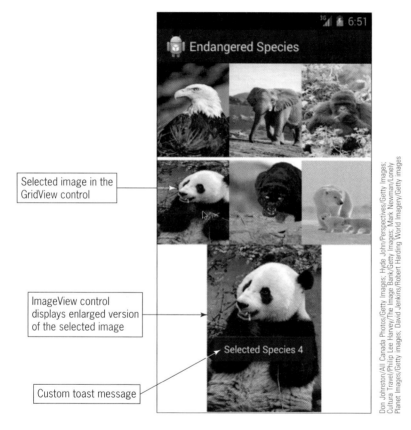

Selected image in the GridView control

ImageView control displays enlarged version of the selected image

Custom toast message

Don Johnston/All Canada Photos/Getty Images; Hyde John/Perspectives/Getty Images; Cultura Travel/Philip Lee Harvey/The Image Bank/Getty Images; Mark Newman/Lonely Planet Images/Getty images; David Jenkins/Robert Harding World Imagery/Getty images

Figure 7-2 Panda image selected in the grid

GTK

A GridView control of images is typically used to select a wallpaper image for the background of an Android device.

To create this application, the developer must understand how to perform the following processes, among others:

1. Add a GridView control and an ImageView control to the emulator.

2. Update the XML code for an ImageView control not linked to a particular image.

3. Place six images in a drawable folder.

4. Define an array to hold the image files.

5. Instantiate the GridView and ImageView controls.

6. Create an ImageAdapter class.

7. Display a custom toast message.

8. Display the selected image.

9. Customize the ImageAdapter class.

10. Define the layout using the getView( ) method.

Adding a GridView Control

The Endangered Species app opens with a horizontal scrolling list of animal pictures in a View container called a GridView, as shown in Figure 7-1. A **View** container is a rectangular area of the screen that displays an image or text object. A View container can include layouts such as GridView, ScrollView, ImageSwitcher, TabHost, and ListView. In Chapter 5, you used the ListView layout to create a vertical list of San Francisco attractions. In the Endangered Species project, the **GridView** container displays a horizontal list of objects with the center item displaying the current image. A GridView is mainly useful when you want to show data in a grid layout to display images or icons, for example. This layout can be used to build applications such as image viewers and audio or video players to show elements in a table or grid. If you have more images than can be displayed on the screen, you can move through the grid by scrolling down the page. The photos in a grid can be sized as small as thumbnail images or as large as full-screen images. The photos can be stored in the drawable folders, in your phone's storage (SD card), or even on a Web site such as Picasa.

The GridView control is a widget in the Composite category of the Palette. Each GridView control can be customized with the attributes shown in Table 7-1.

GridView Attribute Name	Description
android:columnWidth	Specifies the fixed width for each column of the grid
android:numColumns	Defines the number of columns in the grid
android:horizontalSpacing	Defines the default horizontal spacing between columns in the grid
android:verticalSpacing	Defines the default vertical spacing between rows in the grid

Table 7-1   GridView control attributes

To add a GridView control to activity_main.xml, follow these steps to begin the application:

STEP 1

- Open the Eclipse program.

- Type **E:\Workspace** (if necessary, enter a different drive letter that identifies the USB drive) to select a workspace, and then tap or click the OK button.

- Tap or click the New button on the Standard toolbar and then select Android Application Project.

- Tap or click the Next button.

- In the New Android Application dialog box, enter the Application Name **Endangered Species**.

- Enter the Package Name **net.androidbootcamp.endangeredspecies**.

  Notice that the Minimum Required SDK text box displays the API number from the selected Target SDK. If you are deploying to an earlier model of an Android device, you can select an earlier version.

The new Android Endangered Species project has an application name and a package name (Figure 7-3).

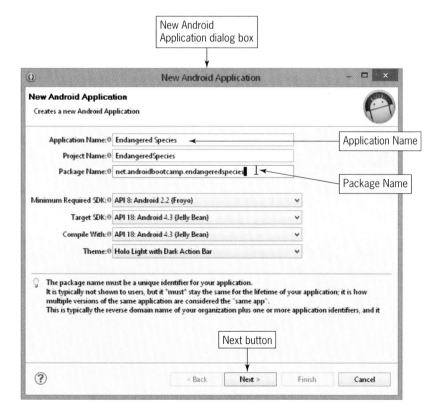

Figure 7-3 Application information for the Endangered Species project

STEP 2

- Tap or click the Next button.

- Tap or click the Create custom launcher icon box to uncheck the option.

- Tap or click the Next button twice.

- Tap or click the Finish button.

- If necessary, expand the Endangered Species project in the Package Explorer.

- Tap or click the Minimize button on the Outline pane.

- On the activity_main.xml tab, tap or click the Hello world! TextView (displayed by default) in the emulator and then press the Delete key.

- In the Composite category of the Palette, drag the GridView control to the top center part of the emulator.

The activity_ main.xml is displayed in the emulator with the GridView control (Figure 7-4).

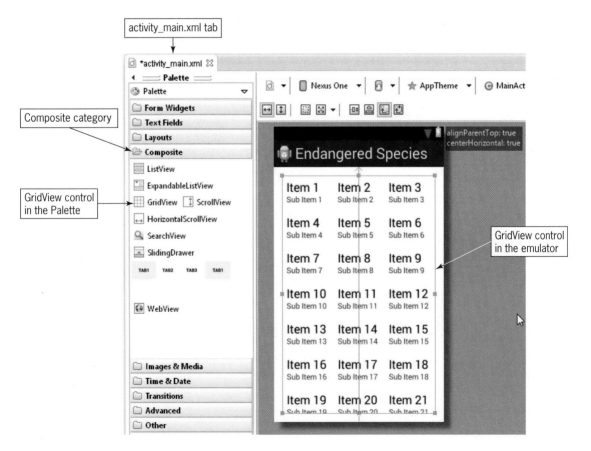

Figure 7-4 GridView control in the emulator for the Endangered Species project

STEP 3

- Tap or click the activity_main.xml tab to display the XML code.

- To customize the layout, change the first and last line of code from RelativeLayout to **LinearLayout**. When you add the ImageView control later, this layout aligns it vertically with the GridView control.

- Delete the padding XML codes from Lines 5–9.

- In Line 5, type **android:orientation="vertical"** > to display controls vertically down the page.

The activity_main.xml is displayed in the emulator with the GridView control (Figure 7-5).

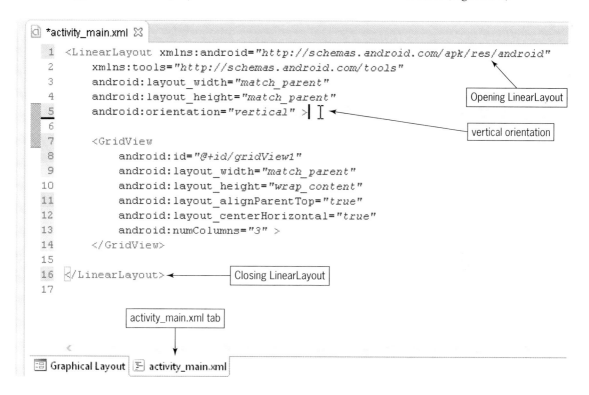

```
 1  <LinearLayout xmlns:android="http://schemas.android.com/apk/res/android"
 2      xmlns:tools="http://schemas.android.com/tools"
 3      android:layout_width="match_parent"
 4      android:layout_height="match_parent"
 5      android:orientation="vertical" >
 6
 7      <GridView
 8          android:id="@+id/gridView1"
 9          android:layout_width="match_parent"
10          android:layout_height="wrap_content"
11          android:layout_alignParentTop="true"
12          android:layout_centerHorizontal="true"
13          android:numColumns="3" >
14      </GridView>
15
16  </LinearLayout>
17
```

Opening LinearLayout

vertical orientation

Closing LinearLayout

activity_main.xml tab

Graphical Layout   activity_main.xml

Figure 7-5 Displaying the LinearLayout XML code

STEP 4

- To customize the GridView control, change the layout_width from "match_parent" to **"wrap_content"** in Line 9. Setting a View's size to wrap_content forces the grid to expand only far enough to contain the image values it contains.

- Change the layout_height in Line 10 from "wrap_content" to **"250dp"**.

- Delete the additional layout commands in Line 11 and Line 12.

- At the end of android:numColumns="3" in Line 11, press the Enter key and type the following XML code before the closing GridView tag:

```
android:columnWidth="100dp"
android:horizontalSpacing="5dp"
android:verticalSpacing="5dp"/>
```

The GridView control is customized with three columns, each 100dp wide, with the horizontal/vertical spacing set to 5dp (Figure 7-6).

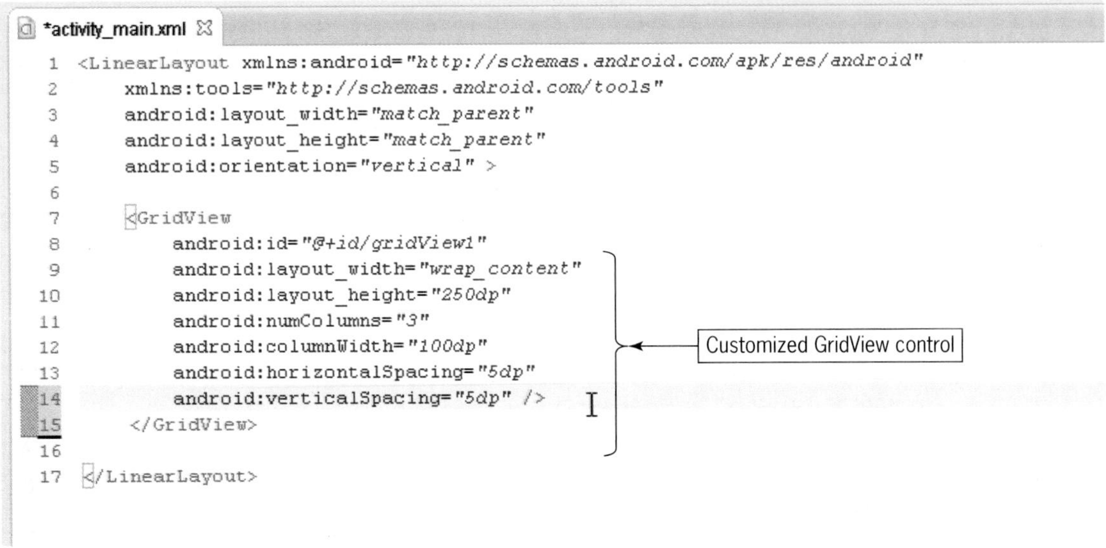

```
 *activity_main.xml
 1  <LinearLayout xmlns:android="http://schemas.android.com/apk/res/android"
 2      xmlns:tools="http://schemas.android.com/tools"
 3      android:layout_width="match_parent"
 4      android:layout_height="match_parent"
 5      android:orientation="vertical" >
 6
 7      <GridView
 8          android:id="@+id/gridView1"
 9          android:layout_width="wrap_content"
10          android:layout_height="250dp"
11          android:numColumns="3"
12          android:columnWidth="100dp"
13          android:horizontalSpacing="5dp"
14          android:verticalSpacing="5dp" />
15      </GridView>
16
17  </LinearLayout>
```

Customized GridView control

Figure 7-6 Custom GridView XML code

Adding the ImageView Control and Image Files

In the Endangered Species chapter project, the GridView control displays a grid containing two rows with three columns of six thumbnail-sized animal photos stored in the drawable-hdpi folder. When the user taps one of these images, a full-size image appears in an ImageView control below the GridView control, as shown in Figure 7-2. Typically, you add an ImageView control by dragging the control onto the emulator. A dialog box automatically opens requesting which image file in the drawable folders should be displayed. In the case of the chapter project, an image appears in the ImageView only if the user taps the thumbnail image in the grid. Otherwise, no image should appear in the ImageView control. To prevent an image from being assigned to (and displayed in) the ImageView control, you must enter the XML code for the ImageView control in the activity_main.xml file. The ImageView source will be displayed in the control when the user selects a particular animal. The source display will be coded in the MainActivity.java file. To add the XML code for the ImageView control named imgLarge, add the strings table, and add the six image files to the drawable folder, follow these steps:

STEP 1

- On the line below the closing GridView XML code, press the Enter key twice to insert two blank lines, and then type the following custom ImageView XML code on Line 16 using auto-completion as much as possible:

```
<ImageView
android:id="@+id/imgLarge"
android:layout_width="match_parent"
android:layout_height="match_parent"
android:contentDescription="@string/imgLarge" />
```

The ImageView control is coded in the activity_main.xml file (Figure 7-7).

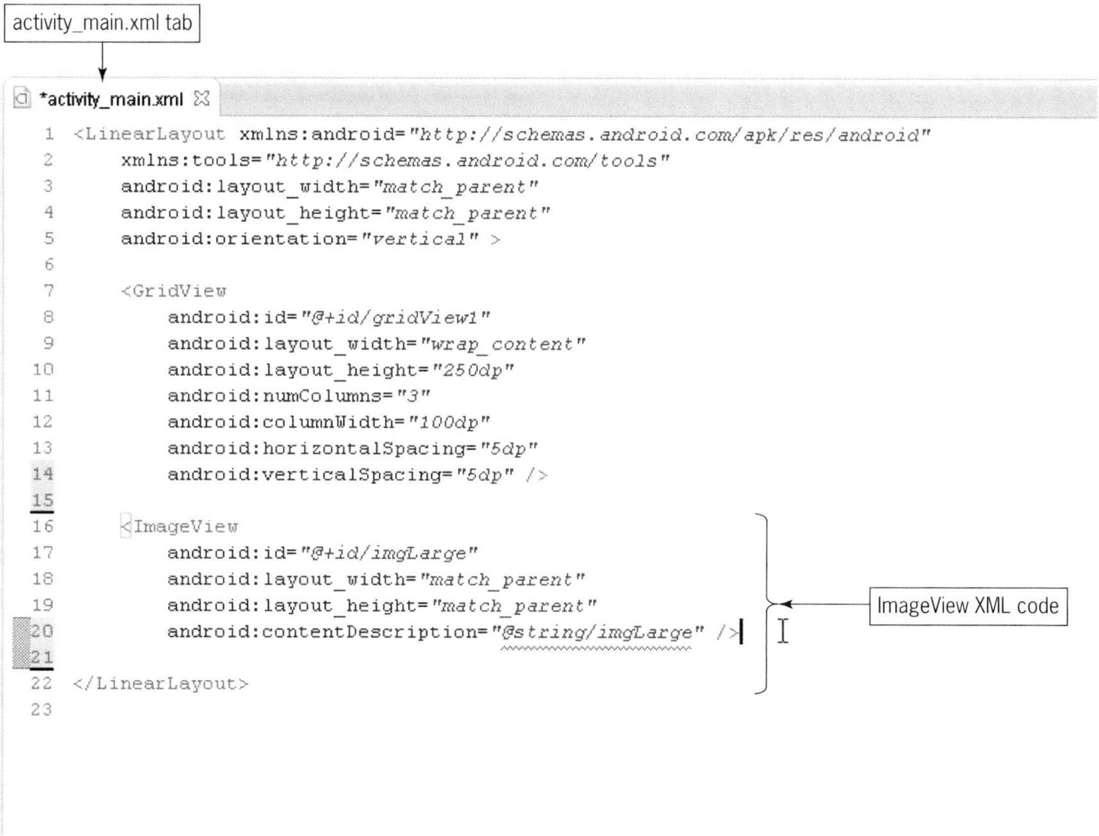

activity_main.xml tab

```
 *activity_main.xml ⊠
 1  <LinearLayout xmlns:android="http://schemas.android.com/apk/res/android"
 2      xmlns:tools="http://schemas.android.com/tools"
 3      android:layout_width="match_parent"
 4      android:layout_height="match_parent"
 5      android:orientation="vertical" >
 6
 7      <GridView
 8          android:id="@+id/gridView1"
 9          android:layout_width="wrap_content"
10          android:layout_height="250dp"
11          android:numColumns="3"
12          android:columnWidth="100dp"
13          android:horizontalSpacing="5dp"
14          android:verticalSpacing="5dp" />
15
16      <ImageView
17          android:id="@+id/imgLarge"
18          android:layout_width="match_parent"
19          android:layout_height="match_parent"
20          android:contentDescription="@string/imgLarge" />
21
22  </LinearLayout>
23
```

ImageView XML code

Figure 7-7 ImageView XML code

STEP 2

- Close and save the activity_main.xml tab.

- To add the content description to the strings table, in the values folder in the Package Explorer, open strings.xml.

- Tap or click the Add button, select String, and then tap or click the OK button.

- Type **imgLarge** in the Name text box and type **Endangered Species Images** in the Value text box.

The strings.xml file contains the String value necessary in this app (Figure 7-8).

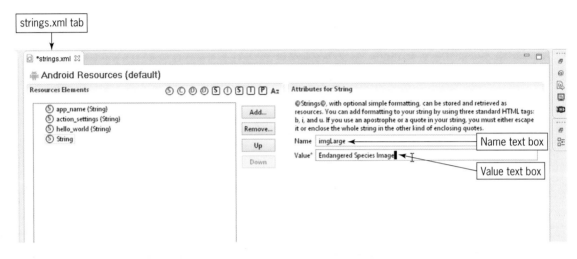

Figure 7-8 String table

STEP 3

- To add the six image files to the drawable folder, if necessary, copy the student files to your USB drive.

- Open the USB folder containing the student files. In the Package Explorer, expand the drawable-hdpi folder in the res folder.

- To add the six image files to the drawable-hdpi resource folder, drag the eagle.png, elephant.png, gorilla.png, panda.png, panther.png, and polar.png files to the drawable-hdpi folder until a plus sign pointer appears. Release the mouse button.

- If necessary, tap or click the Copy files option button, and then tap or click the OK button.

Copies of the six files appear in the drawable-hdpi folder with the default ic_launcher image file (Figure 7-9).

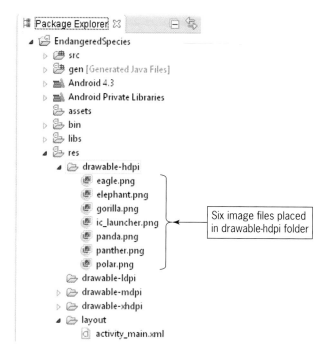

Figure 7-9   Images copied

IN THE TRENCHES

If you are creating an Android application that can be installed on a variety of Android platforms, it is best to create extra high-, high-, medium-, and low-density photos. Typically, you should provide alternative layouts for some of the different screen sizes and alternative bitmap images for different screen densities. At runtime, the system uses the appropriate resources for your application based on the generalized size or density of the current device screen.

Creating an Array for the Images

Before the images can be displayed in the GridView control, the images in the drawable folder must be referenced in the code and assigned to an array. By using an array variable, which can store more than one value, you can avoid assigning a separate variable for each image in the folder. You could add tens of images to be displayed in the GridView control based on the need of your app. For example, an app can display three rows of four images each in a grid to represent the top 12 selling Android phones on the market, and then users can scroll over the grid to select an image of their favorite phone. If more phone images are added to the grid, the GridView control automatically becomes scrollable, allowing users to view every image in the grid.

Arrays provide access to data by using a numeric index, or subscript, to identify each element in the array. In the chapter project, the images are assigned to an integer array named Animals and each image is associated with an integer value. For example, the first image of the eagle is assigned to the subscript of 0, as shown in Table 7-2. Typically an array is used to assign values to a GridView control that has multiple items.

Element of Array	Image File
Animals[0]	eagle.png
Animals[1]	elephant.png
Animals[2]	gorilla.png
Animals[3]	panda.png
Animals[4]	panther.png
Animals[5]	polar.png

Table 7-2   Animals array

© 2015 Cengage Learning

In MainActivity.java, the Animals array and ImageView control are declared as class-level variables because they are referenced in multiple methods throughout the application. Recall that class-level variables are accessed from anywhere within a Java class. The array is available throughout the entire Activity. To declare the Animals array and ImageView control in MainActivity.java, follow these steps:

STEP 1

- Expand the src and net.androidbootcamp.endangeredspecies folders, and then double-tap or double-click MainActivity.java to open its code window.

- Tap or click at the end of the public class MainActivity extends Activity { line, press the Enter key, and then use auto-completion as much as possible to type the following code to create the Animals array that can be used by multiple methods:

```
Integer[] Animals = {R.drawable.eagle, R.drawable.elephant, R.drawable.gorilla,
R.drawable.panda, R.drawable.panther, R.drawable.polar};
```

The Animals array references the images stored in the drawable folder (Figure 7-10).

```
MainActivity.java ⌘
  1  package net.androidbootcamp.endangeredspecies;
  2
  3⊕ import android.os.Bundle;
  6
  7  public class MainActivity extends Activity {
  8⊖     Integer[] Animals = {R.drawable.eagle, R.drawable.elephant, R.drawable.gorilla,
  9            R.drawable.panda, R.drawable.panther, R.drawable.polar}; I
 10⊖     @Override
▲11     protected void onCreate(Bundle savedInstanceState) {
 12         super.onCreate(savedInstanceState);
 13         setContentView(R.layout.activity_main);
 14     }
 15
 16⊖     @Override
▲17     public boolean onCreateOptionsMenu(Menu menu) {
 18         // Inflate the menu; this adds items to the action bar if it is present.
 19         getMenuInflater().inflate(R.menu.main, menu);
 20         return true;
 21     }
 22
 23  }
 24
```

Animals array

Figure 7-10   Animals Array declared

STEP 2

- Press the Enter key.

- To declare ImageView as a class variable, type **ImageView pic;**.

- Point to ImageView and then tap or click Import 'ImageView' (android.widget).

ImageView is referenced as a class variable (Figure 7-11).

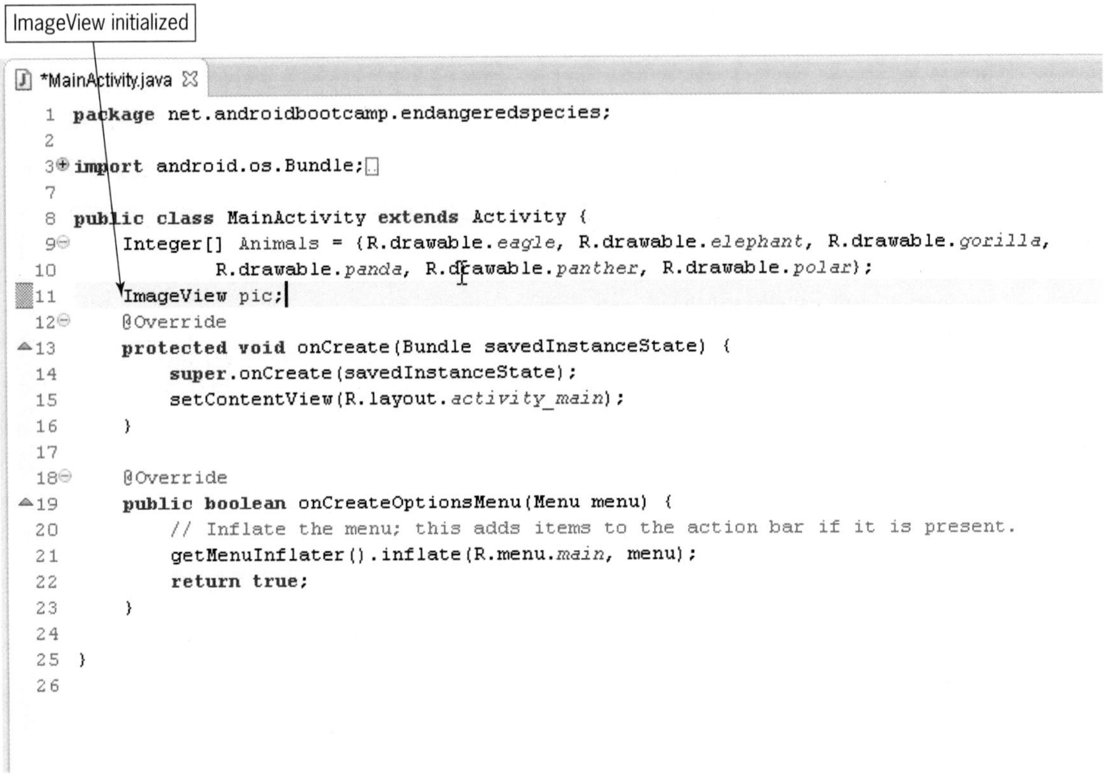

ImageView initialized

```
🎵 *MainActivity.java ✖

  1  package net.androidbootcamp.endangeredspecies;
  2
  3⊕ import android.os.Bundle;▯
  7
  8  public class MainActivity extends Activity {
  9⊝      Integer[] Animals = {R.drawable.eagle, R.drawable.elephant, R.drawable.gorilla,
 10              R.drawable.panda, R.drawable.panther, R.drawable.polar};
 11      ImageView pic;|
 12⊝      @Override
▲13      protected void onCreate(Bundle savedInstanceState) {
 14          super.onCreate(savedInstanceState);
 15          setContentView(R.layout.activity_main);
 16      }
 17
 18⊝      @Override
▲19      public boolean onCreateOptionsMenu(Menu menu) {
 20          // Inflate the menu; this adds items to the action bar if it is present.
 21          getMenuInflater().inflate(R.menu.main, menu);
 22          return true;
 23      }
 24
 25  }
 26
```

Figure 7-11   ImageView referenced

Instantiating the GridView and ImageView Controls

The GridView and ImageView controls in activity_main.xml must be instantiated in the onCreate( ) method of MainActivity.java. The first GridView control in a project is named gridView1 by default. The code to instantiate the GridView assigns the control created in activity_main.xml the name gridView1, as shown in the following code syntax:

Code Syntax

```
GridView gr = (GridView)findViewById(R.id.gridView1);
```

To instantiate the GridView and ImageView controls, follow these steps:

STEP 1

- To instantiate the GridView, in the onCreate( ) method of MainActivity.java, tap or click at the end of the setContentView(R.layout.*activity_main*); line, and then press the Enter key.

- Type **GridView gr = (GridView)findViewById(R.id.*gridView1*);**.

- Point to GridView, and then tap or click Import 'GridView' (android.widget).

The GridView control is instantiated (Figure 7-12).

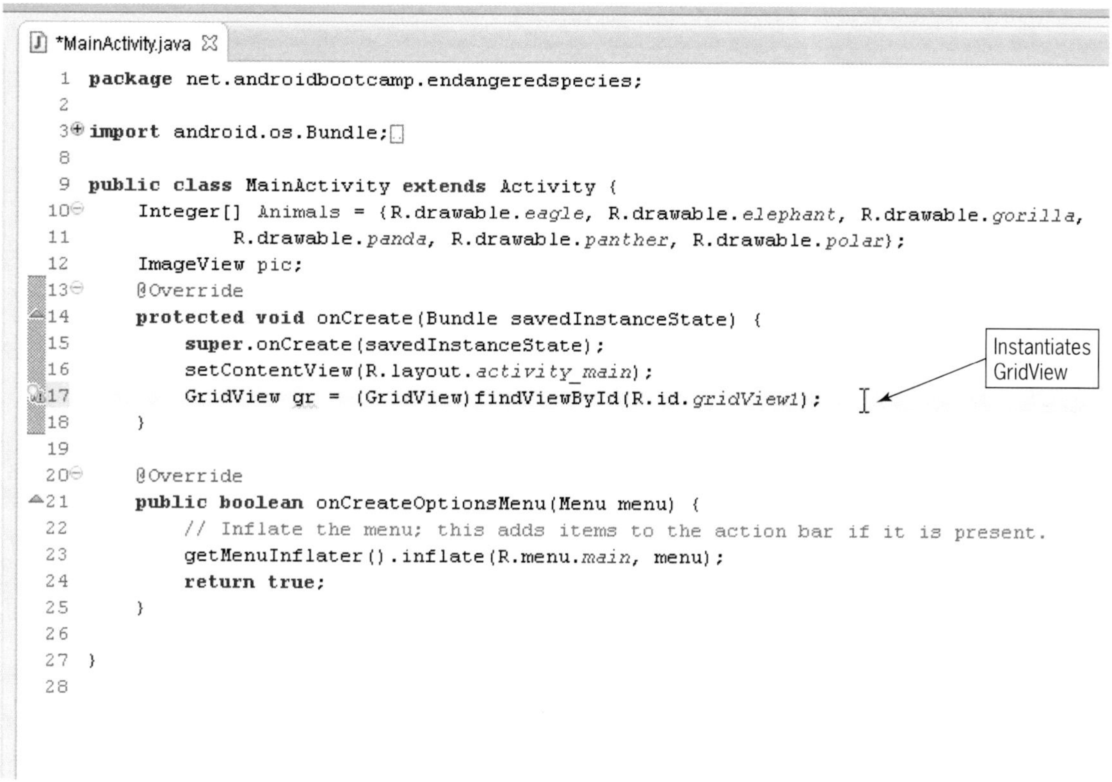

```
J  *MainActivity.java ⊠

 1   package net.androidbootcamp.endangeredspecies;
 2
 3⊕ import android.os.Bundle;☐
 8
 9   public class MainActivity extends Activity {
10⊖      Integer[] Animals = {R.drawable.eagle, R.drawable.elephant, R.drawable.gorilla,
11              R.drawable.panda, R.drawable.panther, R.drawable.polar};
12       ImageView pic;
13⊖      @Override
14       protected void onCreate(Bundle savedInstanceState) {
15           super.onCreate(savedInstanceState);
16           setContentView(R.layout.activity_main);
17           GridView gr = (GridView)findViewById(R.id.gridView1);    I
18       }
19
20⊖      @Override
21       public boolean onCreateOptionsMenu(Menu menu) {
22           // Inflate the menu; this adds items to the action bar if it is present.
23           getMenuInflater().inflate(R.menu.main, menu);
24           return true;
25       }
26
27   }
28
```

Instantiates
GridView

Figure 7-12   GridView control is instantiated

STEP 2

- Press the Enter key.

- To instantiate the ImageView that is assigned as a class variable, type
  final ImageView pic= (ImageView)findViewById(R.id.*imgLarge*);.

The ImageView control is instantiated (Figure 7-13).

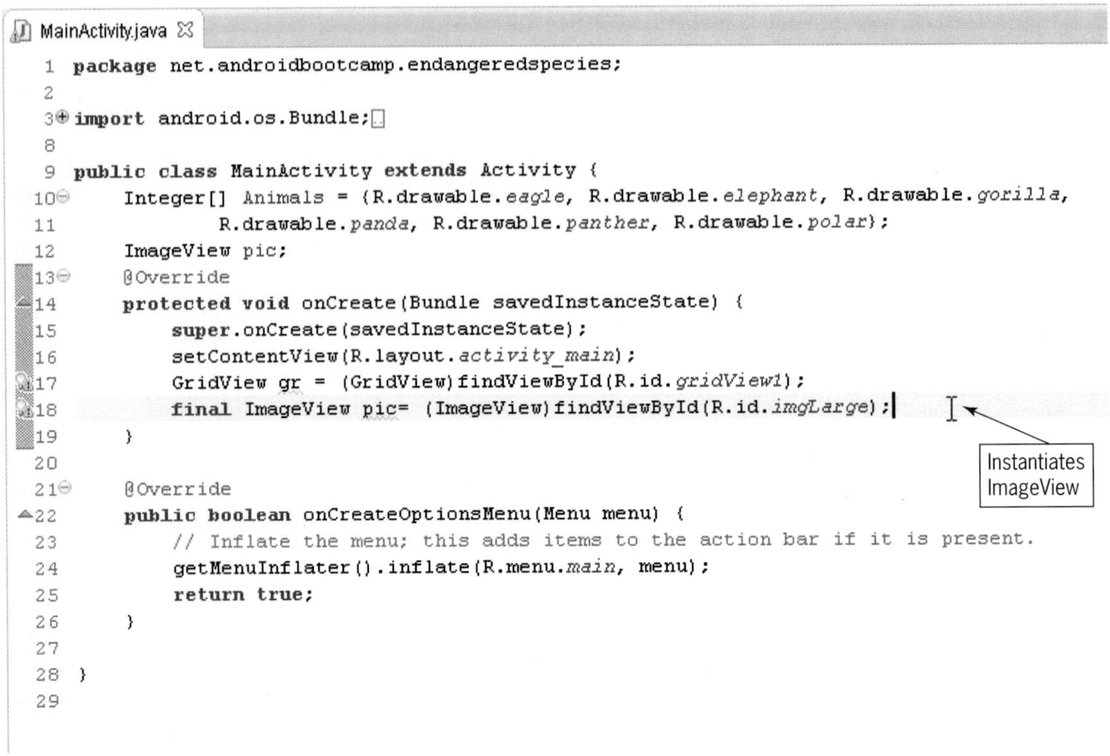

```
   MainActivity.java ⊠

 1  package net.androidbootcamp.endangeredspecies;

 2

 3⊕ import android.os.Bundle;▯

 8

 9  public class MainActivity extends Activity {
10⊖     Integer[] Animals = {R.drawable.eagle, R.drawable.elephant, R.drawable.gorilla,
11             R.drawable.panda, R.drawable.panther, R.drawable.polar};
12     ImageView pic;
13⊖     @Override
14     protected void onCreate(Bundle savedInstanceState) {
15         super.onCreate(savedInstanceState);
16         setContentView(R.layout.activity_main);
17         GridView gr = (GridView)findViewById(R.id.gridView1);
18         final ImageView pic= (ImageView)findViewById(R.id.imgLarge);|
19     }
20
21⊖     @Override
22     public boolean onCreateOptionsMenu(Menu menu) {
23         // Inflate the menu; this adds items to the action bar if it is present.
24         getMenuInflater().inflate(R.menu.main, menu);
25         return true;
26     }
27
28  }
29
```

Instantiates ImageView

Figure 7-13   ImageView control is instantiated

Using a setAdapter with an ImageAdapter

In Chapter 5, an adapter was used to display a ListView control. Similarly, a **setAdapter** provides a data model for the GridView layout. The GridView data model functions as a photo GridView in touch mode. The following code syntax shows how to instantiate a custom BaseAdapter class called ImageAdapter and apply it to the GridView using setAdapter( ):

Code Syntax

```
gr.setAdapter(new ImageAdapter(this));
```

After the ImageAdapter is instantiated, the Android Java ImageAdapter class must be added to extend the custom BaseAdapter class. Using controls such as the GridView, ListView, and Spinner, the adapter binds specific types of data and displays that data in a particular layout. To instantiate the ImageAdapter class for the GridView control, follow these steps:

STEP 1

- Press the Enter key and type **gr.setAdapter(new ImageAdapter(this));**.

- A red error line appears under ImageAdapter. Instead of automatically creating the class, a custom ImageAdapter class is added in the next step, so do not import the class now.

The ImageAdapter is coded for the GridView control. A red error line appears below ImageAdapter (Figure 7-14).

```
🗋 *MainActivity.java ⊠
  1  package net.androidbootcamp.endangeredspecies;
  2
  3⊕ import android.os.Bundle;☐
  8
  9  public class MainActivity extends Activity {
 10⊖     Integer[] Animals = {R.drawable.eagle, R.drawable.elephant, R.drawable.gorilla,
 11              R.drawable.panda, R.drawable.panther, R.drawable.polar};
 12      ImageView pic;
 13⊖     @Override
 14      protected void onCreate(Bundle savedInstanceState) {
 15          super.onCreate(savedInstanceState);
 16          setContentView(R.layout.activity_main);
 17          GridView gr = (GridView)findViewById(R.id.gridView1);
 18          final ImageView pic= (ImageView)findViewById(R.id.imgLarge);
 19          gr.setAdapter(new ImageAdapter(this));|     I←        ImageAdapter class
 20      }
 21
```

Figure 7-14   Instance of the ImageAdapter class

STEP 2

- To add an ImageAdapter class that extends the BaseAdapter custom class, tap or click after the first closing brace at the end of Line 20.

- Press the Enter key and type **public class ImageAdapter extends BaseAdapter {**.

- Press the Enter key to display a closing brace.

- Point to BaseAdapter and tap or click Import 'BaseAdapter' (android.widget).

- Point to ImageAdapter in the same line and tap or click Add unimplemented methods.

- Point to ImageAdapter in the gr.setAdapter(new ImageAdapter (this)); line and select Create constructor 'ImageAdapter(MainActivity)'.

The ImageAdapter class is coded to handle the image display (Figure 7-15). The methods within the ImageAdapter are auto-generated.

```
 📄 *MainActivity.java ☒
    2
    3⊕ import android.os.Bundle;▯
   11
   12 public class MainActivity extends Activity {
   13⊖     Integer[] Animals = {R.drawable.eagle, R.drawable.elephant, R.drawable.gorilla,
   14              R.drawable.panda, R.drawable.panther, R.drawable.polar};
   15     ImageView pic;
   16⊖     @Override
  ▲17     protected void onCreate(Bundle savedInstanceState) {
   18         super.onCreate(savedInstanceState);
   19         setContentView(R.layout.activity_main);
  ⚠20         GridView gr = (GridView)findViewById(R.id.gridView1);
  ⚐21         final ImageView pic= (ImageView)findViewById(R.id.imgLarge);
   22         gr.setAdapter(new ImageAdapter(this));
   23     }
   24⊖     public class ImageAdapter extends BaseAdapter {                    ImageAdapter class added
   25
   26⊖         public ImageAdapter(MainActivity mainActivity) {
  ☑27             // TODO Auto-generated constructor stub
   28         }
   29
   30⊖         @Override
  ▲31         public int getCount() {
  ☑32             // TODO Auto-generated method stub
   33             return 0;
   34         }
   35
   36⊖         @Override
  ▲37         public Object getItem(int arg0) {
  ☑38             // TODO Auto-generated method stub
   39             return null;
   40         }                                                             Auto-generated
   41                                                                       methods
   42⊖         @Override
  ▲43         public long getItemId(int arg0) {
  ☑44             // TODO Auto-generated method stub
   45             return 0;
   46         }
   47
   48⊖         @Override
  ▲49         public View getView(int arg0, View arg1, ViewGroup arg2) {
  ☑50             // TODO Auto-generated method stub
   51             return null;
   52         }
   53
   54     }
   55
```

Figure 7-15   ImageAdapter class

Coding the OnItemClickListener

Like the OnClickListener used for a Button control in previous chapter projects, the
OnItemClickListener awaits user interaction within the GridView control. When the user
touches the GridView display layout, the OnItemClickListener processes an event called onItemClick.

The **onItemClick** method defined by OnItemClickListener provides a number of arguments, which are listed in the parentheses included in the line of code. The two controls—ListView and GridView—enable the Android device to monitor for tap or click events using the OnItemClickListener and onItemClick commands. The following code syntax shows how to use onItemClick in the chapter project.

Code Syntax

```
gr.setOnItemClickListener(new OnItemClickListener( ) {
   @Override
   public void onItemClick(AdapterView<?> arg0,
     View arg1, int arg2, long arg3) {
   }
}};
}
```

In this code syntax example, gr is the instance of the GridView control. The OnItemClickListener executes the onItemClick method as soon as the user touches any image within the GridView control. The onItemClick method has four arguments. Table 7-3 describes the role of the four arguments in the onItemClick method.

Argument	Purpose
AdapterView<?> arg0	The AdapterView records "where" the user actually touched the screen in the argument variable arg0. In other words, if the app has more than one View control, the AdapterView determines if the user touched this GridView control or another control in the application.
View arg1	The View parameter is the specific View within the item that the user touched. This is the View provided by the adapter.
int arg2	This is one of the most important portions of this statement in the chapter project. The arg2 argument is an integer value that holds the position of the View in the adapter. For example, if the user taps the elephant picture, the integer value of 1 is stored in arg2 because the elephant picture is the second image in the Animals array.
long arg3	The GridView control is displayed across multiple rows of the Android device. The argument arg3 determines the row id of the item that was selected by the user. This is especially useful for a GridView control that has multiple rows in the layout.

Table 7-3 Arguments in the onItemClick method

© 2015 Cengage Learning

Users can change their minds more than once when selecting picture images in the GridView. The onItemClick method responds an unlimited number of times throughout the life of the class based on the user's interaction with the GridView control. To code the OnItemClickListener and onItemClick method, follow these steps:

STEP 1

- In MainActivity.java, press the Enter key after the gr.setAdapter command line.

- To set up the OnItemClickListener, type **gr.setOnItemClickListener(new OnItemClickListener( ) {**.

- Press the Enter key to display a closing brace.

- A red error line appears under OnItemClickListener. Point to OnItemClickListener and import the 'OnItemClickListener' (android.widget.AdapterView).

- After the closing brace, type a closing parenthesis and a semicolon to complete the statement.

The GridView OnItemClickListener awaits user interaction. A red error line appears below OnItemClickListener (Figure 7-16).

```java
*MainActivity.java ░
 1  package net.androidbootcamp.endangeredspecies;
 2
 3  import android.os.Bundle;
12
13  public class MainActivity extends Activity {
14      Integer[] Animals = {R.drawable.eagle, R.drawable.elephant, R.drawable.gorilla,
15              R.drawable.panda, R.drawable.panther, R.drawable.polar};
16      ImageView pic;
17      @Override
18      protected void onCreate(Bundle savedInstanceState) {
19          super.onCreate(savedInstanceState);
20          setContentView(R.layout.activity_main);
21          GridView gr = (GridView)findViewById(R.id.gridView1);
22          final ImageView pic= (ImageView)findViewById(R.id.imgLarge);
23          gr.setAdapter(new ImageAdapter(this));
24          gr.setOnItemClickListener(new OnItemClickListener() {
25
26          });
27      }
28      public class ImageAdapter extends BaseAdapter {
29
30          public ImageAdapter(MainActivity mainActivity) {
31              // TODO Auto-generated constructor stub
32          }
33
34          @Override
35          public int getCount() {
36              // TODO Auto-generated method stub
37              return 0;
38          }
39
40          @Override
41          public Object getItem(int arg0) {
42              // TODO Auto-generated method stub
```

OnItemClickListener( )

Closing brace, parenthesis, and semicolon

Figure 7-16 GridView OnItemClickListener

STEP 2

- To add the onItemClick method within the OnItemClickListener, point to the red error line under the OnItemClickListener and select Add unimplemented methods. Save your work.

The onItemClick method stub appears automatically (Figure 7-17).

```
1   package net.androidbootcamp.endangeredspecies;
2
3⊕  import android.os.Bundle;⬚
13
14  public class MainActivity extends Activity {
15⊝      Integer[] Animals = {R.drawable.eagle, R.drawable.elephant, R.drawable.gorilla,
16              R.drawable.panda, R.drawable.panther, R.drawable.polar};
17      ImageView pic;
18⊝      @Override
19      protected void onCreate(Bundle savedInstanceState) {
20          super.onCreate(savedInstanceState);
21          setContentView(R.layout.activity_main);
22          GridView gr = (GridView)findViewById(R.id.gridView1);
23          final ImageView pic= (ImageView)findViewById(R.id.imgLarge);
24          gr.setAdapter(new ImageAdapter(this));
25⊝          gr.setOnItemClickListener(new OnItemClickListener() {
26
27⊝              @Override
28              public void onItemClick(AdapterView<?> arg0, View arg1, int arg2,
29                      long arg3) {
30                  // TODO Auto-generated method stub
31
32              }
33
34          });
35      }
36⊝      public class ImageAdapter extends BaseAdapter {
37
38⊝          public ImageAdapter(MainActivity mainActivity) {
39              // TODO Auto-generated constructor stub
40          }
41
```

onItemClick auto-generated method stub

Figure 7-17   The onItemClick method

Coding a Custom Toast Notification

A toast notification in the Endangered Species program provides feedback as to which animal image is selected. When the toast message is shown to the user, it floats over the application so it will never receive focus. In earlier chapters, you entered a toast notification displaying a temporary message in this form:

```
Toast.makeText(MainActivity.this, "Typical Toast Message",Toast.LENGTH_SHORT).show( );
```

In the Endangered Species project, the toast notification message is different in two ways. First, the toast message in the GridView control appears in the onItemClick method that is executed only when the user makes a selection. Because the toast notification is not used directly in the MainActivity, the reference to MainActivity.this in the toast statement creates an error. To use a toast message within an onItemClick method, considered an AlertDialog class, you must replace MainActivity.this with a Context class called getBaseContext( ). In Android programs, you can place the **getBaseContext( )** method in another method (such as onItemClick) that is triggered only when the user touches the GridView control. If you do, the getBaseContext( ) method obtains a Context instance.

A second difference is that the toast message includes a variable. The variable indicates which image number is selected in the Animals array. Figure 7-18 shows the message when the user selects the panda.

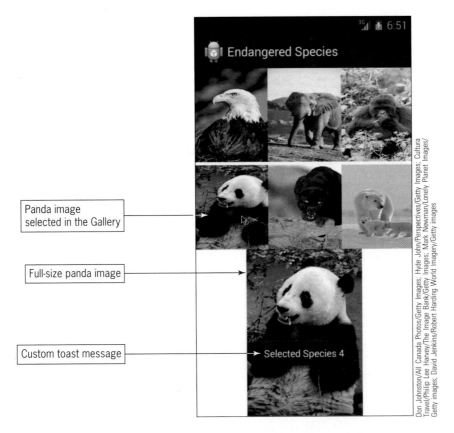

Panda image selected in the Gallery

Full-size panda image

Custom toast message

Selected Species 4

Don Johnston/All Canada Photos/Getty Images; Hyde John/Perspectives/Getty Images; Cultura Travel/Philip Lee Harvey/The Image Bank/Getty Images; Mark Newman/Lonely Planet Images/ Getty Images; David Jenkins/Robert Harding World Imagery/Getty images

Figure 7-18   Toast message displayed when user selects the panda image

Notice that even though the panda is in position Animals[3] in Table 7-2, the custom toast message states "Selected Species 4." Array position 3 is really the fourth image because the array values begin with 0. The value of 1 is added in the toast message shown in the following code syntax to the integer position value of arg2. The arg2 argument is an integer value that holds the position number of the View in the adapter that was an argument of the onItemClick( ) method. The position identifies the image placement in the array.

Code Syntax

```
Toast.makeText(getBaseContext( ), "Selected Species " + (arg2 + 1), Toast.LENGTH_
SHORT).show( );
```

To code the custom toast message that includes a getBaseContext( ) method and variables, follow this step:

STEP 1

- In MainActivity.java, tap or click the blank line after the first TODO comment in Line 30 to add the custom toast message.

- Use auto-completion to type **Toast.makeText(getBaseContext( ), "Selected Species " + (arg2 + 1), Toast.LENGTH_SHORT).show( );**.

- Import 'Toast' (android.widget).

The custom toast message provides feedback to the user of his or her picture selection from the GridView (Figure 7-19).

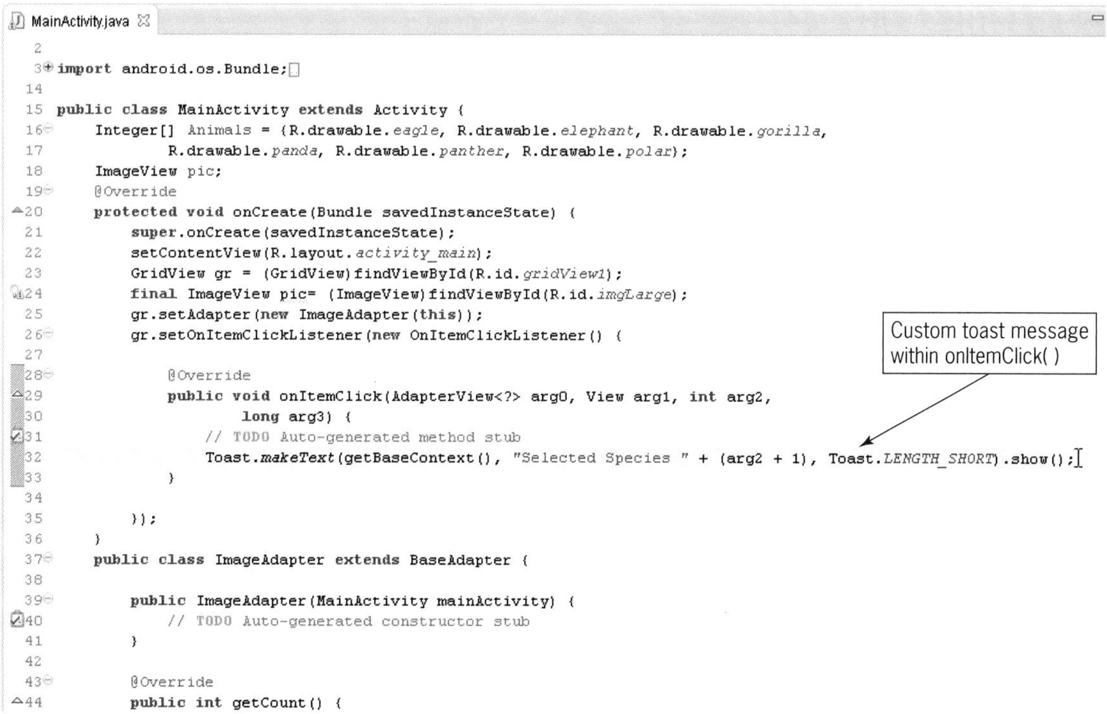

```
MainActivity.java ⊠
  2
  3⊕ import android.os.Bundle;
 14
 15 public class MainActivity extends Activity {
 16⊖     Integer[] Animals = {R.drawable.eagle, R.drawable.elephant, R.drawable.gorilla,
 17             R.drawable.panda, R.drawable.panther, R.drawable.polar};
 18     ImageView pic;
 19⊖     @Override
▲20     protected void onCreate(Bundle savedInstanceState) {
 21         super.onCreate(savedInstanceState);
 22         setContentView(R.layout.activity_main);
 23         GridView gr = (GridView)findViewById(R.id.gridView1);
 24         final ImageView pic= (ImageView)findViewById(R.id.imgLarge);
 25         gr.setAdapter(new ImageAdapter(this));
 26⊖         gr.setOnItemClickListener(new OnItemClickListener() {
 27
 28⊖             @Override
 29             public void onItemClick(AdapterView<?> arg0, View arg1, int arg2,
 30                     long arg3) {
 31                 // TODO Auto-generated method stub
 32                 Toast.makeText(getBaseContext(), "Selected Species " + (arg2 + 1), Toast.LENGTH_SHORT).show();
 33             }
 34
 35         });
 36     }
 37⊖     public class ImageAdapter extends BaseAdapter {
 38
 39⊖         public ImageAdapter(MainActivity mainActivity) {
 40             // TODO Auto-generated constructor stub
 41         }
 42
 43⊖         @Override
▲44         public int getCount() {
```

Custom toast message within onItemClick( )

Figure 7-19 Custom toast message

Displaying the Selected Image

When the user touches an animal picture in the GridView, a toast message appears with an ImageView control displaying the selected image. The ImageView control was previously coded in activity_main.xml, though a specific image was not selected in the code. Instead, the full-sized picture in the ImageView control should be displayed dynamically to the user. An ImageView control is defined either by the android:src attribute in the XML element or by the setImageResource(int) method. The setImageResource method indicates which image is selected, as shown in the following code syntax:

Code Syntax

```
pic.setImageResource(Animals[arg2]);
```

Animals is the name of the array and arg2 represents the index of the array. The argument arg2 is defined as the position of the selected image in the GridView. To assign a picture to the Image View control, follow this step:

STEP 1

- In MainActivity.java, tap or click at the end of the line you just entered, if necessary, and press the Enter key.

- To display the selected image, type **pic.setImageResource(Animals[arg2]);**.

The selected image is displayed in the ImageView with the use of setImageResource (Figure 7-20).

```
26     gr.setOnItemClickListener(new OnItemClickListener() {
27
28     @Override
29     public void onItemClick(AdapterView<?> arg0, View arg1, int arg2,
30             long arg3) {
31         // TODO Auto-generated method stub
32         Toast.makeText(getBaseContext(), "Selected Species " + (arg2 + 1), Toast.LENGTH_SHORT).show();
33         pic.setImageResource(Animals[arg2]);
34     }
35
36     });
37     }
38     public class ImageAdapter extends BaseAdapter {
```

setImageResource
displays the selected image

Figure 7-20   ImageView control displays selected GridView picture

IN THE TRENCHES

An image can also be placed on the surface of a Button control by the android:src attribute in the XML code or by the setImageResource(int) method of a button.

Customizing the ImageAdapter Class

At this point in the chapter project code, the GridView and ImageView are initialized, the onClickListener awaits interaction, the toast message and ImageView are prepared for display, but the ImageAdapter class is simply a set of auto-generated method stubs. The ImageAdapter class was called with this line of code: gr.setAdapter(new ImageAdapter (this));. Recall that the ImageAdapter class determines the layout of the GridView. The context and images of the GridView need to be referenced within the ImageAdapter class. The task to complete inside the ImageAdapter class is to manage the layout of the GridView and connect the data sources from the array for display within the GridView control.

Defining the Context of the ImageAdapter Class

The ImageAdapter class must provide the information to set up the GridView with data and specifications necessary for the display. A Context variable is used to load and access resources for the application. In the following code syntax, the class variable named context is initialized so it can hold each image in the GridView temporarily before it is displayed. The ImageAdapter constructor is changed from the MainActivity to handle the Context resources necessary for the GridView. **Constructors** are used to initialize the instance variables of an object. Constructors enable the programmer to set default values, limit instantiation, and write code that is flexible and easy to read. This command is called a constructor because it constructs the values of data members of the class.

Code Syntax

```
private Context context;
public ImageAdapter(Context c){
    // TODO Auto-generated constructor stub
    context=c;
}
```

This ImageAdapter class constructor is where the Context for an ImageAdapter instance is defined. To define the Context for the ImageAdapter, follow these steps:

STEP 1

- Save your work. Tap or click the blank line after the public class ImageAdapter extends BaseAdapter { line.

- Initialize the Context variable by typing **private Context context;**.

- Point to Context, and then select Import 'Context' (android.content).

The Context variable named context is initialized (Figure 7-21).

```
△30        public void onItemClick(AdapterView<?> arg0, View arg1, int arg2,
 31               long arg3) {
☑32            // TODO Auto-generated method stub
 33            Toast.makeText(getBaseContext(), "Selected Species " + (arg2 + 1), Toast.LENGTH_SHORT).show();
 34            pic.setImageResource(Animals[arg2]);
 35        }
 36
 37     });
 38    }
 39⊖ public class ImageAdapter extends BaseAdapter {
 40        private Context context;   I
 41⊖        public ImageAdapter(MainActivity mainActivity) {
☑42            // TODO Auto-generated constructor stub
 43        }
 44
 45⊖        @Override
△46        public int getCount() {
```

> context variable is
> initialized in the
> ImageAdapter class

Figure 7-21 Context variable

STEP 2

- To change the ImageAdapter constructor to define the Context in the next statement, change public ImageAdapter(MainActivity mainActivity) { on the next line to **public ImageAdapter (Context c) {**.

- At the end of the TODO comment on the next line, press the Enter key to insert a blank line. Type **context=c;**.

The ImageAdapter constructor for the ImageAdapter class holds the Context (Figure 7-22).

```
 39⊖ public class ImageAdapter extends BaseAdapter {
 40        private Context context;
 41⊖        public ImageAdapter (Context c) {
☑42            // TODO Auto-generated constructor stub
 43            context=c;  I
 44        }
 45
 46⊖        @Override
△47        public int getCount() {
☑48            // TODO Auto-generated method stub
 49            return 0;
 50        }
 51
 52⊖        @Override
△53        public Object getItem(int arg0) {
☑54            // TODO Auto-generated method stub
 55            return null;
 56        }
 57
 58⊖        @Override
△59        public long getItemId(int arg0) {
```

> ImageAdapter is
> customized to hold
> Context resources

Figure 7-22 ImageAdapter constructor

Calculating the Length of an Array

The next method in the ImageAdapter class is the getCount( ) method. When the ImageAdapter class is called, the getCount( ) method determines how many pictures should be displayed in the GridView control. It does so by finding the length of the Animals array, which references the pictures of the endangered species. To determine the length of an array, Java provides a method named length( ) that returns an integer value of any given string or array. For example, if a variable named phone is assigned the text Android, the integer phoneLength is assigned the integer value of 7, representing the length of the word "Android".

```
String phone = "Android";
int phoneLength = phone.length( );
```

The length of an array is determined by the number of elements in the array. The length of the Animals array is an integer value of 6. The getCount( ) method must return the number of elements in the GridView in order to create the correct layout for the GridView control. To do so, include in the getCount( ) method a return statement as shown in the following code syntax:

Code Syntax

```
    return Animals.length;
```

A Java **method** is a series of statements that perform some repeated task. In the case of the chapter project, the method is called within the ImageAdapter class. The purpose of the getCount( ) method is to return the number of elements in the array. You declare a method's return type in its method declaration. In the following syntax, the declaration statement public int getCount( ) includes int. The data type int indicates that the return data type is an integer. Within the body of the method, you use the return statement to return the value. Any method declared void does not return a value because it returns to the method normally. Therefore, no return statement is necessary. Any method that is not declared void must contain a return statement with a corresponding return value such as the length of an array.

Code Syntax

```
    public int getCount( ) {
        // TODO Auto-generated constructor stub
        return Animals.length;
    }
```

To return the length of an array from the getCount( ) method, follow this step:

STEP 1

- In the return statement for public int getCount( ), change the return type from return 0; to **return Animals.length;**.

The getCount( ) method returns the length of the Animals array (Figure 7-23).

```
42              // TODO Auto-generated constructor stub
43              context=c;
44          }
45
46      @Override
47      public int getCount() {
48              // TODO Auto-generated method stub
49              return Animals.length;           ◄──── Returns the length
50          }                                          of the Animals array
51
52      @Override
53      public Object getItem(int arg0) {
54              // TODO Auto-generated method stub
55              return null;
56          }
57
58      @Override
59      public long getItemId(int arg0) {
60              // TODO Auto-generated method stub
61              return 0;
62          }
63
64      @Override
```

Figure 7-23   Length of the Animals array

GTK
The length of an array is one more than the maximum subscript number.

Coding the getView Method

The most powerful method in the ImageAdapter class is the getView( ) method. The getView( )
method uses Context to create a new ImageView instance that temporarily holds each image
displayed in the GridView. In addition, the ImageView is scaled to fit the GridView control and sized
according to a custom height and width. The following code syntax shows how the chapter project
uses the getView( ) method:

Code Syntax

```
public View getView(int arg0, View arg1, ViewGroup arg2){
    // TODO Auto-generated method stub
    pic = new ImageView(context);
    pic.setImageResource(Animals[arg0]);
    pic.setScaleType(ImageView.SealeType.FIT_XY) ;
    pic.setLayoutParams(new GridView.LayoutParams(188,200));
    return pic;
}
```

In the getView( ) method, notice that a return type of View is expected (in the View convert View argument). Recall that a View occupies a rectangular area on the screen and is responsible for drawing the GridView component. When pic is returned at the end of the method, it includes a scaled, resized image, ready to display in the GridView control.

In the getView( ) method, an instance of an ImageView control named pic is established in the pic = new ImageView(context); Java code. On the next line, pic is given an image to display in the GridView as defined by a position in the Animals array. As each position is passed to the getView( ) method, the ImageView control changes to hold each of the images referenced in the Animals array. The setImageResource method assigns an image from the drawable folder to the ImageView control. After an animal picture is assigned to pic, the layout of the ImageView control needs to be established. In the next statement, setScaleType scales the image to the bounds of the ImageView. Scaling keeps or changes the aspect ratio of the image within the ImageView control. When an image is scaled, the aspect ratio is changed; for example, the picture may be stretched horizontally, but not vertically. Notice that the ScaleType is set to the option FIT_XY. Several ScaleType options are available, but the most popular options are listed in Table 7-4.

ScaleType Option	Meaning
ImageView.ScaleType.CENTER	This option centers the image within the View type, but does not change the aspect ratio (no scaling).
ImageView.ScaleType.CENTER_CROP	This option centers the image within the View type and scales the image uniformly, maintaining the same aspect ratio.
ImageView.ScaleType.FIT_XY	This option scales the image to fit the View type. The aspect ratio is changed to fit within the control.

Table 7-4   Popular ScaleType options

After the image is scaled, the GridView images are resized to fit the custom layout. The design of the Endangered Species app calls for small thumbnail-sized images, so the setLayoutParams are set to the GridView.LayoutParams(188,200). The first value, 188, represents the number of pixels across the width of the image. The second value, 200, determines a height of 200 pixels. If you want to display a large GridView, the setLayoutParams can be changed to larger dimensions. The last statement in the getView( ) method (return pic;) must return the instance of the ImageView control named pic to display in the GridView control. To code the getView( ) method, follow these steps:

STEP 1

- Scroll down to the statement beginning with public View getView. Tap or click at the end of the TODO comment and press the Enter key to insert a blank line.

- To create an ImageView control that holds the images displayed in the GridView, type **pic = new ImageView(context);**.

An instance of ImageView named pic is created (Figure 7-24).

```
57
58⊖        @Override
△59        public long getItemId(int arg0) {
☑60            // TODO Auto-generated method stub
61            return 0;
62        }
63
64⊖        @Override
△65        public View getView(int arg0, View arg1, ViewGroup arg2) {
☑66            // TODO Auto-generated method stub
67            pic = new ImageView(context);      I ◄── pic in this statement is
68            return null;                              an instance of ImageView
69        }
70
71    }
72
```

Figure 7-24   Code for the ImageView control

STEP 2

- Press the Enter key.
- To assign each of the images referenced in the Animals array, type **pic.setImageResource(Animals[arg0]);**.

The instance of pic holds each of the images within the array (Figure 7-25).

```
△65        public View getView(int arg0, View arg1, ViewGroup arg2) {
☑66            // TODO Auto-generated method stub
67            pic = new ImageView(context);
68            pic.setImageResource(Animals[arg0]);   I ◄── Each image reference
69            return null;                                  in the Animals array is
70        }                                                 displayed in pic
71
```

Figure 7-25   Assigning images in the Animals array to the pic ImageView control

STEP 3

- Press the Enter key.
- To set the scale type of the ImageView control, type **pic.setScaleType(ImageView.ScaleType.FIT_XY);**.

The scale type for the ImageView pic is set to FIT_XY (Figure 7-26).

```
64    @Override
65    public View getView(int arg0, View arg1, ViewGroup arg2) {
66        // TODO Auto-generated method stub
67        pic = new ImageView(context);
68        pic.setImageResource(Animals[arg0]);
69        pic.setScaleType(ImageView.ScaleType.FIT_XY);        ImageView
70        return null;                                         control is
71    }                                                        scaled to fit
72
```

Figure 7-26   Setting the scale type for the ImageView control

STEP 4

- Press the Enter key.

- To resize the images displayed in the GridView control to 188 pixels wide and 200 pixels tall, type **pic.setLayoutParams(new GridView.LayoutParams(188,200));**.

The size of the images displayed in the GridView is set to 188 pixels wide by 200 pixels tall (Figure 7-27).

```
64    @Override
65    public View getView(int arg0, View arg1, ViewGroup arg2) {
66        // TODO Auto-generated method stub
67        pic = new ImageView(context);                        GridView images
68        pic.setImageResource(Animals[arg0]);                 are resized
69        pic.setScaleType(ImageView.ScaleType.FIT_XY);
70        pic.setLayoutParams(new GridView.LayoutParams(188,200));
71        return null;
72    }
73
```

Figure 7-27   Resizing the GridView images

STEP 5

- To return pic to the MainActivity, change the return null; statement to **return pic;**.

The pic instance is returned to the MainActivity (Figure 7-28).

```
 MainActivity.java 

  1  package net.androidbootcamp.endangeredspecies;
  2
  3  import android.os.Bundle;
 15
 16  public class MainActivity extends Activity {
 17      Integer[] Animals = (R.drawable.eagle, R.drawable.elephant, R.drawable.gorilla,
 18          R.drawable.panda, R.drawable.panther, R.drawable.polar);
 19      ImageView pic;
 20      @Override
 21      protected void onCreate(Bundle savedInstanceState) {
 22          super.onCreate(savedInstanceState);
 23          setContentView(R.layout.activity_main);
 24          GridView gr = (GridView)findViewById(R.id.gridView1);
 25          final ImageView pic= (ImageView)findViewById(R.id.imgLarge);
 26          gr.setAdapter(new ImageAdapter(this));
 27          gr.setOnItemClickListener(new OnItemClickListener() {
 28
 29              @Override
 30              public void onItemClick(AdapterView<?> arg0, View arg1, int arg2,
 31                      long arg3) {
 32                  // TODO Auto-generated method stub
 33                  Toast.makeText(getBaseContext(), "Selected Species " + (arg2 + 1), Toast.LENGTH_SHORT).show();
 34                  pic.setImageResource(Animals[arg2]);
 35              }
 36
 37          });
 38      }
 39      public class ImageAdapter extends BaseAdapter {
 40          private Context context;
 41          public ImageAdapter (Context c) {
 42              // TODO Auto-generated constructor stub
 43              context=c;
 44          }
 45
 46          @Override
 47          public int getCount() {
 48              // TODO Auto-generated method stub
 49              return Animals.length;
 50          }
 51
 52          @Override
 53          public Object getItem(int arg0) {
 54              // TODO Auto-generated method stub
 55              return null;
 56          }
 57
 58          @Override
 59          public long getItemId(int arg0) {
 60              // TODO Auto-generated method stub
 61              return 0;
 62          }
 63
 64          @Override
 65          public View getView(int arg0, View arg1, ViewGroup arg2) {
 66              // TODO Auto-generated method stub
 67              pic = new ImageView(context);
 68              pic.setImageResource(Animals[arg0]);
 69              pic.setScaleType(ImageView.ScaleType.FIT_XY);
 70              pic.setLayoutParams(new GridView.LayoutParams(188,200));
 71              return pic;                              Return variable pic
 72          }
 73
 74      }
 75
 76      @Override
 77      public boolean onCreateOptionsMenu(Menu menu) {
 78          // Inflate the menu; this adds items to the action bar if it is present.
 79          getMenuInflater().inflate(R.menu.main, menu);
 80          return true;
 81      }
 82
 83  }
 84
```

Figure 7-28   Complete code of Main_Activity.java

GTK

Aspect ratio is the fractional relation of the width of an image compared with its height. The two most common aspect ratios are 4:3 and 16:9 in HDTV. Keeping the aspect ratio means that an image is not distorted from its original ratio of width to height.

Running and Testing the Application

It is time to see your finished product. Tap or click Run on the menu bar, and then select Run to save and test the application in the emulator. A dialog box requesting how you would like to run the application opens the first time the application is executed. Select Android Application and tap or click the OK button. Save all the files in the next dialog box, if necessary, and unlock the emulator. The application opens in the emulator window where you can touch the GridView to view the images and select an image, as shown in Figures 7-1 and 7-2.

Wrap It Up—Chapter Summary

Many Android applications display a GridView to easily accommodate viewing a large amount of pictures. Creating a GridView in this chapter to dynamically display images from an array provided experience with using a second class, a custom toast message, methods with return variables, and the length of an array. Creating a second class called the ImageAdapter class provided the customization for the GridView layout.

- A View container is a rectangular area of the screen that displays an image or text object. It can include various layouts, including a GridView layout, which displays a grid of objects such as images, songs, or text. Users can scroll the GridView list to select an object such as a photo and display it in another control such as an ImageView control.

- To display an image in an ImageView control only if the user selects the image in the GridView, you must enter XML code for the ImageView control in activity_main.xml.

- An array variable can store more than one value. Arrays provide access to data by using a numeric index, or subscript, to identify each element in the array. For example, the first element in the array is assigned to the subscript of 0. An array can assign more than one image to a GridView control to eventually display only one image.

- A setAdapter provides a data model for the GridView layout. With the GridView control, the adapter binds certain types of data and displays that data in a specified layout.

- Like the OnClickListener used for a Button control, the OnItemClickListener waits for user interaction in a GridView control. When the user selects an item in the GridView, the OnItemClickListener processes an onItemClick event, which includes four arguments. The arg2 argument is an integer value that contains the position of the View in the adapter. For example, if the user taps the second image in the GridView, the integer value of 2 is stored in arg2.

- By including a toast notification in the onItemClick method, you can display a message indicating which image is selected in a GridView control. The message can include a variable to display the number of the image selected in the GridView. The toast message can float over the other controls so it never receives focus.

- Because the toast notification is not used directly in the Main Activity, you must replace Main.this in the onItemClick method with a Context class called getBaseContext( ). In Android programs, you use the getBaseContext( ) method to obtain a Context instance. This Context instance is triggered only when the user touches the GridView control.

- To display in an ImageView control the image selected in the GridView, you use the setImageResource( ) method with an int argument. The setImageResource command inserts an ImageView control and the int argument specifies which image is selected for display. If you are using an array to identify the images, you can use arg2 as the int argument because it represents the position of the selected image in the GridView.

- The ImageAdapter class must provide information to set up the GridView so it can display the appropriate images. You use the Context class to load and access resources for the application. A class variable can hold each image in the GridView temporarily before it is displayed. To handle the Context resources necessary for the GridView, you use the ImageAdapter constructor. A constructor can initialize the instance variables of an object. In other words, it constructs the values of data members of the class. You define the Context for an ImageAdapter instance in the ImageAdapter class constructor.

- The chapter project uses the getCount( ) method to determine how many pictures to display in the GridView control. It does so by referencing the array specifying the images for the GridView. To determine the length of an array, Java provides a method named length( ) that returns an integer type value of any given string or array. The length of an array is determined by the number of its elements. The getCount( ) method uses length( ) to return the number of elements in the GridView.

- The declaration statement public int getCount( ) indicates that the return data type (int) is an integer. Because the getCount( ) method is not declared void, it must contain a return statement with a corresponding return value such as the length of an array.

- In the chapter project, the getView( ) method uses Context to create a new ImageView instance to temporarily hold each image displayed in the GridView. The getView( ) method also contains statements that scale the ImageView to fit the GridView control and a specified height and width.

Key Terms

constructor—A part of the Java code used to initialize the instance variables of an object.

GridView—A View container that displays a grid of objects with rows and columns.

getBaseContext()—A Context class method used in Android programs to obtain a Context instance. Use getBaseContext( ) in a method that is triggered only when the user touches the GridView control.

method—In Java, a series of statements that perform some repeated task.

onItemClick—An event the OnItemClickListener processes when the user touches the GridView display layout. The onItemClick method is defined by OnItemClickListener and sends a number of arguments in the parentheses included within the line of code.

setAdapter—A command that provides a data model for the GridView layout, similar to an adapter, which displays a ListView control.

View—A rectangular container that displays a drawing or text object.

Developer FAQs

1. Which Android control displays a two-dimensional grid of images?

2. In which category on the Palette is the GridView control located?

3. Name three locations where photos that are used in the Android environment can be stored.

4. Why was the ImageView control coded in the XML code in the chapter project instead of dragging the ImageView control onto the emulator?

5. Name six View containers.

6. Write a line of code that uses an instance of a GridView control named grLayout in a new ImageAdapter class using setAdapter( ).

7. Write a line of code that creates a reference array named Games for the images named callofduty, candycrush, halo, and sonicdash.

8. What are the array name and index of halo in question 7?

9. What is the array length of the Games array in question 7?

10. Write a line of code that determines the length of the Games array from question 7 and assigns the value to an int variable named numberOfGames.

11. Write a line of code that assigns dentalLength to the length of a string named dental.

12. What is the purpose of the argument arg2 in the chapter project?

13. In the chapter project, if the user selects panda, what is the value of arg2?

14. Write a custom toast message that resides within an onItemClick( ) method and states *You have selected picture 4 of the political photos* when arg2 is 4.

15. What do the numbers in the following statement represent?

```
pic.setLayoutParams(new GridView.LayoutParams(300,325));
```

16. What does the aspect ratio 3:2 mean?

17. In the following method, what does int (integer) represent?

```
public int getCount( ) {
    return Soccer.length;
}
```

18. What would be returned in the method in question 17 if the Soccer array has the maximum index of 22?

19. What term does the following define? Constructs the values of data members of the class.

20. Write a statement that sets the scale type to CENTER for an ImageView instance named tower.

Beyond the Book

Using the Internet, search the Web for the answers to the following questions to further your Android knowledge.

1. Find GridView images from three Web sites that display a GridView with images and provide a URL and screenshot of each Web site.

2. Name five types of apps not discussed in this chapter and how they would each use a GridView control.

3. An excellent Web site that provides up-to-date information about the Android world can be found at *http://android.alltop.com*. Read an article that interests you and write a summary of that article of at least 100 words.

4. One of the major issues in the Android world is the multiple operating systems currently running on Android devices. Write a one-page report about the issue of upgrading Android devices to the newest OS available.

Case Programming Projects

Complete one or more of the following case programming projects. Use the same steps and techniques taught within the chapter. Submit the program you create to your instructor. The level of difficulty is indicated for each case programming project.

Easiest: ⋆

Intermediate: ⋆ ⋆

Challenging: ⋆ ⋆ ⋆

Case Project 7–1: Quick Healthy Snack Ideas App ✶

Requirements Document

Application title: Quick Healthy Snack Ideas App

Purpose: Stocking your fridge with quick and healthy snacks helps you resist eating diet-damaging foods. The Snack apps displays five healthy snack options.

Algorithms: 1. The screen displays five snacks with three on each row in a GridView control (Figure 7-29).

2. When the user selects a thumbnail image of a healthy snack, a small image appears below the GridView (Figure 7-30).

Conditions: 1. The pictures of the five healthy snacks are provided with your student files with the names snack1 through snack5.

2. Display each image in the GridView with layout height of 400dp, use 2 columns, use 2dp for horizontal and vertical spacing, and use a column width of 150dp.

Figure 7-29

Figure 7-30

Case Project 7-2: New Seven Wonders of the World App ★

Requirements Document

Application title:	New Seven Wonders of the World (Monuments)
Purpose:	Wikipedia would like you to build an app to showcase the new seven wonders of the world and allow users to select any monument to see a large picture.
Algorithms:	1. The opening screen should display in a grid the seven images representing the new seven wonders of the world—Great Wall of China, Petra, The Redeemer, Machu Picchu, Chichen Itza, Colosseum, and Taj Mahal (Figure 7-31).
	2. When the user selects a monument image in the GridView control, a larger version of the image appears below the GridView. A toast message states which monument image the user selected by number (Figure 7-32).
Conditions:	1. The pictures of the seven wonders of the world are provided with your student files with the names wonder1 through wonder7.
	2. Display each image in the GridView control with 4 images across each row, use a column width of 60dp, use horizontal spacing of 3dp, and use vertical spacing of 3dp.

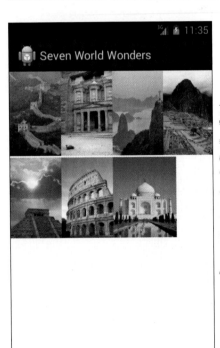

best-photo/E+/Getty Images; HUGHES HervÃ©/hemis.fr/Getty Images; Stuart Dee/Photolibrary/Getty Images; Jeffrey Bosdet/All Canada Photos/Getty Images; Images Etc Ltd/Getty Images; xenotar/E+/Getty Images; Feverstockphoto/E+/Getty Images

Figure 7-31

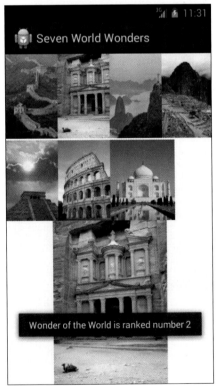

Wonder of the World is ranked number 2

best-photo/E+/Getty Images; HUGHES HervÃ©/hemis.fr/Getty Images; Stuart Dee/Photolibrary/Getty Images; Jeffrey Bosdet/All Canada Photos/Getty Images; Images Etc Ltd/Getty Images; xenotar/E+/Getty Images; Feverstockphoto/E+/ Getty Images

Figure 7-32

Case Project 7–3: S.P.C.A. Rescue Shelter App ⋆

Requirements Document

Application title: S.P.C.A. Rescue Shelter App

Purpose: Your local S.P.C.A. needs an app to display the dogs in need of a home.

Algorithms: 1. The screen displays six dogs from the shelter in a large GridView control.

2. When the user selects a thumbnail image of a dog, a full-size image appears below the GridView.

Conditions: 1. Find six pictures of the dogs eligible for adoption online.

2. Display each image in the GridView with the size 300, 250.

Case Project 7–4: Car Rental App ⋆ ⋆

Requirements Document

Application title: Car Rental App

Purpose: A car rental company would like to display its car rental choices in a GridView.

Algorithms: 1. The opening screen displays images of six rental car models in a GridView control.

2. When the user selects a car thumbnail image, a full-size image appears below the GridView. Using an If statement, a toast message states the types of car and cost of each rental car.

Conditions: 1. Locate six rental car images on the Internet.

2. Create a custom layout using the CENTER scale type.

Case Project 7–5: Anthology Wedding Photography App ★ ★ ★

Requirements Document

Application title:	Anthology Wedding Photography App
Purpose:	Anthology Wedding Photography would like to display a sample of its work with 10 wedding images in a GridView.
Algorithms:	1. Create a GridView that displays 10 wedding photos.
	2. When the user selects a specific wedding image in the GridView, a large image appears with a custom toast message that displays *Anthology Wedding Photo* and the image number.
	3. A text line appears at the bottom of the screen: *Contact us at anthology@wed.com.*
Conditions:	1. Select wedding images from the Internet.
	2. Use a layout of your choice.

Case Project 7–6: Personal Photo App ★ ★ ★

Requirements Document

Application title:	Personal Photo App
Purpose:	Create your own photo app with eight images of your family and friends in a GridView control.
Algorithms:	1. Create a GridView that displays eight images of your friends and family.
	2. When the user selects a specific thumbnail image in the GridView, a large image appears with a custom toast message that states the first name of the pictured person.
Conditions:	1. Select your own images.
	2. Use a layout of your choice.

Design! Using a DatePicker on a Tablet

In this chapter, you learn to:

- ◎ Create an Android project on a tablet
- ◎ Understand tablet specifications
- ◎ Follow design principles for the Android tablet
- ◎ Add a second Android Virtual Device
- ◎ Add a custom launcher and tablet theme
- ◎ Understand the Calendar class
- ◎ Use date, time, and clock controls
- ◎ Determine the system date
- ◎ Display a DatePicker control
- ◎ Launch a dialog box containing a DatePicker control
- ◎ Code an onDateSetListener method to await user interaction
- ◎ Determine the date entered on a calendar control
- ◎ Test an application on a tablet emulator

The explosion of the Android market is not limited to the phone platform. Android tablet sales are successfully competing with the Apple iPad as well, proving that consumers are ready for a tablet environment. Now more than ever, mobile designers are being asked to create experiences for a variety of tablet devices. In today's post-PC world, the tablet market provides the mobility and simplicity users demand for connecting to the Internet, playing games, using Facebook, checking email, and more. Lower price points and a large app marketplace are driving growth in the Android tablet market. Android tablets come in various sizes, often ranging from 7.3 inches to 10.1 inches, comparable to the iPad Mini and the full-size iPad. To understand the process of designing an application on the Android tablet, in this chapter you design a calendar program on a 10.1-inch tablet that books a reservation on a deep sea fishing boat in Hawaii called Sailing Adventures. The Sailing Adventures application shown in Figure 8-1 provides information about one of its fishing adventures located in Kona, Hawaii. This single-screen experience could be part of a larger app featuring fishing trips throughout the world.

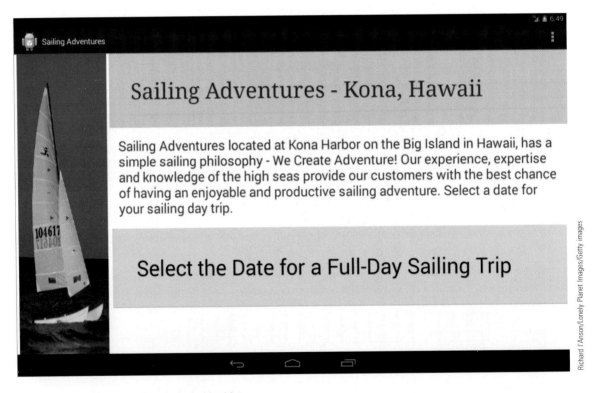

Richard l'Anson/Lonely Planet Images/Getty images

Figure 8-1   Sailing Adventures Android tablet app

The Android tablet app in Figure 8-1 appears on a 10.1-inch WXGA display. When the user makes a reservation by touching the button control, a floating dialog box opens with a DatePicker calendar control, as shown in Figure 8-2. When the date is set by the user, a TextView control confirms the reservation for the deep sea fishing day trip, as shown in Figure 8-3.

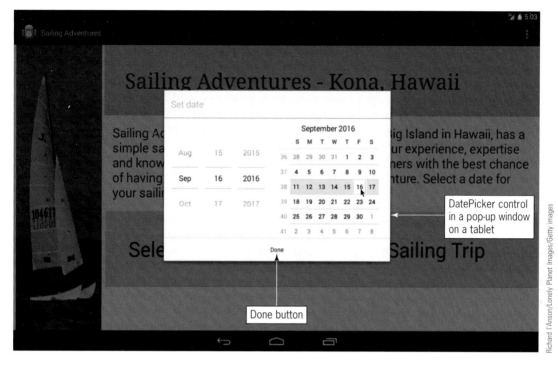

Figure 8-2 DatePicker calendar control in a dialog box

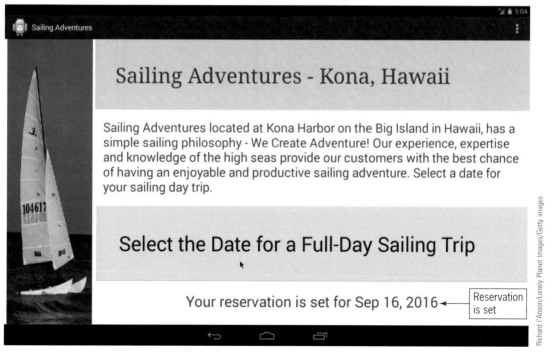

Figure 8-3 TextView control displays reservation

IN THE TRENCHES
The Android platform has been ported to many kinds of devices beyond phones and tablets, such as toasters, televisions, microwaves, and laptops.

To create this application, the developer must understand how to perform the following processes, among others:

1. Add an Android Virtual Device specifically designed for tablets.

2. Add the images used in this project.

3. Change the theme and icon for the tablet display.

4. Create a custom XML file with a Table layout.

5. Add and initialize the TextView controls and the Button control.

6. Initialize a DatePickerDialog with the present date and listen for the user to select a date.

7. Return the selected date.

8. Display the selected reservation date in the TextView control.

Designing a Tablet Application

The Android market initially only included mobile phone devices, but the recent popularity of the tablet device provides a new platform for Android app programming. The growth of the Android tablet market goes hand in hand with dedicated applications designed especially for the tablet, not just enlarged versions of a phone app. **Native applications** are programs locally installed on a specific platform such as a phone or tablet. A native application is typically designed for a specific platform such as a phone on a 3.7-inch screen or a tablet on a 10.1-inch screen. In contrast, an **emulated application** is converted in real time to run on a variety of platforms such as a Web page, which can be displayed on various screen sizes through a browser. A native Android tablet app creates an optimal user experience based on the most common tablet screen sizes between approximately 7.3 and 10.1 inches, a 1280 × 800 pixel resolution, and a 16:9 screen ratio, as shown in Figure 8-4. In comparison, an Apple iPad has a 9.7-inch screen, a 1024 × 768 pixel resolution, and a screen ratio of 4:3. If you plan to create apps on multiple platforms, the different screen specifications will affect your design.

© iStockphoto.com/picmov

Figure 8-4   Android tablet

As you consider creating an Android tablet application, remember that tablets are not simply huge smartphones. Even the primary use of each device is different. A smartphone is most likely used on the go in a truly mobile fashion to quickly check email, update your Facebook status, or send a text message between classes or as you run errands. Tablets are typically used for longer periods of time. This prolonged interaction on tablets is more involved, with users sitting down at a table in Starbucks, riding a train, or relaxing with the tablet positioned in their laps while watching a movie. Whereas phone app design relies on simplicity, a tablet can handle the complexity of more graphics, more text, and more interaction during longer sessions.

IN THE TRENCHES

Android tablet apps are still a relatively new space. To gain some inspiration for your tablet design best practices, download the YouTube, CNN, CNBC, Pulse, WeatherBug, and Kindle apps.

Design Best Practices for Tablets

As you begin designing an Android app, first consider how the user most likely will interact with your app. Will the tablet be in his or her lap, held with two hands (games often require this), or in a tablet stand? Will the user spend seconds, minutes, or hours using your app?

What is the optimal way to deliver the content? As you consider the answers to each of these questions, also keep these design guidelines in mind:

- Keep screens uncluttered and ensure touch controls such as buttons and radio buttons are of sufficient size for user interaction. Larger controls are easier to find and enable simpler interaction for the user.

- Focus apps on the task at hand. Keep the design simple. Do not force the user to spend undue time figuring out how to use the application.

- Resist filling the large screen with "cool" interactions that distract the user without adding to the quality of the program.

- Use flexible dimension values such as dp and sp instead of px or pt.

- Provide higher resolution resources for screen densities (DPI) to ensure that your app looks great on any screen size.

- Create a unique experience for both the phone and tablet designs.

- Use larger fonts than with a phone app. Consider printing your user interface design to see how it looks. Do not make users double-tap or pinch your content to read it clearly. Instead, increase the font size to at least 16dp.

IN THE TRENCHES

Consumers of all ages are spending more time playing games on tablets. This trend affects the retail market sales of console-based video games and traditional children's toys. This shift leaves retailers out of the sales streams because most digital content is distributed within the different phone platform markets.

Adding an Android Virtual Device for the Tablet

To make sure your Android tablet app deploys to any device in the Android platform starting with Android Honeycomb 3.0 operating system (API11), which is the first API dedicated to tablet applications, you can add multiple Android Virtual Devices (AVDs) in Eclipse for your intended device and platform. Honeycomb was initially designed for the Android Xoom, the first tablet introduced, but newer SDKs support the full range of new Android tablet devices on the market. When you create an Android tablet app, the minimum required SDK should be set to API 11: Android 3.0 (Honeycomb) to cover the oldest Android tablets and set the Target SDK to the newest SDK available. Each Android device configuration is stored in AVD.

To use the most recent tablet emulator, you first add the appropriate AVD configuration. To download the Android Development Tools for Honeycomb 3.0, follow these steps:

STEP 1

- Open the Eclipse program and tap or click Window on the menu bar to add a second emulator.

- Tap or click Android Virtual Device Manager to open the Android Virtual Device Manager dialog box.

- Tap or click the New button to open the Create new Android Virtual Device (AVD) dialog box.

- To name the tablet Android emulator, type **Tablet** in the AVD Name text box.

- Tap or click the Device arrow to display a listing of emulator devices.

- 10.1" WXGA (Tablet) (1280 × 800: mdpi). Please note that most computers cannot handle a higher dpi resolution emulator (above 1280 × 800) such as the Nexus 10.

- To target your Android app to appear in the newest Android version, select the latest Android version in the Target list.

A new AVD named Tablet is set up to emulate a tablet device (Figure 8-5).

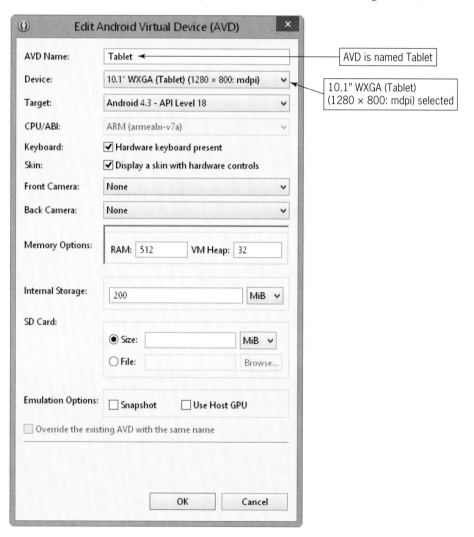

Figure 8-5   Edit Android Virtual Device (AVD) dialog box

STEP 2

- Tap or click the OK button.

The Android Virtual Device Manager dialog box lists the new AVD Name (Tablet) for the Android tablet emulator along with the existing Android smartphone target device (Figure 8-6).

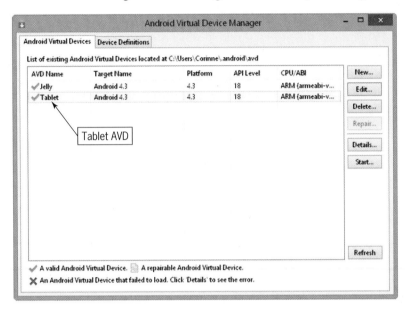

Figure 8-6   Android Virtual Device Manager dialog box

Creating a Tablet App

To create an Android tablet application for the Sailing Adventures app, follow these steps to begin the application and change the emulator:

STEP 1

- Close the Android Virtual Device Manager dialog box.

- Tap or click the New button on the Standard toolbar and then select Android Application Project.

- Tap or click the Next button.

- In the New Android Application dialog box, enter the Application Name **Sailing Adventures**.

- Enter the Package Name **net.androidbootcamp.sailingadventures**.

- Change the Minimum Required SDK to API 11: Android 3.0 (Honeycomb), the first API designed for a tablet.

The new Android Sailing Adventures project has an application name, a package name, and a minimum SDK of API 11, which supports tablet design (Figure 8-7).

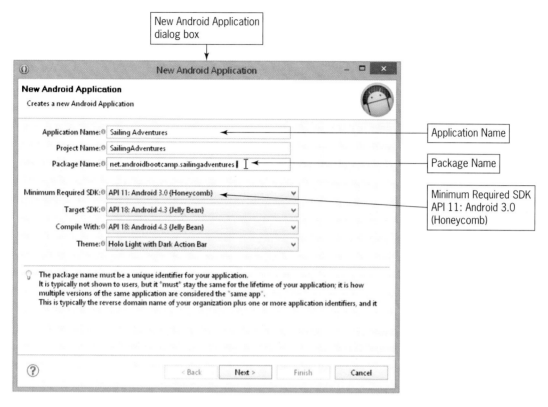

Figure 8-7 Setting up the Sailing Adventures project

STEP 2

- Tap or click the Next button.

- Tap or click the Create custom launcher icon box to uncheck the option.

- Tap or click the Next button twice.

- Tap or click the Finish button.

- If necessary, expand the Sailing Adventures project in the Package Explorer.

- On the activity_main.xml tab, tap or click the Hello world! TextView (displayed by default) in the emulator and press the Delete key.

- To change the emulator display for activity_main.xml, tap or click the Screen Preview arrow presently set to Nexus One and select 10.1" WXGA (Tablet).

- To display the tablet emulator preview in the Landscape state, tap or click the Go to next state arrow and select Landscape.

The activity_main.xml file is displayed in Landscape state as a 10.1-inch tablet on the Graphical Layout tab and the Hello world TextView widget is deleted (Figure 8-8).

10.1in WXGA (Tablet)

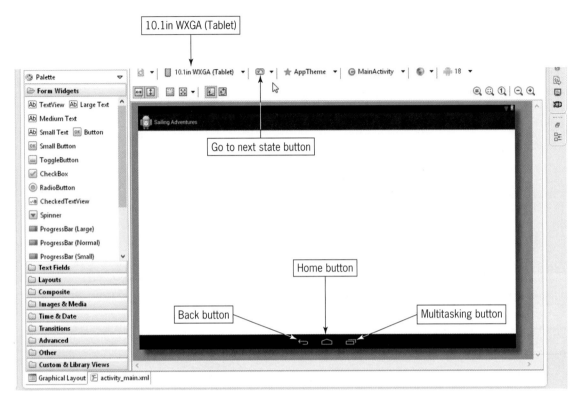

Figure 8-8   activity_main.xml for the Sailing Adventures project as a landscape tablet

GTK

The three navigation buttons centered on the bottom of the Android tablet are Back, Home, and Multitasking. The Back button returns to the previous action. The Home button returns to the default home screen. The Multitasking button opens a list of the apps that have been used recently.

Creating the String Table

The chapter project app contains four text strings—the content description for the image as shown in Figure 8-1, the text title in the first TextView object, the description about the sailing trip, and the Button control text. To add the image to the drawable folder and text values to strings.xml, follow these steps.

STEP 1

- In the Package Explorer, expand the values folder within the res folder.

- Double-tap or double-click the strings.xml file to display the Android Resources.

- Tap or click the Add button.

- If necessary, tap or click String and then tap or click the OK button.

- In the Name text box, type **imgSail** to name the String.
- In the Value text box, type **Sailing Image** to define the text that will be displayed as a content description for the ImageView control.
- Tap or click the Add button.
- If necessary, tap or click String and then tap or click the OK button.
- In the Name text box, type **txtTitle** to name the String.
- In the Value text box, type **Sailing Adventures - Kona, Hawaii** to define the text that will be displayed in the first TextView control.
- Tap or click the Add button.
- If necessary, tap or click String and then tap or click the OK button.
- In the Name text box, type **txtDescription** to name the String.
- In the Value text box, type the following text: **Sailing Adventures located at Kona Harbor on the Big Island in Hawaii, has a simple sailing philosophy - We Create Adventure! Our experience, expertise and knowledge of the high seas provide our customers with the best chance of having an enjoyable and productive sailing adventure. Select a date for your sailing day trip.**
- Tap or click the Add button.
- If necessary, tap or click String and then tap or click the OK button.
- In the Name text box, type **btnDate** to name the String.
- In the Value text box, type **Select the Date for a Full-Day Sailing Trip** to define the text. Save strings.xml.

The Name and Value of the ImageView, TextView, and Button controls are entered into the strings.xml file (Figure 8-9).

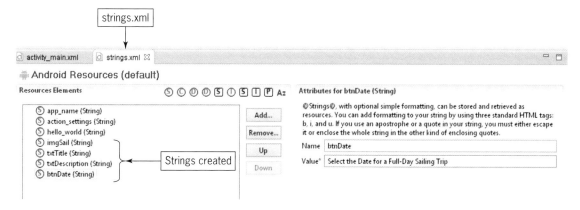

Figure 8-9 String table completed

STEP 2

- Close the strings.xml file tab.

- Open the USB folder containing the student files.

- In the Package Explorer, expand the drawable-hdpi folder. Drag the sailing.png file to the drawable-hdpi folder until a plus sign pointer appears. Release the mouse button.

- Tap or click the OK button in the File Operation dialog box.

The sailing.png image is placed in the drawable folder (Figure 8-10).

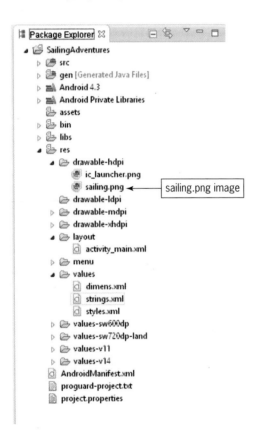

Figure 8-10   Image added to drawable folder

GTK

Google created an Android Design Web site *(http://developer.android.com/design)* to assist in best practices and to set a uniform look and feel across the various Android platforms.

Designing a Tablet Table Layout

In the Sailing Adventures application, two layouts are combined in activity_main.xml to organize the tablet user interface controls. The Linear layout and the Table layout create a simple, clean interface on the tablet containing both rows and columns. The left column described in Table 8-1 uses the Linear layout to display the sailing.png image. On the right side of Table 8-1, four rows are inserted in a Table layout to display the title, description, button, and reservation result. (Figure 8-3 shows this layout with all the design elements.)

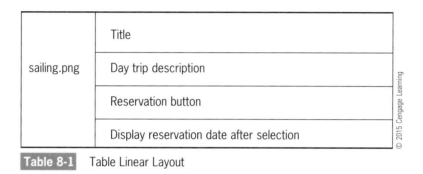

sailing.png	Title
	Day trip description
	Reservation button
	Display reservation date after selection

© 2015 Cengage Learning

Table 8-1   Table Linear Layout

A user interface design layout named **TableLayout** is composed of TableRow controls—one for each row in your table in activity_main.xml. In Table 8-1, the layout consists of four rows and one column. The contents of each TableRow are the view controls that will go in each cell of the table grid. The TableLayout shown in the following code has four TableRow controls with either a TextView or Button control within each row within a LinearLayout:

Code Syntax

```
<?xml version="1.0" encoding="utf-8"?>
<LinearLayout
xmlns:android="http://schemas.android.com/apk/res/android"
    <ImageView />
    <TableLayout
      <TableRow>
         <TextView />
      </TableRow>
      <TableRow>
         <TextView />
      </TableRow>
      <TableRow>
         <Button />
      </TableRow>
      <TableRow>
         <TextView />
      </TableRow>
    </TableLayout>
</LinearLayout>
```

To create additional columns, you add a view to a row. Adding a view in a row forms a cell, and the width of the largest view determines the width of the column.

Within the XML layout file, an Android property named padding is used to spread out the content displayed on the tablet. The **padding property** can be used to offset the content of the control by a specific number of pixels. For example, if you set a padding of 20 pixels, the content of a control is distanced from other controls by 20 pixels. Another Android property named **typeface** sets the style of the text to font families that include monospace, sans_serif, and serif.

The Sailing Adventure app displays the table within a horizontal LinearLayout. By default, the Android layout is set to RelativeLayout, which allows you to place controls anywhere on the emulator. Follow these steps to change the layout of activity_main.xml for the tablet to a LinearLayout.

STEP 1

- Press and hold or right-click the activity_main.xml emulator.

- Tap or click Change Layout to open the Change Layout dialog box.

- Tap or click the New Layout Type arrow to display the layout types.

The layout types are displayed in the Change Layout dialog box (Figure 8-11).

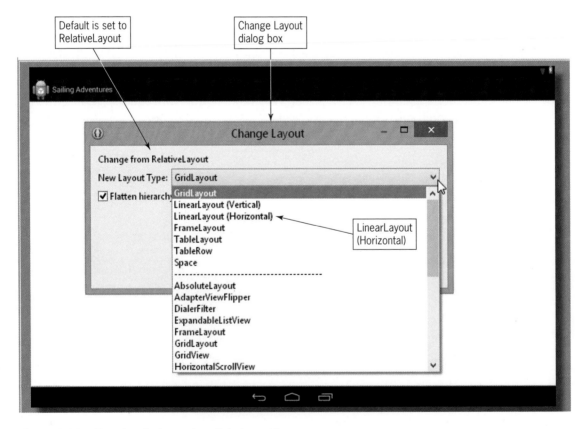

Figure 8-11 Changing the layout from Relative to Linear

STEP 2

- Select LinearLayout (Horizontal) to change the layout.

- Tap or click the OK button.

- Tap or click the activity_main.xml tab at the bottom of the emulator.

The activity_main.xml displays the LinearLayout code, which will horizontally align the elements on the emulator (Figure 8-12).

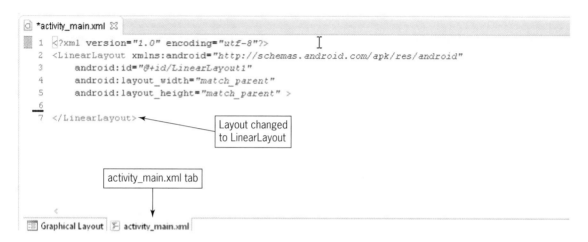

```
*activity_main.xml ⊠
 1  <?xml version="1.0" encoding="utf-8"?>
 2  <LinearLayout xmlns:android="http://schemas.android.com/apk/res/android"
 3      android:id="@+id/LinearLayout1"
 4      android:layout_width="match_parent"
 5      android:layout_height="match_parent" >
 6
 7  </LinearLayout>
```

Layout changed to LinearLayout

activity_main.xml tab

🔲 Graphical Layout 🗎 activity_main.xml

Figure 8-12 LinearLayout set

After the layout is set, the ImageView control and the table can be coded with four rows within the activity_main.xml file by following these steps.

STEP 1

- To the right of the > bracket in Line 5, press the Enter key twice to insert a blank line and then type **<ImageView** in the new line.

- Press the Enter key.

- Type the following code to add the ImageView control using auto-completion as much as possible:

```
android:id="@+id/imgSail"
android:layout_width="220dp"
android:layout_height="685dp"
android:contentDescription="@string/imgSail"
android:src="@drawable/sailing" />
```

The ImageView control is coded in activity_main.xml (Figure 8-13).

```
a  *activity_main.xml ⊠
  1  <?xml version="1.0" encoding="utf-8"?>
  2  <LinearLayout xmlns:android="http://schemas.android.com/apk/res/android"
  3       android:id="@+id/LinearLayout1"
  4       android:layout_width="match_parent"
  5       android:layout_height="match_parent" >
  6
  7       ImageView
  8          android:id="@+id/imgSail"
  9          android:layout_width="220dp"
 10          android:layout_height="685dp"
 11          android:contentDescription="@string/imgSail"
 12          android:src="@drawable/sailing" />
 13
 14  </LinearLayout>
 15
 16
```

ImageView displays sailing.png

Figure 8-13 ImageView control coded in the LinearLayout

STEP 2

- To code the TableLayout for the first two table rows to display the title and description TextView controls, press the Enter key.

- Type the following code using auto-completion as much as possible:

```
<TableLayout
    android:layout_width="fill_parent"
    android:layout_height="wrap_content" >
<TableRow>
<View android:layout_height="60dp" />
<TextView
    android:id="@+id/txtTitle"
    android:layout_width="wrap_content"
    android:background="#B0C4DE"
    android:gravity="fill_horizontal"
    android:padding="50dp"
    android:text="@string/txtTitle"
    android:textSize="50sp"
    android:typeface="serif" />

</TableRow>
<TableLayout
    android:layout_width="fill_parent"
    android:layout_height="wrap_content" >
```

```
<TableRow>
<View android:layout_height="60dp" />
<TextView
    android:id="@+id/txtDescription"
    android:layout_width="wrap_content"
    android:layout_gravity="left"
    android:padding="20dp"
    android:text="@string/txtDescription"
    android:textSize="30sp" />
</TableRow>
</TableRow>
```

The first two rows of the table display the title and description of Sailing Adventures (Figure 8-14).

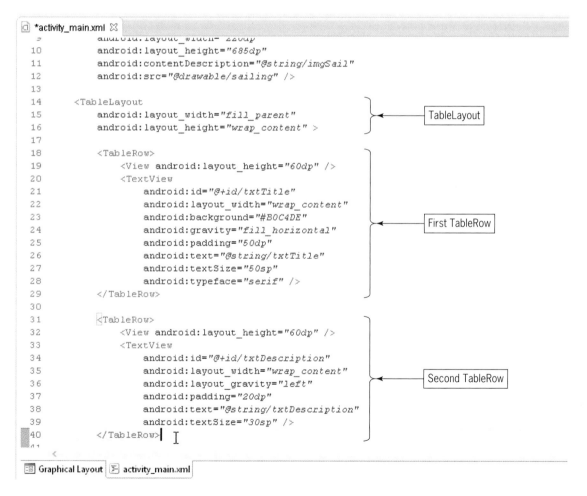

Figure 8-14   TableLayout XML code for first two TableRows

STEP 3

●   Next, write the XML code for the third and fourth table rows, which display a Button and TextView control. Press the Enter key after the closing </TableRow> tag, and then type the following code using auto-completion as much as possible:

```xml
<TableRow>
<View android:layout_height="50dp" />
<Button
    android:id="@+id/btnDate"
    android:layout_width="wrap_content"
    android:gravity="fill_horizontal"
    android:padding="20dp"
    android:text="@string/btnDate"
    android:textSize="36sp" />
</TableRow>

<TableRow>
<View android:layout_height="60dp" />
<TextView
    android:id="@+id/txtReservation"
    android:layout_gravity="center"
    android:padding="20dp"
    android:textSize="36sp" />
</TableRow>
</TableLayout>
```

The last two rows of the table display the button and reservation date of Sailing Adventures (Figure 8-15). To view the finished design, tap or click the Graphical Layout tab at the bottom of the window (Figure 8-16).

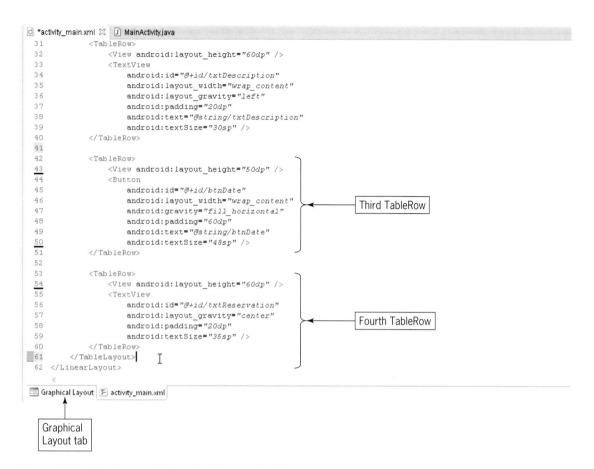

Figure 8-15   TableLayout XML code for last two TableRows

Figure 8-16   activity_main.xml Tablet layout

IN THE TRENCHES
After an app is published, it is the developer's responsibility to monitor comments and reviews for the app at Google Play. Consider conducting user surveys and doing further usability testing to update new versions to create a popular application.

Date, Time, and Clocks

A common Android application topic is managing calendars and time. Whether you are a student or a businessperson, a solid scheduling app can assist in personal organization to remind you about that upcoming test or to pay that bill, and an alarm clock app can help you wake up each morning. Android provides controls for the user to pick a time or a date as ready-to-use controls or to code using Java called dialogs. In the chapter project, a calendar tool called a DatePicker control is displayed in a dialog box to determine the user's preferred date for a full-day fishing trip. In the Time & Date category in the Palette, many calendar controls are available: TimePicker, DatePicker, CalendarView, Chronometer, and AnalogClock, as shown in Figure 8-17. Each picker provides controls for selecting each part of the time (hour, minute, AM/PM) or date (month, day, year).

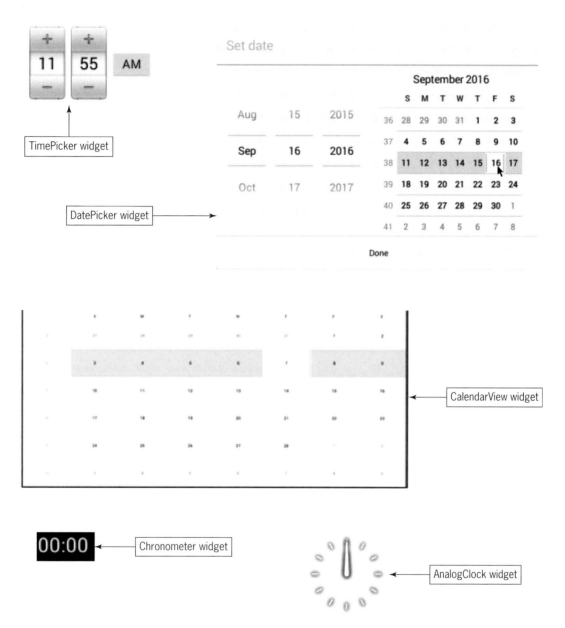

Figure 8-17 TimePicker, DatePicker, CalendarView, Chronometer, and AnalogClock widgets

All Android devices keep a numeric representation of the system's current date and time. These numbers can be displayed in multiple formats based on the cultural preferences of the user's location. For example, in the United States, the format of dates looks like this: March 17th, 2016, or 03/17/2016. In Canada and Europe, the day value normally precedes the month, like this: 17 March 2016 or 17/03/2016. Similarly, some countries use the concept of AM and PM with a 12-hour clock, whereas others commonly use a 24-hour clock. Developers often program these cultural differences based on user preference and location.

Creating a control to enter the date is crucial because requiring users to type the date in a text box can lead to multiple errors, including incorrect format or typos. Web sites primarily rely on some type of calendar control for input in the same way that the Sailing Adventures app requests the reservation in a DatePicker control to streamline the process. Initially, the Sailing Adventures app does not display a DatePicker widget. The user clicks the button to launch a dialog box that includes a coded DatePicker widget displaying today's date. Date and time controls are often launched in dialog boxes to keep the user interface uncluttered.

Instantiating the Objects

In the Sailing Adventures app, the activity_main layout opens, displaying the btnDate button. When the user interacts with the app and taps the btnDate button, a DatePickerDialog box opens and displays today's current date in the calendar. After the user selects the date of the desired sailing date using the calendar and taps Done at the bottom of the calendar, the reservation date is displayed within the txtReservation TextView control. The txtReservation TextView control is referenced in multiple methods, so this instantiation must be declared as a class variable. To instantiate the TextView control, Button control, and the Button OnClickListener, follow these steps.

STEP 1

- Save your work and then close the activity_main.xml window.

- In the Package Explorer, expand the src folder, expand net.androidbootcamp.sailingadventures, and then double-tap or double-click MainActivity.java to open it.

- In MainActivity.java, tap or click after the public class MainActivity extends Activity { statement and press the Enter key to insert a blank line.

- To initialize the class variable, type **private TextView reservation;**.

- Point to TextView and then tap or click Import 'TextView' (android.widget).

A class variable that can be accessed by the rest of the program is initialized (Figure 8-18).

```
 MainActivity.java ⊠
   1  package net.androidbootcamp.sailingadventures;
   2
   3⊕ import android.app.Activity;
   7
   8  public class MainActivity extends Activity {
   9        private TextView reservation; I◄────────────── Class variable
  10⊝       @Override                                        initialized
▲11        public void onCreate(Bundle savedInstanceState) {
  12            super.onCreate(savedInstanceState);
  13            setContentView(R.layout.activity_main);
  14    }
  15
  16⊝       @Override
▲17        public boolean onCreateOptionsMenu(Menu menu) {
  18            // Inflate the menu; this adds items to the action bar if it is present.
  19            getMenuInflater().inflate(R.menu.main, menu);
  20            return true;
  21    }
  22  }
  23
```

Figure 8-18　Date class variable

STEP 2

- In the onCreate( ) method, tap or click at the end of the setContentView(*R.layout.activity_main*); line and press the Enter key to insert a blank line.

- To reference the txtReservation id, type **reservation = (TextView) findViewById(R.id.txtReservation);**.

- To create an instance of the Button control from the XML layout, type **Button btDate = (Button) findViewById(*R.id.btnDate*);** *and then press the Enter key.*

- Point to Button and then tap or click Import 'Button' (android.widget).

The Button and TextView controls named btnDate and txtReservation are referenced in MainActivity. java (Figure 8-19).

```
 *MainActivity.java ⊠
  1   package net.androidbootcamp.sailingadventures;
  2
  3⊕ import android.app.Activity;☐
  8
  9   public class MainActivity extends Activity {
 10       private TextView reservation;
 11⊖      @Override
 12       public void onCreate(Bundle savedInstanceState) {
 13           super.onCreate(savedInstanceState);
 14           setContentView(R.layout.activity_main);
 15           reservation = (TextView) findViewById(R.id.txtReservation);
 16           Button btDate = (Button) findViewById(R.id.btnDate);
 17       }
 18
 19⊖      @Override
 20       public boolean onCreateOptionsMenu(Menu menu) {
 21           // Inflate the menu; this adds items to the action bar if it is present.
 22           getMenuInflater().inflate(R.menu.main, menu);
 23           return true;
 24       }
 25   }
 26
```

TextView class variable

Button instantiated

Figure 8-19   Class variables for Button and TextView controls

STEP 3

- To create the btDate button setOnClickListener method necessary to wait for the user to tap or click the button, on the next line type **btDate.setOnClickListener(new View.OnClickListener( ) {** and then press the Enter key to insert the closing brace.

- This onClickListener is designed for a Button control's variable. Point to View and then tap or click Import 'View' (android.view).

- Point to the red error line below View.OnClickListener and select Add unimplemented methods to add the quick fix.

- Type a right parenthesis and semicolon to complete the statement in Line 27.

An onClick auto-generated stub appears in the code for the button (Figure 8-20).

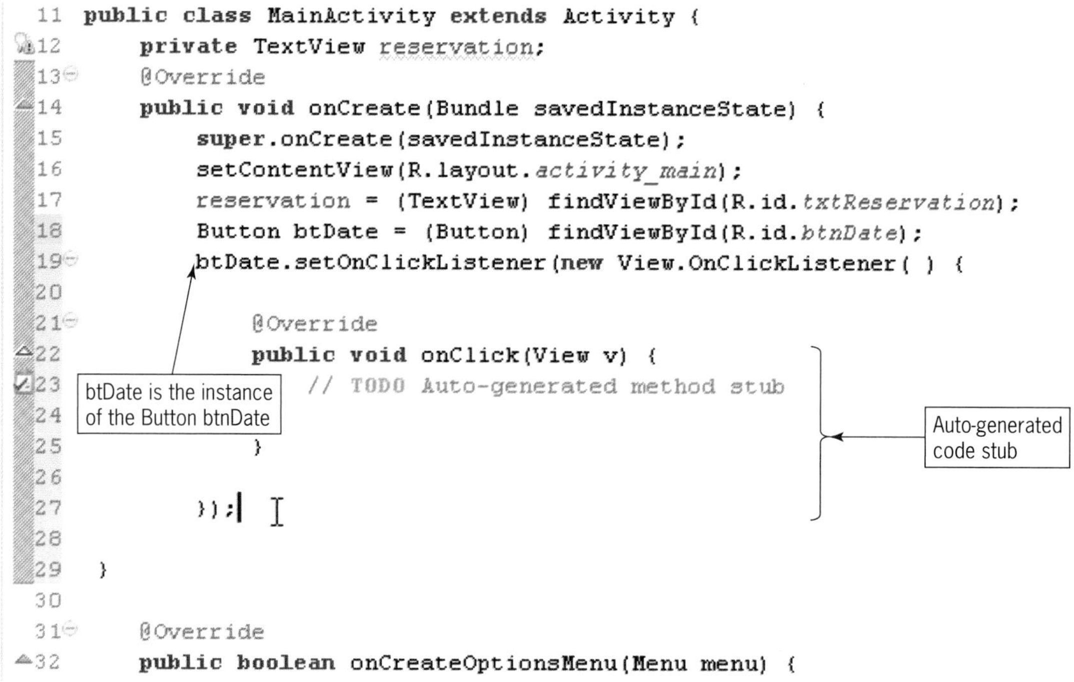

```
11  public class MainActivity extends Activity {
12      private TextView reservation;
13⊝     @Override
14      public void onCreate(Bundle savedInstanceState) {
15          super.onCreate(savedInstanceState);
16          setContentView(R.layout.activity_main);
17          reservation = (TextView) findViewById(R.id.txtReservation);
18          Button btDate = (Button) findViewById(R.id.btnDate);
19⊝         btDate.setOnClickListener(new View.OnClickListener( ) {
20
21⊝             @Override
22              public void onClick(View v) {
23                  // TODO Auto-generated method stub
24
25              }
26
27          });
28
29      }
30
31⊝     @Override
32      public boolean onCreateOptionsMenu(Menu menu) {
```

btDate is the instance of the Button btnDate

Auto-generated code stub

Figure 8-20   OnClickListener( )

Using the Calendar Class

The Android system date can be accessed by using the Java **Calendar class**, which is responsible for converting between a Date object and a set of integer fields such as YEAR, MONTH, and DAY_OF_MONTH. Typically, an Android mobile device connects to a cell phone tower or wireless network, which automatically updates the time zone and date. When using the Calendar class, a method of this class called **getInstance** returns a calendar date or time based on the system settings. The date constants in this class are **YEAR**, **MONTH**, and **DAY_OF_MONTH**; they retrieve an integer value of the system's current year, month, and day, respectively. Another Calendar constant includes **DAY_OF_YEAR**, which displays the day number of the current year, as shown in the following code. For example, February 1 would be identified as the value 32 for the 32nd day of the year.

To request the local date from your computer, the following syntax creates an instance of the Calendar class named c. The Calendar class is part of the java.util.Calendar class.

Code Syntax

```
Calendar c = Calendar.getInstance( ) ;
```

Date Format

The DateFormat class in Java, as the name suggests, formats the date into a String value and is part of the java.text.DateFormat class. By default, the DateFormat class sets the date to the default long style for your default country format with a full representation of the date such as March 17, 2016, in the United States. If you were in France, the default format and the country format for the same date would be 17 March 2016 because most countries list the day before the month.

Code Syntax

```
DateFormat fmtDate = DateFormat.getDateInstance();
```

DatePickerDialog Input

The Android platform has multiple dialog boxes that allow different types of user input. Each input dialog box has a specialized purpose, for example, the DatePickerDialog allows you to select a date from a DatePicker View, the TimePickerDialog allows you to select a time from the TimePicker View, and ProgressDialog displays a progress bar below a message text box to inform you of how long a time-consuming operation is taking. In the Sailing Adventures app, a DatePickerDialog box opens when the user taps the Button object. The DatePickerDialog is launched in the onClick method, and must be passed the values for the present year, month, and day. The values for the present date must be set for the DatePicker to display today's date. When the DatePickerDialog opens, an OnDateSetListener is necessary to await the user's selection of the desired reservation date.

In the code syntax discussed earlier, notice that c is an instance of the Calendar class. The statement c.set(Calendar.YEAR, year) represents the device system's year, c.set(Calendar. MONTH, monthOfYear) represents the system's month, and c.set(Calendar.DAY_OF_MONTH, dayOfMonth) represents which day of the month is set on the system calendar. The field manipulation method called **get** accesses the system date or time, and **set** changes the current date or time.

Code Syntax

```
public void onClick(View v) {
    // TODO Auto-generated method stub
    new DatePickerDialog(MainActivity.this, d,
        c.get(Calendar.YEAR), c.get(Calendar.MONTH),
        c.get(Calendar.DAY_OF_MONTH)).show();

}
```

The variable d in the code syntax is assigned later in the code to the date selected by the user for the sailing reservation, when the OnDateSetListener is established. Just like the button listener that awaits user interaction, a second listener is necessary to "listen" for the user to select a date after the dialog box displays a DatePicker control. To get an instance to the Calendar and DateFormat class, and get the current date from the system calendar within the onClick method, follow these steps:

STEP 1

- In MainActivity.java, tap or click to the right of the closing brace of the onCreate method and press the Enter key.

- To create an instance of the Calendar class, type **Calendar c = Calendar.getInstance( );**.

- Point to Calendar and tap or click Import 'Calendar' (java.util).

An instance of the Calendar class named c is created (Figure 8-21).

```
MainActivity.java ☒
  1  package net.androidbootcamp.sailingadventures;
  2
  3⊕ import java.util.Calendar;
 13
 14  public class MainActivity extends Activity {
 15      private TextView reservation;
 16⊖     @Override
 17      public void onCreate(Bundle savedInstanceState) {
 18          super.onCreate(savedInstanceState);
 19          setContentView(R.layout.activity_main);
 20          reservation = (TextView) findViewById(R.id.txtReservation);
 21          Button btDate = (Button) findViewById(R.id.btnDate);
 22⊖         btDate.setOnClickListener(new View.OnClickListener( ) {
 23
 24⊖             @Override
 25             public void onClick(View v) {
 26                 // TODO Auto-generated method stub
 27
 28             }
 29         });
 30
 31      }
 32      Calendar c = Calendar.getInstance();|  ◄————————  Calendar.getInstance( )
 33
 34⊖     @Override
 35      public boolean onCreateOptionsMenu(Menu menu) {
 36          // Inflate the menu; this adds items to the action bar if it is present.
 37          getMenuInflater().inflate(R.menu.main, menu);
 38          return true;
 39      }
 40  }
 41
```

Figure 8-21   Calendar instance

STEP 2

- Press the Enter key and type **DateFormat fmtDate = DateFormat.getDateInstance();** to set the default format of the date.

- Point to DateFormat and tap or click Import 'DateFormat' (java.text). *Note*: Do not import 'DateFormat' (android.text.format).

An instance of the DateFormat class named fmtDate is created (Figure 8-22).

```
18    public void onCreate(Bundle savedInstanceState) {
19        super.onCreate(savedInstanceState);
20        setContentView(R.layout.activity_main);
21        reservation = (TextView) findViewById(R.id.txtReservation);
22        Button btDate = (Button) findViewById(R.id.btnDate);
23        btDate.setOnClickListener(new View.OnClickListener( ) {
24
25            @Override
26            public void onClick(View v) {
27                // TODO Auto-generated method stub
28
29            }
30        });
31
32    }
33    Calendar c = Calendar.getInstance();
34    DateFormat fmtDate = DateFormat.getDateInstance();    ◄────── DateFormat
35
36        @Override
```

Figure 8-22 Format set with DateFormat

STEP 3

- To display the DatePicker dialog box after the user selects the Button object, tap or click within the onClick(View v) method (Line 28 in Figure 8-22; your line number may vary).

- To show the device's system year, month, and day of the month in the DatePicker, type **new DatePickerDialog(MainActivity.this, d, c.get(Calendar.YEAR), c.get(Calendar.MONTH), c.get(Calendar.DAY_OF_MONTH)).show();**

- Import 'DatePickerDialog' (android.app).

The calendar instance named c is assigned the current system date. The variable d displays a red curly line. It will be assigned the date that the user selects for the sailing reservation in the next steps (Figure 8-23).

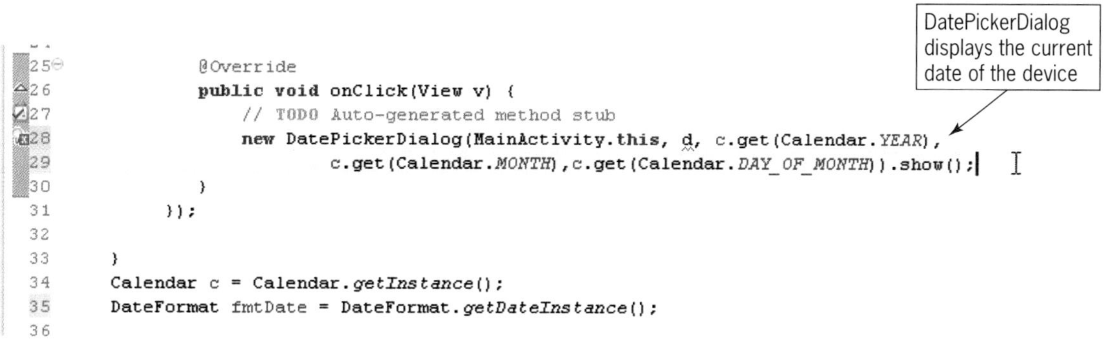

```
25      @Override
26      public void onClick(View v) {
27          // TODO Auto-generated method stub
28          new DatePickerDialog(MainActivity.this, d, c.get(Calendar.YEAR),
29              c.get(Calendar.MONTH),c.get(Calendar.DAY_OF_MONTH)).show();  I
30      }
31  });
32
33  }
34  Calendar c = Calendar.getInstance();
35  DateFormat fmtDate = DateFormat.getDateInstance();
36
```

DatePickerDialog displays the current date of the device

Figure 8-23   DatePickerDialog launched within the onClick method

Selecting the Date from the DatePickerDialog

When the app launches the DatePickerDialog control after tapping the Button control, the Android system date is initially displayed, making it easier for the user to select a future date without having to move forward in a calendar from a date decades ago. To access the system date, the variables are initialized and displayed for the present YEAR, MONTH, and DAY_OF_MONTH. Next, the DatePickerDialog control must await user interaction by coding an OnDateSetListener named d, which listens for a callback, indicating the user is done filling in the reservation date.

Code Syntax

```
DatePickerDialog.OnDateSetListener d = new DatePickerDialog.OnDateSetListener() {

}
```

Adding the onDateSet( ) Method

When the user selects a date from the DatePickerDialog, the **onDateSet( ) method** automatically obtains the date selected by the user. Three portions of the date must be set for the YEAR, MONTH, and DAY_OF_MONTH of the new reservation. The Sailing Adventures application calls the onDateSet( ) method in reaction to the user tapping Done at the bottom of the DatePickerDialog. Notice earlier in the code, the statement get was used to display the current system date and the statement, and set is now used to hold the selected date.

Code Syntax

```
public void onDateSet(DatePicker view, int year,
        int monthOfYear, int dayOfMonth) {
    c.set(Calendar.YEAR, year);
    c.set(Calendar.MONTH, monthOfYear);
    c.set(Calendar.DAY_OF_MONTH, dayOfMonth);
}
```

The next set of steps code the onDateSetListener and onDateSet methods that respond to the user's selected date.

STEP 1

- Save your work.

- After the DateFormat statement (Line 35 in Figure 8-23), press the Enter key and type

  DatePickerDialog.OnDateSetListener d = new DatePickerDialog.OnDateSetListener() {

- Press the Enter key to display a closing brace.

- Type a semicolon after the closing brace to complete the statement.

- Point to the OnDateSetListener( ) and select Add unimplemented methods.

The auto-generated stub for onDateSet( ) method is displayed (Figure 8-24).

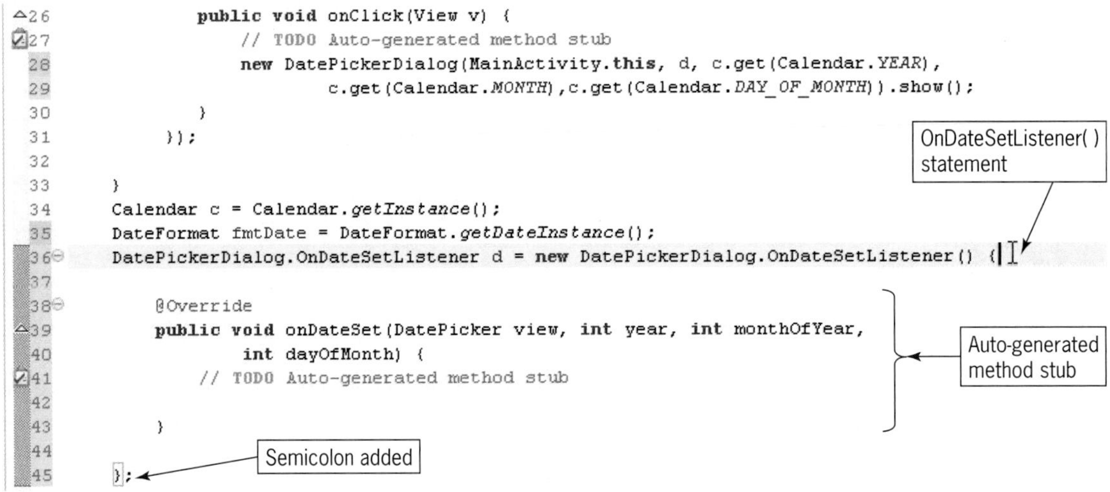

```
26      public void onClick(View v) {
27          // TODO Auto-generated method stub
28          new DatePickerDialog(MainActivity.this, d, c.get(Calendar.YEAR),
29              c.get(Calendar.MONTH),c.get(Calendar.DAY_OF_MONTH)).show();
30      }
31  });
32
33  }
34  Calendar c = Calendar.getInstance();
35  DateFormat fmtDate = DateFormat.getDateInstance();
36  DatePickerDialog.OnDateSetListener d = new DatePickerDialog.OnDateSetListener() {
37
38      @Override
39      public void onDateSet(DatePicker view, int year, int monthOfYear,
40          int dayOfMonth) {
41          // TODO Auto-generated method stub
42
43      }
44  };
45
```

OnDateSetListener( ) statement

Auto-generated method stub

Semicolon added

Figure 8-24 OnDateSetListener awaits the user to select reservation date

STEP 2

- Tap or click within the onDateSet method stub and type the following statements to set the desired date for the sailing reservation:

  ```
  c.set(Calendar.YEAR, year);
  c.set(Calendar.MONTH, monthOfYear);
  c.set(Calendar.DAY_OF_MONTH, dayOfMonth);
  ```

The calendar holds the selected reservation date consisting of the YEAR, MONTH, and DAY_OF_MONTH (Figure 8-25).

```
38     @Override
39     public void onDateSet(DatePicker view, int year, int monthOfYear,
40             int dayOfMonth) {
41         // TODO Auto-generated method stub
42         c.set(Calendar.YEAR, year);
43         c.set(Calendar.MONTH, monthOfYear);
44         c.set(Calendar.DAY_OF_MONTH, dayOfMonth);
45     }
46
47     };
```

Selected year, month, and day are set

Figure 8-25 Setting the desired date for the sailing reservation

Displaying the Date Using the getTime( ) Method

After the user has selected the sailing date reservation, the final step is to display the reservation date in the TextView object named txtReservation, with the instance name of reservation. The reservation variable displays the sailing trip date in the default format named fmtDate. The **getTime( ) method** returns the time value in the Date object. The Sailing Adventures application at this point is one of many bookings that might be part of a larger application. Typically, the application would either email the reserved date to the owners or verify the date in a connected database. The final step is to display the selected date in the TextView object.

STEP 1

- Press the Enter key and type **reservation.setText("Your reservation is set for " + fmtDate.format(c.getTime()));** to display the date in the local country default of the device.

- Save your work.

The reservation is displayed in the TextView object (Figure 8-26).

```
J *MainActivity.java ⊠

 1  package net.androidbootcamp.sailingadventures;
 2
 3⊕ import java.text.DateFormat;▯
14
15  public class MainActivity extends Activity {
16      private TextView reservation;
17⊖     @Override
▲18     public void onCreate(Bundle savedInstanceState) {
19          super.onCreate(savedInstanceState);
20          setContentView(R.layout.activity_main);
21          reservation = (TextView) findViewById(R.id.txtReservation);
22          Button btDate = (Button) findViewById(R.id.btnDate);
23⊖         btDate.setOnClickListener(new View.OnClickListener( ) {
24
25⊖             @Override
▲26             public void onClick(View v) {
☑27                 // TODO Auto-generated method stub
28                 new DatePickerDialog(MainActivity.this, d, c.get(Calendar.YEAR),
29                         c.get(Calendar.MONTH),c.get(Calendar.DAY_OF_MONTH)).show();
30             }
31         });
32
33      }
34      Calendar c = Calendar.getInstance();
35      DateFormat fmtDate = DateFormat.getDateInstance();
36⊖     DatePickerDialog.OnDateSetListener d = new DatePickerDialog.OnDateSetListener() {
37
38⊖         @Override
▲39         public void onDateSet(DatePicker view, int year, int monthOfYear,
40                 int dayOfMonth) {
☑41             // TODO Auto-generated method stub
42             c.set(Calendar.YEAR, year);
43             c.set(Calendar.MONTH, monthOfYear);
44             c.set(Calendar.DAY_OF_MONTH, dayOfMonth);
45             reservation.setText("Your reservation is set for " + fmtDate.format(c.getTime()));
46         }
47
48     };
49⊖     @Override
▲50     public boolean onCreateOptionsMenu(Menu menu) {
51         // Inflate the menu; this adds items to the action bar if it is present.
52         getMenuInflater().inflate(R.menu.main, menu);
53         return true;
54     }
55  }
56
```

> getTime( ) displays the selected reservation date in the TextView control

Figure 8-26 Complete code

GTK

This same program would function with a TimePicker control, Calendar.HOUR_OF_DAY, Calendar.MINUTE, and TimePickerDialog method.

Running and Testing the Application

It's time to make your day trip reservation using the Sailing Adventures apps. Tap or click Run on the menu bar, and then select Run to save and test the application in the tablet emulator. A dialog box requesting how you would like to run the application opens the first time the application is executed. Select Android Application and tap or click the OK button. Save all the files in the next dialog box, if necessary, select the 10.1" tablet, and unlock the tablet emulator. If necessary, tap or click Apps and then double-tap or click Sailing Adventures. The application opens in the tablet 10.1-inch emulator window, where you can test the Button and DatePicker controls in the Sailing Adventures app, as shown in Figure 8-1 and Figure 8-2.

IN THE TRENCHES

On the Windows and Mac computer platforms, the newest operating systems are quickly replacing installed programs launched by icons with an app platform that allows full use of download markets such as the Windows Store and the Apple App Store. Sales of desktop tower cases are declining. Most computer devices now are mobile and app driven.

Wrap It Up—Chapter Summary

This chapter described the steps to create a tablet application on a much larger screen. Creating a calendar control is a common specification on many Android applications. This same DatePicker application would work with a smaller Android phone window with a different design, but the code would work the same. Just like a well-made tool, your Android app, whether it is displayed on a phone or tablet, should strive to combine beauty, simplicity, and purpose to create a magical experience that is effortless to the end user.

- When designing apps for an Android tablet, keep your users' objectives and the size of the device in mind.

- To use an Android emulator designed for tablets, you first add AVD configurations appropriate for tablets.

- You can combine the Linear layout and the Table layout to create a simple, clean layout that takes advantage of a tablet's width. The TableLayout contains TableRow controls—one for each row in your table in activity_main.xml. In each TableRow, you can insert a view control such as a Button or TextView.

- You can display a calendar tool called a DatePicker control in a dialog box so users can select a date from the control. The Time & Date category in the Palette contains many calendar controls, including TimePicker, DatePicker, CalendarView, Chronometer, AnalogClock, and DigitalClock.

- To display the current system date when the DatePicker control opens, you use the YEAR, MONTH, and DAY_OF_MONTH class variables to access the system date.

- To create a DatePickerDialog instance, you must create OnDateSetListener( ) method to await user interaction. If you include a control, such as a Button, that users tap to display a calendar, use the setOnClickListener method to implement the Button. The onClick method responds to the user's action, so you place the code to launch the DatePicker dialog box in the onClick method.

- When a dialog box containing a DatePicker appears, users can select a date and tap a Button control. Tapping the Button invokes an onDateSetListener in DatePickerDialog, which passes integers representing the year, month, and day from the DatePicker into onDateSet. The selected date can then be displayed in a TextView control using setText using the getTime( ) method.

Key Terms

Calendar class—A class you can use to access the Android system date. The Calendar class also is responsible for converting between a Date object and a set of integer fields such as YEAR, MONTH, and DAY_OF_MONTH.

DAY_OF_MONTH—A date constant of the Calendar class that retrieves an integer value of the system's current day.

DAY_OF_YEAR—A date constant of the Calendar class that retrieves the day of the current year as an integer. For example, February 1 is day 32 of the year.

emulated application—An application that is converted in real time to run on a variety of platforms such as a Web page, which can be displayed on various screen sizes through a browser.

get—The field manipulation method that accesses the system date or time.

getInstance—A method of the Calendar class that returns a calendar date or time based on the system settings.

getTime( ) method—A method of the Calendar class that returns the time value in the Date object.

MONTH—A date constant of the Calendar class that retrieves an integer value of the system's current month.

native application—A program locally installed on a specific platform such as a phone or tablet.

onDateSet( ) method—A method that automatically obtains the date selected by the user.

padding property—A property that you can use to offset the content of a control by a specific number of pixels.

set—The field manipulation method that changes the system date or time.

TableLayout—A user interface design layout that includes TableRow controls to form a grid.

typeface—A property that you can use to set the style of control text to font families, including monospace, sans_serif, and serif.

YEAR—A date constant of the Calendar class that retrieves an integer value of the system's current year.

Developer FAQs

1. Explain the difference between a native app and a Web page.

2. What is the range of the diagonal measurement of Android tablet screens?

3. What is the diagonal size of the iPad screen?

4. Describe the three most common activities mentioned in the chapter used with an Android phone.

5. How do the activities in question 4 differ from how you would typically use a tablet?

6. Which Android AVD was first designed specifically for tablets? Identify the name and version. It is used for the minimum required SDK.

7. What is the purpose of the three buttons on the bottom of the tablet?

8. Inside of an XML Table layout, what is the XML code name of each row?

9. True or False? A LinearLayout and TableLayout cannot be used in the same XML layout file.

10. Write the single line of XML code to set the padding to 22 density independent pixels.

11. Write the single line of XML code to set the text to the font family of sans serif.

12. Name six calendar widgets.

13. If a date is displayed as 9/30/2015 in the United States, how would that same date be displayed in Europe?

14. Why is it best to use a pop-up dialog box for a DatePicker control?

15. Which method retrieves the selected date of the DatePicker?

16. Name three purposes of a dialog box.

17. Write a line of code that, for the calendar instance named cal, assigns dueDay to the day of the month.

18. Write the New Year's Eve date of the year 2016 in the default layout of your locale.

19. Write a line of code that, for the calendar instance named c, assigns currentHour to the hour of the day.

20. Write a line of code that, for the calendar instance named c, assigns currentMinute to the minute within an hour.

Beyond the Book

Using the Internet, search the Web for the answers to the following questions to further your Android knowledge.

1. Research Android tablet design. Find five design tips not mentioned in the chapter and describe them using complete sentences.

2. Research five popular Android calendar apps available in the Android Market. Write a paragraph about the purpose of each one.

3. In the Information Technology (IT) field, Gartner, Inc., is considered one of the world's leading IT research and advisory companies. Research Gartner's opinion on the growth of the tablet. Locate a recent article by Gartner and write a summary of at least 150 words of the tablet trend.

4. The Android style guide online at *http://developer.android.com/design* provides a foundation in Android best practices. Create a bulleted list of 15 best practices from this site.

Case Programming Projects

Complete one or more of the following case programming projects. Use the same steps and techniques taught within the chapter. Submit the program you create to your instructor. The level of difficulty is indicated for each case programming project.

Easiest: ★

Intermediate: ★★

Challenging: ★★★

Case Project 8–1: Appalachian Trail Festival Tablet App ★

Requirements Document

Application title:	Appalachian Trail Festival Tablet App
Purpose:	The Appalachian Trail Festival would like an Android tablet app that first displays a title and event description, and then when the user taps a button, a calendar for reserving a ticket for the festival appears. The date is then shown as available for a reservation.
Algorithms:	1. The opening tablet screen displays an image, a title, an event description, and a button to create a reservation for a day at the festival (Figure 8-27).
	2. When the user taps a button, a DatePicker is displayed in a dialog box (Figure 8-28). The dialog box allows the user to select the date to attend the year-long festival.
Conditions:	1. The picture named hike.png is provided with your student files.
	2. Write your own description of the festival.
	3. Research the hexadecimal color for red.
	4. Use the Theme.Black theme.
	5. Use a Table layout with four rows within a Linear layout.

Figure 8-27

Figure 8-28

Case Project 8–2: The Dog Sledding Experience Tablet App ★

Requirements Document

Application title:	The Dog Sledding Experience Tablet App
Purpose:	The Dog Sledding Experience tablet app provides a reservation button to select a date to have the full immersion experience for a full-day dog sledding trip in Alaska.
Algorithms:	1. The opening screen displays an image, a tour description, and a button that launches a DatePicker dialog box (Figure 8-29).
	2. When the user taps the button, a DatePicker control is displayed in a dialog box (Figure 8-30). The dialog box confirms the date of the reservation.
Conditions:	1. A picture of the dog sledding experience named sled.png is provided with your student files.
	2. Write your own description of the sledding experience.
	3. Select your own colors and font.
	4. Use a Table layout.

The Dog Sledding Experience

The Dog Sledding Experience in Alaska

You are speeding through Alaskan forest near Denali, sitting on a sled that is being pulled by some of the most powerful Alaskan creatures. This is dog sledding and mushing is not only an Alaskan tradition, but also a state obsession.

Pick a day for your Dog Sledding Experience

Philip and Karen Smith/ Lonely Planet Images/Getty Images

Figure 8-29

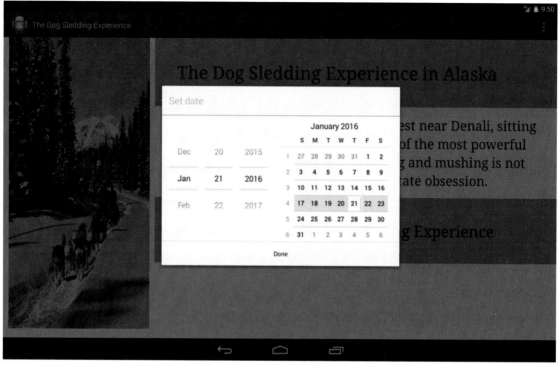

Figure 8-30

Case Project 8–3: Country Cabin Rental Tablet App ★★

Requirements Document

Application title:	Country Cabin Rental Tablet App
Purpose:	The Country Cabin Rental realty agency provides cabins for rental. Two cabins are available for a minimum three-night stay.
Algorithms:	1. The opening screen displays an image, cabin descriptions, two radio button controls with different cabin names, and a button that launches a DatePicker dialog box.
	2. When the user taps the button, a DatePicker control is displayed in a dialog box. The user selects the first night of a three-night reservation. The dialog box displays the date range of the three-night reservation with the name of the selected cabin.
Conditions:	1. Find an appropriate picture on the Web.
	2. Write your own descriptions of the cabins.
	3. Do not use the default theme.
	4. Only one radio button can be selected at a time.
	5. Use a Table layout.

Case Project 8–4: Final Touch Auto Detailing Tablet App ★★

Requirements Document

Application title:	Final Touch Auto Detailing Tablet App
Purpose:	The Final Touch Auto Detailing business provides a variety of detailing services. The company wants an app to list each service and its price and display a calendar for making a service reservation.
Algorithms:	1. The opening screen displays an image, service descriptions, four check boxes offering different detailing services each with different prices, and a button that launches a DatePicker dialog box to make a reservation for the all-day auto-detailing services.
	2. When the user taps the button, a DatePicker control is displayed in a dialog box. The user selects the date for the reservation. The dialog box displays the date and final cost of the detailing services.
Conditions:	1. Select your own image(s).
	2. Write your own descriptions about the car detailing services.
	3. Do not use the default theme.
	4. More than one check box can be checked at once.
	5. Use a Table layout.

Case Project 8–5: Wild Ginger Dinner Delivery Tablet App ★★★

Requirements Document

Application title:	Wild Ginger Dinner Delivery Tablet App with TimePicker
Purpose:	Wild Ginger Dinner Delivery service delivers dinners in the evening. The business wants an app that customers can use to select a dinner and reserve a delivery time.
Algorithms:	1. The opening screen displays an image, a Wild Ginger food description, and a button that launches a TimePicker dialog box to make a reservation for delivery tonight.
	2. When the user taps the button, a TimePicker control is displayed in a dialog box. The user selects the time for delivery, and the app confirms the delivery time, which is available only from 5 pm to 11 pm.
Conditions:	1. Select your own image(s).
	2. Write your own description of the great food offered at Wild Ginger.
	3. Do not use the default theme.
	4. Use a Table layout.

Case Project 8–6: Create Your Own Tablet App ★★★

Requirements Document

Application title:	Create Your Own Tablet App
Purpose:	Create an app with a DatePicker and a TimePicker to create a reservation.
Algorithms:	1. Create an app on a topic of your own choice.
	2. Use two buttons. The first button allows the user to select the date and the second button allows the user to select the time.
Conditions:	1. Select your own image(s).
	2. Use a custom layout and icon.

CHAPTER 9

Customize! Navigating with a Master/Detail Flow Activity on a Tablet

In this chapter, you learn to:

- ◎ Understand responsive design for Android apps
- ◎ Create an Android tablet project using an application template
- ◎ Understand the Master/Detail Flow template
- ◎ Modify the Master/Detail Flow template
- ◎ Add a WebView widget
- ◎ Display a Web browser within a tablet app
- ◎ Add an Internet permission to the Android Manifest
- ◎ Customize the content of the sample template file
- ◎ Display a custom layout in the details pane

Creating an attractive user interface that provides simple navigation can be challenging when programming a tablet app on an Android device. Fortunately, the Android platform provides a flexible way to simplify layout and navigation using built-in Android templates. To construct apps that automatically fit the device, you need design elements such as fluid grids and flexible images that can adapt to various screen sizes. Instead of creating a number of rigid XML layouts heavily optimized to a number of predefined screen sizes, built-in templates are available using the best presentation mode based on the size of the device. Like multiple windows, multipane layouts can be used to show different topics within a single window in an intuitive interface.

In this chapter, you create a multipane interface in an Android application using a template designed to customize a European bike and barge cruise vacation. Bike and barge cruises combine two popular ways of exploring Europe—cycling and river cruising. On a bike and barge experience, you spend your days cycling through historic European sites and your nights cruising down scenic rivers through cities such as Amsterdam and Budapest. The Bike and Barge application shown in Figure 9-1 features a three-item list containing Photos, Tour, and Web Site. When the app first opens, the item list is displayed in the left pane and the right pane is blank.

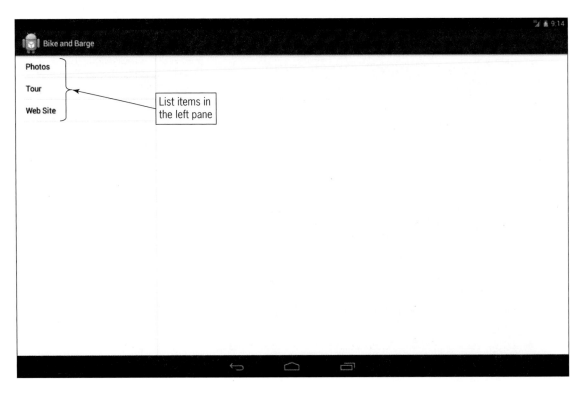

Figure 9-1 Opening screen of the Bike and Barge tablet app

This Android tablet Bike and Barge app provides images, text, and a link that opens a Web page within the Android browser. If the user selects Photos, the first item in the left pane, a TableLayout displays three images with text descriptions in the right pane as shown in Figure 9-2. When the user taps Tour, the second list item on the left, the item details in the right pane change to display tour information, as shown in Figure 9-3. Web Site, the third list item, links to a browser that displays the full Bike and Barge Web site, including tour company contact information, as shown in Figure 9-4. The intuitive list items eliminate the need for additional instructions for navigation.

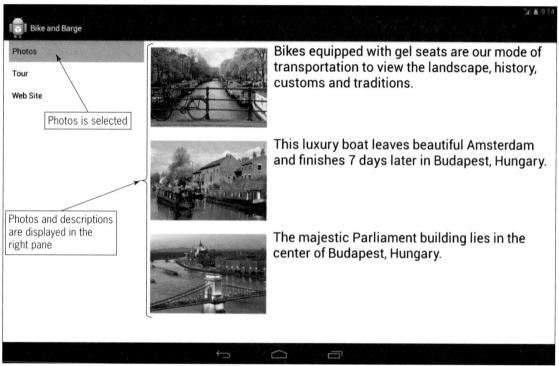

Figure 9-2   Selecting Photos in the left pane

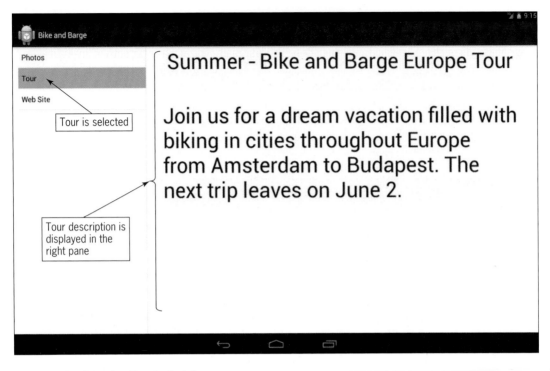

Figure 9-3   Selecting Tour in the left pane

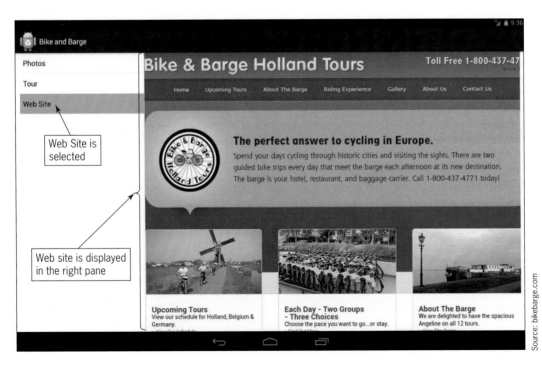

Figure 9-4   Selecting Web Site in the left pane

IN THE TRENCHES
Cycling apps already in Google Play include GPS-based biking routes, personal cycling logs, mountain biking trails, bike repair, distance tracking, and cycling fitness to use on your trip. In addition, these apps can often be used on Android watches.

To create this application, the developer must understand how to perform the following processes, among others:

1. Create a Master/Detail Flow template app.

2. Add the images to the drawable folder.

3. Add text to the Strings table.

4. Create the photos.xml TableLayout XML file for the details pane of the first list item.

5. Create the tour.xml file for the details pane of the second list item.

6. Change the default TextView widget to a WebView widget.

7. Update the Android Manifest file to include an Internet permission.

8. Customize the DummyContent class to display the item list.

9. Customize the DummyContent class to connect to the Web site.

10. Modify the ItemDetailFragment.java class to:

    a. Display the photos.xml in the details pane.

    b. Display the tour.xml in the details pane.

    c. Display a Web site in a browser.

HEADS UP
Watch out for that stretched-out look! On tablets, single-pane layouts lead to awkward whitespace and excessive line lengths. Use padding to reduce the width of UI elements and consider using multipane layouts.

Understanding Responsive Design

When mobile devices first were developed, the apps displayed simple text content designed for small screens, but the tablet and smartphone landscape can now handle complicated processes and full Web access. This design approach is especially true for the Android platform. Instead of developers creating apps for multiple sizes of Android devices, apps and Web pages should be developed once for a wide range of displays. **Responsive design** is an approach to designing apps and Web sites that provide an optimal viewing experience across as many devices as possible. Similarities between Web pages and Android apps do not end with screen sizes. When building for the Web, designers also have to take into account multiple browsers and multiple versions of each one. Earlier in this text, you learned to use scalable pixels to change the size of text or margins, but more tools are necessary for a complete approach to designing for all device sizes. To assist with responsive design in recent Android API versions, Eclipse has responsive design templates, which allow you to build the app once, but display it on multiple devices. You can run the Bike and Barge app on a smartphone emulator as shown in Figure 9-5 without any change in code. The first screen shows the list of items. If you select Web Site, a separate Activity is displayed on the smartphone showing the Bike and Barge Web site.

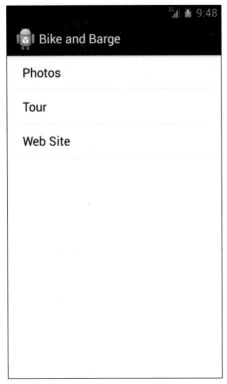

Opening screen

Screen after selecting Web Site

Figure 9-5   Bike and Barge app runs as two Activities on a smartphone

Using Application Templates

The Eclipse software development kit provides tools for fast creation of Android apps that follow the Android design and development guidelines and include code that can be customized to the exact needs of your app. These tools are called **application templates**; you use them to create basic Android applications that you can immediately run and test on an Android device of any size. Android templates are available when you create a new Android project, as shown in Figure 9-6. Throughout this text, you selected the Blank Activity, but in this chapter's project app, you use the Master/Detail Flow application template.

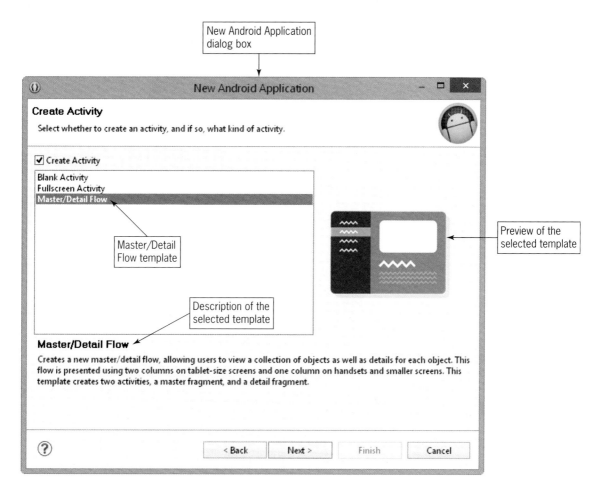

Figure 9-6   Android application templates

Master/Detail Flow Template

The Bike and Barge tablet app features an opening screen with three list items on the left, as shown in Figure 9-1. List items function as they do in a framed browser window. A menu of list items on the left of a browser window displays Web page content using intuitive navigation on the right side of the page. You can switch between items on the list to display new content without opening more browser windows. The **Master/Detail Flow template** creates an adaptive, responsive layout for a set of list items and associated detail content. The Master list appears in a narrow vertical pane along the left edge of the screen. Without any customization, the Master/Detail Flow template as shown in Figure 9-7 can be displayed on a tablet or on a smartphone. On a tablet device, the item list and item details are displayed on the same screen when you select a list item. The remainder of the display is devoted to the detail pane in an arrangement referred to as two-pane layout. On a smaller device, the list and details are displayed on separate screens when you select a list item.

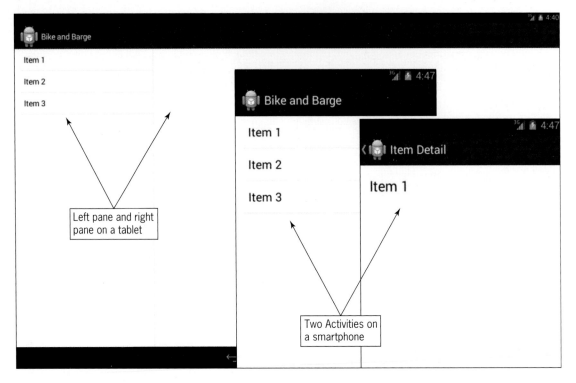

Figure 9-7   Master/Detail Flow template on a tablet and a smartphone

To begin the application using the Master/Detail Flow template on the tablet, follow these steps.

STEP 1

- Open the Eclipse program.
- Type **E:\Workspace** (if necessary, enter a different drive letter that identifies the USB drive) to select a workspace, and then tap or click the OK button.
- Tap or click the New button on the Standard toolbar and then select Android Application Project.
- Tap or click the Next button.
- In the New Android Application dialog box, enter the Application Name **Bike and Barge**.
- Enter the Package Name of **net.androidbootcamp.bikeandbarge**.
- Change the Minimum Required SDK to API 11: Android 3.0 (Honeycomb), the first tablet designed API.

The new Bike and Barge project has an application name and a package name (Figure 9-8).

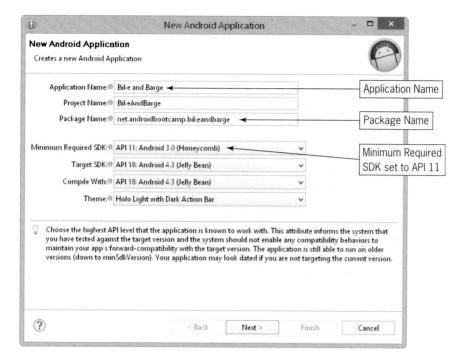

Figure 9-8   Creating the Bike and Barge Android application

STEP 2

- Tap or click the Next button.
- Tap or click the Create custom launcher icon box to uncheck the option.
- Tap or click the Next button.
- Select the Master/Detail Flow template in the list of Activities.

The Master/Detail Flow template is selected (Figure 9-9).

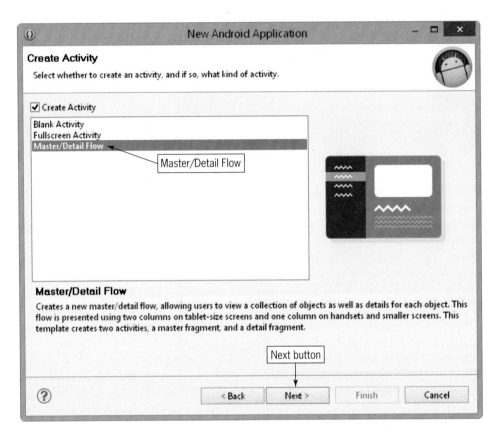

Figure 9-9   Selecting the Master/Detail Flow template

STEP 3

- Tap or click the Next button. By default, the Object Kind is set to Item and the Object Kind Plural is set to Items.

The Master/Detail Flow template automatically enters the Item as the Object Kind and Items as the Object Kind Plural settings (Figure 9-10).

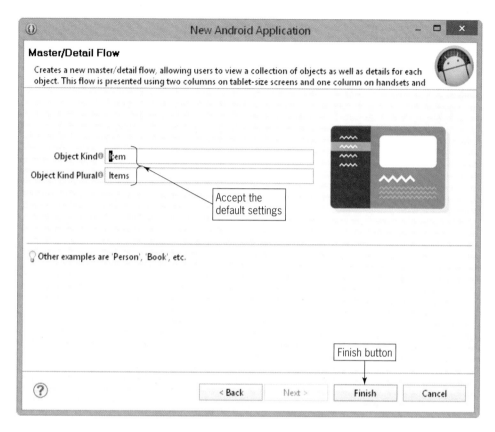

Figure 9-10   Entering the Object Kind and Object Kind Plural settings

STEP 4

- Tap or click the Finish button to create the new application based on the Master/Detail Flow template.

Understanding the Structure of the Master/Detail Flow Template

When the Bike and Barge app is expanded in the Package Explorer as shown in Figure 9-11, notice a number of Java and XML layout resource files have been created automatically.

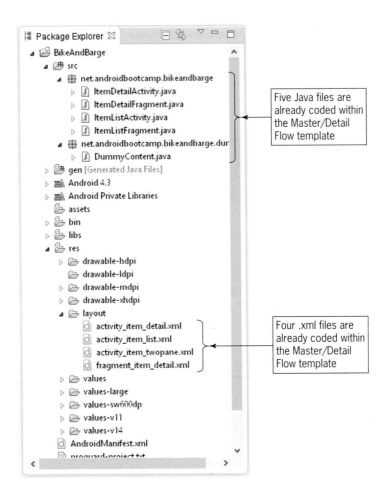

Figure 9-11 Package Explorer displays template code files

Each of the src and layout files in the Master/Detail Flow template has a specific purpose, as described in the following lists. Most of these files will not be altered in the development of the Bike and Barge app.

Src Files

- *ItemDetailActivity.java*: The purpose of this class is to display the activity_item_detail.xml layout file if a smartphone is detected.

- *ItemDetailFragment.java*: The purpose of this class is to display the fragment_item_detail.xml layout file. This class can be customized to determine which detailed items to display.

- *ItemListActivity.java*: The purpose of this initial Activity is to display the master list in a two-pane mode if a tablet device is detected or to launch a second Activity to display the detailed items if a smaller device is detected.

- *ItemListFragment.java*: The purpose of this class is to display the activity_item_list.xml layout file.

- *DummyContent.java*: The purpose of this Java file is to provide sample code you customize to suit your specific app content.

Layout Files

- *activity_item_detail.xml*: When a smartphone is detected, the app uses this layout to display the FrameLayout instance.

- *activity_item_list.xml*: When a smartphone is detected, the app uses this layout to display the master list fragment.

- *activity_item_twopane.xml*: When a tablet is detected, the app is displayed in a two-pane layout containing both the master item list fragment and the item detail container.

- *fragment_item_detail.xml*: When a smartphone or a tablet is detected, this layout file displays the detail pane using the onCreateView( ) method.

Adding Images to the Drawable Folder

Before designing the XML layouts, three images are first placed in the drawable-hdpi folder and then referenced in the photos.xml layout. To add the images for this project, follow this step:

STEP 1

- If necessary, expand the src and layout folders in the Package Explorer.

- Open the USB folder containing the student files.

- To add the three image files to the drawable-hdpi resource folder, drag the bike.png, barge.png, and budapest.png files to the drawable-hdpi folder until a plus sign pointer appears.

- Release the mouse button. Tap or click the Copy files option button, and then tap or click the OK button.

Copies of the three files appear in the drawable-hdpi folder (Figure 9-12).

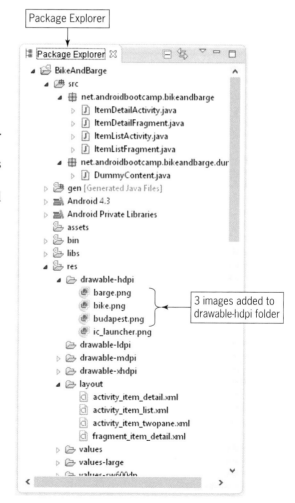

Figure 9-12   Image files for the Bike and Barge app

Designing an XML TableLayout

When the user selects the first list item in the Bike and Barge app, three images are displayed: a bike in Amsterdam, a barge passenger boat on the Danube River, and the Parliament building in Budapest. Each image has a text description in an XML TableLayout as shown in Figure 9-2. The Strings table, responsible for the text displayed in the app, has two initial Strings in the template. The first String named appName is displayed in the title bar of the tablet, and by default is set to Bike and Barge, the application name. The second String named title_item_detail is displayed in the title bar of a smaller device such as a smartphone and is set to Item Detail. This text should be changed to Bike and Barge to create a consistent experience on a tablet or smartphone. One single image description is used for all three images in the app. To create a Strings table for the text descriptions necessary throughout the app and to code the XML layout for photos.xml, follow these steps:

STEP 1

- In the Package Explorer, expand the values folder within the res folder.
- Double-tap or double-click the strings.xml file to display the Android Resources.
- Tap or click the title_item_detail and change the Value text box to the text **Bike and Barge**.
- Tap or click the Add button.
- If necessary, tap or click String and then tap or click the OK button.
- In the Name text box, type **txtBike** to name the String.
- In the Value text box, type the following to specify the text: **Bikes equipped with gel seats are our mode of transportation to view the landscape, history, customs and traditions.**
- Tap or click the Add button.
- If necessary, tap or click String and then tap or click the OK button.
- In the Name text box, type **txtBarge** to name the String.
- In the Value text box, type **This luxury boat leaves beautiful Amsterdam and finishes 7 days later in Budapest, Hungary.**
- Tap or click the Add button.
- If necessary, tap or click String and then tap or click the OK button.
- In the Name text box, type **txtBudapest** to name the String.
- In the Value text box, type **The majestic Parliament building lies in the center of Budapest, Hungary.**
- Tap or click the Add button.
- If necessary, tap or click String and then tap or click the OK button.
- In the Name text box, type **txtTitle** to name the String.
- In the Value text box, type **Summer - Bike and Barge Europe Tour**.

- Tap or click the Add button.

- If necessary, tap or click String and tap or click the OK button.

- In the Name text box, type **txtInfo** to name the String.

- In the Value text box, type **Join us for a dream vacation filled with biking in cities throughout Europe from Amsterdam to Budapest. The next trip leaves on June 2.**

- Tap or click the Add button.

- If necessary, tap or click String and then tap or click the OK button.

- In the Name text box, type **txtDescription** to name the String.

- In the Value text box, type **Bike and Barge Image**.

- Save your work.

The Name and Value of the TextView controls are entered into the strings.xml file (Figure 9-13).

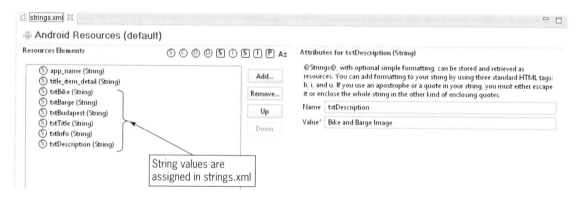

Figure 9-13 Strings table for the Bike and Barge app

STEP 2

- Collapse the drawable-hdpi and values subfolders.

- In the Package Explorer, press and hold or right-click the layout folder.

- On the shortcut menu, point to New and then tap or click Android XML File.

- In the New Android XML File dialog box, type **photos.xml** in the File text box to name the layout file.

- In the Root Element list, select TableLayout.

- Tap or click the Finish button to create an XML layout named photos.xml.

- Tap or click the screen size arrow button and then select 10.1" WXGA (Tablet) (1280 × 800: mdpi).

- Tap or click Go to next state and then select Landscape to display tablet in landscape mode.

- Tap or click the photos.xml tab at the bottom of the window.

The XML file is named photos.xml and the layout is set to TableLayout. The photos.xml code is displayed (Figure 9-14).

```
1  <?xml version="1.0" encoding="utf-8"?>
2  <TableLayout xmlns:android="http://schemas.android.com/apk/res/android"
3      android:layout_width="match_parent"
4      android:layout_height="match_parent" >
5
6  </TableLayout>
7
```

Figure 9-14 photos.xml created

STEP 3

- In Line 6 of photos.xml, type the following code to add a table row that displays an image and text:

```
<TableRow>
    <ImageView
        android:id="@+id/imgBike"
        android:contentDescription="@string/txtDescription"
        android:layout_width="wrap_content"
        android:layout_height="wrap_content"
        android:src="@drawable/bike"
        android:padding="15sp" />
    <TextView
        android:layout_width="700dp"
        android:layout_height="wrap_content"
        android:text="@string/txtBike"
        android:textSize="30sp"
        android:paddingRight="40sp" />
</TableRow>
```

A table row displays an ImageView and TextView control in the TableLayout (Figure 9-15).

```
🎵 ItemDetailActivity.java ⊠  📄 photos.xml ⊠
  1    <?xml version="1.0" encoding="utf-8"?>
  2    <TableLayout xmlns:android="http://schemas.android.com/apk/res/android"
  3         android:layout_width="match_parent"
  4         android:layout_height="match_parent" >
  5
  6         <TableRow>
  7             <ImageView
  8                 android:id="@+id/imgBike"
  9                 android:contentDescription="@string/txtDescription"
 10                 android:layout_width="wrap_content"
 11                 android:layout_height="wrap_content"
 12                 android:src="@drawable/bike"
 13                 android:padding="15sp" />
 14             <TextView
 15                 android:layout_width="700dp"
 16                 android:layout_height="wrap_content"
 17                 android:text="@string/txtBike"
 18                 android:textSize="30sp"
 19                 android:paddingRight="40sp" />
 20         </TableRow>
 21
 22    </TableLayout>
```

TableRow

Figure 9-15   First row of the TableLayout

STEP 4

- Copy the TableRow commands from Step 3, paste them two times in the photos.xml code, and then customize the new commands to match the following code:

```
<TableRow>
    <ImageView
        android:id="@+id/imgBarge"
        android:contentDescription="@string/txtDescription"
        android:layout_width="wrap_content"
        android:layout_height="wrap_content"
        android:src="@drawable/barge"
        android:padding="15sp" />
    <TextView
        android:layout_width="700dp"
        android:layout_height="wrap_content"
        android:text="@string/txtBarge"
        android:textSize="30sp"
        android:paddingRight="40sp" />
    </TableRow>
<TableRow>
    <ImageView
        android:id="@+id/imgBudapest"
        android:contentDescription="@string/txtDescription"
        android:layout_width="wrap_content"
```

```
                android:layout_height="wrap_content"
                android:src="@drawable/budapest"
                android:padding="15sp" />
        <TextView
                android:layout_width="700dp"
                android:layout_height="wrap_content"
                android:text="@string/txtBudapest"
                android:textSize="30sp"
                android:paddingRight="40sp" />
    </TableRow>
```

The second and third table rows display more ImageView and TextView controls in the TableLayout (Figure 9-16).

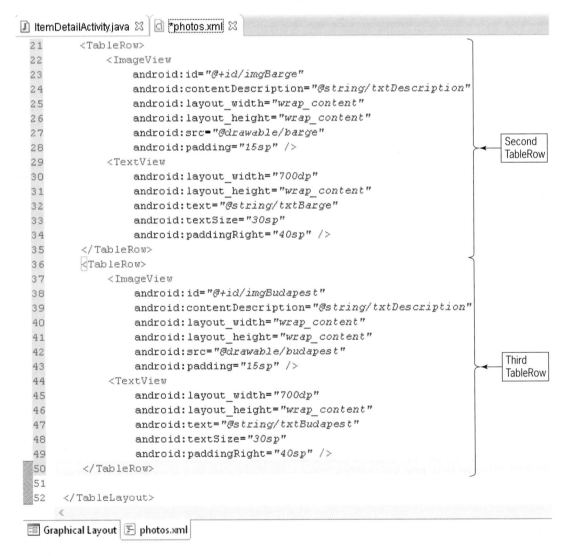

Figure 9-16   Second and third rows of the TableLayout

- Tap or click the Graphical Layout tab.

- Tap or click the Save All button on the Standard toolbar.

The TableLayout is displayed in the Graphical Layout of the emulator for photos.xml (Figure 9-17).

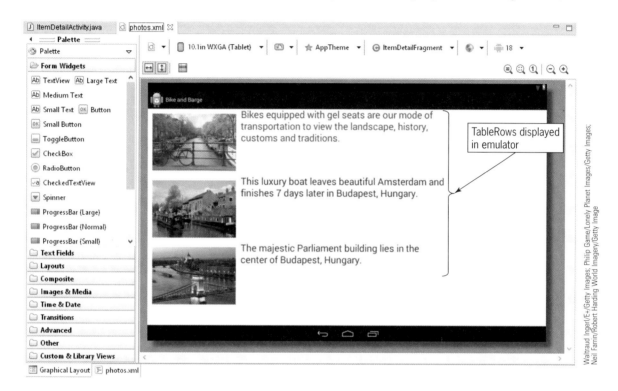

Figure 9-17 Completed TableLayout in photos.xml

Creating a TextView XML Layout for the Second List Item

For the detail content of the second list item, two TextView controls display the tour details for the Bike and Barge application within the LinearLayout. To create an XML layout file that displays two TextView controls, follow these steps:

- Close the photos.xml tab.

- In the Package Explorer, press and hold or right-click the layout folder.

- On the shortcut menu, point to New and then tap or click Android XML File.

- In the New Android XML File dialog box, type **tour.xml** in the File text box to name the layout file.

- In the Root Element list, select LinearLayout.

- Tap or click the Finish button to create an XML layout named tour.xml and open the emulator window.

- Tap or click the screen size arrow button, and then select 10.1" WXGA (Tablet).

- Tap or click Go to next state, and then select Landscape to display the tablet interface in landscape mode.

- Tap or click the tour.xml tab at the bottom of the window.

- In Line 7, type the following XML code for the first TextView control using auto-completion as much as possible:

```
<TextView
    android:id="@+id/txtTitle"
    android:layout_width="wrap_content"
    android:layout_height="wrap_content"
    android:text="@string/txtTitle"
    android:textSize="50sp"
    android:paddingLeft="50sp"
    android:paddingBottom="60sp" />
```

The first TextView control is coded in tour.xml with a LinearLayout (Figure 9-18).

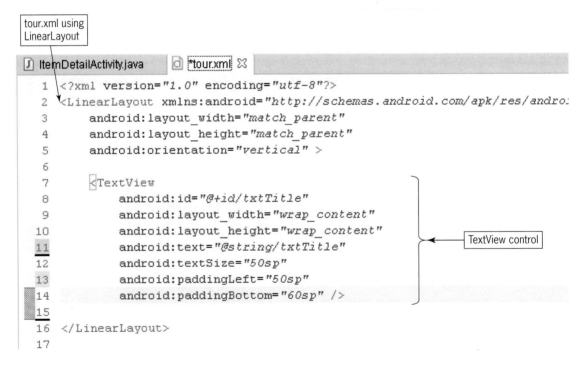

Figure 9-18 LinearLayout for tour.xml

STEP 2

● Press the Enter key twice, and then type the following XML code for the second TextView control using auto-completion as much as possible:

```
<TextView
    android:id="@+id/txtInfo"
    android:layout_width="wrap_content"
    android:layout_height="wrap_content"
    android:text="@string/txtInfo"
    android:textSize="50sp"
    android:paddingLeft="40sp"
    android:paddingRight="40sp" />
```

● Save your work.

The second TextView control is coded in tour.xml (Figure 9-19).

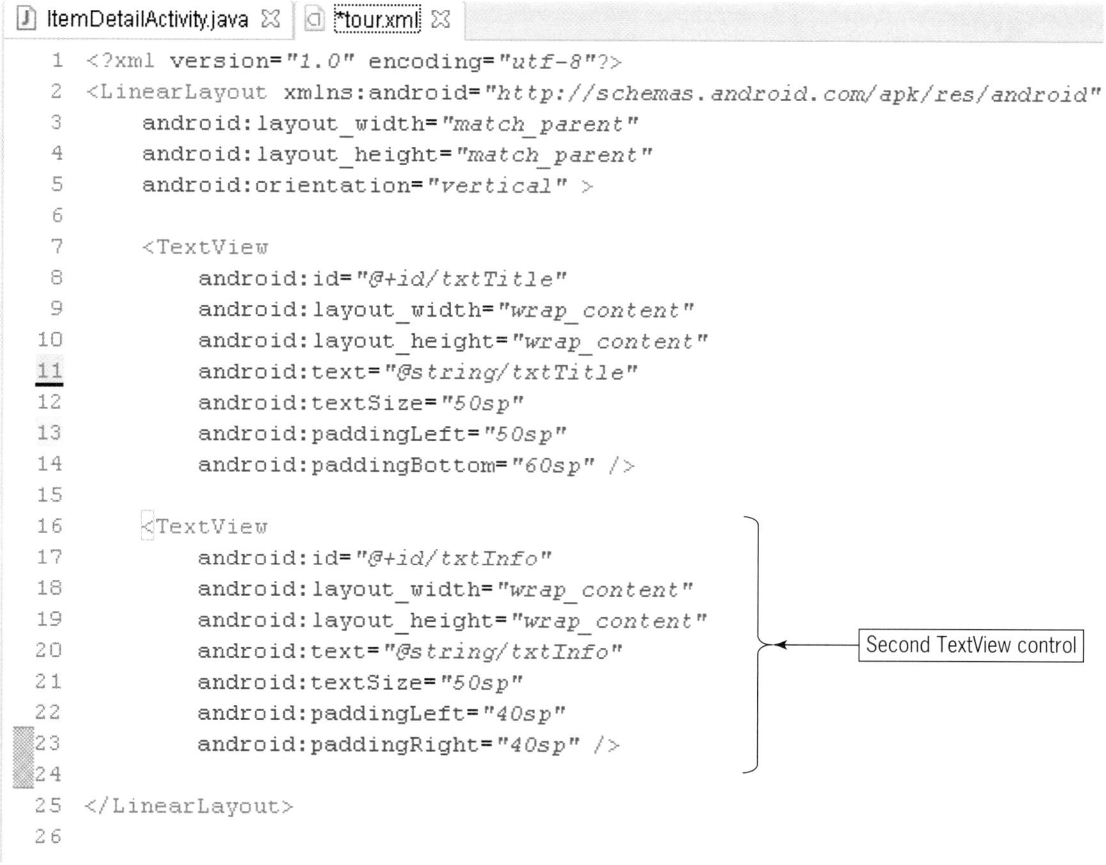

```
ItemDetailActivity.java ⊠    *tour.xml ⊠
1   <?xml version="1.0" encoding="utf-8"?>
2   <LinearLayout xmlns:android="http://schemas.android.com/apk/res/android"
3       android:layout_width="match_parent"
4       android:layout_height="match_parent"
5       android:orientation="vertical" >
6
7       <TextView
8           android:id="@+id/txtTitle"
9           android:layout_width="wrap_content"
10          android:layout_height="wrap_content"
11          android:text="@string/txtTitle"
12          android:textSize="50sp"
13          android:paddingLeft="50sp"
14          android:paddingBottom="60sp" />
15
16      <TextView
17          android:id="@+id/txtInfo"
18          android:layout_width="wrap_content"
19          android:layout_height="wrap_content"
20          android:text="@string/txtInfo"                    ◄── Second TextView control
21          android:textSize="50sp"
22          android:paddingLeft="40sp"
23          android:paddingRight="40sp" />
24
25  </LinearLayout>
26
```

Figure 9-19   Second TextView control in tour.xml

Creating a WebView XML Layout for the Third List Item

Initially the Master/Detail Flow template displays each list item using the TextView object displayed in the fragment_item_detail.xml layout file. In the Bike and Barge app, if the user selects the first list item, the photos.xml layout is displayed, and if the user selects the second list item, the tour.xml layout is shown. The third list item in the Bike and Barge app uses the default fragment_item_detail. xml layout, but the TextView object cannot display a Web page. The TextView control must be changed to a WebView control to accommodate the launch of the site. The **WebView** object is a View widget that displays Web pages. The WebView object allows you to place a Web browser or simply display some online content within your Activity. The WebView object uses a built-in rendering engine to display Web pages.

After the WebView object is placed in the XML layout of the app, you must add the INTERNET permissions to the Android Manifest file in order for your Activity to access the Internet and load Web pages. A **permission** is a restriction limiting access to a part of the code or to data on the device. The permission protects critical data and code that could be misused to cause issues to your app and others. Permissions can be set in the Android Manifest file within an Android app to allow certain actions such as to set the background wallpaper, check the device's power levels, read your contacts, write events to your calendar, and display a Web page. Without the proper permission, attempts to access the Internet or complete similar actions will fail.

Code Syntax

```
android:permission="android.permission.INTERNET"
```

To change the TextView control to a WebView control in the fragment_item_detail.xml layout file and to add permission for the WebView widget to use the Internet within the app, follow these steps:

STEP 1

- Close the tour.xml tab.

- If necessary, expand the layout folder and double-tap or double-click the fragment_item_detail. xml layout file.

- Press and hold or right-click the emulator to display a shortcut menu.

- Tap or click Change Widget Type.

- Tap or click the New Widget Type arrow button.

- Scroll down and select WebView as the new widget type.

The WebView widget is selected, enabling the fragment_item_detail.xml layout to display a Web page (Figure 9-20).

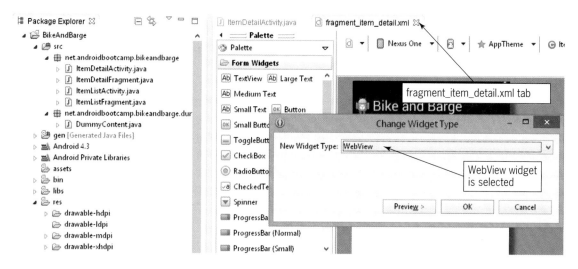

Figure 9-20   Selecting a WebView widget

STEP 2

- Tap or click the OK button in the Change Widget Type dialog box.

- Save your work and close the fragment_item_detail.xml tab.

- To set the permissions for the Web page to open in the app, double-tap or double-click the AndroidManifest.xml file.

- Tap or click the Application tab at the bottom of the AndroidManifest.xml file.

- Tap or click the Permission arrow to display the permissions.

- Scroll down and select android.permission.INTERNET.

- Tap or click the AndroidManifest.xml tab at the bottom to view the permission set in Line 15 of the code.

The permission to connect to the Internet is set within the AndroidManifest.xml file (Figure 9-21).

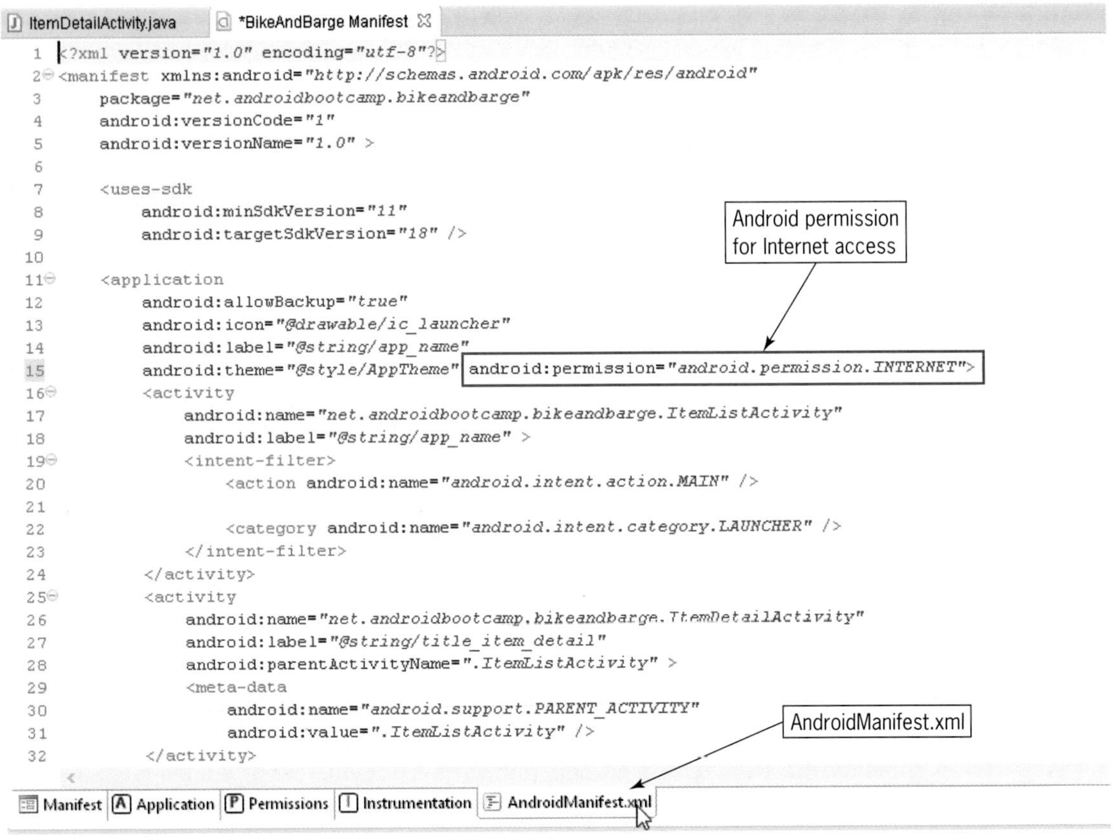

```
[J] ItemDetailActivity.java    [c] *BikeAndBarge Manifest ⊠

 1  <?xml version="1.0" encoding="utf-8"?>
 2  <manifest xmlns:android="http://schemas.android.com/apk/res/android"
 3      package="net.androidbootcamp.bikeandbarge"
 4      android:versionCode="1"
 5      android:versionName="1.0" >
 6
 7      <uses-sdk
 8          android:minSdkVersion="11"
 9          android:targetSdkVersion="18" />
10
11      <application
12          android:allowBackup="true"
13          android:icon="@drawable/ic_launcher"
14          android:label="@string/app_name"
15          android:theme="@style/AppTheme" android:permission="android.permission.INTERNET">
16          <activity
17              android:name="net.androidbootcamp.bikeandbarge.ItemListActivity"
18              android:label="@string/app_name" >
19              <intent-filter>
20                  <action android:name="android.intent.action.MAIN" />
21
22                  <category android:name="android.intent.category.LAUNCHER" />
23              </intent-filter>
24          </activity>
25          <activity
26              android:name="net.androidbootcamp.bikeandbarge.ItemDetailActivity"
27              android:label="@string/title_item_detail"
28              android:parentActivityName=".ItemListActivity" >
29              <meta-data
30                  android:name="android.support.PARENT_ACTIVITY"
31                  android:value=".ItemListActivity" />
32          </activity>

  Manifest  [A] Application  [P] Permissions  [I] Instrumentation  [F] AndroidManifest.xml
```

Android permission for Internet access

AndroidManifest.xml

Figure 9-21   Setting permission to connect to the Internet

Customizing the Item List

The Master/Detail Flow template provides a custom package named net.androidbootcamp. bikeandbarge.dummy that contains a Java class file named DummyContent.java. The purpose of this class is to provide sample content to display in the user interface of the template. This class can be customized or replaced by classes that are fully created from scratch. In Lines 27–30 of the DummyContent.java, three items are added in the following sample code:

Code Syntax

```
// Add 3 sample items.
    addItem(new DummyItem("1", "Item 1"));
    addItem(new DummyItem("2", "Item 2"));
    addItem(new DummyItem("3", "Item 3"));
```

The command addItem displays list items in the left pane of the tablet display or in the first Activity display of a smartphone. You can add more addItem commands if your app has more than three list items. In the Bike and Barge app, the list items should display the text Photos (Item 1), Tour (Item 2), and Web Site (Item 3). The third item is different from the first two items because selecting it displays the *bikebarge.com* site in the right pane of the tablet screen. The Bike and Barge app is different from the San Francisco City Guide app, which launched the phone's built-in browser to display the city Web sites. The Bike and Barge app displays the Web site within the app in the detail pane.

The DummyContent.java file by default is displayed in a two-pane layout on a tablet with a TextView control displayed in the detail pane. Because the TextView control cannot display a Web site, you place the WebView control in the fragment_item_detail.xml page to display the Web site. To display the Bike and Barge Web site, you add code to the addItem statement in the DummyContent.java file. Originally the addItem statement contains two strings: the id number to identify the user's selection and the string Item1 that is displayed in the item list in the left pane of the tablet. When the Web site is added to the third item, you must modify the code to contain three String objects: the id, the item list string, and the Web site URL. The original DummyItem class, which is coded to handle two string objects shown below, must be updated to handle three string objects.

Original DummyItem Class Syntax

```
public static class DummyItem {
    public String id;
    public String content;

    public DummyItem(String id, String content) {
        this.id = id;
        this.content = content;
    }
}
```

Modified DummyItem Class Syntax

```
public static class DummyItem {
    public String id;
    public String content;
    public String item_name;
    public String item_url;

    public DummyItem(String id, String content) {
        this.id = id;
        this.content = content;
    }

    public DummyItem(String id, String item_name, String item_url) {
        // TODO Auto-generated constructor stub
        {
            this.id = id;
            this.item_name = item_name;
            this.item_url = item_url;
            content=item_name;
        }
    }
}
```

The auto-generated construct stub is created when you add the constructor. Constructors are used to initialize the instance variables of an object. The id is the string value assigned to the user's selection in the item list. The item_name is the string value displayed in the list item in the left pane of the tablet. The item_url variable is assigned to the Web site displayed in the detail pane. To customize the display of the list items in the DummyContent.java file within the template, follow these steps:

STEP 1

- Save your work and close the BikeAndBarge Manifest tab.

- If necessary, expand the src folder and the net.androidbootcamp.bikeandbarge.dummy package.

- Double-tap or double-click the DummyContent.java class.

- In Line 28, replace Item 1 with the text **Photos**.

- On the next line, replace Item 2 with the text **Tour**.

- On the next line, replace the existing code with the statement:

   addItem(new DummyItem("3", "Web Site", "http://bikebarge.com"));

The DummyContent.java file is customized with the item list in the left pane of the tablet (Figure 9-22). A red line appears below the code for the third list item.

Figure 9-22   DummyContent.java content file

STEP 2

- To handle the three string addItem statements, which display the three strings, and to modify the DummyItem class, hover over the third list item code and select Create constructor 'DummyItem (String, String, String)' to add an auto-generated constructor stub.

- In the auto-generated constructor stub in Line 50, modify the statement public DummyItem (String string, String string2, String string3) { to:

```
public DummyItem(String id, String item_name, String item_url) {
```

- To declare the item_name and item_url variables in the DummyItem class, add the two declaration statements below the public String content statement:

```
public String item_name;
public String item_url;
```

- Tap or click in the DummyItem auto-generated constructor stub and assign the following variables for the id, item_name, and item_url:

```
this.id = id;
this.item_name = item_name;
this.item_url = item_url;
content = item_name;
```

The DummyContent class is coded to handle the Web site request for the third list item (Figure 9-23).

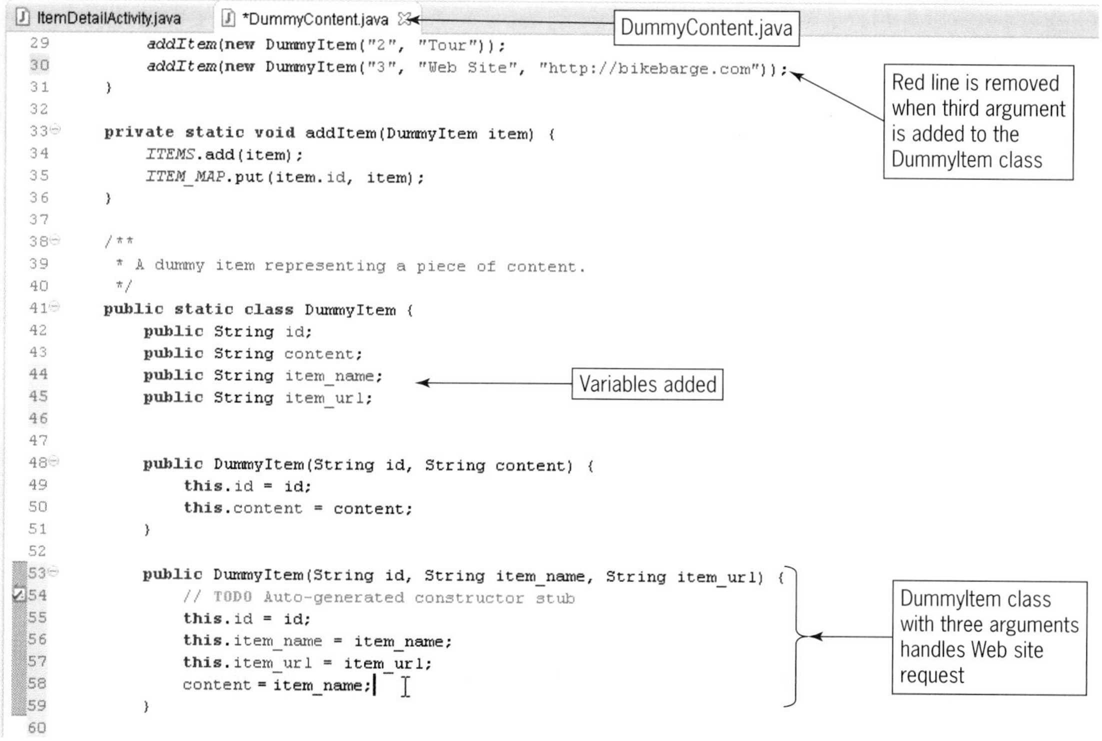

Figure 9-23 Customizing the DummyItem class

Displaying the Custom Layout in the Detail Pane

When the Bike and Barge application starts, it opens to display the three list items in the left pane. To work as designed, the chapter project requires that if the user selects the first item, the photos.xml layout is displayed in the detail pane. If the user selects the second item, the tour. xml is displayed in the detail pane. When the user selects Web Site, the third item, the WebView in the template fragment_item_detail.xml file displays the Bike and Barge Web site. This Java file works with a **fragment**, which is a piece of an application's user interface or behavior that can be placed in an Activity. A fragment is essentially a sub-Activity hosted inside another Activity. By dividing components of the user interface and displaying them in fragments, it is easier for developers to reuse these components across various Activities. For example, in the chapter project, a fragment is displayed in the right pane, while the left pane remains unchanged. Android introduced fragments in Android 3.0, API level 11, primarily to support more dynamic and flexible user interface designs on large screens. Three conditional if statements are necessary in the ItemDetailFragment.java file. In the DummyContent.java file, the variable id was set to the String value of the user's selection of the three list items. To determine if two String objects match exactly, you should use the **.equals method**, and not the == operator. The == operator compares if two objects are exactly the same object. Two strings may be different objects, but have the same exact characters. The .equals() method is used to compare strings for equality. When you compare the value of a String, the following syntax is necessary in Java:

Code Syntax

```
if (mItem.id.equals("1")) {
     }
```

Within the ItemDetailFragment.java file, the following code displays a custom XML layout file named photos.xml in the details pane:

Code Syntax

```
View rootView = inflater.inflate(R.layout.photos, container, false);
```

The inflate method has three arguments: The first part displays the XML layout, the second part applies the layout parameters to the container, and the third part is false, a Boolean type declaring that that layout was already passed to the container.

To display the Web page URL with the variable named item_url within the WebView widget, the following syntax is necessary:

Code Syntax

```
((WebView)
rootView.findViewById(R.id.item_detail)).loadUrl(mItem.item_url);
```

Code the three conditional if statements to display the XML layout and the Web page within the detail pane, as shown in the following steps:

STEP 1

- Save your work and close the DummyContent.java tab.

- If necessary, expand the src and net.androidbootcamp.bikeandbarge folder.

- Tap or click the ItemDetailFragment.java file that displays the layout files for the detail list in the right pane of the tablet.

- Scroll down to Line 55 and delete Lines 55–59, which originally displayed the detail list in a TextView widget.

- Tap or click Line 55 and type the following code to display the XML layout if the first list item is selected:

```
if (mItem.id.equals("1")) {
    rootView = inflater.inflate(R.layout.photos, container, false);
}
```

- On the next line, type the following code to display the XML layout if the second list item is selected:

```
if (mItem.id.equals("2")) {
    rootView = inflater.inflate(R.layout.tour, container, false);
}
```

The first and second list items are displayed in the detail pane with their corresponding XML layout (Figure 9-24).

```
    ItemDetailActivity.java        *ItemDetailFragment.java

    33    public ItemDetailFragment() {                        ItemDetailFragment.java tab
    34    }
    35
    36        @Override
    37    public void onCreate(Bundle savedInstanceState) {
    38            super.onCreate(savedInstanceState);
    39
    40            if (getArguments().containsKey(ARG_ITEM_ID)) {
    41                // Load the dummy content specified by the fragment
    42                // arguments. In a real-world scenario, use a Loader
    43                // to load content from a content provider.
    44                mItem = DummyContent.ITEM_MAP.get(getArguments().getString(
    45                    ARG_ITEM_ID));
    46            }
    47    }
    48                                                             First detail pane displays
    49        @Override                                          photos.xml layout
    50    public View onCreateView(LayoutInflater inflater, ViewGroup container,
    51            Bundle savedInstanceState) {
    52        View rootView = inflater.inflate(R.layout.fragment_item_detail,
    53                container, false);
    54
    55        if (mItem.id.equals("1")) {
    56            rootView = inflater.inflate(R.layout.photos, container, false);
    57        }
    58        if (mItem.id.equals("2")) {
    59            rootView = inflater.inflate(R.layout.tour, container, false);
    60        }
    61
    62        return rootView;
    63    }
    64  }
    65
                                                             Second detail pane
                                                             displays tour.xml layout
```

Figure 9-24   ItemDetailFragment.java class customized for the first and second items

STEP 2

- On the next line, type the following code to display the Bike and Barge Web page if the third list item is selected:

```
if (mItem.id.equals("3")) {
    ((WebView) rootView.findViewById(R.id.item_detail)).loadUrl(mItem.item_url);
}
```

- Hover over the red curly line below WebView and select Import 'WebView' (android.webkit).

The third list item displays the Bike and Barge url in a WebView widget (Figure 9-25).

```
50⊖      @Override
51       public View onCreateView(LayoutInflater inflater, ViewGroup container,
52               Bundle savedInstanceState) {
53           View rootView = inflater.inflate(R.layout.fragment_item_detail,
54                   container, false);
55
56           if (mItem.id.equals("1")) {
57               rootView = inflater.inflate(R.layout.photos, container, false);
58           }
59           if (mItem.id.equals("2")) {
60               rootView = inflater.inflate(R.layout.tour, container, false);
61           }
62           if (mItem.id.equals("3")) {
63               ((WebView) rootView.findViewById(R.id.item_detail)).loadUrl(mItem.item_url);
64           }
65
66           return rootView;
67       }
68   }
69
```

Third detail pane displays Bike and Barge Web site

Figure 9-25   ItemDetailFragment.java class customized for the third item

STEP 3

- Scroll to the top of ItemDetailFragment.java and expand the import list by tapping or clicking the plus sign in Line 3.

- Delete the import android.widget.TextView statement because the TextView library is not necessary.

- Save your work.

Running and Testing the Application

The Android Master/Detail Flow template provides an easy-to-use navigation to display multiple windows within the tablet interface or two separate Activities on a smartphone device. To test the Bike and Barge Android app, tap or click Run on the menu bar, and then select Run to save and test the application in the emulator. A dialog box requesting how you would like to run the application opens the first time the application is executed. Select Android Application and tap or click the OK button. Save all the files in the next dialog box, if necessary, and unlock the emulator. The application opens in the tablet emulator window where you can test list items in the Bike and Barge app, as shown in Figures 9-1, 9-2, 9-3, and 9-4. If your app is not displayed as a tablet emulator, tap or click Run on the menu and select Run Configurations. Tap or click the Target tab and then check the Tablet AVD box. You must have Internet connectivity to open the Web page and enough memory available to handle the app connection to the Web.

GTK

Because a tablet's screen is much larger than that of a smartphone, it provides more room to combine and interchange user interface components.

Wrap It Up—Chapter Summary

Android's diversity provides plenty of challenges, but creating apps that run on an entire ecosystem of devices can be faster using responsive design. A tablet provides a larger screen that allows for easier navigation using list items on the left and the details pane on the right on a tablet. The chapter provided steps to create a custom Master/Detail Flow template that created a simple structure to display three screens of content. The WebView control was introduced for opening Internet content directly within the app using AndroidManifest INTERNET permissions.

- Responsive design is an approach to designing apps and Web sites that provide an optimal viewing experience across as many devices as possible.

- Android templates are available when you create a new Android project. You use them to create basic Android applications that you can run and test on an Android device of any size.

- A tablet app created with the Master/Detail Flow template displays a Master list of items in a narrow vertical pane along the left edge of the screen. When the user selects an item in the list, associated content appears in the detail pane on the right. On a smaller device, such as a smartphone, the Master list and detail content are displayed on separate screens.

- To display the detail content for the first list item in the Bike and Barge app, you provide images and text descriptions in an XML TableLayout. Each row in the TableLayout displays an ImageView and TextView control.

- To display the detail content for the second list item, you code two TextView controls in a Linear layout that include the tour details.

- To display the detail content for the third list item, you customize the default fragment_item_detail.xml layout to use a WebView object instead of a TextView object. A WebView object allows you to place a Web browser or simply display some online content within your Activity, and uses a built-in rendering engine to display Web pages.

- After including a WebView object in the XML layout of an app, you must add the INTERNET permissions to the Android Manifest file so the app can access the Internet and load Web pages.

- To associate the content displayed in the detail pane with each list item in the left pane, you customize the DummyContent.java class file by adding code to the addItem statement so it references three String objects: the id, the item list string, and the Web site URL.

- To handle the responses to user selections, you add conditional statements to the ItemDetailFragment.java file.

Key Terms

.equals method—A method used to compare strings for equality.

Application template—A design you can use to create basic Android applications and then customize them.

fragment—A piece of an application's user interface or behavior that can be placed in an Activity.

Master/Detail Flow template—A template Eclipse provides for creating an Android app with an adaptive, responsive layout; it displays a set of list items on the left and the associated details on the right.

permission—A restriction limiting access to a part of the code or to data on the device.

responsive design—An approach to designing apps and Web sites that provide an optimal viewing experience across as many devices as possible.

WebView—A View widget that displays Web pages.

Developer FAQs

1. In the chapter project, the Master/Detail Flow template was selected when creating the app. Which activity has been used in the first eight chapters of this book?

2. How many list items are in the Master/Detail Flow template by default?

3. Which template XML layout file displays the item list fragment and the item detail container for a tablet?

4. What is the name of the sample Java file that contains content in the Master/Detail Flow template?

5. True or False? Each list item launches a separate Activity on a smartphone.

6. Which layout was used in the photos.xml file?

7. Write a line of code starting with addItem to display the first list item named Reservations.

8. Write a line of code starting with addItem to display the second list item named View Site connecting to the site android.com.

9. In which file would the lines in questions 7 and 8 be written?

10. When a smartphone is detected, the app uses which XML layout to display the FrameLayout instance?

11. What is the lowest API level that you can use with the Master/Detail Flow template?

12. True or False? You cannot add more list items to the Master/Detail Flow template.

13. Does the WebView widget open a full screen browser on the tablet?

14. Which XML file in the chapter project was switched from a TextView widget to a WebView widget?

15. Give four examples of Android device permissions mentioned in this chapter.

16. What type of permission is necessary when using the WebView widget?

17. In which file are permissions set?

18. What do fragments make it easier for developers to code?

19. Write an If structure to compare if mItem is equal to 6. The value 6 has been assigned to an Integer value.

20. Write an If structure to compare if mItem is equal to 6. The value 6 has been assigned to a String value.

Beyond the Book

Using the Internet, search the Web for the answers to the following questions to further your Android knowledge.

1. Research three Android tablet devices. Write a paragraph about the cost, usage, dimensions, and posted reviews of each of these three tablets.

2. Using *cnet.com* (a popular review site), compare the newest Android, iPad, and Windows tablets and summarize their recommendations in a one-page paper.

3. Using *developer.android.com*, research the topic of permissions. After writing many Android projects, the Android help files should be easier to understand now. Explain the use of permissions in your own words (at least 100 words).

4. A common user complaint is that it is difficult to use an onscreen keyboard to type long documents. Discuss three alternatives beyond using the traditional onscreen keyboard layout for input. Write a paragraph about each.

Case Programming Projects

Complete one or more of the following case programming projects. Use the same steps and techniques taught within the chapter. Submit the program you create to your instructor. The level of difficulty is indicated for each case programming project.

Easiest: *

Intermediate: **

Challenging: ***

Case Project 9–1: Oasis Spa Tablet App ⋆

Requirements Document

Application title: Oasis Spa Tablet App

Purpose: This tablet app explains the services of a full-service spa named Oasis Spa.

Algorithms: 1. The opening screen displays three list items titled Spa Services, Spa Address, and Full Web Site. The first list item displays two table rows within a table layout with an image in each row (spa1.png and spa2.png) with the text shown in Figure 9-26.

2. The second item displays the address and phone number of Oasis Spa at 1268 Andrew Lane, Pond, OK 43277, 555-332-3366.

3. The third list item opens *http://www.theoasisspa.net/* in a browser (Figure 9-27).

Conditions: 1. The pictures are provided with your student files.

2. Use the Master/Detail Flow template.

![Oasis Spa app screen]

 Oasis Spa

Spa Services

Spa Address

Full Web Site

 With our spa and massage services you are getting the relaxing touch of an expert. With an aromatic pillow for your eyes, a choice of aroma therapy oil, and a heated pillow for your neck, our massage offerings will restore balance to mind and body.

 Our spa manicure and pedicure services soothe with a warm neck pillow. Skin exfoliation and a hydrating massage are extended to the elbow for manicures and to the knee for pedicures, which also include a customized foot bath with essential oil.

Figure 9-26

Source: www.oasisluxury.net

Figure 9-27

Case Project 9–2: Modern Art Museums

Requirements Document

Application title: Modern Art Museums Tablet App

Purpose: The Modern Art Museum shows many of the world's famous art museum Web sites.

Algorithms:
1. The opening screen displays three list items: MOMA (*moma.org*), Tate Modern Museum (*www.tate.org.uk*), and Van Gogh Museum (*www.vangoghmuseum.nl*).

2. The first list item displays the MOMA Web site in the detail pane.

3. The second list item displays the Tate Modern Museum Web site in the detail pane.

4. The third list item displays the Van Gogh Museum Web site in the detail pane.

Case Project 9–3: Famous Athlete Tablet App ★★

Requirements Document

Application title: Famous Athlete Tablet App

Purpose: Create one tablet screen of a large app that features information about the famous athletes of the world. You can select your favorite athlete to feature.

Algorithms:
1. The first list item uses a TableLayout to display the name of the athlete. The second row should have an image of the athlete and text about the athlete.

2. The second list item displays the athlete's birth date, his or her hometown, and stats. Research the information needed.

3. The third list opens a link about the featured athlete.

Case Project 9–4: Snap Fitness Tablet App ★★

Requirements Document

Application title: Snap Fitness Tablet App

Purpose: The local fitness gym in your area wants an app that provides information about the activities and memberships at the gym.

Algorithms:
1. The list items display the text Site, Info, and Photos. The first list item links to the Web site of a local gym.

2. The second list item displays the costs for the gym:

      Youth (ages 14–17): $25

      Adult (18 and over): $50

      Family/Household: $75

      Active Senior: $50

3. The third list item displays four photos in four rows with information about the gym next to each one.

Case Project 9–5: Go Web 2.0 Tablet App ★★★

Requirements Document

Application title:	Go Web 2.0 Tablet App
Purpose:	The Go Web 2.0 Tablet app displays six of your favorite Web 2.0 technology sites.
Algorithms:	1. An opening screen displays the six names of the Web 2.0 sites.
	2. Each list item opens the corresponding Web 2.0 site.

Case Project 9–6: Pick Your Topic Tablet App ★★★

Requirements Document

Application title:	Pick Your Topic Tablet App
Purpose:	Get creative! Create an app with four list items on a topic of your choice.
Algorithms:	1. Create four list items on the opening screen.
	2. The four list items should link to a TableLayout with three rows, one TextView layout, one large ImageView layout, and a Web page.
Conditions:	Select your own images.

Move! Creating Animation

Unless otherwise noted in the chapter, all screenshots are provided courtesy of Eclipse.

In this chapter, you learn to:

- ◎ Create an Android application with Frame and Tween animation
- ◎ Understand Frame animation
- ◎ Understand Tween animation
- ◎ Add an animation-list XML file
- ◎ Code the AnimationDrawable object
- ◎ Set the background Drawable resource
- ◎ Launch the start( ) and stop( ) methods
- ◎ Add Tween animation to the application
- ◎ Create a Tween XML file that rotates an image
- ◎ Determine the rotation pivot, duration, and repeat count of a Tween animation
- ◎ Load the startActivity Tween animation in a second Activity
- ◎ Change the orientation of the emulator

Computer animation is widely used by television, the video game industry (as on Xbox, Vita, and Wii), and gaming applications on handheld devices. Animation displays many images in rapid succession or displays many changes to one image to create an illusion of movement. Animation is an integral part of many of the most popular Android apps at Google Play, including *Words with Friends, Angry Birds, Cut the Rope,* and *Roller Ball.* Android developers see the value in using 3D graphics to create more graphical apps and in-demand games.

Using Android animation, the chapter project named Wave Animation displays multiple photos of surfing the perfect wave controlled by a Start Frame Animation button that reveals the animated images frame by frame. The app contains five photos of surfing in Hawaii. When the user taps the Stop Frame Animation button, the frame-by-frame animation stops and the last image of the surfer rotates several times using Tween animation. A **motion tween** specifies a start state of an object, and then animates the object using a uniform transition type such as rotating a predetermined number of times or an infinite number of times. The Wave Animation Android smartphone app shown in Figure 10-1 allows the user to start and stop the animated images of a surfer riding a wave at different moments in a frame-by-frame sequence and then launches a second Activity that plays a rotation of the surfer image six times.

Five images are displayed during the Frame animation

© iStockphoto.com/EpicStockMedia

Figure 10-1 Wave Animation Android app using Frame animation

The animation in the Android app in Figure 10-1 displays frame-by-frame animation where the time between each photo is measured in 100-millisecond intervals. Clicking the Start Frame Animation button begins displaying the surfing images, and clicking the Start Tween Animation button stops the continuous Frame animation and begins the Tween animation of rotating the surfing image, as shown in Figure 10-2. The Tween animation rotates the last surfing image six times in a perfect circle. The orientation of the emulator is changed to landscape in Figure 10-2.

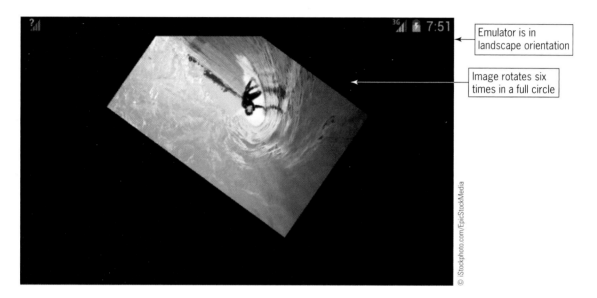

Figure 10-2 Wave Animation Android app using Tween animation

 GTK

Professional Android animation can be created by using complex programs such as Maya or Cinema 4D. A freeware program named Blender develops 3D animated content in the gaming environment.

To create this application, the developer must understand how to perform the following processes:

1. Add the five images to the drawable folder.

2. Add a Frame animation XML file to the project.

3. Add the layout for the image and button objects in activity_main.xml.

4. Set the duration between frames in the frame-by-frame animation.

5. Declare and instantiate the ImageView, Button, and AnimationDrawable controls.

6. Code the OnClickListeners for the Button controls.

7. Run the Frame animation application.

8. Add a layout for an ImageView control for the Tween animation.

9. Add a Tween animation XML file to rotate the last surfing image.

10. Create a second Activity named Tween.java to launch the rotation Tween animation.

11. When the application executes, change the orientation of the emulator.

Android Animation

Android provides two types of animation: Frame and Tween animation. **Frame animation**, also called frame-by-frame animation, assigns a sequence of photos to play as in a slide show with a predefined interval between images. Frame-by-frame animation is typically created to show steps in a process such as how to fly-fish or to play a fast-paced sequence such as in a cartoon. To create the illusion of movement, a cartoon image can be displayed on the screen and repeatedly replaced by a new image that is similar, but slightly advanced in the time sequence.

Instead of using a sequence of images, **Tween animation** creates an animation by performing a series of transformations on a single image such as position, size, rotation, and transparency on the contents of a View object. Text can fly across the screen, an image of an engine can be rotated to display different angles, or the transparency of an image can change from transparent to solid. A sequence of animation instructions defines the Tween animation using either XML or Android code. In this chapter project, the application first displays a frame-by-frame animation. Code is added to the same application to display a second type of animation called a Tween rotation effect.

Adding the Layout for the Frame Image and Button Controls

The layout specifications for the chapter project reside within the activity_main.xml file in a LinearLayout. The single ImageView control named imgSurf displays the surfing images in a frame-by-frame animation. The two Button controls named btnStart and btnStop start and stop the Frame animation, respectively. The layout includes a Relative layout nested within a Linear layout to place the two buttons side by side. In the Linear layout, an ImageView control displays the animation images. Insert this control and its properties in the activity_main.xml file to specify precise settings for the control. Within the structured Linear layout, insert a Relative layout to arrange the buttons side by side, which the Linear layout does not allow. Later in the chapter, a Tween animation is added to the application and launched when the Frame animation ends. To begin the application, set up the String table, and code the activity_main.xml layout, follow these steps:

STEP 1

- Open the Eclipse program.

- Type **E:\Workspace** (if necessary, enter a different drive letter that identifies the USB drive) to select a workspace, and then tap or click the OK button.

- Tap or click the New button on the Standard toolbar and then select Android Application Project.

- Tap or click the Next button.

- In the New Android Application dialog box, enter the Application Name **Wave Animation**.

- Enter the Package Name of **net.androidbootcamp.waveanimation**.

The new Android Wave Animation project has an application name, a package name, and a MainActivity Activity (Figure 10-3).

Figure 10-3   Creating the Wave Animation application

STEP 2

- Tap or click the Next button.

- Tap or click the Create custom launcher icon box to uncheck the option.

- Tap or click the Next button twice.

- Tap or click the Finish button.
- If necessary, open the activity_main.xml Graphical Layout tab. Tap or click the Hello world! TextView in the emulator and press the Delete key.
- In the Package Explorer, expand the values folder within the res folder.
- Double-tap or double-click the strings.xml file to display the Android Resources.
- Tap or click the Add button.
- If necessary, tap or click String and then tap or click the OK button.
- In the Name text box, type **imgDescription** to name the String.
- In the Value text box, type **Surfing Image** to define the text.
- Tap or click the Add button.
- If necessary, tap or click String and then tap or click the OK button.
- In the Name text box, type **btnStart** to name the String.
- In the Value text box, type **Start Frame Animation** to define the text.
- Tap or click the Add button.
- If necessary, tap or click String and then tap or click the OK button.
- In the Name text box, type **btnStop** to name the String.
- In the Value text box, type **Start Tween Animation** to define the text.

The String table includes an image description and two Button control text strings (Figure 10-4).

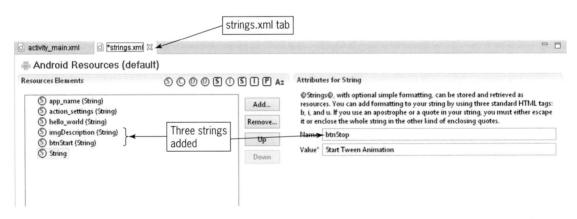

Figure 10-4   String table

STEP 3

- Save and close the strings.xml tab.
- In the res/layout folder, double-tap or double-click activity_main.xml to display the graphical layout.

- If necessary tap or click the activity_main.xml tab at the bottom of the window. By default, RelativeLayout is set.

- Within the RelativeLayout, add the ImageView control by typing the following custom XML code using auto-completion as much as possible:

```
<ImageView
        android:id="@+id/imgSurf"
        android:layout_width="200dp"
        android:layout_height="200dp"
        android:layout_alignParentTop="true"
        android:layout_centerHorizontal="true"
        android:contentDescription="@string/imgDescription" />
```

The ImageView control is coded in activity_main.xml (Figure 10-5).

```
 1  <RelativeLayout xmlns:android="http://schemas.android.com/apk/res/android"
 2          xmlns:tools="http://schemas.android.com/tools"
 3          android:layout_width="match_parent"
 4          android:layout_height="match_parent"
 5          android:paddingBottom="@dimen/activity_vertical_margin"
 6          android:paddingLeft="@dimen/activity_horizontal_margin"
 7          android:paddingRight="@dimen/activity_horizontal_margin"
 8          android:paddingTop="@dimen/activity_vertical_margin"
 9          tools:context=".MainActivity" >
10
11      <ImageView
12          android:id="@+id/imgSurf"
13          android:layout_width="200dp"
14          android:layout_height="200dp"
15          android:layout_alignParentTop="true"
16          android:layout_centerHorizontal="true"
17          android:contentDescription="@string/imgDescription" />
18
19  </RelativeLayout>
20
```

Figure 10-5   ImageView XML code

STEP 4

- Press the Enter key twice, and then add the two Button controls to place the buttons on the same line by typing the following custom XML code, using auto-completion as much as possible:

```
<Button
      android:id="@+id/btnStart"
      android:layout_width="wrap_content"
      android:layout_height="wrap_content"
      android:layout_alignParentLeft="true"
      android:layout_below="@+id/imgSurf"
      android:layout_marginTop="50dp"
      android:text="@string/btnStart"
      android:textSize="12sp" />

<Button
      android:id="@+id/btnStop"
      android:layout_width="wrap_content"
      android:layout_height="wrap_content"
      android:layout_alignBaseline="@+id/btnStart"
      android:layout_alignBottom="@+id/btnStart"
      android:layout_alignParentRight="true"
      android:text="@string/btnStop"
      android:textSize="12sp" />
```

The two Button controls are coded in activity_main.xml (Figure 10-6).

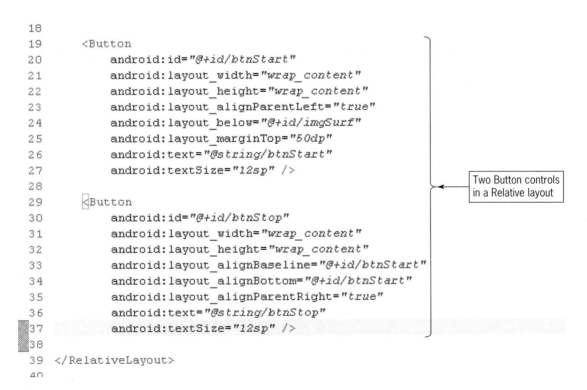

```
18
19        <Button
20             android:id="@+id/btnStart"
21             android:layout_width="wrap_content"
22             android:layout_height="wrap_content"
23             android:layout_alignParentLeft="true"
24             android:layout_below="@+id/imgSurf"
25             android:layout_marginTop="50dp"
26             android:text="@string/btnStart"
27             android:textSize="12sp" />
28
29        <Button
30             android:id="@+id/btnStop"
31             android:layout_width="wrap_content"
32             android:layout_height="wrap_content"
33             android:layout_alignBaseline="@+id/btnStart"
34             android:layout_alignBottom="@+id/btnStart"
35             android:layout_alignParentRight="true"
36             android:text="@string/btnStop"
37             android:textSize="12sp" />
38
39   </RelativeLayout>
40
```

Two Button controls in a Relative layout

Figure 10-6   Two Button controls in the XML code

Creating Frame-by-Frame Animation

In the Wave Animation app, the frame-by-frame animation loads and displays a sequence of surfing images from the drawable folder. A single XML file named frame.xml lists the frames that constitute the surfing animation. You create frame.xml in a new res folder named drawable. In the XML code, an **animation-list** root element references five surfing images stored in the drawable folders. Each item in the animation-list specifies how many milliseconds to display each image. In the chapter project, each image is displayed for 1/10 of a second. The animation-list code includes a oneshot property, which is set to true by default. By setting the **android:oneshot** attribute of the animation-list to false, as shown in the following code, the animation plays repeatedly until the Start Tween Animation button is tapped. If the oneshot attribute is set to true, the animation plays once and then stops and displays the last frame. Note that you add the oneshot attribute to the code in the opening animation-list tag.

Code Syntax

```
<?xml version="1.0" encoding="utf-8"?>
<animation-list xmlns:android="http://schemas.android.com/'apk/'res/android"
android:oneshot="false" >
<item android:drawable="@drawable/surf1" android:duration= "100"/>
<item android:drawable="@drawable/surf2" android:duration= "100"/>
<item android:drawable="@drawable/surf3" android:duration= "100"/>
<item android:drawable="@drawable/surf4" android:duration= "100"/>
<item android:drawable="@drawable/surf5" android:duration= "100"/>
</animation-list>
```

When the XML file is added to the Android project, the Drawable Resource type is selected and animation-list is specified as the root element of the XML code. A folder named drawable is automatically added to the res folder. To copy the images into the drawable folder and code the animation-list XML code, follow these steps:

STEP 1

- Save and close the activity_main.xml file.

- To add the five image files to the drawable-hdpi folder, if necessary, copy the student files to your USB drive. Open the USB folder containing the student files.

- In the Package Explorer, expand the drawable-hdpi folder in the res folder.

- To add the five image files to the drawable-hdpi resource folder, drag the surf1.png, surf2.png, surf3.png, surf4.png, and surf5.png files to the drawable-hdpi folder until a plus sign pointer appears. Release the mouse button.

- Tap or click the Copy files option button, and then tap or click the OK button.

Copies of the five files appear in the drawable-hdpi folder (Figure 10-7).

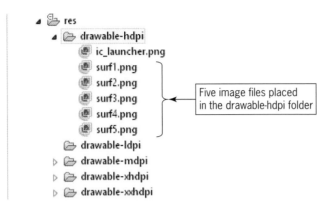

Figure 10-7   Copied images in the drawable-hdpi folder

STEP 2

- Press and hold or right-click the layout folder.

- Point to New on the shortcut menu, and then tap or click Android XML File.

- In the Resource Type drop-down box, select Drawable.

- In the File text box, type the XML filename **animation**.

- In Root Element, select animation-list as the type of element to add to the XML file.

An XML file named animation is created in a folder named drawable with the root element animation-list of resource type Drawable (Figure 10-8).

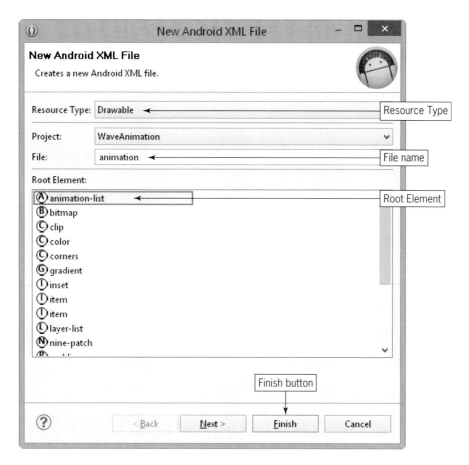

Figure 10-8 Creating the animation.xml file

STEP 3

- Tap or click the Finish button. The animation.xml file opens with the animation-list element already coded.

- Expand the drawable folder.

- Tap or click the animation-list source tag and then tap or click before the closing tag (>) in Line 2.

- To add the oneshot attribute to create a continuous loop of animation, type **android:oneshot="false"**.

In animation.xml, the oneshot attribute is set to false in the animation-list code to animate the frames continuously (Figure 10-9).

Figure 10-9   The oneshot attribute is set to false

STEP 4

- Tap or click Line 3 within the animation-list element to add the five list items that are displayed within the frame-by-frame animation. Type the following five lines to reference the images and millisecond durations:

```
<item android:drawable="@drawable/surf1" android:duration="100"/>
<item android:drawable="@drawable/surf2" android:duration="100"/>
<item android:drawable="@drawable/surf3" android:duration="100"/>
<item android:drawable="@drawable/surf4" android:duration="100"/>
<item android:drawable="@drawable/surf5" android:duration="100"/>
```

In animation.xml, the five frames of the animation are entered as items in the animation-list element (Figure 10-10).

Figure 10-10   Entering the animation-list items

GTK

Android includes support for high-performance 2D and 3D graphics with the Open Graphics Library named OpenGL. OpenGL is a cross-platform graphics API that specifies a standard software interface for 3D graphics processing hardware and uses a coordinate system to map the image to the screen.

Coding the AnimationDrawable Object

The **AnimationDrawable class** provides the methods for Drawable animations to create a sequence of frame-by-frame images. In Android development, frame-based animations and image transitions are defined as drawables. The instance of AnimationDrawable is instantiated as a class variable because it is used in multiple methods within the MainActivity class. To instantiate the AnimationDrawable object in MainActivity.java as a class variable, follow this step:

STEP 1

- Save your work and then close the animation.xml tab.

- Expand the src and net.androidbootcamp.waveanimation folders, and then double-tap or double-click MainActivity.java to open its code window.

- In Line 9 within the MainActivity class, type **AnimationDrawable surfAnimation;** to instantiate the object. (Your line numbers might differ.)

- Point to AnimationDrawable and tap or click Import 'AnimationDrawable' (android.graphics. drawable).

The AnimationDrawable instance named surfAnimation is coded within MainActivity.java (Figure 10-11).

```
                                          MainActivity.java

 J *MainActivity.java ✕
   1  package net.androidbootcamp.waveanimation;
   2
   3⊕ import android.os.Bundle;▢
   7
   8  public class MainActivity extends Activity {
   9      AnimationDrawable surfAnimation;              ← AnimationDrawable
  10⊝     @Override                                        statement
 ▲11     protected void onCreate(Bundle savedInstanceState) {
  12          super.onCreate(savedInstanceState);
  13          setContentView(R.layout.activity_main);
  14      }
  15
  16⊝     @Override
 ▲17     public boolean onCreateOptionsMenu(Menu menu) {
  18          // Inflate the menu; this adds items to the action bar if it is present.
  19          getMenuInflater().inflate(R.menu.main, menu);
  20          return true;
  21      }
  22
  23  }
  24
```

Figure 10-11 Instantiating the AnimationDrawable class variable

Setting the Background Resource

The ImageView control named imgSurf that was coded in activity_main.xml must be coded in MainActivity.java to bind the Drawable resource files to the Background property. The Background property of an image can be set to any full Drawable resource such as a .png file, a 9-patch image file, or a solid color designated with hexadecimal code such as #FF0000 for red. A special image, called a **9-patch image**, has predefined "stretching" areas that maintain the same look on different screen sizes. These 9-patch graphics are named for their nine areas, called patches, that scale separately. For example, a button may change sizes when it is stretched across different form factors.

The images used in the Wave Animation application are .png files, referenced in animation.xml as items in the animation-list. In the following code, a new instance of ImageView named imgFrame is assigned to the ImageView control named imgSurf, which was defined in the activity_main.xml layout. The list of drawable images in the animation-list is connected to the imgFrame instance by the imgFrame.setBackgroundResource method. The **setBackgroundResource** method shown in the following code places the four surfing images in the frame-by-frame display. Each frame points to one of the surfing images that were assembled in the XML resource file.

Code Syntax

```
ImageView imgFrame=(ImageView)findViewById(R.id.imgSurf);
imgFrame.setBackgroundResource(R.drawable.animation);
surfAnimation=(AnimationDrawable) imgFrame.getBackground( );
```

In the third line of the code syntax, the instance of AnimationDrawable called surfAnimation is assigned as the background of the four images to display in the animation. Android constructs an AnimationDrawable Java object before setting it as the background. At this point, the animation is ready to display the four images, but must wait for you to code the start( ) method, which actually begins the movement in the Frame animation. To instantiate the ImageView control and assign the four images to the Background properly, follow these steps:

STEP 1

- Tap or click at the end of the setContentView(R.layout.*activity_main*); line, press the Enter key, and then instantiate the ImageView that accesses imgSurf in the XML layout file by typing **ImageView imgFrame=(ImageView)findViewById(R.id.imgSurf);**.

- Point to ImageView and tap or click Import 'ImageView' (android.widget).

The ImageView control is instantiated (Figure 10-12).

```
 J  *MainActivity.java  ⊠
  1  package net.androidbootcamp.waveanimation;
  2
  3⊕ import android.os.Bundle;▯
  8
  9  public class MainActivity extends Activity {
 10      AnimationDrawable surfAnimation;
 11⊖     @Override
▲12      protected void onCreate(Bundle savedInstanceState) {
 13          super.onCreate(savedInstanceState);
 14          setContentView(R.layout.activity_main);
 15          ImageView imgFrame=(ImageView)findViewById(R.id.imgSurf);  ◄──────  ImageView
 16      }                                                                       instance
 17
 18⊖     @Override
▲19      public boolean onCreateOptionsMenu(Menu menu) {
 20          // Inflate the menu; this adds items to the action bar if it is present.
 21          getMenuInflater().inflate(R.menu.main, menu);
 22          return true;
 23      }
 24
 25  }
```

Figure 10-12   Instantiating the ImageView control

STEP 2

● Press the Enter key to insert a blank line, and then set the background resource image for the
animation-list in animation.xml by typing **imgFrame.setBackgroundResource(R.drawable.
animation);**.

*The animation-list within animation.xml is set as the Background property of the imgFrame
ImageView (Figure 10-13).*

```
J *MainActivity.java ⊠
 1   package net.androidbootcamp.waveanimation;
 2
 3⊕ import android.os.Bundle;□
 8
 9   public class MainActivity extends Activity {
10       AnimationDrawable surfAnimation;
11⊖     @Override
12       protected void onCreate(Bundle savedInstanceState) {
13           super.onCreate(savedInstanceState);
14           setContentView(R.layout.activity_main);
15           ImageView imgFrame=(ImageView)findViewById(R.id.imgSurf);
16           imgFrame.setBackgroundResource(R.drawable.animation);
17       }
18
```

setBackgroundResource

Figure 10-13   Setting setBackgroundResource for the ImageView control

STEP 4

- Next, access the AnimationDrawable object by "getting" the view object. Press the Enter key, and then type **surfAnimation=(AnimationDrawable) imgFrame.getBackground();**.

The AnimationDrawable is ready to display the five images (Figure 10-14).

```
J MainActivity.java ⊠
 1   package net.androidbootcamp.waveanimation;
 2
 3⊕ import android.os.Bundle;□
 8
 9   public class MainActivity extends Activity {
10       AnimationDrawable surfAnimation;
11⊖     @Override
12       protected void onCreate(Bundle savedInstanceState) {
13           super.onCreate(savedInstanceState);
14           setContentView(R.layout.activity_main);
15           ImageView imgFrame=(ImageView)findViewById(R.id.imgSurf);
16           surfAnimation=(AnimationDrawable) imgFrame.getBackground();
17       }
18
```

getBackground

Figure 10-14   getBackground prepares the Animation drawable

IN THE TRENCHES

Common frame-by-frame animations include rotating timers, email symbols, Activity icons, page-loading animations, cartoons, and other useful user interface elements.

Adding Two Button Controls

The Button controls in the Wave Animation project turn the frame-by-frame animation on and off. Both buttons use a setOnClickListener to await user interaction. To instantiate the two Button controls and add the setOnClickListener, follow these steps:

STEP 1

- To code the first button, press the Enter key and then type **Button btFrame=(Button) findViewById(R.id.btnStart);**.

- Point to Button and select Import 'Button' (android.widget).

The first Button control that begins the animation is instantiated (Figure 10-15).

```
 1  package net.androidbootcamp.waveanimation;
 2
 3⊕ import android.os.Bundle;☐
 9
10  public class MainActivity extends Activity {
11      AnimationDrawable surfAnimation;
12⊖     @Override
13      protected void onCreate(Bundle savedInstanceState) {
14          super.onCreate(savedInstanceState);
15          setContentView(R.layout.activity_main);
16          ImageView imgFrame=(ImageView) findViewById(R.id.imgSurf);
17          surfAnimation=(AnimationDrawable) imgFrame.getBackground();
18          Button btFrame=(Button)  findViewById(R.id.btnStart);
19      }
20
```

[Annotation: First Button control instance]

Figure 10-15   btFrame is an instance of the first button

STEP 2

- To code the second button, press the Enter key and type **Button btTween=(Button) findViewById(R.id.btnStop);**.

The second Button control that stops the animation is instantiated (Figure 10-16).

```
J *MainActivity.java ⊠
   1  package net.androidbootcamp.waveanimation;
   2
   3⊕ import android.os.Bundle;▯
   9
  10  public class MainActivity extends Activity {
  11      AnimationDrawable surfAnimation;
  12⊖     @Override
  13      protected void onCreate(Bundle savedInstanceState) {
  14          super.onCreate(savedInstanceState);
  15          setContentView(R.layout.activity_main);
  16          ImageView imgFrame=(ImageView)findViewById(R.id.imgSurf);
  17          surfAnimation=(AnimationDrawable)imgFrame.getBackground();
  18          Button btFrame=(Button) findViewById(R.id.btnStart);
  19          Button btTween=(Button) findViewById(R.id.btnStop);  ◄──── Instance of second
  20          }                                                         Button control
  21
```

Figure 10-16   btTween is an instance of the second button

STEP 3

- To code the first Button listener, press the Enter key and type **btFrame** followed by a period to open a code listing.

- Scroll down to double-tap or double-click the first setOnClickListener displayed in the auto-completion list.

- Inside the parenthesis, type **new on** and then press the Ctrl+spacebar keys to display the auto-completion list.

- Double-tap or double-click the first choice, which is a View.OnClickListener with an Anonymous Inner Type event handler.

- Type **View.** before OnClickListener.

- Insert a semicolon after the closing brace for the auto-generated stub.

The first button OnClickListener awaits user interaction for btFrame (Figure 10-17).

```
 1   package net.androidbootcamp.waveanimation;
 2
 3⊕ import android.os.Bundle;☐
10
11   public class MainActivity extends Activity {
12       AnimationDrawable surfAnimation;
13⊖     @Override
14       protected void onCreate(Bundle savedInstanceState) {
15           super.onCreate(savedInstanceState);
16           setContentView(R.layout.activity_main);
17           ImageView imgFrame=(ImageView)findViewById(R.id.imgSurf);
18           surfAnimation=(AnimationDrawable)imgFrame.getBackground();
19           Button btFrame=(Button) findViewById(R.id.btnStart);
20           Button btTween=(Button) findViewById(R.id.btnStop);
21⊖          btFrame.setOnClickListener(new View.OnClickListener() {
22
23⊖              @Override
24               public void onClick(View arg0) {
25                   // TODO Auto-generated method stub
26
27               }
28           });
29           }
30
31⊖      @Override
32       public boolean onCreateOptionsMenu(Menu menu) {
33           // Inflate the menu; this adds items to the action bar if it is present.
34           getMenuInflater().inflate(R.menu.main, menu);
35           return true;
36       }
37
38   }
39
```

OnClickListener for btFrame button

Semicolon inserted

Figure 10-17   OnClickListener for the first button

STEP 4

- Press the Enter key after the semicolon to code the second Button listener.

- Type **btTween** followed by a period to open a code listing.

- Double-tap or double-click the first setOnClickListener displayed in the auto-completion list.

- Inside the parenthesis, type **new on** and then press the Ctrl+spacebar keys to display the auto-completion list.

- Scroll down and double-tap or double-click the first choice, which is a View.OnClickListener with an Anonymous Inner Type event handler.

- Type **View.** before OnClickListener.

- Insert a semicolon after the closing brace for the auto-generated stub.

The second button OnClickListener awaits user interaction for btTween (Figure 10-18).

```
 1  package net.androidbootcamp.waveanimation;
 2
 3⊕ import android.os.Bundle;▯
10
11  public class MainActivity extends Activity {
12      AnimationDrawable surfAnimation;
13⊝      @Override
14      protected void onCreate(Bundle savedInstanceState) {
15          super.onCreate(savedInstanceState);
16          setContentView(R.layout.activity_main);
17          ImageView imgFrame=(ImageView)findViewById(R.id.imgSurf);
18          surfAnimation=(AnimationDrawable)imgFrame.getBackground();
19          Button btFrame=(Button) findViewById(R.id.btnStart);
20          Button btTween=(Button) findViewById(R.id.btnStop);
21⊝          btFrame.setOnClickListener(new View.OnClickListener() {
22
23⊝              @Override
24              public void onClick(View arg0) {
25                  // TODO Auto-generated method stub
26
27              }
28          });
29⊝          btTween.setOnClickListener(new View.OnClickListener() {
30
31⊝              @Override
32              public void onClick(View arg0) {
33                  // TODO Auto-generated method stub
34
35              }
36          });
37      }
38
39⊝      @Override
```

OnClickListener for btTween button

Semicolon inserted

Figure 10-18 OnClickListener for the second button

Using the Start and Stop Methods

After associating AnimationDrawable with the animation images and coding the buttons, you can use the start( ) and stop( ) methods of the drawable objects to control the Frame animation. When the user taps the Start Frame Animation button, the start( ) method begins the Frame animation continuously because oneshot is set to false. The Frame animation stops only when the user taps the Start Tween Animation button, which launches the stop( ) method and then initiates the startActivity, launching the second Activity named Tween.java. In the following code, the start( ) method is placed within the onClick( ) method for the Start Frame Animation button and the stop( ) method is placed within the onClick( ) method for the Start Tween Animation button:

Code Syntax

```
surfAnimation.start( );
surfAnimation.stop( );
```

The start( ) method launches the surfAnimation.xml file displaying the animation-list items and the stop( ) method ends the display of the animation-list. To add the start( ) and stop() methods, follow these steps:

STEP 1

● Tap or click at the end of the first // TODO comment (for btFrame), press the Enter key, and then type **surfAnimation.start( );**.

The Start Frame Animation button is coded to start surfAnimation.xml (Figure 10-19).

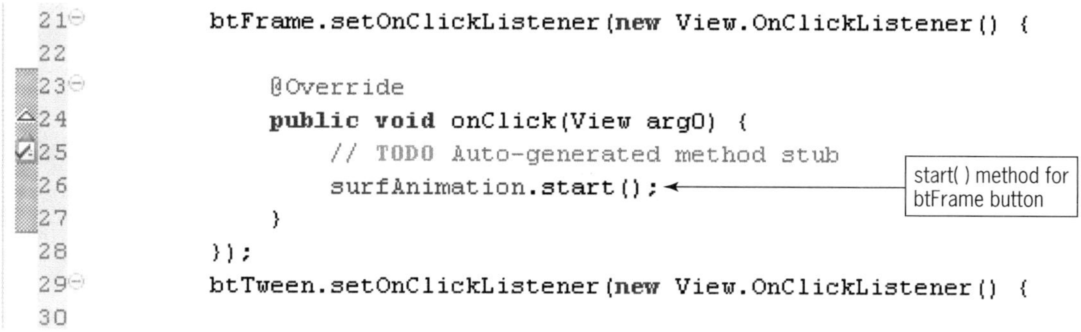

```
21⊖        btFrame.setOnClickListener(new View.OnClickListener() {
22
23⊖            @Override
24            public void onClick(View arg0) {
25                // TODO Auto-generated method stub
26                surfAnimation.start();  ←———————————   start( ) method for
27            }                                           btFrame button
28        });
29⊖        btTween.setOnClickListener(new View.OnClickListener() {
30
```

Figure 10-19   Entering the start( ) method

STEP 2

● Tap or click at the end of the // TODO comment for btTween, press the Enter key, and then type **surfAnimation.stop( );**.

The Start Tween Animation button is coded to stop the Frame animation within surfAnimation.xml (Figure 10-20).

```
23⊖              @Override
△24              public void onClick(View arg0) {
☑25                  // TODO Auto-generated method stub
26                  surfAnimation.start();
27              }
28          });
29⊖          btTween.setOnClickListener(new View.OnClickListener() {
30
31⊖              @Override
△32              public void onClick(View arg0) {
☑33                  // TODO Auto-generated method stub
34                  surfAnimation.stop();◄──────────  stop( ) method for
35              }                                      btTween button
36          });
37      }
38
```

Figure 10-20   Entering the stop( ) method

STEP 3

- To test the Frame animation, tap or click Run on the menu bar, and then tap or click Run to save the application and test it in the emulator.

- A dialog box requesting to run the application opens the first time the application is executed. Select Android Application and tap or click the OK button.

- Save all the files in the next dialog box, if necessary, and unlock the emulator.

- The application opens in the emulator window where you can tap or click the Start Frame Animation button to view the surfing animation.

The emulator displays the frame-by-frame animation (Figure 10-21).

Adding the Layout for the Tween Image

After the user taps the Start Tween Animation button, the Frame animation ends and a second Activity is launched. This second Activity is named Tween.java, and it defines a

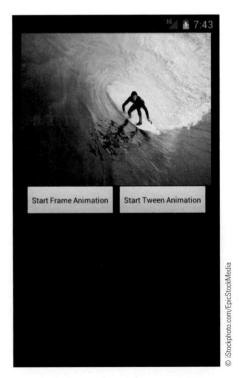

Figure 10-21   Frame-by-frame animation displayed in the emulator

© iStockphoto.com/EpicStockMedia

second layout with a single ImageView control identified with the id imgTween, referencing the fifth image named surf5. To code the tween.xml file layout to display an ImageView control, follow this step:

STEP 1

- Exit the emulator, and then close MainActivity.java.

- In the res folder, press and hold or right-click the layout folder, point to New on the shortcut menu, and then tap or click Android XML Layout File.

- In the New Android XML File dialog box, type **tween.xml** in the File text box to name the layout file.

- In the Root Element list, select LinearLayout, if necessary.

- Tap or click the Finish button.

- When the emulator window opens, tap or click the tween.xml tab, if necessary.

- Add the ImageView control by typing the following custom XML code beginning on Line 7, using auto-completion as much as possible:

```
<ImageView
        android:id="@+id/imgTween"
        android:layout_width="wrap_content"
        android:layout_height="wrap_content"
        android:layout_gravity="center"
        android:contentDescription="@string/imgDescription"
        android:src="@drawable/surf5" />
```

A second XML layout named tween.xml displays an ImageView control (Figure 10-22).

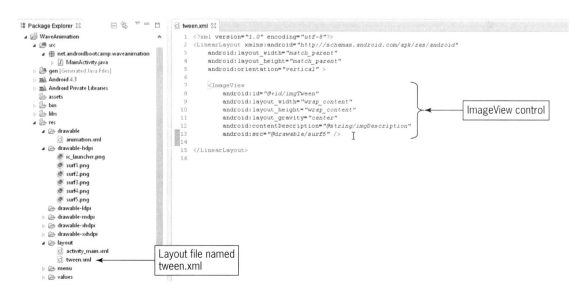

Figure 10-22   ImageView control coded in tween.xml

Creating Tween Animation

Instead of rendering several images in a sequence in Frame animation, Tween animation manipulates a Drawable image by adding tween effects. Defined in an XML file, **tween effects** are transitions that change objects from one state to another. An ImageView or TextView object can move, rotate, grow, or shrink. As shown in Table 10-1, Tween animations include a built-in library of tween effects. These effects are saved within an animation XML file that belongs in the res/anim/ folder of your Android project.

Tween effect	Purpose
Alpha	Transitions an object from one level of transparency to another where 0.0 is transparent and 1.0 is opaque
Rotate	Spins an object from one angular position to another. To rotate an object completely around, start at 0 degrees and rotate to 359 degrees (a full circle). A pivotX and pivotY percentage shows the amount of pivot based on the object's left edge
Scale	Transitions the size of an object (grow or shrink) on an X/Y scale
Translate	Moves the object vertically or horizontally a percentage relative to the element width (e.g., deltaX="100%" would move the image one image width away)

Table 10-1　Tween animation effects

© 2C15 Cengage Learning

The four Tween animation effects in Table 10-1 can be coded in an XML file and individually configured or nested together to animate an object in any possible direction or size.

Coding a Tween Rotation XML File

In the Wave Animation application, the last image named surf5.png is rotated when the user clicks the Start Tween Animation button. Android uses an XML file-creator utility that supports 10 different Resource types. The default Resource type is Layout, but in the chapter project, you select Tween animation. After entering the XML filename as rotation.xml, tap or click the root element of rotate to store the rotation.xml code for a Tween animation in the /res/anim folder. The XML file for a Frame animation is stored in the /res/drawable folder. The rotation.xml statements are shown in the following code:

Code Syntax

```xml
<?xml version="1.0" encoding="utf-8"?>
<rotate
xmlns:android="http://schemas.android.com/apk/res/android"
android:fromDegrees="0"
android:toDegrees="359"
android:pivotX="50%"
android:pivotY="50%"
android:duration="2000"
android:repeatCount="5"
```

The rotation.xml code defines the attributes of the Tween animation. Notice the tween effect is set to rotate in the second line. The fromDegrees and toDegrees rotate attribute spins the object from 0 to 359 degrees, which equals 360 degrees for a full circle. The image in the chapter project completes several clockwise rotations. The pivotX and pivotY attributes pivot an object from its center by setting the pivot point, which can be a fixed coordinate or a percentage. By default, the object pivots around the (0,0) coordinate, or the upper-left corner of the object. Notice pivotX and pivotY are set to 50% in the code example, which determines that the pivot location is from the center of the object. The duration for each rotation is set for 2,000 milliseconds. The repeatCount represents how many times the object rotates after the initial rotation. You can set repeatCount to an integer or to "infinite" if you do not want the rotation to stop. Remember that the number of rotations is always one greater than the repeat value, so if you set the repeatCount to the integer 5, the object rotates six times. It rotates once initially and then repeats the rotation five more times. By creating an XML file, it is easier to make simple changes to fine-tune the animation. You might want to try different values in the rotation.xml file to see how the animation changes. To code the Tween animation to rotate an image, follow these steps:

STEP 1

- Save and close the tween.xml layout file.

- To create a new rotation XML file, press and hold or right-click the layout folder.

- Point to New on the shortcut menu, and then tap or click Android XML File. The New Android XML File dialog box opens.

- In the Resource Type drop-down box, select Tween Animation.

- In the File text box, type the XML filename **rotation**.

- In Root Element, select rotate as the type of element that is added to the XML file.

The New Android XML File dialog box opens and the Resource Type, File, and Root Element are selected (Figure 10-23).

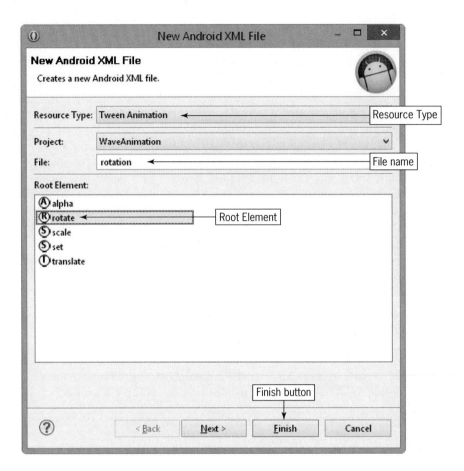

Figure 10-23 New Android XML File dialog box

STEP 2

- Tap or click the Finish button.

- Expand the anim folder. The rotation.xml file opens with the rotate element already coded.

- Delete the closing rotate code and the right angle bracket (>) after rotate on Line 2.

- Tap or click Line 3 and type the following code after the opening rotate root element:

```
xmlns:android="http://schemas.android.com/apk/res/android"
android:fromDegrees="0"
android:toDegrees="359"
android:pivotX="50%"
android:pivotY="50%"
android:duration="2000"
android:repeatCount="5" />
```

In rotation.xml, the Tween animation attributes are coded to rotate the image (Figure 10-24).

```
1   <?xml version="1.0" encoding="utf-8"?>
2   <rotate
3       xmlns:android="http://schemas.android.com/apk/res/android"
4       android:fromDegrees="0"
5       android:toDegrees="359"
6       android:pivotX="50%"
7       android:pivotY="50%"
8       android:duration="2000"
9       android:repeatCount="5" />
10
```

rotation.xml

rotate
attributes

Figure 10-24 rotate attributes in rotation.xml

IN THE TRENCHES
To change an image from transparent to opaque, code an alpha statement in an XML file such as
<alpha xmlns:android=*http://schemas.android.com/apk/res/android* android:fromAlpha="0.0"
android:toAlpha="1.0" android:duration="100">.

Coding a Second Activity to Launch the Tween Animation

When the user taps the Start Tween Animation button in the Wave Animation, two actions are triggered within the second onClick( ) method. The Frame animation is concluded with the stop( ) method and a startActivity intent launches a second Activity named Tween.java. To code a second Activity and launch the startActivity, follow these steps:

STEP 1

- Save and close rotation.xml.

- To create a second class, press and hold or right-click the src/net.androidbootcamp. waveanimation folder, point to New on the shortcut menu, and then tap or click Class.

- Type **Tween** in the Name text box to create a second class that defines the Tween Activity.

- Tap or click the Superclass Browse button, and then type **Activity** in the Choose a type text box. As you type, matching items are displayed.

- Tap or click Activity—android.app and then tap or click the OK button to extend the Activity class.

A new class named Tween.java is created (Figure 10-25).

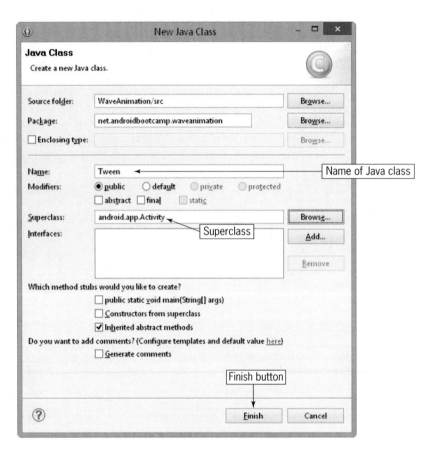

Figure 10-25 Creating the Tween.java class

STEP 2

- Tap or click the Finish button to finish creating the Tween class.

- To launch the Tween Activity class from the MainActivity.java class, open MainActivity.java.

- Scroll down to the statement surfAnimation.stop( ).

- Tap or click at the end of the statement and press the Enter key.

- To launch an intent that starts the second Activity, type **startActivity (new Intent (MainActivity.this, Tween.class));**.

- Point to Intent and then tap or click Import 'Intent' (android.content).

A startActivity launches the Tween.java class (Figure 10-26).

Tween.java   MainActivity.java

```
     *Tween.java        MainActivity.java ✕
  2
  3⊕ import android.os.Bundle;
 11
 12  public class MainActivity extends Activity {
 13      AnimationDrawable surfAnimation;
 14⊝     @Override
▲15     protected void onCreate(Bundle savedInstanceState) {
 16         super.onCreate(savedInstanceState);
 17         setContentView(R.layout.activity_main);
 18         ImageView imgFrame=(ImageView)findViewById(R.id.imgSurf);
 19         surfAnimation=(AnimationDrawable)imgFrame.getBackground();
 20         Button btFrame=(Button) findViewById(R.id.btnStart);
 21         Button btTween=(Button) findViewById(R.id.btnStop);
 22⊝        btFrame.setOnClickListener(new View.OnClickListener() {
 23
 24⊝            @Override
▲25            public void onClick(View arg0) {
 26                // TODO Auto-generated method stub
 27                surfAnimation.start();
 28            }
 29         });
 30⊝        btTween.setOnClickListener(new View.OnClickListener() {
 31
 32⊝            @Override
 33            public void onClick(View arg0) {                    startActivity
 34                // TODO Auto-generated method stub
 35                surfAnimation.stop();
 36                startActivity (new Intent(MainActivity.this, Tween.class));
 37            }
 38         });
 39     }
```

Figure 10-26   MainActivity.java launches the second Activity

IN THE TRENCHES

If you deploy an Android app and receive an error message similar to "Installation error: INSTALL_FAILED_ INSUFFICIENT_STORAGE," the default internal storage is 64 MB or lower. You can override this setting in the Eclipse launch configuration by tapping or clicking Run on the menu bar and then selecting Run Configurations. Tap or click the Target tab and in the Additional Emulator Command Line Options box, type **-partition-size 1024.**

Coding a StartAnimation

Now that the layout, rotation XML file, and second Activity are ready, the Tween animation can be launched using the StartAnimation method. Applying the Tween rotation animation, the **StartAnimation** method begins animating a View object by calling the AnimationUtils class utilities to access the resources necessary to load the animation. To code the StartAnimation method to launch the rotation, follow these steps:

STEP 1

- Save and close MainActivity.java.

- To code the onCreate method in Tween.java, tap or click at the end of the public class Tween extends Activity { line, and then press the Enter key.

- Type **public void onCreate(Bundle savedInstanceState) {** and press the Enter key. A closing brace for the onCreate method appears.

- Point to Bundle and then tap or click Import 'Bundle' (android.os).

The onCreate method for Tween.java is coded (Figure 10-27).

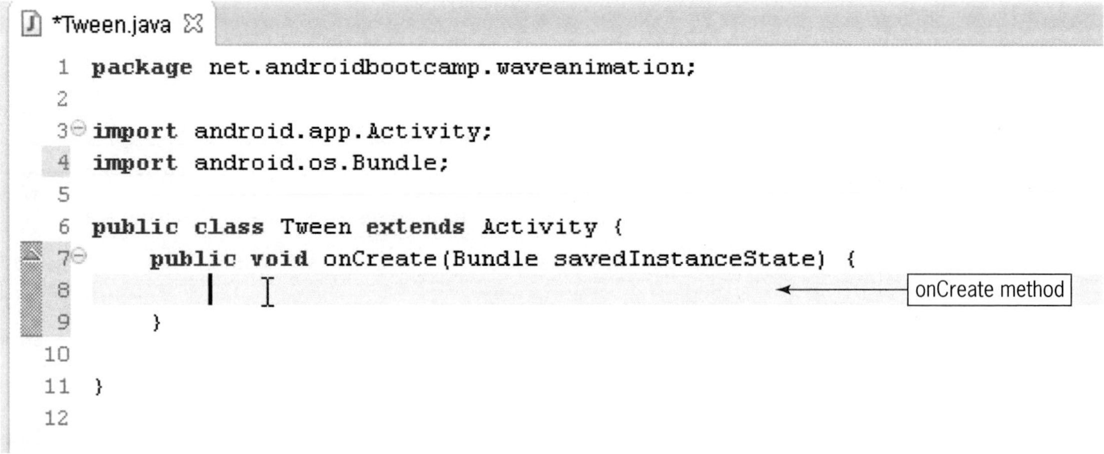

```
*Tween.java
  1  package net.androidbootcamp.waveanimation;
  2
  3  import android.app.Activity;
  4  import android.os.Bundle;
  5
  6  public class Tween extends Activity {
  7      public void onCreate(Bundle savedInstanceState) {          ← onCreate method
  8          |  I
  9      }
 10
 11  }
 12
```

Figure 10-27   Entering the onCreate method in Tween.java

STEP 2

- To display the tween.xml layout, type **super.onCreate(savedInstanceState);**.

- Press the Enter key and then type **setContentView(R.layout.tween);**.

A tween.xml layout is displayed for the Tween class (Figure 10-28).

Figure 10-28 Setting the layout in tween.xml

STEP 3

- To instantiate the ImageView control named imgTween, press the Enter key and type **ImageView imgRotate = (ImageView) findViewById(R.id.imgTween);**.

- Point to ImageView and then tap or click Import 'ImageView' (android.widget).

An instance of the ImageView control named imgRotate is instantiated (Figure 10-29).

Figure 10-29 Instantiating the ImageView

STEP 4

- To begin the Tween rotation animation, press the Enter key and type **imgRotate.startAnimation (AnimationUtils.loadAnimation(this, R.anim.rotation));**.

- Point to AnimationUtils and then tap or click Import 'AnimationUtils' (android.view.animation), if necessary.

The Tween animation is started. The fifth image rotates six times and stops (Figure 10-30).

```
Tween.java  ⊠
 1  package net.androidbootcamp.waveanimation;
 2
 3⊕ import android.app.Activity;
 7
 8  public class Tween extends Activity {
 9⊖     public void onCreate(Bundle savedInstanceState) {
10          super.onCreate(savedInstanceState);
11          setContentView(R.layout.tween);
12          ImageView imgRotate = (ImageView) findViewById(R.id.imgTween);
13          imgRotate.startAnimation(AnimationUtils.loadAnimation(this, R.anim.rotation));
14      }
15
16  }
17                           ┌──────────────────────┐
                             │ startAnimation rotation │
                             └──────────────────────┘
```

Figure 10-30 Image rotates using Tween animation (complete code for Tween.java)

Updating the Android Manifest File

The Android Manifest file must be updated to include the second Activity named Tween.java and to remove the title bar in the theme of both Activities to provide more display room for the animation, if necessary. To add the second Activity to the Android Manifest file, follow these steps:

STEP 1

- Save your work and close the Tween.java file.

- In the Package Explorer, double-tap or double-click the AndroidManifest.xml file.

- To add the Tween class to the Android Manifest file, tap or click the Application tab at the bottom of the WaveAnimation Manifest page.

- If necessary, scroll down to display the Application Nodes section.

- In the Application Nodes section, tap or click the Add button.

- Select Activity in the Create a new element at the top level, in Application dialog box.

- Tap or click the OK button.

- The Attributes for Activity section opens in the Application tab.

- In the Name text box, type the class name preceded by a period (.**Tween**) to add the Tween Activity to the AndroidManifest.xml file.

- Save your work.

The class .Tween is entered in the Name text box of the Attributes for Activity section (Figure 10-31).

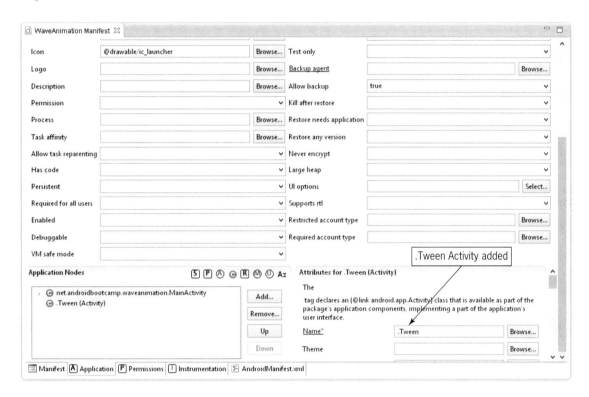

Figure 10-31 Adding the Tween Activity to the Android Manifest file

STEP 2

- To change the Android theme, tap or click the AndroidManifest.xml tab at the bottom of the window.

- Inside the Activity code, tap or click at the end of the code that states android:icon="@drawable/ ic_launcher". Press the Enter key to insert a new blank line.

- Type **android:theme="@android:style/Theme.Black.NoTitleBar"**.

- The theme also needs to be changed for the second Activity. Before the closing brace of <activity android: name=".Tween", press the Enter key.

- Type **android:theme="@android:style/Theme.Black.NoTitleBar"**. If a right angle bracket does not appear at the end of the line, type > to insert the closing bracket.

The Android theme is coded within both Activities in the Android Manifest file (Figure 10-32).

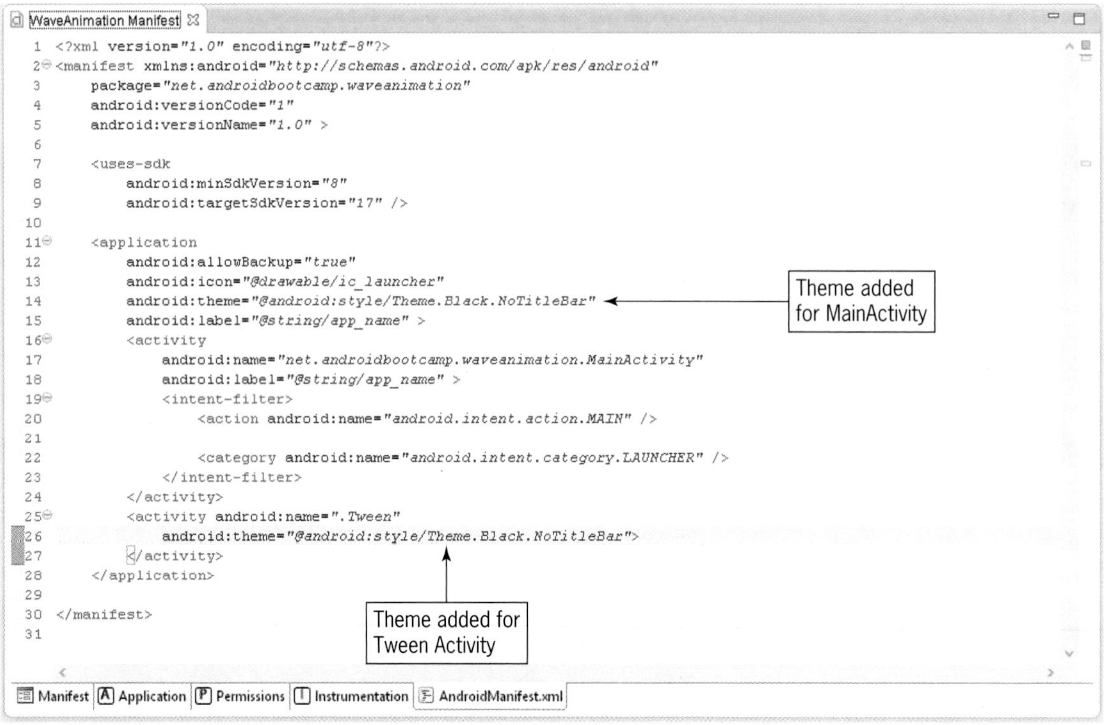

```
WaveAnimation Manifest ⊠

 1  <?xml version="1.0" encoding="utf-8"?>
 2  <manifest xmlns:android="http://schemas.android.com/apk/res/android"
 3      package="net.androidbootcamp.waveanimation"
 4      android:versionCode="1"
 5      android:versionName="1.0" >
 6
 7      <uses-sdk
 8          android:minSdkVersion="8"
 9          android:targetSdkVersion="17" />
10
11      <application
12          android:allowBackup="true"
13          android:icon="@drawable/ic_launcher"
14          android:theme="@android:style/Theme.Black.NoTitleBar"      Theme added
15          android:label="@string/app_name" >                         for MainActivity
16          <activity
17              android:name="net.androidbootcamp.waveanimation.MainActivity"
18              android:label="@string/app_name" >
19              <intent-filter>
20                  <action android:name="android.intent.action.MAIN" />
21
22                  <category android:name="android.intent.category.LAUNCHER" />
23              </intent-filter>
24          </activity>
25          <activity android:name=".Tween">
26              android:theme="@android:style/Theme.Black.NoTitleBar">
27          </activity>
28      </application>
29
30  </manifest>                        Theme added for
31                                     Tween Activity
```

Manifest | Application | Permissions | Instrumentation | AndroidManifest.xml

Figure 10-32   Adding the theme to the Android Manifest file

STEP 3

●   Close the WaveAnimation Manifest tab and save your work.

Changing the Emulator to Landscape Orientation

Most Android phones and tablets automatically rotate the display from portrait to landscape orientation when the user turns the device 90 degrees. Throughout this text, the emulator has been shown in a portrait orientation because when you first install the Android emulator, the default screen orientation layout is vertical. To switch the emulator to a landscape orientation on a PC, press the Ctrl+F12 keys simultaneously (or press the 7 key on the keypad when Num Lock is turned off) when the emulator is displayed during execution, as shown in Figure 10-2. To rotate the phone emulator back to the initial portrait position, press the Ctrl+F12 keys again. Mac users can press the Fn+Ctrl+F12 keys to change the orientation.

Running and Testing the Application

With all this exciting animation, it is time to see both types of animation running in the Android emulator. Tap or click Run on the menu bar, and then select Run to save and test the application in the emulator. Save all the files, if necessary, and unlock the emulator. The application opens in the emulator window where you can tap or click the Start Frame Animation button to begin the Frame animation of the four surfing images, as shown in Figure 10-1. To end the Frame animation and begin the rotation shown in Figure 10-2, tap or click the Start Tween Animation button. The Tween animation rotates the image six times in a complete circle and ends.

Wrap It Up—Chapter Summary

Android supports two types of animations: frame-by-frame and Tween animations, as shown in the Wave Animation application in this chapter. Frame-by-frame animation shows different drawable images in a View in the opening window. The second Activity displays a Tween animation that rotates an image. Using the animation methods provided in the Android environment, developers can explore the user interface layouts that provide more usability and interest.

- Frame animation assigns a sequence of images to play as in a slide show with a specified interval between images. Tween animation performs a series of transformations on a single image, such as to change its position, size, rotation, and transparency.

- To create a layout that displays two controls side by side, you can nest a Relative layout within a Linear layout.

- To create a Frame animation, you write code in an XML file to load a sequence of images from the drawable folder. In the XML code, an animation-list root element references these images. Each item in the animation-list specifies how many milliseconds to display the image.

- In the animation-list code, you can include the oneshot property to determine how many times to play the animation. The oneshot property is set to true by default, meaning the animation plays once and then stops. Set the oneshot property to false to have the animation repeatedly play through to the end and then play again from the beginning.

- When you add the XML file with the animation-list code to the Android project, select Drawable as the Resource type and select animation-list as the root element so that Android stores the XML file in the res/drawable folder.

- The AnimationDrawable class provides the methods for Drawable animations to create a sequence of frame-by-frame images. In Android development, frame-based animations and image transitions are defined as drawables.

- You can set the Background property of an image to any full Drawable resource such as a .png file. In MainActivity.java, you must specify the ImageView control that contains the animation images so you can bind the Drawable resource files to the Background property. Assign a new instance of ImageView to the ImageView control that was originally defined in the activity_main.xml layout.

Use the setBackgroundResource method to connect the images in the animation-list to the instance of ImageView.

- In MainActivity.java, also include an instance of AnimationDrawable and assign it as the background of the animation images. Android constructs an AnimationDrawable Java object before setting it as the background. The animation is now ready to display the images, though it does not actually start playing them until the start( ) method is triggered.

- You can use the start( ) and stop( ) methods of the drawable objects to control a Frame animation. When the user taps one button, the start( ) method begins playing the animation continuously if the oneshot property is set to false. The animation stops only when the user taps another button to execute the stop( ) method. The code can then initiate a startActivity that launches another Activity.

- A Tween animation manipulates a Drawable image by adding tween effects, which are predefined transitions that change an object from one state to another. Save a tween effect within an animation XML file. Specify the Resource type of this XML file as Tween animation so that Android stores the file in the res/anim/ folder of your Android project.

- The XML file for a Tween animation defines rotate attributes such as the number of degrees to spin, the pivot location, the rotation duration, and the number of times to repeat the rotation.

- To launch a Tween animation, use the startAnimation method, which begins animating a View object by calling the AnimationUtils class utilities to access the resources it needs to play the animation.

- To switch the emulator to use a landscape orientation on a PC, press the Ctrl+F12 keys. To rotate the emulator to the original portrait position, press the Ctrl+F12 keys again. Mac users can press the Fn+Ctrl+F12 keys to change the orientation.

Key Terms

9-patch image—A special image with predefined stretching areas that maintain the same look on different screen sizes.

android:oneshot—An attribute of the animation-list that determines whether an animation plays once and then stops or continues to play until the Stop Animation button is tapped.

AnimationDrawable class—A class that provides the methods for Drawable animations to create a sequence of frame-by-frame images.

animation-list—An XML root element that references images stored in the drawable folders and used in an animation.

Frame animation—A type of animation, also called frame-by-frame animation, that plays a sequence of images, as in a slide show, with a specified interval between images.

motion tween—A type of animation that specifies the start state of an object, and then animates the object a predetermined number of times or an infinite number of times using a transition.

setBackgroundResource—A method that places images in the frame-by-frame display for an animation, with each frame pointing to an image referenced in the XML resource file.

startAnimation—A method that begins the animation process of a View object by calling the AnimationUtils class utilities to access the resources necessary to load the animation.

Tween animation—A type of animation that, instead of using a sequence of images, creates an animation by performing a series of transformations on a single image, such as position, size, rotation, and transparency, on the contents of a View object.

tween effect—A transition that changes objects from one state to another, such as by moving, rotating, growing, or shrinking.

Developer FAQs

1. What are the two types of built-in Android animation?

2. Which type of animation displays a slide show type of presentation?

3. Which type of animation is applied to a single image?

4. What is the root element of a Frame animation within the XML file?

5. Write the code that sets an attribute to play a Frame animation until the app ends.

6. Write the code that sets an attribute to play a Frame animation for three seconds.

7. Would the oneshot property be set to true or false in question 6?

8. Which type of Drawable image stretches across different screen sizes?

9. Name three types of Drawable objects that can be set as a Background drawable.

10. Which method launches a Frame animation?

11. Which method ends a Frame animation?

12. Name four tween effects.

13. Which tween effect shrinks an image?

14. Which tween effect changes the transparency of the image?

15. When you create a Tween XML file, which folder is the file automatically saved in?

16. If you wanted to turn an image one-quarter of a circle starting at 0 degrees, write two lines of the code necessary to make that rotation.

17. Write the attribute for a rotation that repeats 8 times.

18. When an emulator launches, which orientation type is displayed?

19. Which keys change the orientation of the emulator on a PC?

20. Which keys change the orientation of the emulator on a Mac?

Beyond the Book

Using the Internet, search the Web for the answers to the following questions to further your Android knowledge.

1. Research how smartphone animation games have changed the sales of console games in the gaming industry. Write at least 200 words on this topic.

2. Research OpenGL graphic development. Write at least 150 words on this topic.

3. A new player to the mobile platform is the Windows 8 smartphone. Research why this phone might or might not be successful in the long term. Write at least 150 words on this topic.

4. At the Google Play site, determine the top five grossing apps. Write a paragraph about each.

Case Programming Projects

Complete one or more of the following case programming projects. Use the same steps and techniques taught within the chapter. Submit the program you create to your instructor. The level of difficulty is indicated for each case programming project.

Easiest: ⋆

Intermediate: ⋆

Challenging: ⋆⋆

Case Project 10–1: Facial Expressions App ⋆

Requirements Document	
Application title:	Facial Expressions App
Purpose:	A series of images use Frame animation to demonstrate seven facial expressions of an actor.
Algorithms:	1. The opening screen displays the first image of a man with a happy facial expression (Figure 10-33).
	2. When the user taps the See the Actor button, the seven facial expressions are each displayed for two seconds. After each image is shown once, the animation ends.
Conditions:	1. The pictures of the seven facial expressions of the actor are provided with your student files with the names face1 through face7.
	2. Display each image in the Frame animation with the size 210, 300.
	3. Code a theme with no title bar.

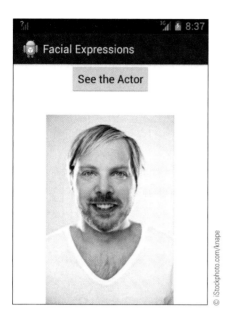

Figure 10-33

Case Project 10–2: Improve Your Golf Stroke App ⋆

Requirements Document

Application title: Improve Your Golf Stroke App

Purpose: A series of images use Frame animation to demonstrate the proper positions
                      of the perfect golf swing.

Algorithms: 1. The screen displays six images, each showing the proper position during the
                         process of making a golf swing. Display the images in a Frame animation with 0.5
                         seconds between each image. Each image should only be displayed once when
                         the user taps the Perfect Golf Swing button.

                      2. When the user taps the Rotate Your Swing button, rotate the fifth
                         image around 270 degrees nine times with an interval of three seconds.

Conditions: 1. Find six pictures online of a golfer at different moments in a golf stroke.

                      2. Display each image with the size 200, 400.

                      3. Code a theme with no title bar.

Case Project 10–3: Android Rotation App ★★

Requirements Document

Application title:	Android Rotation App
Purpose:	As an advertisement at the end of a television commercial, an Android phone rotates in a perfect circle four times.
Algorithms:	1. The opening screen displays an Android phone in the center and automatically begins rotating the image four times in a perfect circle with an interval of 1.5 seconds.
Conditions:	1. Find a picture online of an Android phone.
	2. Display the image with the size 100, 170.
	3. Code a theme with no title bar.

Case Project 10–4: Cartoon Animation App ★★

Requirements Document

Application title:	Cartoon Animation App
Purpose:	A sequence of cartoon images is displayed to create the sense of motion.
Algorithms:	1. The opening screen displays one of four cartoon images of a man with an idea. When the user taps the Start Cartoon button, each image is displayed for 0.15 seconds.
	2. When the user taps the Stop Cartoon button, the current image rotates once and then stops.
Conditions:	1. Find cartoons online to create a moving animation.
	2. Display each image with the size 300, 400.
	3. Code a theme with no title bar.

Case Project 10–5: Flags of the World App ★★★

Requirements Document

Application title: Flags of the World App

Purpose: A sequence of flag images appears when the app starts.

Algorithms:

1. The opening screen displays images of seven world flags. When the user taps a Start Flags button, a Frame animation displays each flag for 0.75 seconds until the app ends.

2. When the user taps the Stop Flags button, the Frame animation stops. The last flag image fades away for 10 seconds until it is no longer visible.

Conditions:

1. Find pictures of the seven world flags online.

2. Display each image with the size 170, 100.

3. Code a theme with no title bar.

Case Project 10–6: Frame and Tween Animation Game App ★★★

Requirements Document

Application title: Frame and Tween Animation Game App

Purpose: Display images of your favorite game in action.

Algorithms:

1. Locate at least four images of your favorite game character (such as one in *Angry Birds)* and create a custom Frame animation of your choice.

2. Create a Tween animation with one of the images that uses at least two of the tween effects.

Conditions:

1. Select your own images.

2. Use a layout of your choice.

3. Code a theme with no title bar.

Discover! Persistent Data

In this chapter, you learn to:

◎ Create an Android project using persistent data

◎ Understand different types of persistent data

◎ Understand SharedPreferences persistent data

◎ Understand internal storage

◎ Understand external storage

◎ Understand saving data using a network connection

◎ Understand saving to a database connection

◎ Write data using SharedPreferences

◎ Instantiate a SharePreferences object

◎ Write data using getString( ) method

◎ Retrieve data from SharedPreferences

◎ Read data using a putString( ) method

◎ Display an ImageView control using code

An Android app typically requests data and then modifies that data to produce a result throughout multiple activities. To demonstrate the use of storing that data across classes, this chapter's ClearJet Rewards project requests the flyer's name and miles flown for the given year. The opening screen (Figure 11-1a) provides two EditText controls to accept the name and number of miles flown. The two variables are stored in a local variable on the computer (Figure 11-1b). These values will persist throughout the life of the app and after the program stops execution. After the user taps the button on the opening screen, a second Activity (Figure 11-2) opens and the number of miles flown, entered in the first Activity, determines if the customer has reached bronze, silver, or gold status with the airline for the upcoming year. To reach the bronze status, the customer must reach the 25,000 mile threshold. To reach the silver status, the customer must reach the 50,000 mile threshold. To reach the gold status, the customer must reach the 75,000 mile threshold. Each status level provides benefits such as free upgrades to first class, free airline lounge benefits, and first seating. The image shown on the second activity changes to an appropriate image based on the frequent flier status level.

(a) Opening screen

(b) Persistent data entered

© iStockphoto.com/Franck-Boston

Figure 11-1 ClearJet Rewards Android app

Figure 11-2   Reward level displayed on second activity

IN THE TRENCHES
The persistent data structure is available in some form in every programming language.

To create this application, the developer must understand how to perform the following processes, among others:

1. Add strings to the String table.
2. Add images to the drawable folder.
3. Design two XML layouts for the first and second Activity.
4. Instantiate the XML controls in the first Activity.
5. Establish a SharedPreferences object to store the data entered.
6. Write data to the SharedPreferences object.
7. Launch a second Activity.

8. Initialize the XML controls on the second Activity.

9. Retrieve the data from the SharedPreferences object.

10. Determine the status of the frequent flier using an If structure.

11. Display the results on the second Activity.

Understanding Persistent Data

The ClearJet Rewards app opens with a window that requests user input. Unlike the project in Chapter 2 (Healthy Recipes), this program allows input that is stored within the device. That data survives to be used in the second Activity class. With the programs that you have written so far, the values entered did not persist beyond the Activity in which they were created. The data was lost because the data is stored in RAM (random access memory), which is cleared when the app (or the device) stops running. Android applications can save data on the device's drive or other storage media such as a memory card or cloud service so that the data be retrieved later within the app or after the termination of the program. **Persistent data** stores values permanently by placing the information in a file.

Android provides several options for you to save persistent application data. Persistent data can be saved within a variable or within a database, based on the specific need of the app. Some apps may require private storage, while others should be accessible to other applications. Persistent data can be stored in five different ways in Android applications:

- Shared preferences—Stores private data in key–value pairs

- Internal storage—Stores private data in the memory of the device

- External storage—Stores data, which can be available to other apps on shared external storage

- SQLite database—Stores structured data in a private database

- Network connection—Stores data on a Web server

Using Shared Preferences

The SharedPreferences class provides one of the easiest ways to save and load primitive data, whether you are looking to save the user's name or settings such as the font size the user prefers. In the ClearJet Rewards app, the SharedPreferences object is used to store user data even if the user closes the application. Shared preferences can save any data including user preferences, such as what wallpaper a user has chosen or individual values entered by the user in an EditText control.

SharedPreferences can be used to save any primitive data: Booleans, floats, ints, longs, and strings. In the chapter project app, the frequent flier user enters their full name (string) and the number of miles flown for the current year (int). In the first Activity, these values are saved using SharedPreferences, and in the second Activity, they are retrieved to determine if the miles flown qualify for bronze, silver, or gold status for the airlines. SharedPreferences are best when your app needs to save small chunks of data such as a name–value pair. The two-part pair specifies a name for the data you want to save and the actual value. The pair is saved to an XML file that can be retrieved later in the app or after the app closes. To save data in SharedPreferences file, the following steps must be completed when writing persistent data:

- Obtain an instance of the SharedPreferences file.

- Create a SharedPreferences.Editor object.

- Assign values into SharedPreferences objects using the putString( ) method.

- Save the values to the preferences file using the commit( ) method.

Using Internal Storage

Another option when saving persistent data is to store the information directly on the device's internal drive. The saved files on the device are available only to the app that created the files. Other applications cannot access files saved with the internal storage method. Use caution when storing internal files, because low internal storage space can drastically affect the speed of an Android device and battery life.

Using External Storage

Android apps can save persistent data to external storage, for example, the device's SD (Secure Digital) card. All applications can read and write files placed on the external storage and the Android smartphone or tablet owner can remove them. To use external storage, the following permissions are necessary in the Android Manifest file:

```
<uses-permission android:name="android.permission.WRITE_EXTERNAL_STORAGE"/>
<uses-permission android:name="android.permission.READ_EXTERNAL_STORAGE"/>
```

Using SQLite Databases

If you have a large amount of data to store as persistent data, a database is the perfect choice. The default database engine for Android is SQLite. **SQLite** (SQL stands for Structured Query Language) is a lightweight, preloaded mobile database engine, which has been available since the Cupcake 1.5 version of Android and occupies a small amount of disk memory. The data is stored within the SQLite database so that it persists even after the app is terminated. Using a SQLite database, Android apps model data items in tables and columns, with optional relationships between the entities within the database. The tables can be queried using SQL statements.

Using a Network Connection

If your device is connected to the Internet, persistent data can be stored and retrieved on a Web service. Before an app attempts to connect to a network connection, it should check to see whether an Internet connection is available. The device may be out of range of a 3G/4G network or the user may have disabled both Wi-Fi and mobile data access. If a connection is not available, the user cannot save or retrieve the persistent data.

Creating XML Layout Files

The ClearJet Rewards app begins with the activity_main.xml layout, which displays a title, a Plain Text and a Number EditText control, and a Button control. A second XML layout named status.xml displays an ImageView control with the appropriate image of the earned status level and a TextView control. To start the ClearJet Rewards application by adding images, a String table and two XML layout files, complete the following steps:

STEP 1

- Open the Eclipse program.

- Type **E:\Workspace** (if necessary, enter a different drive letter that identifies the USB drive) to select a workspace, and then tap or click the OK button.

- Tap or click the New button on the Standard toolbar and then select Android Application Project.

- Tap or click the Next button.

- In the New Android Application dialog box, enter the Application Name **ClearJet Rewards**.

- Enter the Package Name **net.androidbootcamp.clearjetrewards**.

The new Android ClearJet Rewards project has an application name and a package name (Figure 11-3).

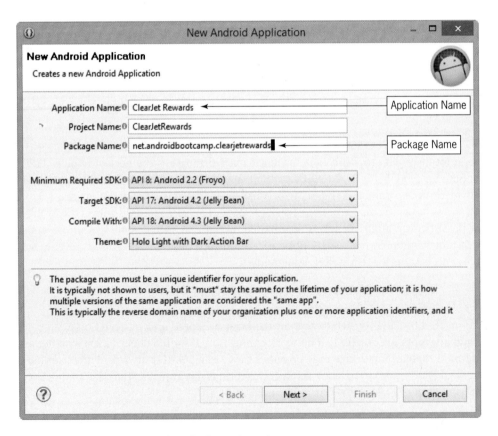

Figure 11-3   Setting up the ClearJet Rewards project

STEP 2

- Tap or click the Next button.

- Tap or click the Create custom launcher icon box to uncheck the option.

- Tap or click the Next button twice, and then click Finish.

- To add the four image files to the drawable-hdpi resource folder, drag bronze.png, gold.png, rewards.png, and silver.png to the drawable-hdpi folder until a plus sign pointer appears. Release the mouse button.

- If necessary, tap or click the Copy files option button, and then tap or click the OK button.

Copies of the three image files appear in the drawable-hdpi folder (Figure 11-4).

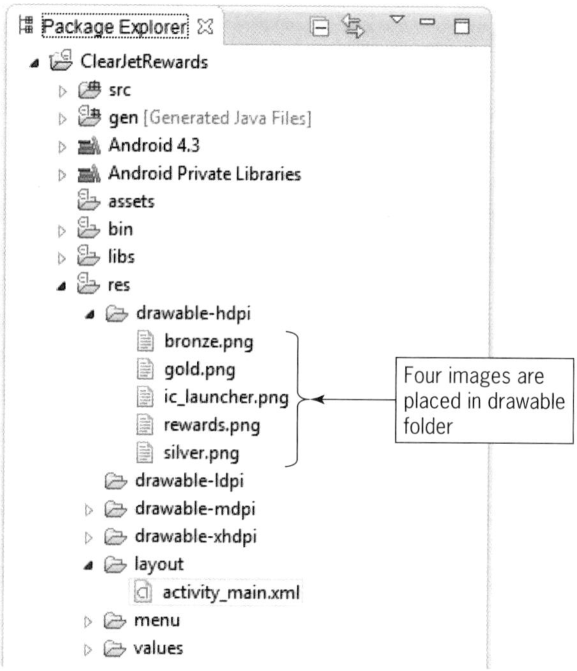

Figure 11-4   Image files in the drawable-hdpi folder

STEP 3

- Expand the res\values folder and then double-tap or double-click the strings.xml file.

- Tap or click the Add button, if necessary, select String, and then tap or click the OK button.

- Type **txtTitle** in the Name text box and type **Frequent Flier Miles** in the Value text box.

- Repeat the process of adding the following strings shown in Table 11-1 to the strings.xml file:

String Name	String Value
hint1	Name
hint2	Miles Flown
btnStatus	Find Status
imgDescription	Status Level Image
txtStatus	Reward Level

Table 11-1 String table

© 2015 Cengage Learning

- Save your work.

The strings.xml file contains the string values necessary in this app (Figure 11-5).

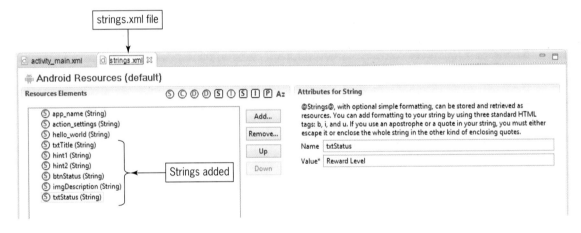

Figure 11-5 strings.xml file

STEP 4

- Close the strings.xml tab.

- If necessary, open the activity_main.xml layout file, and then delete the Hello world! placeholder.

- Drag a TextView control to the top center of the emulator.

- Drag a Plain Text EditView control from the Text Fields category of the Palette, and then center the EditView control below the TextView control.

- Drag a Number EditView control to the emulator, and then center it below the first EditView control.

- Drag Button control from the Form Widgets category, and then center it below the second EditText control.

- Drag an ImageView control from the Images & Media category, and then center it below the Button control.

- Select rewards from the Resource Chooser dialog box.

- Tap or click the OK button.

- Tap or click the activity_main.xml tab at the bottom of the window to view the XML code.

- Alter the XML code to match the following customized code:

```
<TextView
    android:id="@+id/txtTitle"
    android:layout_width="wrap_content"
    android:layout_height="wrap_content"
    android:layout_centerHorizontal="true"
    android:text="@string/txtTitle"
    android:textSize="30sp" />

<EditText
    android:id="@+id/txtName"
    android:layout_width="wrap_content"
    android:layout_height="wrap_content"
    android:layout_below="@+id/txtTitle"
    android:layout_centerHorizontal="true"
    android:layout_marginTop="19dp"
    android:ems="10"
    android:hint="@string/hint1">

    <requestFocus />
</EditText>

<EditText
    android:id="@+id/txtMiles"
    android:layout_width="wrap_content"
    android:layout_height="wrap_content"
    android:layout_below="@+id/txtName"
    android:layout_centerHorizontal="true"
    android:layout_marginTop="21dp"
    android:ems="10"
    android:inputType="number"
    android:hint="@string/hint2" />
```

```
<Button
    android:id="@+id/btnStatus"
    android:layout_width="wrap_content"
    android:layout_height="wrap_content"
    android:layout_below="@+id/txtMiles"
    android:layout_centerHorizontal="true"
    android:layout_marginTop="17dp"
    android:text="@string/btnStatus"
    android:textSize="40sp" />

<ImageView
    android:id="@+id/imgRewards"
    android:layout_width="wrap_content"
    android:layout_height="wrap_content"
    android:layout_alignTop="@+id/btnStatus"
    android:contentDescription="@string/imgDescription"
    android:src="@drawable/rewards" />
```

The activity_main.xml file contains a TextView, two EditText, a Button, and ImageView controls (Figure 11-6).

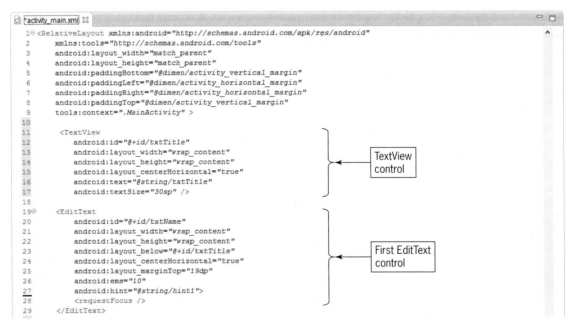

(a) First two controls

Figure 11-6   First XML layout *(continues)*

(continued)

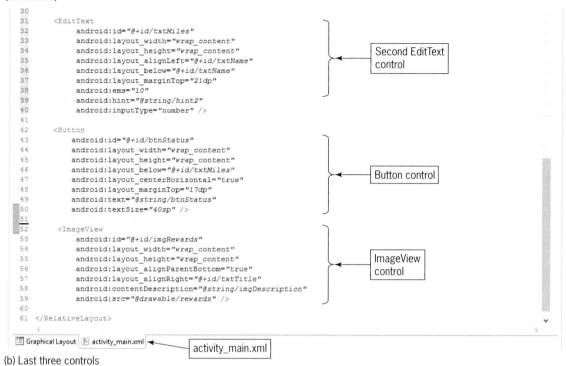

```
30
31    <EditText
32          android:id="@+id/txtMiles"
33          android:layout_width="wrap_content"
34          android:layout_height="wrap_content"
35          android:layout_alignLeft="@+id/txtName"
36          android:layout_below="@+id/txtName"
37          android:layout_marginTop="21dp"
38          android:ems="10"
39          android:hint="@string/hint2"
40          android:inputType="number" />
41
42    <Button
43          android:id="@+id/btnStatus"
44          android:layout_width="wrap_content"
45          android:layout_height="wrap_content"
46          android:layout_below="@+id/txtMiles"
47          android:layout_centerHorizontal="true"
48          android:layout_marginTop="17dp"
49          android:text="@string/btnStatus"
50          android:textSize="40sp" />
51
52    <ImageView
53          android:id="@+id/imgRewards"
54          android:layout_width="wrap_content"
55          android:layout_height="wrap_content"
56          android:layout_alignParentBottom="true"
57          android:layout_alignRight="@+id/txtTitle"
58          android:contentDescription="@string/imgDescription"
59          android:src="@drawable/rewards" />
60
61 </RelativeLayout>
```

Second EditText control

Button control

ImageView control

Graphical Layout activity_main.xml ← activity_main.xml

(b) Last three controls

Figure 11-6 First XML layout

STEP 5

- Close the activity_main.xml tab and save your work.
- To add the second XML layout file, press and hold or right-click the layout folder.
- On the shortcut menu, point to New, and then tap or click Android XML File.
- In the New Android XML File dialog box, type **status.xml** in the File text box to name the layout file. In the Root Element list, select RelativeLayout.
- Tap or click the Finish button. The emulator window opens.

The second layout file named status.xml is created (Figure 11-7).

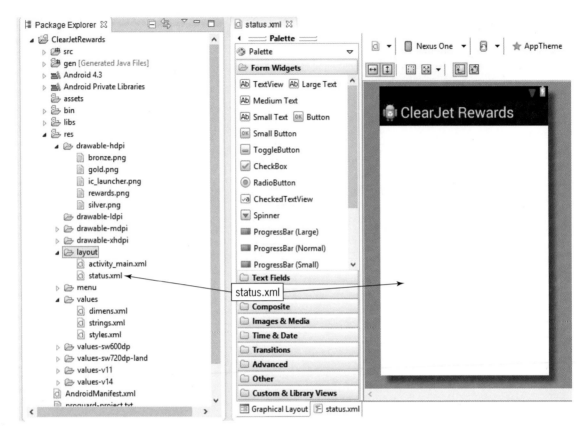

Figure 11-7   Second XML layout

STEP 6

- Drag a TextView control from the Palette to the top center of the emulator.

- Drag a second TextView to the emulator, and then center it below the TextView control.

- Open the Images & Media category of the Palette, drag an ImageView control below the two TextView controls, and then center it horizontally.

- When the Resource Chooser dialog box opens, tap or click the Cancel button because an image will be coded later to display in the ImageView control in Status.java.

- Tap or click the status.xml tab at the bottom of the window to display the XML code for this layout.

- Alter the XML code to match the following customized code, and then save your work:

```
<TextView
    android:id="@+id/txtTitle"
    android:layout_width="wrap_content"
    android:layout_height="wrap_content"
    android:layout_centerHorizontal="true"
    android:layout_marginTop="30dp"
    android:text="@string/txtTitle"
    android:textSize="30sp" />
```

```
<TextView
    android:id="@+id/txtResult"
    android:layout_width="wrap_content"
    android:layout_height="wrap_content"
    android:layout_below="@+id/txtTitle"
    android:layout_centerHorizontal="true"
    android:layout_marginTop="40dp"
    android:textSize="20sp" />

<ImageView
    android:id="@+id/imgStatus"
    android:layout_width="250dp"
    android:layout_height="150dp"
    android:layout_alignParentBottom="true"
    android:layout_centerHorizontal="true"
    android:layout_marginBottom="65dp"
    android:contentDescription="@string/imgDescription" />
```

The status.xml file contains two TextView controls and an ImageView control (Figure 11-8).

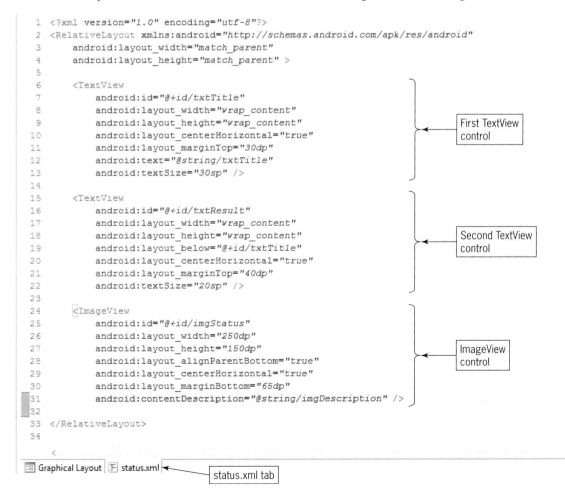

Figure 11-8   Two TextView and an ImageView controls for status.xml

Instantiating the XML Controls

When the ClearJet Rewards app starts, the activity_main.xml layout opens, displaying the TextView control title and requests the user to enter their name and the number of airline miles flown this year. When the user taps the Button control, the values are assigned to the variables within the MainActivity class. To instantiate the XML controls from the first Activity, follow these steps:

STEP 1

- In the Package Explorer, expand the src folder, expand net.androidbootcamp.clearjetrewards, and then double-tap or double-click MainActivity.java to open the code window.

- Press the Enter key to insert a new line after Line 12, type **final EditText name=(EditText) findViewById(R.id.txtName);** to instantiate the first EditText control, and then press the Enter key.

- Type **final EditText miles=(EditText)findViewById(R.id.txtMiles);** to instantiate the second EditText control, and then press the Enter key.

- Point to EditText and import the statement by tapping or clicking Import 'EditText' (android. widget).

The two EditText controls are instantiated (Figure 11-9).

```
📄 *MainActivity.java ⊠
 1  package net.androidbootcamp.clearjetrewards;
 2
 3⊕ import android.os.Bundle;▢
 7
 8  public class MainActivity extends Activity {
 9
10⊖     @Override
11      protected void onCreate(Bundle savedInstanceState) {
12          super.onCreate(savedInstanceState);
13          setContentView(R.layout.activity_main);
14          final EditText name=(EditText)findViewById(R.id.txtName);
15          final EditText miles=(EditText)findViewById(R.id.txtMiles);
16      }
17
18⊖     @Override
19      public boolean onCreateOptionsMenu(Menu menu) {
20          // Inflate the menu; this adds items to the action bar if it is present.
21          getMenuInflater().inflate(R.menu.main, menu);
22          return true;
23      }
24
25  }
26
```

Two EditText controls instantiated

Figure 11-9 EditText controls instantiated

STEP 2

- Press the Enter key to insert a new line, type **Button btStatus = (Button)findViewById(R.id. btnStatus);** to instantiate the Button control, and then press the Enter key twice.

- Select Import 'Button' (android.widget) to import the Button library.

- To create a setOnClickListener method so the btStatus Button waits for the user's tap or click, type **btStatus.seton** and press Ctrl+spacebar.

- Double-tap or double-click the first setOnClickListener to select it from the auto-complete listing.

- In the parentheses, type **new on** and press Ctrl+spacebar to display an auto-complete listing.

- Double-tap or double-click the first choice, which lists a View.OnClickListener with an Anonymous Inner Type event handler.

- Point to the red curly line below OnClickListener.

- Select Import 'OnClickListener' (android.view.View).

- Type **;** (semicolon) after the closing parenthesis on Line 28 to complete the auto-generated stub.

An OnClickListener auto-generated stub appears in the code (Figure 11-10).

```
J  *MainActivity.java  ⊠

 1  package net.androidbootcamp.clearjetrewards;
 2
 3⊕ import android.os.Bundle;☐
10
11  public class MainActivity extends Activity {
12
13⊝     @Override
14      protected void onCreate(Bundle savedInstanceState) {
15          super.onCreate(savedInstanceState);
16          setContentView(R.layout.activity_main);
17          final EditText name=(EditText)findViewById(R.id.txtName);
18          final EditText miles=(EditText)findViewById(R.id.txtMiles);
19          Button btStatus = (Button)findViewById(R.id.btnStatus);
20
21⊝         btStatus.setOnClickListener(new OnClickListener() {
22
23⊝             @Override
24              public void onClick(View v) {
25                  // TODO Auto-generated method stub
26
27              }
28          });
29      }
```

Button control instantiated

OnClickListener( ) stub

Figure 11-10   Button OnClickListener stub

STEP 3

- On Line 11, initialize the variables by typing **String strName;** and then press Enter. (Your line numbers might differ.)

- On the next line type **int intMiles;**.

- Tap or click within the onClick method on Line 27 and assign the name to strName by typing **strName = name.getText().toString();**.

- On the next line, assign the number of miles flown to an integer value by typing **intMiles = Integer.parseInt(miles.getText( ).toString( ));**.

The variables strName and intMiles are assigned to the entered name and flown miles (Figure 11-11).

```
 1   package net.androidbootcamp.clearjetrewards;
 2
 3⊕  import android.os.Bundle;☐
10
11   public class MainActivity extends Activity {
12       String strName;             ⎱  Class variables
13       int intMiles;               ⎰
14⊝       @Override
▲15       protected void onCreate(Bundle savedInstanceState) {
16           super.onCreate(savedInstanceState);
17           setContentView(R.layout.activity_main);
18           final EditText name=(EditText)findViewById(R.id.txtName);
19           final EditText miles=(EditText)findViewById(R.id.txtMiles);
20           Button btStatus = (Button)findViewById(R.id.btnStatus);
21
22⊝          btStatus.setOnClickListener(new OnClickListener() {
23
24⊝              @Override
▲25              public void onClick(View v) {
26                  // TODO Auto-generated method stub
27                  strName = name.getText().toString();
28                  intMiles = Integer.parseInt(miles.getText().toString());
29              }
30          });
31       }
```

> **Class variables** ← (pointing to lines 12–13)

> **strName is assigned to the name entered by the user** ← (pointing to line 27)

> **intMiles assigned to the mileage entered by the user** ← (pointing to line 28)

Figure 11-11   Variables strName and intMiles are assigned

IN THE TRENCHES

When you write data using SharedPreferences, you can make changes to the data by using the SharedPreferences. Editor.

Writing Persistent Data with SharedPreferences

One of the most effective ways to save simple application data to an Android device is by using the SharedPreferences object. The data is saved to an XML file as a key–value pair. The **key** is a string such as "key1" that uniquely identifies the preference, and the **value** is the data represented as a string, int, long, float, or Boolean. Android SharedPreferences can store data that can be used in different Activities of your application or by another application. A common example of using SharedPreferences may be in a game like Angry Birds. The Angry Birds app needs to save the high score from game to game, the user name, and current level achieved. Preferences can be stored at the Activity or application level.

In the chapter project app, the first data to be stored is the frequent flier's name. The SharedPreference for this name data is a set of data values: key1 uniquely identifies the preference and strName represents the actual value of the string. A preference can be any of a number of different data types. The following data types are supported by the SharedPreferences class:

- putString( )—Stores string values
- putInt( )—Stores integer values
- putLong( )—Stores long values
- putFloat( )—Stores float values
- putBoolean( )—Stores Boolean values

To create an instance of the SharedPreferences object from an Activity, you use the following code syntax:

Code Syntax

```
final SharedPreferences sharedPref = PreferenceManager.
getDefaultSharedPreferences(this);
SharedPreferences.Editor editor = sharedPref.edit();
editor.putString("key1", strName);

editor.putInt("key2", intMiles);

editor.commit();
```

In the first line, a valid SharedPreferences object is instantiated. Next, a SharedPreferences.Editor provides a method to add, modify, or delete preference content. Within the editor, you can also remove a specific preference by name using the remove( ) method, or remove all preferences within the set using the clear( ) method. The putString and putInt methods are not called immediately. The commit( ) method must be called to actually write the values to the XML file. Save values as persistent data using SharedPreferences by following these steps:

STEP 1

- In the code on the MainActivity.java tab, after the Button is instantiated (Line 21), type **final SharedPreferences sharedPref = PreferenceManager.getDefaultSharedPreferences(this);**.

- Point to SharedPreferences and tap or click Import 'SharedPreferences' (android.content).

- Point to PreferenceManager and tap or click Import 'PreferenceManager' (android.preference).

An instance of the SharedPreferences class is created named sharedPref in the MainActivity class (Figure 11-12).

```
 1  package net.androidbootcamp.clearjetrewards;
 2
 3⊕ import android.os.Bundle;▢
12
13  public class MainActivity extends Activity {
14      String strName;
15      int intMiles;
16⊖     @Override
17      protected void onCreate(Bundle savedInstanceState) {
18          super.onCreate(savedInstanceState);
19          setContentView(R.layout.activity_main);
20          final EditText name=(EditText)findViewById(R.id.txtName);
21          final EditText miles=(EditText)findViewById(R.id.txtMiles);
22          Button btStatus = (Button)findViewById(R.id.btnStatus);
23          final SharedPreferences sharedPref =PreferenceManager.getDefaultSharedPreferences(this);
24⊖         btStatus.setOnClickListener(new OnClickListener() {
25
26⊖             @Override
27              public void onClick(View v) {
28                  // TODO Auto-generated method stub
29                  strName = name.getText().toString();
30                  intMiles = Integer.parseInt(miles.getText().toString());
31              }
32          });
33      }
34
```

Instantiate the SharedPreferences object

Figure 11-12   SharedPreferences class

STEP 2

- Tap or click at the end of Line 30 (assignment of intMiles) and add a new line within the OnClick method.

- To store data using the editor, type **SharedPreferences.Editor editor = sharedPref.edit();**.

- On the next line, assign the first key–value pair by typing **editor.putString("key1", strName);**.

- On the next line, assign the second key–value pair by typing **editor.putInt("key2", intMiles);**.

- To write the values to the XML data file, on the next line type **editor.commit();**.

Two values are saved to the SharedPreferences XML data file (Figure 11-13).

```
  1  package net.androidbootcamp.clearjetrewards;
  2
  3⊕ import android.os.Bundle;☐
 12
 13  public class MainActivity extends Activity {
 14      String strName;
 15      int intMiles;
 16⊖     @Override
▲17     protected void onCreate(Bundle savedInstanceState) {
 18          super.onCreate(savedInstanceState);
 19          setContentView(R.layout.activity_main);
 20          final EditText name=(EditText)findViewById(R.id.txtName);
 21          final EditText miles=(EditText)findViewById(R.id.txtMiles);
 22          Button btStatus = (Button)findViewById(R.id.btnStatus);
 23          final SharedPreferences sharedPref =PreferenceManager.getDefaultSharedPreferences(this);
 24⊖         btStatus.setOnClickListener(new OnClickListener() {
 25
 26⊖             @Override
▲27             public void onClick(View v) {
☑28                 // TODO Auto-generated method stub
 29                 strName = name.getText().toString();
 30                 intMiles = Integer.parseInt(miles.getText().toString());
 31                 SharedPreferences.Editor editor = sharedPref.edit();
 32                 editor.putString("key1", strName);
 33                 editor.putInt("key2", intMiles);
 34                 editor.commit();
 35             }
 36         });
 37  }
```

Persistent data written to the SharedPreferences object

Figure 11-13   Values written in an XML data file

IN THE TRENCHES
There is no limit to the number of different shared preferences you can create.

Launching the Second Activity

After the persistent data is saved to a local XML file, MainActivity starts a second Activity named Status.java. The second Activity is responsible for retrieving the persistent data, which is tested using a conditional If statement to determine if the frequent flier has reached reward status. The Android Manifest file must be updated to include the second Activity. To create a second class, update the Android Manifest file, and launch the second class, follow these steps:

STEP 1

- In the Package Explorer, press and hold or right-click the net.androidbootcamp.clearjetrewards folder, point to New on the shortcut menu, and then tap or click Class.

- Type **Status** in the Name text box.

- Tap or click the Superclass Browse button.

- Type **Activity** in the Choose a type text box.

- Tap or click Activity—android.app and then tap or click the OK button to extend the Activity class.

- Tap or click the Finish button to finish creating the Status class.

A second class named Status is created (Figure 11-14).

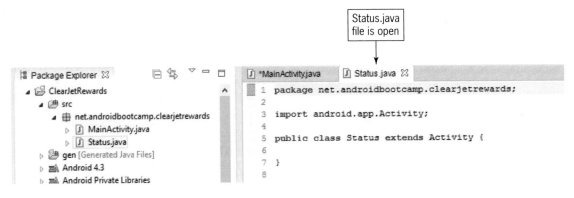

Figure 11-14   Status class created

STEP 2

- In the Package Explorer, scroll down, if necessary, and double-tap or double-click the AndroidManifest.xml file.

- To add the Status class to the Android Manifest, tap or click the Application tab at the bottom of the Android Manifest page.

- Scroll down to display the Application Nodes section.

- Tap or click the Add button. Select Activity in the Create a new element at the top level, in Application dialog box.

- Tap or click the OK button.

- The Attributes for Activity section opens in the Application tab. In the Name text box in this section, type **.Status**.

- Save your work.

The Status class is added to the Android Manifest file (Figure 11-15).

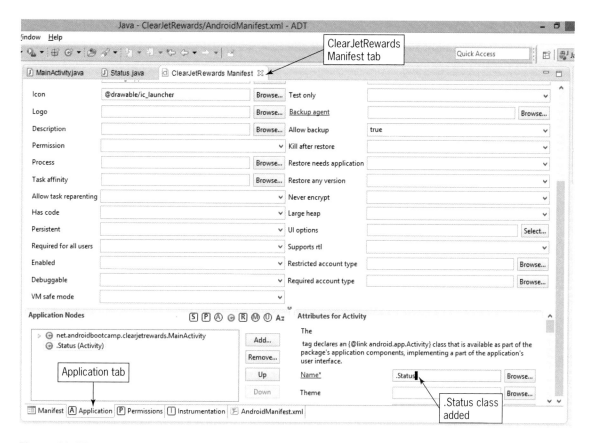

Figure 11-15   Adding the Status class to the Android Manifest

STEP 3

- Close the ClearJetRewards Manifest tab.

- To launch the Status class from the first Activity, open the MainActivity.java tab.

- Insert a new line in the onClick(View v) auto-generated method stub after the editor.commit(); statement.

- Type **startActivity(new Intent(MainActivity.this, Status.class));** to launch the second Activity.

- Point to the red error line below Intent, and then select Import 'Intent' (android.content). Save your work.

The second Activity named Status is launched with an Intent statement (Figure 11-16).

```
 *MainActivity.java 23    Status.java
 1  package net.androidbootcamp.clearjetrewards;
 2
 3⊕ import android.os.Bundle;
13
14  public class MainActivity extends Activity {
15       String strName;
16       int intMiles;
17⊖      @Override
▲18      protected void onCreate(Bundle savedInstanceState) {
19           super.onCreate(savedInstanceState);
20           setContentView(R.layout.activity_main);
21           final EditText name=(EditText)findViewById(R.id.txtName);
22           final EditText miles=(EditText)findViewById(R.id.txtMiles);
23           Button btStatus = (Button)findViewById(R.id.btnStatus);
24           final SharedPreferences sharedPref =PreferenceManager.getDefaultSharedPreferences(this);
25⊖          btStatus.setOnClickListener(new OnClickListener() {
26
27⊖               @Override
▲28               public void onClick(View v) {
☑29                   // TODO Auto-generated method stub
30                   strName = name.getText().toString();
31                   intMiles = Integer.parseInt(miles.getText().toString());
32                   SharedPreferences.Editor editor = sharedPref.edit();
33                   editor.putString("key1", strName);
34                   editor.putInt("key2", intMiles);
35                   editor.commit();
36                   startActivity(new Intent(MainActivity.this, Status.class)); I
37               }
38           });
39       }
40
41⊖       @Override
▲42       public boolean onCreateOptionsMenu(Menu menu) {
```

Launches
second Activity

Figure 11-16 Status class launched

Instantiating the Second Activity Controls

As soon as the second Activity launches, the status.xml layout file is displayed. Next, the Status class must instantiate the TextView control that displays the frequent flier status of bronze, silver, or gold and an ImageView control displaying the appropriate image denoting the reward achieved. To set the layout and instantiate the TextView and ImageView controls, follow these steps:

STEP 1

- Close the MainActivity.java tab.

- If necessary, open Status.java and tap or click Line 6 to move the insertion point between the two curly braces that open and close the method.

- Type **oncreate**, and then press Ctrl+spacebar.

- Double-tap or double-click the first onCreate method in the auto-complete listing to generate the method structure.

- Tap or click at the end of Line 10 and then press Enter to insert a blank line.

- Type **setContentView(R.layout.status);** to display the status.xml layout.

The setContentView command is entered to open the status.xml layout file (Figure 11-17).

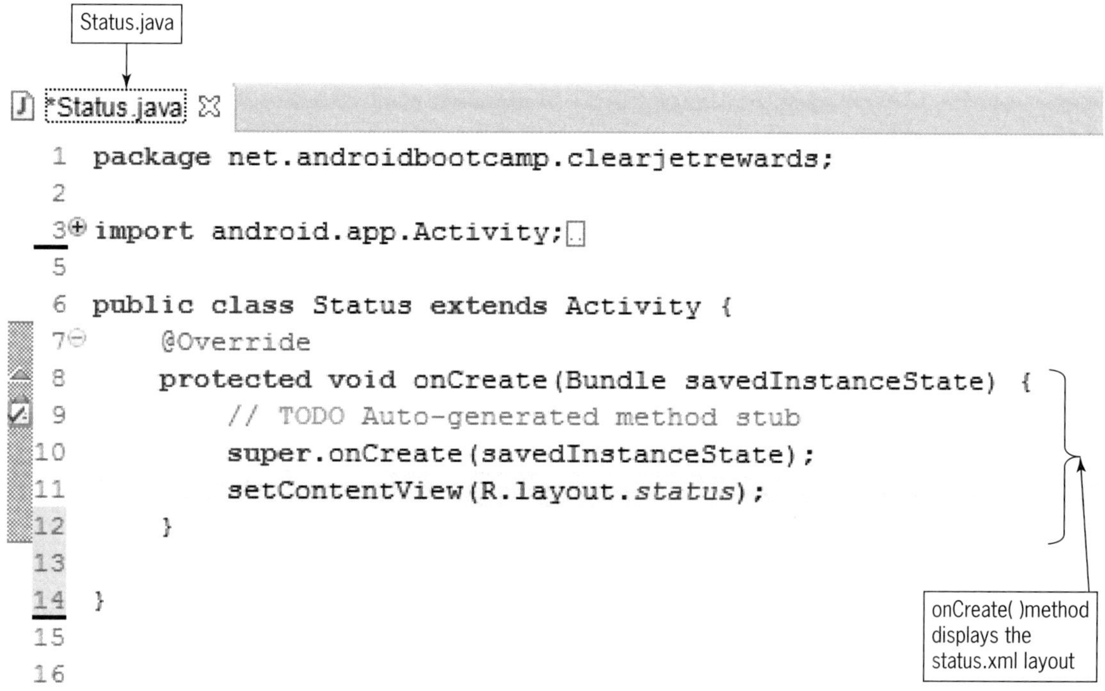

Status.java

```
 1  package net.androidbootcamp.clearjetrewards;
 2
 3⊕ import android.app.Activity;⬚
 5
 6  public class Status extends Activity {
 7⊖      @Override
 8      protected void onCreate(Bundle savedInstanceState) {
 9          // TODO Auto-generated method stub
10          super.onCreate(savedInstanceState);
11          setContentView(R.layout.status);
12      }
13
14  }
15
16
```

onCreate( )method displays the status.xml layout

Figure 11-17   Status.java code is displayed

STEP 2

- To create an instance of the TextView control, press the Enter key and type **TextView result = (TextView)findViewById(R.id.txtResult);**.

- Point to TextView and import the statement by tapping or clicking Import 'TextView' (android. widget).

- To create an instance of the ImageView control, press the Enter key and then type **ImageView image=(ImageView)findViewById(R.id.imgStatus);**. Import 'ImageView' (android.widget).

The TextView and ImageView controls named result and image are referenced in Status.java (Figure 11-18).

```
[J] *Status.java ⊠
  1  package net.androidbootcamp.clearjetrewards;
  2
  3⊕ import android.app.Activity;[]
  7
  8  public class Status extends Activity {
  9⊖     @Override
 10      protected void onCreate(Bundle savedInstanceState) {
 11          // TODO Auto-generated method stub
 12          super.onCreate(savedInstanceState);
 13          setContentView(R.layout.status);
 14          TextView result = (TextView)findViewById(R.id.txtResult);
 15          ImageView image=(ImageView)findViewById(R.id.imgStatus);
 16      }
 17
 18  }
 19
```

TextView control instantiated

ImageView control instantiated

Figure 11-18   Instance of TextView and ImageView controls

Retrieving Preferences

Retrieving Android data is just as easy as saving it when you are working with SharedPreferences. Loading data saved in the SharedPreferences XML file begins in the second Activity by instantiating the SharedPreferences object. You do not need an editor to read the saved data in the SharedPreferences. Instead, retrieve the SharedPreferences object and use the appropriate method to retrieve a key's value by name:

- getString( )—Retrieves string values

- getInt( )—Retrieves integer values

- getLong( )—Retrieves long values

- getFloat( )—Retrieves float values

- getBoolean( )—Retrieves Boolean values

Each of these methods has two parameters: the preference key string and a default value to return if the preference is undefined. If a string value is undefined, it is set to a null value, represented by empty quotes. If a numeric value is undefined, the variable is assigned the value of zero. If the key is not found, the default value is given in response. To create an instance of the SharedPreferences object and to load the data from the persistent data XML file, use the following code syntax:

Code Syntax

```
SharedPreferences sharedPref = PreferenceManager.getDefaultSharedPreferences(this);
String strFlier = sharedPref.getString("key1", "");
int intMileage = sharedPref.getInt("key2", 0);
```

In this code, strFlier is assigned the name of the frequent flier and the value for their flown miles is assigned to intMileage stored in the XML persistent data file. To retrieve the data from the SharedPreferences object, follow these steps:

STEP 1

● To create an instance within the Status class of the SharedPreferences object, type **SharedPreferences sharedPref = PreferenceManager.getDefaultSharedPreferences(this);** and then press Enter key. Select Import 'SharedPreferences' (android.content), and then select Import 'PreferenceManager' (android.preference).

An instance of the SharedPreferences class is created named sharedPref in the Status class (Figure 11-19).

```
1   package net.androidbootcamp.clearjetrewards;
2
3⊕  import android.app.Activity;▯
9
10  public class Status extends Activity {
11⊖      @Override
12      protected void onCreate(Bundle savedInstanceState) {
13          // TODO Auto-generated method stub
14          super.onCreate(savedInstanceState);
15          setContentView(R.layout.status);
16          TextView result = (TextView)findViewById(R.id.txtResult);
17          ImageView image=(ImageView)findViewById(R.id.imgStatus);
18          SharedPreferences sharedPref = PreferenceManager.getDefaultSharedPreferences(this);
19      }
20
21  }
```

SharedPreferences object instantiated

Figure 11-19   SharedPreferences instance in the Status class

STEP 2

● To read the first value written in the XML file and assign the string value to strFlier, type **String strFlier = sharedPref.getString("key1", "");**.

● On the next line, to read the second value saved as persistent data and assign the integer value to intMileage, type **int intMileage = sharedPref.getInt("key2", 0);**.

● Save your work.

The two values are retrieved from the SharedPreferences object (Figure 11-20).

```
J *Status.java ⊠
  1  package net.androidbootcamp.clearjetrewards;
  2
  3⊕ import android.app.Activity;▢
  9
 10  public class Status extends Activity {
 11⊖     @Override
 12      protected void onCreate(Bundle savedInstanceState) {
 13          // TODO Auto-generated method stub
 14          super.onCreate(savedInstanceState);
 15          setContentView(R.layout.status);
 16          TextView result = (TextView)findViewById(R.id.txtResult);
 17          ImageView image=(ImageView)findViewById(R.id.imgStatus);
 18          SharedPreferences sharedPref = PreferenceManager.getDefaultSharedPreferences(this);
 19          String strFlier = sharedPref.getString("key1", "");
 20          int intMileage = sharedPref.getInt("key2", 0);
 21      }
 22
 23  }
```

> strFlier retrieves the user's name

> intMileage retrieves the user's flown miles

Figure 11-20   SharedPreferences values are retrieved

IN THE TRENCHES
You can assign literal text to the SharedPreferences object by coding:

```
editor.putString("key", "literal text");
```

Coding an ImageView Control

In an Android project, an ImageView control can display an image by assigning a source path (android:src="drawable/filename") in the XML layout file or by dynamically assigning the image within the Java code.

Code Syntax

```
image.setImageResource(R.drawable.bronze);
```

In the ClearJet Rewards app, the image displayed in Status.java depends on which reward level is reached. The value of miles flown retrieved from the SharedPreferences object named intMileage is compared in the nested If structure. If the frequent flier reaches 25,000 flown miles, the bronze.png image is displayed. If the 50,000 mile mark is reached, the silver.png file is shown, and if the 75,000 mile mark is reached, the gold.png file is shown. A nested If decision structure is used to determine the result text and the image displayed. If the user has not reached the minimum reward level, no image is displayed and a text response appears stating that the user has not reached an award. To code the nested Else If decision structure and display the TextView and ImageView controls, follow these steps:

STEP 1

- Press Enter two times to skip a line.

- To determine if the flier has achieved gold status, type the following If structure:

```
if (intMileage >= 75000) {
    image.setImageResource(R.drawable.gold);
    result.setText(strFlier + " has reached Gold status");

}
```

The gold reward status text is displayed with an appropriate image (Figure 11-21).

```
J *Status.java ⌗
 1  package net.androidbootcamp.clearjetrewards;
 2
 3⊕ import android.app.Activity;▢
 9
10  public class Status extends Activity {
11⊖     @Override
12      protected void onCreate(Bundle savedInstanceState) {
13          // TODO Auto-generated method stub
14          super.onCreate(savedInstanceState);
15          setContentView(R.layout.status);
16          TextView result = (TextView)findViewById(R.id.txtResult);
17          ImageView image=(ImageView)findViewById(R.id.imgStatus);
18          SharedPreferences sharedPref = PreferenceManager.getDefaultSharedPreferences(this);
19          String strFlier = sharedPref.getString("key1", "");
20          int intMileage = sharedPref.getInt("key2", 0);
21
22          if (intMileage >= 75000){
23              image.setImageResource(R.drawable.gold);
24              result.setText(strFlier + " has reached Gold status");
25          }
26      }
27
28  }
29
```

If structure for displaying gold.png file and the result text

Figure 11-21 Status text and image for the gold reward within If structure

STEP 2

- To determine the silver status, on the same line as the curly brace, type **else if (intMileage >= 50000) {** and press the Enter key to create the closing brace.

- To display the silver.png image and display the text for the silver status type:

```
image.setImageResource(R.drawable.silver);
result.setText(strFlier + " has reached Silver status");
```

- To reward bronze status, on the same line as the closing curly brace type **else if (intMileage >= 25000) {** and press the Enter key to create the closing brace.

- To display the bronze.png image and display the text for the bronze status type:

```
image.setImageResource(R.drawable.bronze);
result.setText(strFlier + " has reached Bronze status");
```

The images and text appear for the silver and bronze status rewards (Figure 11-22).

```
Status.java ✕
  1  package net.androidbootcamp.clearjetrewards;
  2
  3⊕ import android.app.Activity;▯
  9
 10  public class Status extends Activity {
 11⊖     @Override
 12      protected void onCreate(Bundle savedInstanceState) {
 13          // TODO Auto-generated method stub
 14          super.onCreate(savedInstanceState);
 15          setContentView(R.layout.status);
 16          TextView result = (TextView)findViewById(R.id.txtResult);
 17          ImageView image=(ImageView)findViewById(R.id.imgStatus);
 18          SharedPreferences sharedPref = PreferenceManager.getDefaultSharedPreferences(this);
 19          String strFlier = sharedPref.getString("key1", "");
 20          int intMileage = sharedPref.getInt("key2", 0);
 21
 22          if (intMileage >= 75000){
 23              image.setImageResource(R.drawable.gold);
 24              result.setText(strFlier + " has reached Gold status");
 25          } else if (intMileage >= 50000){
 26              image.setImageResource(R.drawable.silver);
 27              result.setText(strFlier + " has reached Silver status");
 28          } else if (intMileage >=25000){
 29              image.setImageResource(R.drawable.bronze);
 30              result.setText(strFlier + " has reached Bronze status");
 31          }
 32      }
 33
 34  }
```

Else If structure for silver status

Else If structure for bronze status

Figure 11-22 Else If structure for silver and bronze rewards

STEP 3

- If the user has not reached reward status, the following text displays by typing after the curly brace:

```
else {
    result.setText("You have not reached an award");
}
```

A closing else displays a message if the user has not reached any status (Figure 11-23).

```
J Status.java ⊠
 1  package net.androidbootcamp.clearjetrewards;
 2
 3⊕ import android.app.Activity;▯
 9
10  public class Status extends Activity {
11⊝      @Override
 12      protected void onCreate(Bundle savedInstanceState) {
 13          // TODO Auto-generated method stub
 14          super.onCreate(savedInstanceState);
 15          setContentView(R.layout.status);
 16          TextView result = (TextView)findViewById(R.id.txtResult);
 17          ImageView image=(ImageView)findViewById(R.id.imgStatus);
 18          SharedPreferences sharedPref = PreferenceManager.getDefaultSharedPreferences(this);
 19          String strFlier = sharedPref.getString("key1", "");
 20          int intMileage = sharedPref.getInt("key2", 0);
 21
 22          if (intMileage >= 75000){
 23              image.setImageResource(R.drawable.gold);
 24              result.setText(strFlier + " has reached Gold status");
 25          } else if (intMileage >= 50000){
 26              image.setImageResource(R.drawable.silver);
 27              result.setText(strFlier + " has reached Silver status");
 28          } else if (intMileage >=25000){
 29              image.setImageResource(R.drawable.bronze);
 30              result.setText(strFlier + " has reached Bronze status");
 31          } else {
 32              result.setText("You have not reached an award");
 33          }
 34      }
 35
 36  }
 37
```

> Closing else statement for users that have not reached an award

Figure 11-23   Closing Else structure

Running and Testing the Application

Your first experience with persistent saved data in an Android application is complete. Tap or click Run on the menu bar, and then select Run to save and test the application in the emulator. Select Android Application and tap or click the OK button. Save all the files in the next dialog box, if necessary, and unlock the emulator. The application opens in the emulator window, as shown in Figure 11-1a, Figure 11-1b, and Figure 11-2. The first Activity opens requesting the frequent flier's name and mileage, which is saved to an XML file by use of the SharedPreferences object. The second Activity launches the Status.java file, which retrieves your stored data and compares the mileage in a decision structure to determine the earned status. An appropriate image denotes the earned status.

Wrap It Up—Chapter Summary

In this chapter, the Android SharedPreferences object was used to easily store application persistent data. Application preferences are stored as key–value pairs and can be many different data types, including numbers, strings, and Boolean values. Different sets of preferences can be stored in named preference sets. Use shared preferences to store simple application primitive data in a persistent manner such as the user's name or mileage flown.

- When data users enter in an Android app is stored in RAM, it is lost when the app or the device stops running. Persistent data, on the other hand, is stored on the device's drive or other storage medium such as a memory card or cloud service so that the data can be retrieved later within the app or after the termination of the program.

- Persistent data can be stored using shared preferences, internal storage, external storage, a SQLite database, or a network connection. Use the SharedPreferences object to save any primitive data: Booleans, floats, ints, longs, and strings.

- When you save application data using the SharedPreferences object, the data is saved to an XML file as a key–value pair. The key is a string such as "key1" that uniquely identifies the preference, and the value is the data represented as a string, int, long, float, or Boolcan.

- You can use the key–value pairs stored in SharedPreferences in different Activities of your application or in another application.

- Use a put*DataType*( ) method to store the data in a SharedPreferences object, and use a get*DataType*( ) method to retrieve the data.

Key Terms

key—The string part of a key-value pair that uniquely identifies a preference.

Persistent data—Stores values permanently by placing the information in a file.

SQLite—Structured Query Language) is a lightweight, preloaded mobile database engine, which has been available since the Cupcake 1.5 version of Android and occupies a small amount of disk memory.

value—The data part of a key-value pair that represents a string, int, long, float, or Boolean value.

Developer FAQs

1. What is the general name of the type of data that is saved after the app is executed?

2. Name five ways to store data in an app.

3. When is it best to use SharedPreferences to save persistent data?

4. What does each part of the SharedPreferences data pair represent? Explain each part of the pair.

5. True or False. When you save persistent data with internal storage, other apps can access and use the data.

6. Why should an app not store massive amounts of data using internal storage?

7. You can save data using external storage to your SD card. What does SD stand for?

8. What does SQL stand for?

9. If you decide to use a network connection to save an app's persistent data, what is the limitation?

10. What kind of file does persistent data save in when using the SharedPreferences object?

11. Which method stores a float value using the SharedPreferences object?

12. Write a statement that assigns the variable intAge with the key of key1 to the SharedPreferences object.

13. The preference values are not saved until which method is executed?

14. What is the maximum number of preferences saved to a SharedPreferences object?

15. Write a line of Java code that displays an image named bacon.

16. Which method retrieves an integer value?

17. If a float value is retrieved from the SharedPreferences object and the value does not exist, which value is retrieved?

18. Write a line of Java code to retrieve an integer value that is referenced by the key, key1, and saves the value to intClassSize.

19. Write a line of Java code to retrieve a string value that is referenced by the key, key3, and saves the value to strPolitician.

20. In a single line of Java code, assign a string value of "Kindness" to a SharedPreferences object with a key value named key5.

Beyond the Book

Using the Internet, search the Web for the answers to the following questions to further your Android knowledge.

1. Research the SD cards that are available for Android devices. Write 100 words about your findings.

2. Find five apps in the Google Play store that use mobile databases to save the data used in the app. Name and describe the reason the database connection is necessary.

3. Google Maps now require a paid account to access map features as an Android developer. Write a summary of at least 100 words describing some of the latest Google mapping features.

4. Research more information about saving to an SQLite database. Write a 200-word paragraph and show sample code of saving information to a local mobile database.

Case Programming Projects

Complete one or more of the following case programming projects. Use the same steps and techniques taught within the chapter. Submit the program you create to your instructor. The level of difficulty is indicated for each case programming project.

Easiest: ⋆
Intermediate: ⋆⋆
Challenging: ⋆⋆⋆

Case Project 11–1: BMI Calculator App ⋆

Requirements Document

Application title:	Body Mass Index (BMI) Calculator App
Purpose:	A body mass index calculator app computes your BMI using a formula.
Algorithms:	1. The first Activity opens displaying the bmi1.png image with the title "BMI Calculator".
	2. The first screen requests your weight in pounds to the nearest whole pound and your height in inches to the nearest whole inch (Figure 11-24). These values are saved in persistent data using SharedPreferences.
	3. The second Activity opens and retrieves the saved values.
	4. The BMI formula needed is:

$$\frac{\textbf{Weight in pounds} * \textbf{703}}{\textbf{height in inches}^2}$$

	5. The body mass index is displayed to one-tenth of a decimal place and the image bmi2.png is displayed (Figure 11-25).
Conditions:	1. The two image files are provided with your student files.

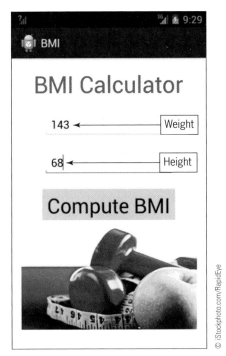

Figure 11-24

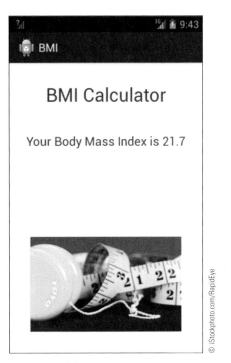

Figure 11-25

Case Project 11–2: Home Mortgage Interest App ★★

Requirements Document

Application title:	Home Mortgage Interest App
Purpose:	The Home Mortgage Interest App computes the total interest paid for the life of a home mortgage loan.
Algorithms:	1. The opening screen displays an image (mortgage.png) and the title Mortgage Interest.
	2. The user enters the amount of their monthly mortgage payment, number of years (10, 20, or 30) which must be converted to months, and the initial principal of the loan. Save these values using the SharedPreferences object (Figure 11-26).
	3. In the second Activity, retrieve the three values and compute the total interest paid over the life of the loan with this formula:

Total Interest = (Monthly Payment * Number of Months) – Initial Principal

4. The second screen displays the result of interest paid with an appropriate image (ten.png, twenty.png, or thirty.png) for a 10, 20, or 30 year loan (Figure 11-27).

Conditions:	1. The four images are provided with your student files.
	2. The result should appear in currency format.

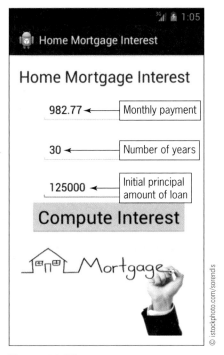

Figure 11-26

Figure 11-27

Case Project 11–3: Relocation Moving Truck Rental App ★★

Requirements Document

Application title:	Relocation Moving Truck Rental App
Purpose:	A relocation moving truck app provides the costs of renting a truck.
Algorithms:	1. An opening screen displays an image of a moving truck and a title.
	2. The first Activity requests whether you are renting a 10-foot truck ($19.95), 17-foot truck ($29.95), or a 26-foot truck ($39.95) for a one-day rental. The number of miles is also requested (99 cents per mile). This data is saved to the SharedPreferences object.
	3. The second screen displays a picture of a rental truck the same size that you are renting and the full cost of the rental for one day with the cost of mileage included.
Conditions:	1. Choose your own images available on the Web.
	2. The moving costs should be displayed as currency.

Case Project 11–4: Marathon Race App ★

Requirements Document

Application title:	Marathon Race App
Purpose:	Your city is planning a full 26-mile marathon race. Your time is ranked in the top, middle, or bottom third of runners.
Algorithms:	1. The opening screen displays the text "Marathon Race" and an image of a marathon.
	2. Your total time to run the entire race is requested in two TextView controls, which save the hour and the minutes (for example, 3 hours and 27 minutes).
	3. A second screen displays the average time that it took to run one mile.
	4. If your average time to run each mile is under 11 minutes, display a top one-third gold medal image.
	5. If your average time to run each mile in under 15 minutes, display a middle-third silver medal image.
	6. If your average time to run each mile is equal to or more than 15 minutes, display a completion bronze medal image.
Conditions:	1. The completion time for the marathon cannot be more than 10 hours.
	2. The number of minutes entered cannot be more than 59 minutes.
	3. Locate images for this app online.

Case Project 11–5: Amtrak Train App ★★★

Requirements Document

Application title:	Amtrak Train App
Purpose:	The Amtrak Train app determines your arrival time after you enter the boarding time and length of trip.
Algorithms:	1. Create an app that opens with a picture of the Amtrak logo and a title. This activity should request:

    a. The boarding time with separate input for hour and minutes on a 24-hour clock.

    b. The length of the entire train trip in minutes only.

    c. The three values are saved using SharedPreferences.

    2. The second screen shows the arrival time of the train by hour and minutes of a 24-hour clock.

    3. If the arrival is past midnight, display the message "Red-Eye Arrival" in addition to an appropriate image.

Conditions:	1. Select your own images available by searching the Web.

    2. The maximum hour entered for the boarding time is 23 and the minutes is 59.

    3. The maximum number of minutes for length of travel entered is 1500 minutes.

Case Project 11–6: Your Personal Limerick App ★★★

Requirements Document

Application title:	Your Personal Limerick App
Purpose:	Get creative! Request a city, an occupation, a number, and an action verb and create a happy limerick with the text entered.
Algorithms:	1. Create an app that opens with an image and title and requests a city, occupation, number, and action verb. Save these four items to an XML file using SharedPreferences.

    2. The second screen should display a limerick with the four requested items in a poem-like fashion with an image.

Conditions:	1. Select your own images and limerick wording.

Finale! Publishing Your Android App

In this chapter, you learn to:

- ◎ Understand Google Play
- ◎ Target various device configurations and languages
- ◎ Prepare your app for publishing
- ◎ Create an APK package by exporting an app
- ◎ Prepare promotional materials
- ◎ Publish your app on Google Play

After all the work of designing your Android app, the time to publish it has arrived. Similar to the many Android devices available, an Android app can be published to a variety of application distribution networks. As an Android developer, you can publish your app to Google Play, as well as many others, such as Amazon Appstore, AppBrain, and SlideME. Because Google Play is the largest marketplace, this chapter targets the publication of apps on this Android network. The process to publish an app consists of preparing your app for publication, and then registering, configuring, uploading, and finally publishing it.

Before publishing an application, the developer must understand how to perform the following processes, among others:

1. Test your app.

2. Prepare the app for publication.

3. Create an APK package and digitally sign your application.

4. Prepare promotional materials.

5. Publish your app to Google Play.

Understanding Google Play

Google Play *(https://play.google.com)* is a digital repository that serves as the storefront for Android devices and apps. It includes an online store for paid and free Android apps as well as music, movies, books, and games. Android phones, tablets, and Google television can all access the Google Play services. The Google Play Web site, shown in Figure 12-1, includes the features and services of Android apps, Google Music, and Google e-books. In addition, Google Play provides free cloud storage services, which saves space on an Android device. Google Play is entirely cloud based, so you can store all your music, movies, books, and apps online and have them always available to you. Over 130 countries around the world presently use Google Play. Competing companies such as the Apple App Store and Windows Store also market their applications within a similar structure. When you select an app on Google Play, the app installs directly to your Android device. Google Play is part of the default setup on new Android devices.

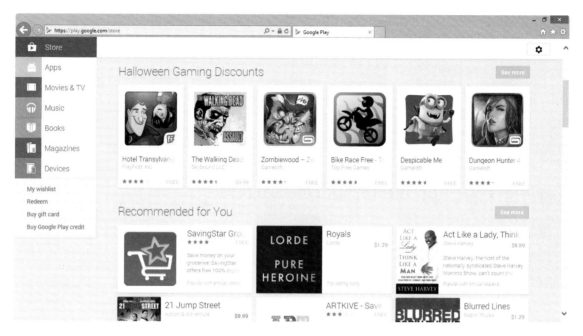

Figure 12-1   Google Play

Source: Google

GTK
With Google Play, you can store up to 20,000 songs for free using the cloud services.

Targeting Different Device Configurations and Languages

To reach a larger audience within the Google Play market, consider targeting multiple Android devices and translating your app into multiple languages. The Android platform runs on a variety of devices that offer different screen sizes and pixel densities. With over a hundred Android handheld devices, using flexible design layouts that work on many screen sizes and resolutions ensures that your app works on a wider range of Android phones and tablets. Creating a custom experience for different screen sizes, pixel densities, orientations, and resolutions guarantees that each user feels that the app was designed specifically for his or her phone or tablet.

Android users live in every corner of the world and speak hundreds of different languages. As you design an Android app, you can provide alternate resources such as app text translated into multiple languages that change depending on the default locale detected on the device. For example, if your home country is Spain, most likely your phone's locale for the dialect selection is set to Spanish (Spain). If you want your application to support both English and Spanish text, you can create two resource directories in the strings directory (the strings.xml file). By customizing the strings resource files, you can write one application that recognizes many local languages. When creating your app in English, remember that the majority of the world does not speak English and consider extending your app's reach to a worldwide pool of Android users.

GTK

To translate the languages used in your app, you can use Google Translate (*http://translate.google.com*), a free translation service that provides instant translations among 70 different languages. If you use any translation service, it is still important to have a native speaker test your app.

Testing Your App on an Android Device

After completing your Android app, you must test your application on various devices before publication. Using different built-in emulators in Eclipse, you can test the design and functionality of your application on a wide range of devices. You can also see how your development application will perform in a real-world environment by using Eclipse to install and test it directly on an Android phone. With an Android-powered device, you can develop and debug your Android applications just as you would on the emulator. After you change the settings on your Android phone or tablet, you can use a versatile tool called the **Android Debug Bridge (ADB)** to communicate with a connected Android device. To set up a device for testing your app, follow these steps:

STEP 1

- On the home screen of an Android device, tap the Settings app to display the device settings.

- If your device is running Android 3.2 or older, select Applications, and then select Development.

  If your device is running Android 4.0 or newer, select Developer options. The Developer options command is hidden by default. To make it available, select Settings, select About phone (or About device), and then tap Build number seven times.

- Enable the USB debugging option and then tap or click the OK button.

The Android device changes the settings to enable USB debugging.

STEP 2

- To set up your computer to detect your Android device, first install a USB driver for Android Debug Bridge on a Windows computer following the steps at ***http://developer.android.com/ sdk/oem-usb.html***.

- Each Android phone brand, such as Motorola and Samsung, has its own drivers that must be installed on your Windows computer. Be sure to install the drivers for the appropriate device brand. If you are using a Mac, you do not need to install a driver.

The USB drivers are installed on a Windows computer.

- Attach an Android device to a USB cable.

- Run your application from Eclipse as usual.

- The Android Device Chooser dialog box opens, listing the available emulator(s) and connected device(s).

- Select the device upon which you want to install and run the application, and then tap or click the OK button.

The Android application is tested on your Android device.

Creating an APK Package

After your Android application is successfully tested, you must create a release-ready package that users can install and run on their Android phones and tablets. The release-ready package is called an **.apk file (application package file)**, which is a compressed archive similar to a .zip file that contains the application, the manifest file, and all associated resources, such as image files, music, and other required content. An .apk file is a file format created by Google. Using the Eclipse Export Wizard, you can build a release-ready .apk file that is signed with your private key and optimized for publication. A private key digitally signs your application with your local system. All Android applications must be digitally signed with a certificate before the system can create an .apk package of your app for distribution. The Android system uses the certificate as a means of identifying the author of an application and establishing trust relationships between applications. To create an .apk package that generates a private key for your local system, follow these steps:

- Open a completed project in Eclipse that has been tested and runs properly.

- To export the project and create an .apk package, tap or click File on the menu bar and then tap or click Export.

The Export dialog box opens (Figure 12-2).

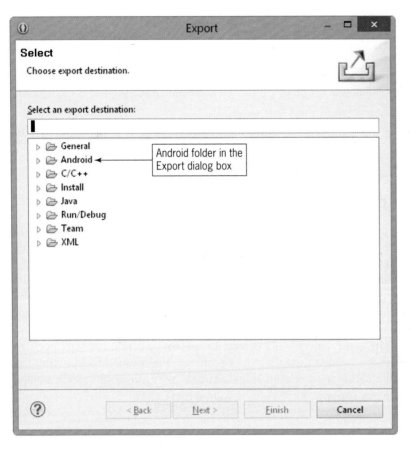

Figure 12-2 Export dialog box

STEP 2

- Expand the Android folder in the Export dialog box.

- Tap or click Export Android Application.

The Export Android Application option is selected in the Android folder of the Export dialog box (Figure 12-3).

Export dialog box

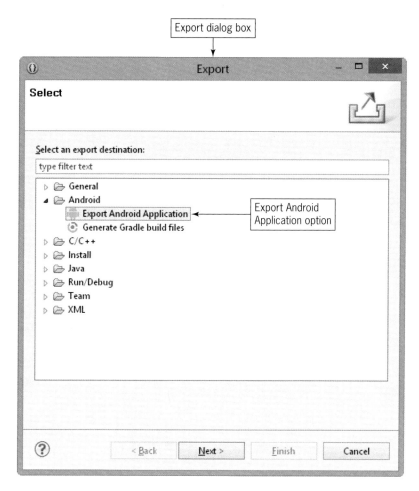

Figure 12-3   Exporting an Android application

STEP 3

- Tap or click the Next button.

- In the Export Android Application dialog box, tap or click the Browse button. The Project Selection dialog box opens.

- Tap or click the name of the application that you are exporting.

The Android app project name is selected (Figure 12-4).

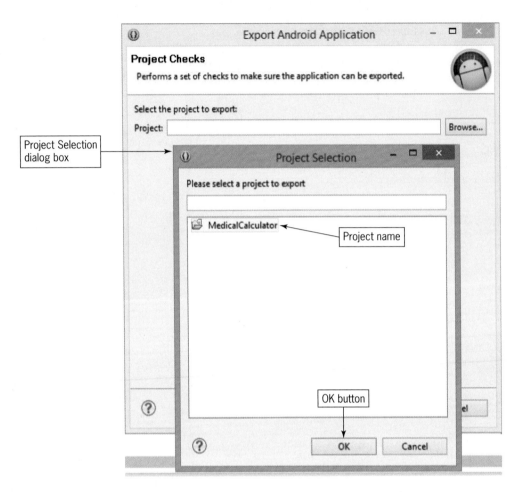

Figure 12-4 Selecting the project

STEP 4

- Tap or click the OK button, and then tap or click the Next button.

The Export Android Application dialog box displays the Keystore selection options (Figure 12-5).

Figure 12-5   Selecting the keystore

STEP 5

- Tap or click the Create new keystore option button.

- In the Location text box, type the file path to your .android file and the name of the keystore file (such as C:\Users\yourcomputer\.android\debug.keystore).

The debug.keystore file is selected in the Select Keystore Name dialog box (Figure 12-6). In the path, yourcomputer must be replaced with the login name of your computer, in my case, Corinne Hoisington.

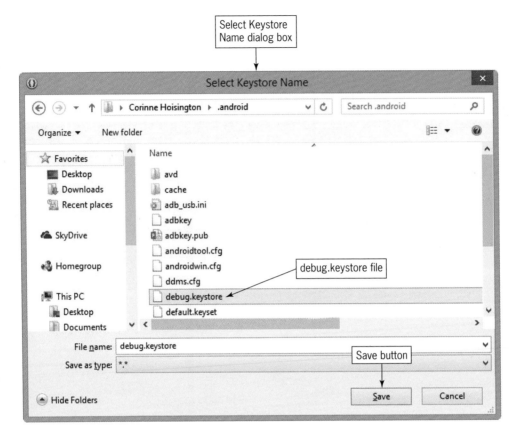

Figure 12-6 Keystore file is selected

STEP 6

- Click the Save button.

- Enter a password of your own choosing in the Password text box.

- Type the same password again in the Confirm text box.

Your password is typed twice in the Export Android Application dialog box (Figure 12-7).

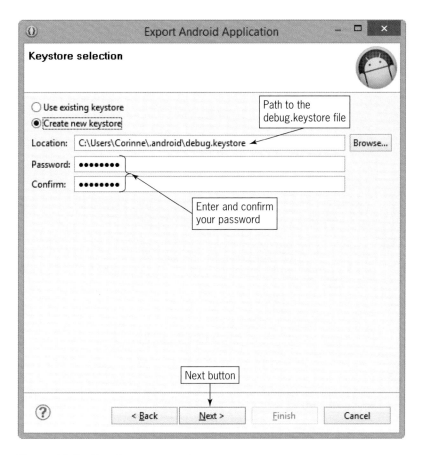

Figure 12-7   Entering a password

STEP 7

- Click the Next button. To create a key, you must fill out the Key Creation form with your personal information.

- In the Alias text box, enter **androiddebugkey**.

- In the Password and Confirm text boxes, enter your keystore password.

- In the Validity (years) text box, enter a valid number of years from 50 to 1,000 years. You can leave the Organization text box empty if you do not belong to an organization.

The Key Creation form is filled out with your personal information (Figure 12-8).

Figure 12-8 Key Creation form

STEP 8

- Click the Next button. The Destination and key/certificate checks form opens.
- Click the Browse button, and then save the APK key file within the application folder.

The Destination APK file is saved within the application folder (Figure 12-9).

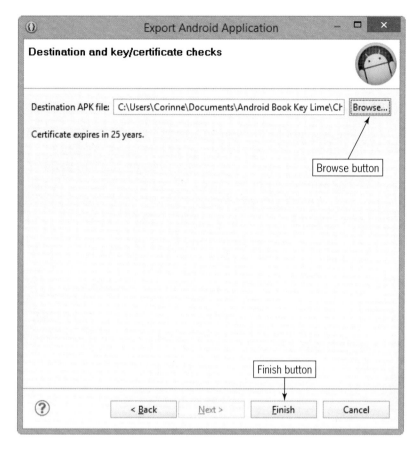

Figure 12-9 Selecting a location for the destination APK file

STEP 9

- Click the Finish button.

The Android app is now signed and ready to be saved to Google Play.

GTK

Android .apk files can be installed and run directly on an Android device.

IN THE TRENCHES

The keystore creates your private key for Android deployment. It is best to back up your keystore in a safe file location. If you lose your keystore file, you will not be able to upgrade your Android Google Play app.

Preparing Promotional Materials to Upload

When you publish your app in Google Play, you are required to post several images that accompany your app to assist with marketing. With hundreds of thousands of apps in the store, you must publicize your app so it stands out and is noticed by casual visitors. To leverage your app in the Google Play store, you can upload your app with screenshots, a video link, promotional graphics, and descriptive text, as in the Angry Birds Space page at Google Play, which is shown in Figure 12-10.

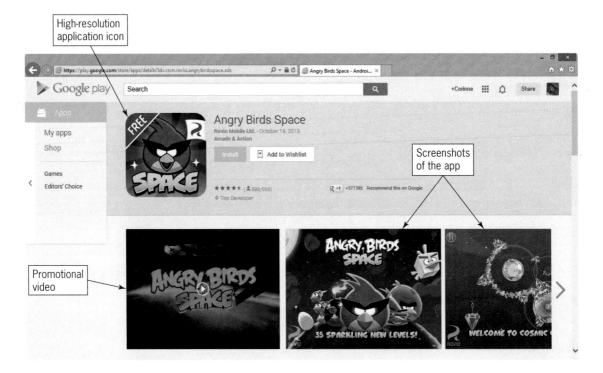

Figure 12-10   Angry Birds Space Android app from Google Play

Source: Angry Birds © 2014 Roxio Entertainment Ltd.

Providing Images

In the Angry Birds Android app, a high-resolution application icon is displayed in the left pane by default. The application icon does not replace your launcher icon, but serves to identify and brand your app. The size of the application icon should be 512 × 512 pixels and stored in a PNG file. In addition, Google Play requires a minimum of two screenshots of the app to display on the details page of your application. A large image (typically in the PNG format) is displayed at the top (Figure 12-10) with any of the following dimensions: 480 × 320, 800 × 480, or 854 × 480 pixels. You can upload up to eight screenshots for the app page. The screenshots appear before the description. You can also display a video to demo your app, though Google Play does not require one. As an alternative, you can upload with your app a video link to your demo video from *YouTube.com*. The short video should highlight the top features of your app and last between 30 seconds and 2 minutes. Remember that these visual elements are the first impression potential users have of your app. Quality media helps improve an app's marketability.

GTK

Google Play has over 1 million published apps and over 60 billion downloads.

Providing a Description

In addition to the promotional media items, an app description provides a quick overview of the purpose of the app and what it does. To intrigue your readers, you can include some of the features your application provides and describe why your app is unique in comparison with other competitors without mentioning their names. The description needs to sell your app to the widest audience possible. The description of the Angry Birds Space app in Figure 12-11 appeals to a gaming audience searching for a new Angry Birds experience in space. Notice that the bullets used in the Angry Birds Space description showing the features and benefits of the app are clear and concise. A good description is written to motivate users to download the app. Revise the description with each update of your app, adding new information such as new features and user reviews. In Figure 12-11, notice the Review section and the ratings. If you scroll down the site, you can also display the date of last update, current version, Android platform requirement, category, size, price, and content rating. Users search for the most popular apps as measured by their ratings. Prospective app buyers read user reviews to determine if your app is worth their time and money. When a visitor writes a good review about your application, you can quote the review within your description. Customers value a large number of good reviews and are more likely to download your app if it has them.

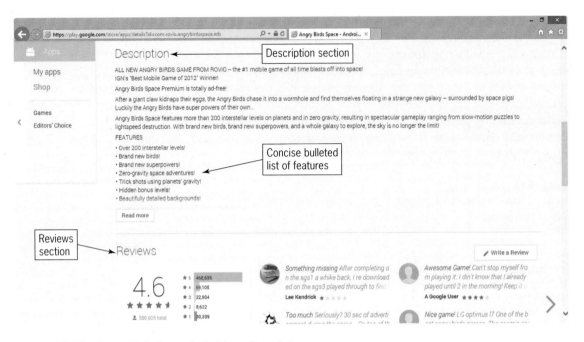

Figure 12-11   Angry Birds Space Android app Description page

Source: Google

The Angry Birds Space game on Google Play is free. So how do the developers make money? At the bottom of the Google Play Angry Birds page, a list of other products created by this developer, including a second version of Angry Birds Space HD, is available for $2.99. Upon mastering the free game, users are often motivated to buy the full version of this product. As you price your app, consider that some users will never want to pay for an app, but many will pay for a great app. Consider also adding Facebook, Twitter, and other social networking links on your app's page at Google Play so users can also market your app within their friend networks.

When you upload your app into Google Play, you select one of the application categories shown in Table 12-1. If your app fits into more than one category, be sure to include each category to attract visitors in each category searched.

Category	Example Types of Apps
Comics	Comic players, comic titles
Communications	Messaging, chat/IM, dialers, address books, browsers, and call management
Finance	Banking, payment, ATM finders, financial news, insurance, taxes, portfolio/trading, and tip calculators
Health & Fitness	Personal fitness, workout tracking, diet and nutritional tips, and health and safety
Medical	Drug and clinical references, calculators, handbooks for healthcare providers, and medical journals and news
Lifestyle	Recipes and style guides
Media & Video	Subscription movie services, remote controls, and media/video players
Music & Audio	Music services, radios, and music players
Photography	Cameras, photo-editing tools, and photo management and sharing
News & Magazines	Newspapers, news aggregators, magazines, and blogging
Weather	Weather reports
Productivity	Notepad, to-do list, keyboard, printing, calendar, backup, calculator, and conversion
Business	Document editor/reader, package tracking, remote desktop, email management, and job search
Books & Reference	Book readers, reference books, text books, dictionaries, thesaurus, and wikis
Education	Exam preparations, study-aids, vocabulary, educational games, and language learning
Shopping	Online shopping, auctions, coupons, price comparison, grocery lists, and product reviews
Social	Social networking, check-in, and blogging
Sports	Sports news and commentary, score tracking, fantasy team management, and game coverage
Personalization	Wallpapers, live wallpapers, home screen, lock screen, and ring tones
Tools	System utility tools
Travel & Local	City guides, local business information, and trip management tools
Libraries & Demo	Software libraries

Table 12-1   Category types

Including Social Networks

On the Angry Birds Space page, a Read more button within the Description provides links to social networks. You can become a fan of Angry Birds on Facebook or follow Angry Birds on Twitter (Figure 12-12). By creating a social networking presence for your app, you can build a social relationship among your customers who share common interests, backgrounds, or hobbies. By creating a Facebook and Twitter page, you have the advantage of communicating with your fans in a more entertaining manner. Customers might suggest what they would like added to the app in future versions.

Figure 12-12   Angry Birds Space app Twitter page
Source: Angry Birds © 2014 Roxio Entertainment Ltd.

Registering for a Google Play Account

Google Play is a publishing platform that helps you distribute your Android apps to users around the world. Before you can publish apps through Google Play you must register as a developer using your Gmail account username and password at *http://play.google.com/apps/publish*. Registering at Google Play requires a one-time-only payment of $25, which registers you as an Android application developer and enrolls you in a Google Merchant account. In order to receive payment for the purchased apps, you must first specify a bank account. Bank account information is not added or updated within your Google Checkout account, but rather in the Google Wallet Merchant Center. Google states that they charge this fee to encourage higher quality products on Google Play and fewer products with spam. You can allow an unlimited number of people to access your Google Play developer's account. You will remain the owner of the account and will be the only person who can grant or revoke access to other users.

The registration process requires you to have a Google account, agree to the legal terms, and pay the fee via your Google Merchant account. If you charge for your app, Google Merchant disperses revenue for application sales. If you register to sell applications, you must also be registered as a Google Merchant with your Google wallet. As a developer, you have access to your app ratings, comments, and number of downloads. If you charge for your application, you will receive 70 percent of the application price, with the remaining 30 percent distributed among the phone carriers. The profit after your first sale arrives in your Google Merchant account 24 hours later. After a purchaser buys and installs an app, his or her credit card is charged 24 hours later. If the user uninstalls the app before the 24-hour time period, Google issues a full refund of the purchase price. To register as a Google Play Android developer, follow these steps:

STEP 1

- To register at Google Play, open a browser and go to the site ***http://play.google.com/apps/publish***.

- If necessary, enter your Gmail account information. Enter the password for your Gmail account.

Your Gmail account username and password are entered in the Google Play Developer Console (Figure 12-13).

Figure 12-13   Signing into a Google developer's account

Source: Google

STEP 2

- Tap or click the Sign in button to sign in with your Google account information.

- Tap or click the check box acknowledging that you read the Google Play Developer distribution agreement, and then click the Continue to payment button.

- Complete the payment process.

- If necessary, tap or click Settings (the gear icon) to view the Account details tab.

- To register for a developer's Google Play account, in the Developer name text box, type your name. The email address is already added based on your Google account.

- In the Phone Number text box, type your phone number.

On the Account details tab of the Settings page in the Google Play Developer Console, the developer's name and phone number are entered (Figure 12-14).

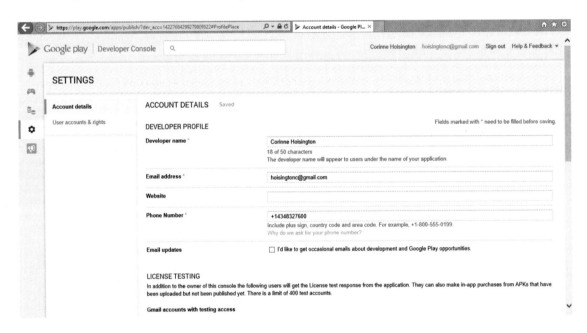

Figure 12-14   Entering account details
Source: Google

STEP 3

- Scroll down the page and tap or click Learn more.

You can open the categories Manage Your Account, Manage Your Apps, Sell Your Apps, Policy and Best Practices, and Troubleshooting to learn the latest updates about publishing your apps (Figure 12-15).

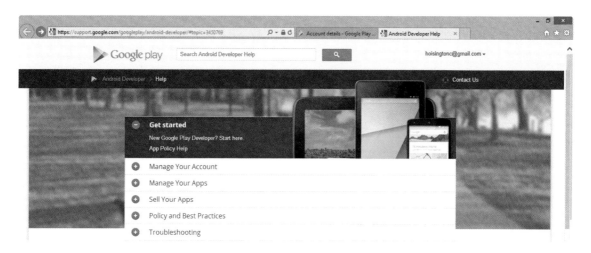

Figure 12-15   Getting help about being a Google Play developer
Source: Google

IN THE TRENCHES
After creating your account in Google Play, it may take up to 24 hours for your account to be approved for publishing Android apps.

Uploading an App to Google Play

As you upload your app to Google Play, you will be prompted to enter information about your application. Once you create an account, the Developer Console pages take you through the steps to upload your unlocked application .apk file and the promotional assets. The maximum supported file size for the .apk file at Google Play is 50 MB. After your app is posted and rises in popularity, Google Play gives you higher placement in weekly "top" lists and in promotional slots in collections such as Top Free Apps. To upload an Android application to Google Play, follow these steps:

STEP 1

- To upload your app at Google Play, tap or click the first tab to reopen the Developer's Console.

- Tap or click the All applications icon (Android symbol) in the left column.

The All Applications page opens and displays a list of any apps (if any) previously uploaded (Figure 12-16).

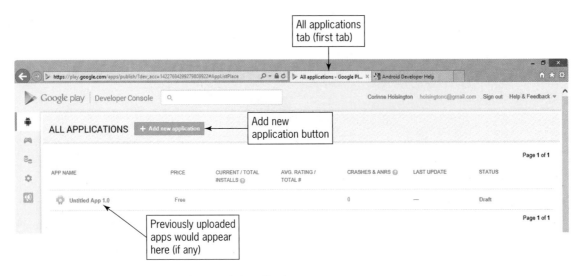

Figure 12-16   Displaying previously uploaded applications

Source: Google

STEP 2

- Tap or click the Add new application button to upload the .apk file.

The Add New Application dialog box opens (Figure 12-17).

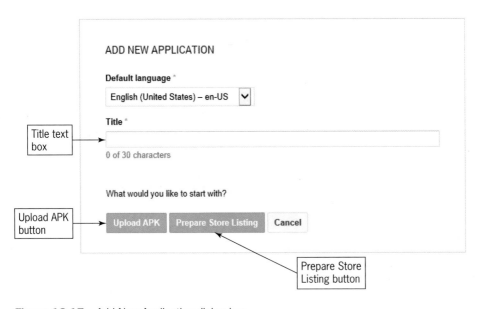

Figure 12-17   Add New Application dialog box

Source: Google

STEP 3

- Type the name of the app in the Title text box.

The APK tab on the left side of the window opens within the browser (Figure 12-18).

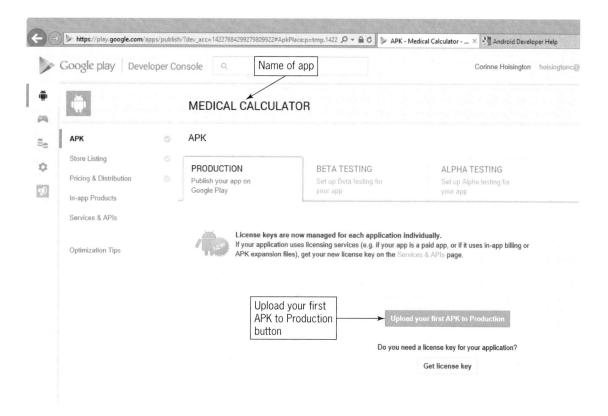

Figure 12-18 Uploading the APK

Source: Google

STEP 4

- To upload your .apk file, tap or click the Upload your first APK to Production button.
- Tap or click the Browse files button and locate the .apk file for the app that you are publishing.
- Tap or click the Open button to upload the app.
- If necessary, tap or click the Store Listing tab in the left column.

The app uploads to the Google Play store (Figure 12-19).

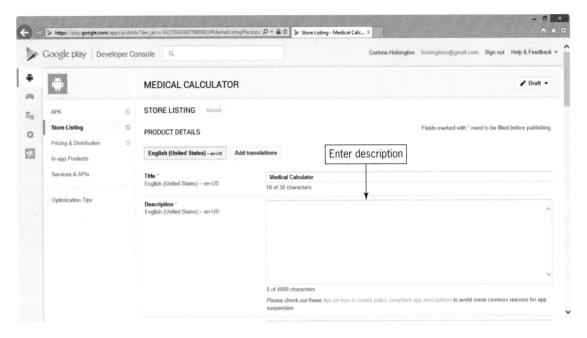

Figure 12-19   Store Listing Product Details page

Source: Google

STEP 5

- In the Store Listing Product Details page, you can enter a Description, Promo text, and Recent changes, and upload screenshots of phone, 7-inch tablet, 10-inch tablet, High-res icon, Feature Graphic, Promo Graphic, and Promo Video URL link.

After scrolling down the page, the Categorization, Contact Details, and Privacy Policy settings for the app are displayed (Figure 12-20).

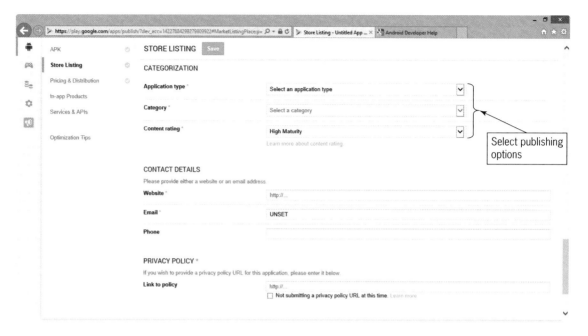

Figure 12-20   Publishing options

Source: Google

STEP 6

- In the Store Listing Product Details page, enter the information requested in the Categorization, Contact Details, and the Privacy Policy sections.

- Tap or click the Pricing & Distribution tab in the left column.

The Pricing & Distribution page is displayed for the app (Figure 12-21).

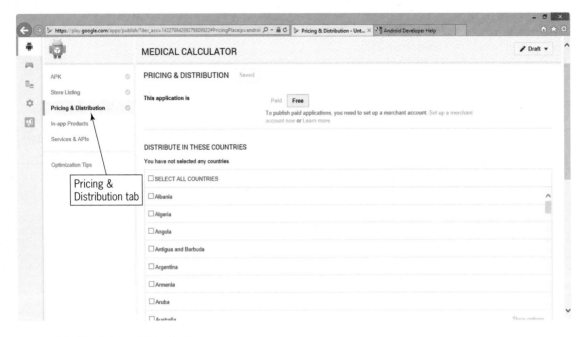

Figure 12-21   Pricing & Distribution page

Source: Google

STEP 7

- In the Pricing & Distribution page, enter whether application is Free or Paid, and then enter information in the Distribute in These Countries, Google Play for Education, Consent for Marketing opt-out, Content guidelines, and US export laws sections.

Wrap It Up—Chapter Summary

Before you can publish your application on Google Play, the app should be fully tested in the emulator and on multiple Android devices. To prepare your app for publishing, an APK package is exported using Eclipse. Successful app marketing requires paying attention to promotional materials that appear on Google Play, such as images, videos, and clear descriptions of the app. Publishing your app involves uploading the promotional materials that accompany the .apk file.

- Google Play is the storefront for Android devices and apps, and provides access to Android apps, Google Music, and Google e-books. It includes an online store for paid and free Android apps, music, movies, books, and games. Android phones, tablets, and Google television can access the Google Play services.

- To reach a larger audience within the Google Play market, you should target multiple Android devices and translate your app into multiple languages. Create a custom experience for devices with different screen sizes, pixel densities, orientations, and resolutions so that each user feels that the app was designed specifically for his or her phone or tablet.

- As you design an Android app, you can provide alternate resources such as strings of text translated into multiple languages that change depending on the default locale detected on the device.

- Before publishing an Android app, test it on various devices. Using different built-in emulators in Eclipse, you can test the design and functionality of your application on a wide range of devices and see how your development application performs in a real-world environment. Using the Android Debug Bridge (ADB) tool in Eclipse, you can develop and debug an Android application on an Android device.

- After testing an Android app, you must create an .apk file (application package file), which is a release-ready package that users can install and run on their Android phones and tablets. An .apk file is a compressed archive that contains the application, the manifest file, and all associated resources, such as image files, music, and other required content. Using the Eclipse Export Wizard, you can build a release-ready .apk file that is signed with your private key and optimized for publication.

- When you publish your app in Google Play, you must post several images, including an application icon and screenshots. You can also post an optional video or link to a video that demonstrates your app. You must also provide a description that provides an overview of the purpose and features of the app. Finally, include app information such as ratings, Android platform requirement, category, and price.

- To publish apps through Google Play, you must register as a developer using your Gmail account username and password at *https://play.google.com/apps/publish*. The registration process requires you to have a Google account, agree to the legal terms, and pay a $25 fee via your Google Checkout account.

- After creating a Google Play account, the Developer Console pages at the Google Play Web site step you through uploading your unlocked application .apk file and its promotional assets.

Key Terms

.apk file (application package file)—A release-ready package of an Android app stored in a compressed archive similar to a Zip file that contains the application, the manifest file, and all associated resources, such as image files, music, and other required content.

Android Debug Bridge (ADB)—An Android tool you use to communicate with a connected Android device.

Google Play—A digital repository that serves the Android Market and includes an online store for paid and free Android apps, as well as music, movies, books, and games.

Developer FAQs

1. What is the URL of Google Play?

2. Approximately how many countries use Google Play?

3. Name four services of Google Play.

4. What is the name of the two largest competitors to Google Play?

5. To increase your target audience in Google Play, what two considerations should you make?

6. How do you change your app to multiple languages?

7. What is the address of the Google Web site that assists with language translation?

8. What does ADB stand for?

9. What does APK stand for?

10. Can you deploy your app to your Android phone?

11. Do you have to install ADB drivers on a Mac computer?

12. Name four promotional assets that you can upload with your app at Google Play.

13. What is the maximum number of screenshots of your app in action that you can post in Google Play?

14. Where must you post your promotional video?

15. What are the minimum length and maximum length of the promotional video?

16. In which two social networking sites should you create a marketing presence?

17. Which category would you select at Google Play for a calendar app?

18. Which category would you select for a recipe app?

19. How much is the registration fee to publish Android apps at Google Play?

20. What is the maximum size of an .apk file at Google Play?

Beyond the Book

To answer the following questions, create an idea for an app that you think would sell well at Google Play.

1. Write about 200 words describing your Google Play app idea, beginning with a catchy title for the app.

2. Locate an image link that you would consider to be your application icon for your Android app idea. (If you plan to use the icon, you would of course need to properly obtain this image following copyright guidelines.)

3. Consider the price for selling your app. Write at least 150 words explaining why you selected this price after researching the Internet for price points for Android apps.

4. Create a short YouTube video to market your app idea, and provide the link to your instructor.

Glossary

.apk file (application package file) A release-ready package of an Android app stored in a compressed archive similar to a Zip file that contains the application, the manifest file, and all associated resources, such as image files, music, and other required content.

.equals method A method used to compare strings for equality.

9-patch image A special image with predefined stretching areas that maintain the same look on different screen sizes.

ACTION_VIEW A generic action you can use to send any request to get the most reasonable action to occur.

Activity An Android component that represents a single screen with a user interface.

Adapter Provides a data model for the layout of a list and for converting the data from the array into list items.

Android Debug Bridge (ADB) An Android tool you use to communicate with a connected Android device.

Android Development Tools (ADT) An Eclipse plug-in that extends the capabilities of Eclipse to create Android projects.

Android Library A project folder that contains the android.jar file, which includes all the class libraries needed to build an Android application for the specified version.

Android Manifest A file with the filename AndroidManifest.xml that is required in every Android application. This file provides essential information to the Android device, such as the name of your Java application and a listing of each Activity.

android:oneshot An attribute of the animation-list that determines whether an animation plays once and then stops or continues to play until the Stop Animation button is tapped.

AndroidManifest.xml A file containing all the information Android needs to run an application.

animation-list An XML root element that references images stored in the drawable folders and used in an animation.

AnimationDrawable class A class that provides the methods for Drawable animations to create a sequence of frame-by-frame images.

app A mobile application.

Application template A design you can use to create basic Android applications and then customize them.

array variable A variable that can store more than one value.

ArrayAdapter<String> i A ListAdapter that supplies string array data to a ListView object.

assets folder A project folder containing any asset files that are accessed through classic file manipulation.

break A statement that ends a case within a Switch statement and continues with the statement following the Switch decision structure.

Calendar class A class you can use to access the Android system date. The Calendar class also is responsible for converting between a Date object and a set of integer fields such as YEAR, MONTH, and DAY_OF_MONTH.

case A keyword used in a Switch statement to indicate a condition. In a Switch statement, the case keyword is followed by a value and a colon.

Change Gravity A tool that changes the linear alignment of a control, so that it is aligned to the left, center, right, top, or bottom of an object or the screen.

class A group of objects that establishes an introduction to each object's properties.

class variable A variable with global scope; it can be accessed by multiple methods throughout the program.

codec A computer technology used to compress and decompress audio and video files.

compound condition More than one condition included in an If statement.

constructor A part of the Java code used to initialize the instance variables of an object.

DAY_OF_MONTH A date constant of the Calendar class that retrieves an integer value of the system's current day.

DAY_OF_YEAR A date constant of the Calendar class that retrieves the day of the current year as an integer. For example, February 1 is day 32 of the year.

DecimalFormat A class that provides patterns for formatting numbers in program output.

decision structure A fundamental control structure used in computer programming that deals with the different conditions that occur based on the values entered into an application.

Eclipse The most popular IDE for writing Java programs and for building and integrating application development tools and open-source projects.

element A single individual item that contains a value in an array.

emulated application An application that is converted in real time to run on a variety of platforms such as a Web page, which can be displayed on various screen sizes through a browser.

emulator Software that duplicates how an app looks and feels on a particular device.

Entries A Spinner property that connects a string array to the Spinner control for display.

equals method A method of the String class that Java uses to compare strings.

event handler A part of a program coded to respond to the specific event.

final A type of variable that can only be initialized once; any attempt to reassign the value results in a compile error when the application is executed.

fragment A piece of an application's user interface or behavior that can be placed in an Activity.

Frame animation A type of animation, also called frame-by-frame animation, that plays a sequence of images, as in a slide show, with a specified interval between images.

gen folder A project folder that contains automatically generated Java files.

get The field manipulation method that accesses the system date or time.

getBaseContext( ) A Context class method used in Android programs to obtain a Context instance. Use getBaseContext( ) in a method that is triggered only when the user touches the GridView control.

getInstance A method of the Calendar class that returns a calendar date or time based on the system settings.

GetSelectedItem( ) A method that returns the text of the selected Spinner item.

GetText( ) A method that reads text stored in an EditText control.

getTime( ) method A method of the Calendar class that returns the time value in the Date object.

Google Play A digital repository that serves the Android market and includes an online store for paid and free Android apps, as well as music, movies, books, and games.

GridView A View container that displays a grid of objects with rows and columns.

hexadecimal color code A triplet of three colors using hexadecimal numbers, where colors are specified first by a pound sign followed by how much red (00 to FF), how much green (00 to FF), and how much blue (00 to FF) are in the final color.

hint A short description of a field that appears as light text in a Text Field control.

If Else statement A statement that executes one set of instructions if a specified condition is true and another set of instructions if the condition is false.

If statement A statement that executes one set of instructions if a specified condition is true and takes no action if the condition is not true.

ImageView control A control that displays an icon or a graphic from a picture file.

import To make the classes from a particular Android package available throughout the application.

import statement A statement that makes more Java functions available to a program.

instantiate To create an object of a specific class.

intent Code in the Android Manifest file that allows an Android application with more than one Activity to navigate among Activities.

isChecked( ) method A method that tests a checked property to determine if a RadioButton object has been selected.

item In a Spinner control, a string of text that appears in a list for user selection.

Java An object-oriented programming language and a platform originated by Sun Microsystems.

key The string part of a key-value pair that uniquely identifies a preference.

launcher icon An icon that appears on the home screen to represent the application.

layout A container that can hold widgets and other graphical elements to help you design an interface for an application.

life cycle The series of actions from the beginning, or birth, of an Activity to its end, or destruction.

Linear layout A layout that arranges components in a vertical column or horizontal row.

ListActivity A class that displays a list of items within an app.

local variable A variable declared by a variable declaration statement within a method.

localization The use of the String table to change text based on the user's preferred language.

margin Blank space that offsets a control by a certain amount of density independent pixels (dp) on each of its four sides.

Master/Detail Flow template A template Eclipse provides for creating an Android app with an adaptive, responsive layout; it displays a set of list items on the left and the associated details on the right.

MediaPlayer class The Java class that provides the methods to control audio playback on an Android device.

method A set of Java statements that can be included inside a Java class.

method body The part of a method containing a collection of statements that defines what the method does.

MONTH A date constant of the Calendar class that retrieves an integer value of the system's current month.

motion tween A type of animation that specifies the start state of an object, and then animates the object a predetermined number of times or an infinite number of times using a transition.

native application A program locally installed on a specific platform such as a phone or tablet.

nest To place one statement, such as an If statement, within another statement.

object A specific, concrete instance of a class.

object-oriented programming language A type of programming language that allows good software engineering practices such as code reuse.

onDateSet( ) method A method that automatically obtains the date selected by the user.

onDestroy( ) method A method used to end an Activity. Whereas the onCreate( ) method sets up required resources, the onDestroy( ) method releases those same resources to free up memory.

onItemClick An event the OnItemClickListener processes when the user touches the GridView display layout. The onItemClick method is defined by OnItemClickListener and sends a number of arguments in the parentheses included within the line of code.

onListItemClick( ) A method called when an item in a list is selected.

Open Handset Alliance An open-source business alliance of 80 firms that develop open standards for mobile devices.

open-source operating system Organizations and developers can extract, modify, and use the source code free of charge and copyright restrictions.

Package Explorer A pane on the left side of the Eclipse program window that contains the folders for the current project.

padding property A property that you can use to offset the content of a control by a specific number of pixels.

Parse A class that converts a string into a number data type.

Pascal case Text that begins with an uppercase letter and uses an uppercase letter to start each new word.

permission A restriction limiting access to a part of the code or to data on the device.

Persistent data Stores values permanently by placing the information in a file.

position The placement of an item in a list. When an item in a list is selected, the position of the item is passed from the onListItemClick method and evaluated with a decision structure. The first item is assigned the position of 0, the second item is assigned the position of 1, and so forth.

prompt Text that displays instructions at the top of the Spinner control.

RadioGroup A group of RadioButton controls; only one RadioButton control can be selected at a time.

Relative layout A layout that arranges components in relation to each other. Relative layout is the default layout of the emulator.

res folder A project folder that contains all the resources, such as images, music, and video files, that an application may need.

responsive design An approach to designing apps and Web sites that provide an optimal viewing experience across as many devices as possible.

scope The scope of a variable refers to the variable's visibility within a class.

set The field manipulation method that changes the system date or time.

setAdapter A command that provides a data model for the GridView layout, similar to an adapter, which displays a ListView control.

setBackgroundResource A method that places images in the frame-by-frame display for an animation, with each frame pointing to an image referenced in the XML resource file.

setContentView The Java code necessary to display the content of a specific screen.

setListAdapter A command that projects your data to the onscreen list on your device by connecting the ListActivity's ListView object to array data.

soft keyboard An onscreen keyboard positioned over the lower part of an application's window.

Software Development Kit (SDK) A package containing development tools for creating applications.

sp A unit of measurement that stands for scaled-independent pixels.

Spinner control A widget similar to a drop-down list for selecting a single item from a fixed listing.

SQLite A lightweight, preloaded mobile database engine, which has been available since the Cupcake 1.5 version of Android and occupies a small amount of disk memory.

src folder A project folder that includes the Java code source files for the project.

startAnimation A method that begins the animation process of a View object by calling the AnimationUtils class utilities to access the resources necessary to load the animation.

state A stage in an Activity's life cycle that determines whether the Activity is active, paused, stopped, or dead.

string A series of alphanumeric characters that can include spaces.

string array Two or more text strings.

strings.xml A default file that is part of every Android application and holds commonly used strings in an application.

stub A piece of code that serves as a placeholder to declare itself, containing just enough code to link to the rest of the program.

Switch A type of decision statement that allows you to choose from many statements based on an integer or a char input.

TableLayout A user interface design layout that includes TableRow controls to form a grid.

Text property A property that changes the text written within a control.

Text Size property A property that sets the size of text in a control.

theme A style applied to an Activity or an entire application.

thread A single sequential flow of control within a program.

Timer A Java class that creates a timed event when the schedule method is called.

timer A tool that performs a one-time task such as displaying an opening splash screen or performs a continuous process such as a morning wake-up call set to run at regular intervals.

TimerTask A Java class that invokes a scheduled timer.

toast notification A message that appears as an overlay on a user's screen, often displaying a validation warning.

Tween animation A type of animation that, instead of using a sequence of images, creates an animation by performing a series of transformations on a single image, such as position, size, rotation, and transparency, on the contents of a View object.

tween effect A transition that changes objects from one state to another, such as by moving, rotating, growing, or shrinking.

typeface A property that you can use to set the style of control text to font families, including monospace, sans_serif, and serif.

URI An acronym for Uniform Resource Identifier, a URI is a string that identifies the resources of the Web. Similar to a URL, a URI includes additional information necessary for gaining access to the resources required for posting the page.

URL An acronym for Uniform Resource Locator, a URL is a Web site address.

value The data part of a key-value pair that represents a string, int, long, float, or Boolean value.

variable A name used in a Java program to contain data that changes during the execution of the program.

View A rectangular container that displays a drawing or text object.

Visibility property The Java property that controls whether a control is displayed on the emulator.

WebView A View widget that displays Web pages.

widget A single element such as a TextView, Button, or CheckBox control, and is also called an object.

XML An acronym for Extensible Markup Language, a widely used system for defining data formats. XML assists in the layout of the Android emulator.

YEAR A date constant of the Calendar class that retrieves an integer value of the system's current year.

Index

Note: Page numbers in **bold** indicate where keywords are defined.